Lecture Notes in Artificial Intelligence (LNAI)

Vol. 345: R. T. Nossum (Ed.), Advanced Topics in Artificial Intelligence. VII, 233 pages. 1988.

Vol. 346: M. Reinfrank, J. de Kleer, M. L. Ginsberg, E. Sandewall (Eds.), Non-Monotonic Reasoning. Proceedings, 1988. XIV, 237 pages. 1989.

Vol. 347: K. Morik (Ed.), Knowledge Representation and Organization in Machine Learning. XV, 319 pages. 1989.

Vol. 353: S. Hölldobler, Foundations of Equational Logic Programming. X, 250 pages. 1989.

Vol. 383: K. Furukawa, H. Tanaka, T. Fujisaki (Eds.), Logic Programming '88. Proceedings, 1988. IX, 251 pages. 1989.

Vol. 390: J. P. Martins, E. M. Morgado (Eds.), EPIA 89. Proceedings, 1989. XII, 400 pages. 1989.

Vol. 395: M. Schmidt-Schauß, Computational Aspects of an Order-Sorted Logic with Term Declarations. VIII, 171 pages. 1989.

Vol. 397: K. P. Jantke (Ed.), Analogical and Inductive Inference. Proceedings, 1989. IX, 338 pages. 1989.

Vol. 406: C. J. Barter, M. J. Brooks (Eds.), AI '88. Proceedings, 1988. VIII, 463 pages. 1990.

Vol. 419: K. Weichselberger, S. Pöhlmann, A Methodology for Uncertainty in Knowledge-Based Systems. VIII, 132 pages. 1990.

Vol. 422: B. Nebel, Reasoning and Revision in Hybrid Representation Systems. XII, 270 pages. 1990.

Other volumes of the Lecture Notes in Computer Science relevant to Artificial Intelligence:

Vol. 221: E. Wada (Ed.), Logic Programming '85. Proceedings, 1985. IX, 311 pages. 1986.

Vol. 225: E. Shapiro (Ed.), Third International Conference on Logic Programming. Proceedings, 1986. IX, 720 pages. 1986.

Vol. 230: J. H. Siekmann (Ed.), 8th International Conference on Automated Deduction. Proceedings, 1986. X, 708 pages. 1986.

Vol. 231: R. Hausser, NEWCAT: Parsing Natural Language Using Left-Associative Grammar. II, 540 pages. 1986.

Vol. 232: W. Bibel, Ph. Jorrand (Eds.), Fundamentals of Artificial Intelligence. VII, 313 pages. 1986. Reprint as Springer Study Edition 1987.

Vol. 238: L. Naish, Negation and Control in Prolog. IX, 119 pages. 1986.

Vol. 256: P. Lescanne (Ed.), Rewriting Techniques and Applications. Proceedings, 1987. VI, 285 pages. 1987.

Vol. 264: E. Wada (Ed.), Logic Programming '86. Proceedings, 1986. VI, 179 pages. 1987.

Vol. 265: K. P. Jantke (Ed.), Analogical and Inductive Inference. Proceedings, 1986. VI, 227 pages. 1987.

Vol. 271: D. Snyers, A. Thayse, From Logic Design to Logic Programming. IV, 125 pages. 1987.

Vol. 306: M. Boscarol, L. Carlucci Aiello, G. Levi (Eds.), Foundations of Logic and Functional Programming. Proceedings, 1986. V, 218 pages. 1988.

Vol. 308: S. Kaplan, J.-P. Jouannaud (Eds.), Conditional Term Rewriting Systems. Proceedings, 1987. VI, 278 pages. 1988.

Vol. 310: E. Lusk, R. Overbeek (Eds.), 9th International Conference on Automated Deduction. Proceedings, 1988. X, 775 pages. 1988.

Vol. 315: K. Furukawa, H. Tanaka, T. Fujisaki (Eds.), Logic Programming '87. Proceedings, 1987. VI, 327 pages. 1988.

Vol. 320: A. Blaser (Ed.), Natural Language at the Computer. Proceedings, 1988. III, 176 pages. 1988.

Vol. 336: B. R. Donald, Error Detection and Recovery in Robotics. XXIV, 314 pages. 1989.

Lecture Notes in Artificial Intelligence

Subseries of Lecture Notes in Computer Science
Edited by J. Siekmann

Lecture Notes in Computer Science

Edited by G. Goos and J. Hartmanis

Editorial

Artificial Intelligence has become a major discipline under the roof of Computer Science. This is also reflected by a growing number of titles devoted to this fast developing field to be published in our Lecture Notes in Computer Science. To make these volumes immediately visible we have decided to distinguish them by a special cover as Lecture Notes in Artificial Intelligence, constituting a subseries of the Lecture Notes in Computer Science. This subseries is edited by an Editorial Board of experts from all areas of AI, chaired by Jörg Siekmann, who are looking forward to consider further AI monographs and proceedings of high scientific quality for publication.

We hope that the constitution of this subseries will be well accepted by the audience of the Lecture Notes in Computer Science, and we feel confident that the subseries will be recognized as an outstanding opportunity for publication by authors and editors of the AI community.

Editors and publisher

Lecture Notes in Artificial Intelligence

Edited by J. Siekmann

Subseries of Lecture Notes in Computer Science

422

Bernhard Nebel

Reasoning and Revision in Hybrid Representation Systems

Springer-Verlag

Berlin Heidelberg New York London Paris Tokyo Hong Kong

Author

Bernhard Nebel
Deutsches Forschungszentrum für Künstliche Intelligenz (DFKI)
Stuhlsatzenhausweg 3, D-6600 Saarbrücken 11, FRG

CR Subject Classification (1987): I.2.3−4

ISBN 3-540-52443-6 Springer-Verlag Berlin Heidelberg New York
ISBN 0-387-52443-6 Springer-Verlag New York Berlin Heidelberg

© Springer-Verlag Berlin Heidelberg 1990
Printed in Germany

Printing and binding: Druckhaus Beltz, Hemsbach/Bergstr.
2145/3140-543210 − Printed on acid-free paper

Preface

The dynamic aspects of knowledge representation systems, namely, *reasoning* with represented knowledge and *revising* represented knowledge, are the most important aspects of such systems. In this book, these aspects are investigated in the context of hybrid representation systems based on KL-ONE.

After a general introduction to knowledge representation, reasoning, and revision, a typical member of the family of hybrid representation systems based on KL-ONE is introduced and analyzed from a semantic and algorithmic point of view. This analysis leads to new complexity results about subsumption determination and a characterization of a proposed hybrid inference algorithm as conditionally complete. Additionally, it is shown that so-called terminological cycles can be integrated smoothly into the framework.

Based on the analysis of representation and reasoning in KL-ONE-based systems, the revision problem is investigated. A survey of some approaches to belief revision leads to a reconstruction of symbol-level belief revision on the knowledge level. A conceptual analysis of terminological revision demonstrates that belief revision techniques developed for the revision of assertional knowledge are not adequate for the revision of terminological knowledge. For this reason, a literal revision approach is adopted. Essentially, it amounts to minimal mutilations in the literal description of definitions. Finally, implementation techniques for terminological revision operations are described, and the interface problem for a knowledge acquisition system is discussed.

This book is a revised version of my doctoral dissertation, accepted by the University of Saarland in June 1989. Most of the work was carried out while I was a member of the KIT-BACK project at the Technical University of Berlin. The final version was written up while I participated in the LILOG project as a guest researcher at the Scientific Center IBM Germany, Institute for Knowledge-Based Systems, Stuttgart.

I am indebted to my thesis advisor Wolfgang Wahlster, who stimulated my interest in knowledge representation in the first place while I was a member of the HAM-ANS project and who encouraged me in the following years to carry out the research described here.

Additionally, I would like to express my thanks to all those people without whom this book would not be what it is now. Foremost, there are my colleagues in the KIT group at the Technical University of Berlin and in the LILOG project at the Scientific Center of IBM Germany, Stuttgart. In particular, working with Kai von Luck, Christof Peltason, and Albrecht Schmiedel in the KIT-BACK project was a pleasure and played a central role in starting the research described here.

Once started, Kai played a driving force by always asking for the next chapter.

Furthermore, I would like to thank Peter Gärdenfors for making available the manuscript of his book and for his comments on some points concerning base revision; Otthein Herzog and Claus Rollinger for inviting me to participate in the LILOG project; Bob MacGregor for a number of discussions and suggestions, including the hint that realization must be easier than subsumption; Bernd Mahr for comments on the semantics of cycles; Peter Patel-Schneider for making the KANDOR system available and for discussions on semantics and complexity; Klaus Schild for showing me that subsumption in general terminological languages is undecidable; Jim Schmolze for pointing out that cycles are a serious problem; Jörg Siekmann, who was the second reader of the thesis, for asking the right questions and giving some valuable hints; Gert Smolka for numerous helpful discussions on semantic specification, algorithms, and the relationship between feature logic and KL-ONE; Norm Sondheimer for inviting me to ISI as a guest researcher and for showing me how to use KL-TWO in a natural language system; Jay Tucker for proof-reading various versions of the thesis (I take credit for any remaining flaws, of course); Marc Vilain for discussions on realization algorithms; and a number of other people too many to be listed here.

Contents

III   Revision

List of Figures

List of Tables

Part I

Representation, Reasoning and Revision – The Idea

1. Introduction

One of the key assumptions in Artificial Intelligence is that intelligent behavior requires vast amounts of knowledge. Therefore, any computer system supposed to exhibit some form of intelligent behavior has to provide means for representing knowledge and drawing conclusions from it. This makes the study of knowledge representation a central field in Artificial Intelligence.

Main research topics in knowledge representation are the development of formalisms capable for explicating knowledge and the design of systems which apply the explicated knowledge inside of a computer effectively – systems which *reason* with the represented knowledge. If knowledge were a static entity, there would be nothing left to do. However, as it turns out, we are constantly confronted with new discoveries (for example, of our own mistakes) and a changing world – thus, the represented knowledge has to be *revised*.

1.1 A Dynamic View of Knowledge Bases

One view of knowledge representation focusses on the static aspects of represented knowledge. This includes the question of what kind of formal language we should use to represent a given body of knowledge and how we can assign *meaning* to the expressions of the formal language. Although such questions are important, it turns out that the real work begins after we have answered those questions.

If we have committed ourselves to a *semantics* of a knowledge representation language, it usually turns out that what is stored *explicitly* in a *knowledge base* is only a fraction of what is represented *implicitly*. In fact, if this were not the case, we would not talk about knowledge representation but about data-structures. In a nutshell, knowledge representation and reasoning are two sides of the same coin. This introduces one of the dynamic aspects of knowledge bases. How do we *derive* knowledge represented only implicitly, and how do we *control* the amount of computational resources dedicated to this purpose? Although we are interested in discovering all things implied by some body of knowledge stored in a knowledge base, this turns out to be impossible in most cases. This is true even in cases when we are only interested in some seemingly "simple" relationships. Half of this book deals with the reason for this fact and how to characterize reasoning processes in this context.

The other half is devoted to another aspect of the dynamics of knowledge bases, namely, the way knowledge bases are *changed*. Supporting the *revision* of knowledge bases is a crucial topic in building increasingly larger knowledge-based systems. How important this issue is might become apparent upon considering how much effort is spent in maintaining realistic knowledge bases, for instance, the R1 knowledge base [Bachant and McDermott, 1984]. This problem, however, does not only come up in systems when they are applied in real world situations. Even systems in research environments are "suffering" from large knowledge bases. For example, the knowledge base used in the JANUS project [Sondheimer and Nebel, 1986], contains 850 concepts and 150 relationships between concepts, and the knowledge base used in the FAME system contains over 1500 concepts with an average of 25 relationships per concept [Mays et al., 1988]. However, this is just the beginning. There is evidence for the fact that for any domain of expertise $70,000 \pm 20,000$ chunks of knowledge are necessary [Reddy, 1988, p. 14].

Clearly, such an amount of represented knowledge cannot be handled merely by pencil, paper, and concentration. The usual answer is to employ some sort of *knowledge base editor*, such as KREME [Abrett and Burstein, 1987]. These systems usually directly manipulate the data-structures used to implement the knowledge base. A more principled solution is, of course, to divide the task of revising a knowledge base into a formal task which is concerned only with formal manipulations of the expressions in the knowledge base – based on the semantics of those expressions – and another task responsible for the interaction with a human user. Such a distinction would open up the way to use the first subtask for purposes other than just knowledge base editing – for instance, it might be used inside a *machine learning system* – and it would also enhance our understanding of the general process of revising knowledge bases.

1.2 Hybrid Systems Based on KL-ONE

The two problems sketched above will be investigated in the context of the family of hybrid systems based on KL-ONE [Brachman and Schmolze, 1985]. This family includes, for instance, KL-TWO [Vilain, 1985], KRYPTON [Brachman et al., 1985], and BACK [Nebel and von Luck, 1988]. Any such hybrid system consists of at least two subsystems: a *terminological representation system* (the *TBox*) and an *assertional representation system* (the *ABox*). The former subsystem is concerned with representing the terminology and relationships between terms, the latter is used to describe the world by making assertions.

All these systems employ representation formalisms with quite well-defined semantics – a property which distinguishes them from many other representation systems, such as KRL [Bobrow and Winograd, 1977], FRL [Roberts and Goldstein, 1977], KODIAK [Wilensky, 1984], and KEE [IntelliCorp, 1985]. However, having a well-defined semantics does not imply that the associated reasoning processes are well-understood. Although much research effort has been devoted to this subject in recent years, it turns out that there are still a number of unexplored areas and ignored issues. Based on the experience I gained in the development of the BACK system, these points will be analyzed, which will lead to some new and interesting insights into the reasoning processes in hybrid systems based on

KL-ONE.

While reasoning in KL-ONE-based systems has been investigated before, revision has usually been neglected in such systems. Patel-Schneider, for instance, pointed out that in KANDOR, another member of the family mentioned, *knowledge base revision* has been left out "...partly because its semantics are unclear and partly because it is computationally expensive to perform" [Patel-Schneider, 1984, p. 15].

One effort to integrate knowledge base revision in hybrid systems based on KL-ONE is the KL-TWO system [Vilain, 1985]. KL-TWO consists of the terminological representation system NIKL [Moser, 1983] and the *reason maintenance system* RUP [McAllester, 1982], which is used as the assertional component. This special architecture permits revision of the assertional knowledge, but not the revision of terminological knowledge.

My personal experience in both working with such a system [Sondheimer and Nebel, 1986] and developing one [Nebel and von Luck, 1987] has convinced me, however, that a theoretically clean and principled solution supporting revision of assertional *and* terminological knowledge is needed.

1.3 An Introductory Example

In order to make things a little more concrete, a small, informal example might be appropriate to demonstrate where reasoning and revision come into play and how they are interrelated. Let us assume that the bureaucrats who manage your research department throw away the old-fashioned relational database system and put a brand-new advanced knowledge representation system in charge of supporting the management of the department. This is perhaps an unexpected use. Nevertheless, it seems worthwhile to consider such applications.

Assume that for the purpose of managing the department, it is necessary to classify all projects which are currently running. Let us further assume that the bureaucrats have introduced the *terminology* in Fig. 1.1.

Terms intended to describe classes of individuals (e.g. Small-team) will be called *concepts* (using the notions and terms introduced in [Brachman and Schmolze, 1985]). Concepts introduced with the phrase "a X is (defined as) a ..." are called *defined concepts*. These concepts are introduced by giving all *necessary* and *sufficient* conditions, i.e., any individual satisfying the associated description will be considered as a member of the class the concept denotes. All other concepts are called *primitive concepts*; the associated descriptions name only the *necessary* conditions.

Terms intended to denote relationships between individuals (e.g. member) are called *roles*.[2] *Restrictions on roles* are used to define concepts. For instance, the definition of Small-team means that an individual i is a member of the class

---

[1]I will use this font when referring to symbols of a knowledge base in order to avoid confusion between the formal meaning of a term and the ordinary meaning of the word.

[2]In order to distinguish roles and concepts lexically, role names are written in lowercase and concept names are capitalized.

A Man[1] is a
  Human.
A Woman is a
  Human.
No Man is a Woman, and *vice versa*.
A Team is (defined as) a
  Set with at least 2 members which are all Humans.
A Small-team is (defined as) a
  Team with at most 5 members.
A Modern-team is (defined as) a
  Team with at most 4 members and
  with at least 1 leader, which is a member, and
  all leaders are Women.

Fig. 1.1. Informal Example of a Terminological Knowledge Base

denoted by the concept Small-team if and only if the individual *i* belongs to the class denoted by Team and if there are at most five other individuals being in the member relationship to *i*.

A visualization of the relations between the terms of our small terminology is given in Fig. 1.2. The similarity of this network to a special class of semantic networks – *structural inheritance networks* [Brachman, 1979] – is not incidental, but intended. Terminological knowledge representation has its roots there.

Note that Fig. 1.2 does not simply depict the terminology in Fig. 1.1, but shows a couple of *inferred* properties as well. For instance, the specialization relationship – called *subsumption* – (depicted by a double-lined arrow) between the concepts Small-team and Modern-team, which is only implicit in Fig. 1.1, is made explicit in the graphical depiction. Furthermore, the role restrictions are all completed according to obvious *inheritance* rules.

While this gives us a first indication of where *reasoning* comes into play, the role of reasoning becomes more obvious when propositions about entities in the world are added. Assume that the knowledge base of our bureaucrats contains the fact that the object TEAM-A[3] is a Modern-team with TOM, DICK, HARRY, and KIM as members, and that they are all Men. Obviously, we have an *inconsistency*. At least one of the members must be a Woman. Supposing that KIM is the Woman – and thus also the leader – we can *infer* that TEAM-A must be a Small-team, although nobody specified this explicitly. All this looks very easy and natural, but, as we will see, specifying general *inference algorithms* which come to the same conclusions presents considerable problems.

Ignoring these difficulties for a while, let us assume that the terminology has to be changed. This might be necessary because the knowledge base contains an error, because the knowledge base has to be adapted for new purposes, or because

---

[3]Identifiers denoting "real-world objects" are written in uppercase.

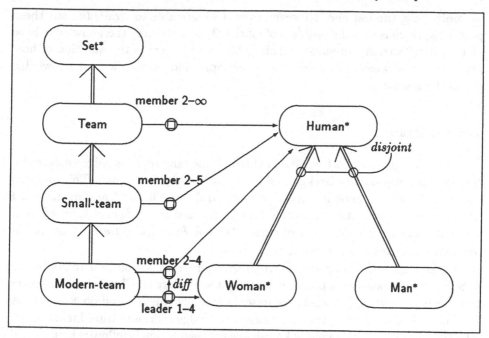

Fig. 1.2. Graphical Depiction of the Example Knowledge Base

laws have changed. For instance, the following *revision requests* are reasonable:

- Because the classification scheme changes, a Small-team is redefined as a Team with at most 3 members. Should this imply that a Modern-team is no longer a Small-team?

- Somebody changes his mind about what a Modern-team is. He thinks that a Modern-team can have up to ten members. Should such a revision request result in the automatic removal of the original restriction on the member role?

- One of the more sexist bureaucrats changes the definition of Modern-team so that all members have to be Men. What should be done with such a revision operation? Obviously, no Modern-team could satisfy such a description because at least one member has to be a Woman – the leader.

- For legal reasons, the distinction between Man and Woman is dropped. Thus, the corresponding concepts are deleted. How should we update the definition of Modern-Team?

- Since it becomes necessary to have information about children of employees, we would like to add to the knowledge base the fact that all offspring of Humans are Humans as well. Does such a change make sense? Are circularly defined concepts meaningful?

Some of the problems are obviously of a pragmatic nature, i.e., what intentions do revision requests have? Others are concerned solely with semantics and reasoning, e.g. the last one. However, even if we are able to straighten out these problems, there is still the problem of efficiently maintaining the knowledge base so that it reflects the intended meaning. Moreover, there is the question of how interactions between the revision of assertional and terminological knowledge should be handled.

1.4 Outline

Chapter 2 contains a short excursion through the land of knowledge representation in order to provide a background for the following discussions. This includes the introduction of some important notions and some lines of argumentation I will rely on – arguments which could be summarized as the *logical point of view*. We will also take a quick view of what is called *Knowledge Base Management Systems* nowadays and relate our work to it.

Backed up with arguments from Chap. 2, representation and reasoning in hybrid systems based on KL-ONE is investigated in Part II. Chapter 3 introduces one particular hybrid knowledge representation formalism based on KL-ONE. A brief historical account of terminological knowledge representation including an intuitive approach to this kind of knowledge representation is followed by a formal treatment. In particular, it is shown how to reduce the problem of determining *subsumption* between concepts *in a terminology* to the problem of determining subsumption between *terms*. Additionally, a simple assertional representation formalism is introduced, a unified model-theoretic semantics for the resulting hybrid formalism is specified, and possible inferences are sketched. The chapter closes with a discussion of some conceivable extensions and relates terminological formalisms to other, similar formalisms.

Having a knowledge representation formalism is one thing. Getting the computer to reason with it is another thing. Chapter 4 is devoted to this subject. Some implementation techniques are described, and the computational complexity is analyzed, which reveals new insights about reasoning in such systems. In Sect. 4.2, an analysis of the computational complexity of the *subsumption problem* shows that a *complete* and *computationally tractable subsumption algorithm* for the *term-forming formalism* introduced in Chap. 3 is impossible. Furthermore, in Sect. 4.3 it is shown that subsumption in almost any *terminological formalism* is *intractable* in the formal sense, but well-behaved in practice. In Sect. 4.5, an interesting type of hybrid inferences which has been neglected by all other similar systems based on KL-ONE is studied. Integrating this type of inference results in a complete hybrid inference algorithm in the limiting case that *canonical models* can be identified – which enables us to the characterize the hybrid inference algorithm as *conditionally complete*.

With these two chapters, we could close the discussion on representation and reasoning in hybrid representation systems. However, terminological representation formalisms, as viewed so far, contain a semantic gap: *Circular concept introductions* are not sanctioned because they create a number of problems from a semantic and algorithmic point of view. Instead of subscribing to the traditional point of view in this matter, this semantic gap will be removed in Chap. 5 since *terminological cycles* often seem to be useful and, more importantly, may easily be created when revising a terminological knowledge base. The intuitive semantics of terminological cycles are studied, and different formal semantics are investigated. What I call *descriptive semantics* seems to cover our intuitions best and, for this reason, will be adopted and used to derive an extension of the basic inference algorithm.

Part III of the book tackles the revision problem. Chapter 6 introduces the topic of belief revision. Current approaches to belief revision in the areas of the dynamics of epistemic states, database theory, nonmonotonic reasoning, and reason maintenance systems are surveyed. In the course of the study of these topics, an interesting result concerning the relation between the revision of *symbol-level* knowledge bases and *knowledge-level* knowledge bases will be presented in Sect. 6.3. It is shown that the former can be reconstructed as belief revision on the knowledge-level, taking into account the notion of *epistemic relevance*. Based on this result, I will argue that, from a theoretical point of view, *reason maintenance* need not to be integrated as a primitive notion into a theoretical framework of belief revision. Nevertheless, on the implementational level, this is an important notion. Surveying work done in the area of *reason maintenance systems*, some points critical for revision of assertional knowledge are identified.

Equipped with a thorough understanding of terminological knowledge representation, the accompanying reasoning processes, and the theory of belief revision, we are prepared to tackle the revision problem in terminological representation systems. Chapter 7 starts off with a discussion of principles any knowledge base revision system should follow and a description of the conceptual problems in revising terminological knowledge, followed by a survey of approaches to knowledge base revision in terminological representation systems pursued so far. Reflections about the pragmatics of terminological knowledge bases finally lead us to a specification of a revision facility based on *minimal changes of literal definitions*. The chapter closes with an outlook on revision in hybrid systems involving assertional and terminological knowledge.

The techniques necessary to implement terminological revision operations efficiently are described in Chap. 8. In essence, they amount to employing a *reason-maintenance system*. However, because an approach based solely on such a system would be too expensive in terms of computational costs, a balanced solution is chosen which employs a data-dependency network as well as optimizations derived from semantic properties of revision operations. Finally, we will discuss how a knowledge acquisition system can make use of the knowledge base revision facility.

2. Representation and Management of Knowledge

Knowledge, its representation and its management play a central role in Artificial Intelligence. However, it cannot be said that the views and approaches in this field are converging. As Brachman and Levesque [1985] pointed out in the introduction of an anthology of papers on knowledge representation, there is no textbook available on this subject, and, probably, it would be impossible to write one at this point.

The following sections certainly cannot compensate for this deficiency. However, what I will try to achieve is a presentation of my basic assumptions about what knowledge representation amounts to. These assumptions can be roughly characterized as the *logical point of view*. Additionally, in the last section, I will briefly relate my work to what is called *Knowledge Base Management Systems*.

2.1 Knowledge and its Representation

Research in Artificial Intelligence (henceforth AI) started off by trying to identify the *general mechanisms* responsible for intelligent behavior. One instance for this line of research is the General Problem Solver[1] GPS [Ernst and Newell, 1969]. The main paradigm was that "One had not to 'cheat' by 'giving' the problem-solver the solution in any sense" as Hayes [1974] characterized it. However, it quickly became obvious that general and powerful methods are not enough to get the desired result, namely, intelligent behavior. Almost all tasks a human can perform which are considered to require intelligence are also based on a huge amount of knowledge. For instance, understanding and producing natural language heavily relies on knowledge accumulated during our life time, knowledge about the language, about the structure of the world, social relationships etc. Therefore, it seems to be inevitable that this knowledge must be utilized in some way.

The most straightforward solution would be that the programmer of an AI system just "programs the knowledge into the system," using an AI programming language, such as LISP [Winston and Horn, 1981] or PROLOG [Clocksin and Mellish, 1981]. The outcome of this effort would be a system based on the knowledge of its programmer, a "knowledge-based" system. However, something seems fun-

---

[1]This system is not only an example of the mentioned paradigm, but also a very striking instance of what D. McDermott [1976, p. 4] calls the fallacy of "wishful mnemonics": "...it originally meant 'General Problem Solver,' which caused everybody a lot of excitement and distraction. It should have been called LFGNS – 'Local-Feature-Guided Network Searcher'."

damentally wrong with this solution: we are giving up on generality. Although the program might exhibit an interesting intelligent behavior in some special field, we get no hints of how general the solution is, whether it can be moved to other application areas, or how it relates to intelligence (whatever that may be). We – and the system as well – may even be unable to explain which knowledge is responsible for a particular system behavior. Thus, such an approach precludes the realization of something like an *explanation facility* for such a system, a capability often explicitly required for complex systems [Wahlster, 1981]. Furthermore, there seems to be no difference from other programming activities in computer science.[2]

Of course, knowledge in AI is utilized in a different way, and here *knowledge representation* (henceforth KR, or simply representation) comes into play. Knowledge is not just programmed into a system, but *explicitly* and *declaratively represented* by using some kind of formal language – a *KR formalism*. Explicit means that the system architecture contains an *explicit knowledge base* (henceforth KB), which, in turn, contains expressions of the KR formalism. These expressions describe in a (more or less) declarative way the knowledge the system relies on to solve a given problem. Only if these conditions are met, we call a system *knowledge-based* [Brachman and Levesque, 1985, p. xiv].

This characterization implies a couple of other properties a KB and a knowledge-based system must possess. However, it also leaves some questions unanswered, namely:

- What is the relationship between knowledge and represented knowledge? This includes a question of what the *nature of knowledge* is (from the point of view of AI).

- What are the *necessary properties* of KR formalisms? Stated in another way, is any formal language a KR formalism?

- What does *declarativity* mean, or, stated differently, where do expressions get their *meaning* from?

- What are the *services* a system manipulating represented knowledge should provide?

- What are the appropriate *techniques* to implement a system dealing with represented knowledge – a *KR system*?

2.1.1 Knowledge and Data

One way of approaching the question of what knowledge is might be to contrast the notion of *data* as understood in the data-base field with *knowledge* as used in AI. Wiederhold [1986, p. 79] characterizes the difference in the following way:

---

[2]Although such a view is possible [Stoyan, 1987], I believe that there are a number of differences, which hopefully become obvious in this chapter.

If we can trust an automatic process or clerk to collect the material then we are talking about *data*. ...

If we look for an expert to provide the material then we are talking about *knowledge*. Knowledge includes abstraction and generalization of voluminous data. ...

This point of view, however, is influenced by the systems Wiederhold [1986, p. 78] intends to describe, namely, information systems "to be used for decision-making in enterprises". Furthermore, the characterization seems to be influenced by one very prominent kind of AI systems: expert systems [Waterman, 1986]. Even though it often might seem that AI consists mainly of research in this field, in particular if AI is seen from the outside, representation of expert knowledge is only one topic. For instance, AI and KR are very much concerned about the representation of *common-sense* knowledge [Hobbs and Moore, 1985], which, apparently, is possessed not only by experts. Additionally, as Wiederhold himself admits, the definition is only of a pragmatic nature. The distinction between what knowledge is and what data is may change according to who is interpreting the information.

Wong and Mylopoulos [1977, p. 344] tried to characterize the difference indirectly by specifying what is stored in knowledge bases and data bases. Knowledge bases will

include large amounts of abstract knowledge ... and a small amount of (less interesting) concrete knowledge ...

while data bases

were designed mostly for concrete knowledge, and the modelling methods were inadequate for representing abstract knowledge.

Here again, we meet the distinction between raw data (by the way, what does *raw* data really mean?) and abstractions. However, it is clearly spelled out that both are considered as some kind of knowledge.

Obviously, it does not give a satisfying answer to our question. The only hint we got is that data stored in data bases could be viewed as represented knowledge, albeit a very limited sort. All in all, it does not seem that this small excursion into the data-base field contributed to any deeper understanding of knowledge or how it could be represented.

2.1.2 The Knowledge Level

If in AI the term *represented knowledge* is used, it most often refers to the expressions of a KR formalism. In addition to that, of course, there must be some processes using the KR expressions which assign the (structural, internal) meaning to the expressions [Barr and Feigenbaum, 1979, p. 143]:

We can say, metaphorically, that a book is a source of knowledge, but without a reader, the book is just ink on paper. Similarly, we often talk about of the list-and-pointer data structures in an AI data-base as knowledge per se, when we really mean that they represent facts or rules when used by a certain program to behave in a knowledgeable way.

This leads to a totally different perspective on knowledge and data than the one in the last subsection, namely, something like

$$Knowledge = Data + Interpreter$$

This sounds simple and plausible, but it is quite misleading. Consider, for instance, two different Data/Interpreter pairs. Are they necessarily different bodies of knowledge? Even if they behave identically? Certainly not.

Knowledge does not seem to be describable in mechanical terms. It seems to be a property we ascribe to an agent when it is acting. And this ascription is not just arbitrary or accidental, but rather serves as an important abstraction which permits the explanation of behavior. If we observe someone we consider as a *rational agent*, we may explain the agent's actions in the following way [Newell, 1982, pp. 105]:

1. The rational agent has some *knowledge* about the environment and how it could be affected by actions.

2. The rational agent has some *goals* (also a kind of knowledge).

3. Then the agent's actions are based on the knowledge and aimed at achieving some of the goals.

This explanation does not give us any predictive power because we do not know what will happen in the case of conflicting goals, when goals can be achieved by different actions, or in the case of inaccurate knowledge. It is more a competence-like notion. Nevertheless, it permits us to characterize knowledge in an important way [Newell, 1982, p. 105]:

Knowledge is to be characterized entirely *functionally*, in terms of what it does, not *structurally*, in terms of physical objects with particular properties and relations. This still leaves open the requirement for a physical structure that can fill the functional role.

Newell [1982, p. 99] goes as far as postulating an additional computer system level distinct from all other levels (as the symbol level, the register-transfer level, etc.) – the *knowledge level*:

There exists a distinct computer system level, lying immediately above the symbol level, which is characterized by knowledge as the medium and the *principle of rationality* as the law of behavior.

Although this level has some very weird properties compared with other computer system levels – it is only approximative, there exist no laws of composition, etc., and therefore its existence may be arguable – it does give us the opportunity to analyze knowledge at a very abstract level. Furthermore, KR systems can also be analyzed at this level. Instead of going into the details of how knowledge is represented symbolically in a particular KR system we may just view it on the knowledge level and ask how it behaves on particular inputs. This enables us, for instance, to compare such different representation formalisms as *semantic networks* as described in Sect. 3.1.1, *frame systems* as sketched in Sect. 3.1.2, *production-rule systems, relational data base system*, etc. Certainly, we cannot perform the comparison without an appropriate analytical tool. Newell [1982, p. 121] suggests for that purpose logic:

> Just as talking of *programmer-less* programming violates truth in packaging, so does talking of *non-logical analysis* of knowledge.

If anybody has the feeling that, besides the fact that the term *knowledge* was used very often above, the ideas sound very familiar and similar to *abstract data types* [Liskov and Zilles, 1974], he or she is not completely misled. As a matter of fact, Levesque [1984a] describes KBs on the knowledge level in terms of abstract data types using two operations: TELL to add more knowledge to a KB and ASK to query the KB.

2.1.3 The Knowledge Representation Hypothesis

In agreeing with the above point of view, we may arrive at the question of how it is possible to find a way to *represent* knowledge, this rather abstract object. Although there is, or at least was, a broad diversity of opinions of what representation of knowledge amounts to, as Brachman and Smith [1980] concluded from a questionnaire, there seems to be at least one common assumption, namely, that "knowledge is representational." That means first, if we "know something," then there is an object of our knowledge, i.e., we know something *about some particular entity.*[3] Second, this knowledge can be in some way symbolically encoded,[4] and if the knowledge is applied then the symbols are manipulated without regard to the entities the symbols refer to. This point of view is spelled out by Brian C. Smith [1982, p. 2] as the *Knowledge Representation Hypothesis*:

> Any mechanically embodied intelligent process will be comprised of structural ingredients that a) we as external observers naturally take to represent a propositional account of the knowledge the overall process exhibits, and b) independent of such external semantical attribution, play a formal but causal and essential role in engendering the behavior that manifests that knowledge.

---

[3]Entity here is meant to be a very general category. It could be an existing object in the world, relationships between objects, nonexistent objects, ideas, events, etc.

[4]This is not a commitment to any particular kind of representation, e.g. propositional or analogical, or whatever [Hayes, 1974, Levesque, 1986], as Schefe [1982, p. 43] seems to assume.

Whether we subscribe to this point of view in the strong version – *any* knowledge is representational – or in a weak version – knowledge is *possibly* representational – or whether we deny both as, for example, Dreyfus [1981] does,[5] we have to admit that

- AI and the paradigm of KR has some success. Expert systems, a now very popular species of knowledge-based systems, proved that KR can be applied successfully.

- If we want to build "smarter computer systems" – one goal of AI [Winston, 1984, p. 3] – it seems that we really do not have a better hypothesis today than Smith's.

- Even if the hypothesis may be wrong for the human as a whole, the analysis of mind – another goal of AI – can rest on this hypothesis, provided that some significant aspect of thought can be understood in this way [Haugeland, 1985, pp. 246–254].

To summarize, the knowledge representation hypothesis seems to be reasonable.[6] If we accept the hypothesis as a base for further investigation (and we will do so in the following), this yields some consequences. An important one is that KR is a kind of *reconstruction* of human knowledge.[7] We do not directly represent the human knowledge by a mapping from "objects of the mind" to expressions of some KR formalism (in the first place), but instead we try to establish a system which is *functionally similar* to human knowledge.

2.1.4 Three Approaches to Knowledge Representation

In the extreme, a KR formalism could be viewed as "mentalese" (as B. C. Smith [1982, p. 3] termed it), the language our mind uses. Of course, nobody holds this view. We are just too far away from a complete understanding of what is going on in our brain.

Nevertheless, in KR, as well in AI in general, there are at least two different intentions in working out solutions. One is to build performance systems, i.e., systems which act intelligently. In this case, only engineering principles are important in building a system (let us call it the engineering perspective). The other intention is to get insights into the mind. Here, the physical structure of a process is much more important for the realization of a solution than before. In fact, the structure of the system is considered to be more important than

---

[5]Dreyfus denies that knowledge *can* be representational. He argues that intelligence instead depends on skills acquired by practice and training and that this cannot be formalized.

[6]Furthermore, no empirical evidence or arguments, in particular by connectionists [Rumelhart and McClelland, 1986], show that the hypothesis is mistaken. On the contrary, it seems likely that connectionism will have to adopt organizing principles that resemble the knowledge representation hypothesis [Chandrasekaran et al., 1988].

[7]An observation also mentioned by Schefe [1982] leading him to coin the term *knowledge reconstruction*. We, however, will stick to the established terminology and will continue to use the term *knowledge representation*.

the system's being used for some purpose (this is usually called the cognitive perspective).

Examples of these two different approaches are HAM-RPM [von Hahn et al., 1980], a natural language system which was used to investigate the cognitive abilities of an agent engaging in a natural language dialog, and HAM-ANS [Hoeppner et al., 1983], a natural language access system to different background systems. These two systems present also a good example for the fact that even though the goals seem to be fundamentally different both approaches are fertilizing each other: HAM-ANS is the descendant of HAM-RPM. Another good example of cross-fertilization in the field of KR are production-rule systems. In the early days of AI, they were used as a tool for demonstrating some cognitive properties; later on, they were employed by expert systems [Davis and King, 1984].

The reasons for this cross-fertilization are obvious. In trying to build an AI performance system, we have to create at least a human-friendly interface, often resulting in a human-like interface. In a natural language system, for instance, we have to account for misunderstandings [McCoy, 1984]. Furthermore, instead of interpreting a question literally, we had better infer the intention of the human questioner and answer appropriately [Marburger and Wahlster, 1983].

In research oriented around cognition, on the other hand, it is known that the human mind does extraordinarily well on cognitive tasks, so that a good engineering solution might show us the way to the structure we are looking for. An example of this, at least partly, is the work of Winograd [1972]. Of course, an efficient solution is not enough. Often, timing considerations and the ability to produce human-like failures are also important in evaluating a solution [Christaller, 1985, pp. 9ff].

Returning to our subject – knowledge representation – we can identify another perspective which does not fit into the scheme established so far. I would like to call that the epistemological perspective [McCarthy and Hayes, 1969, McCarthy, 1977]. The focus of research guided by this perspective is neither to build performance systems nor to investigate cognitive structures, but to develop a *theory of common-sense knowledge* and *reasoning* based on well-founded formalization, which might just be viewed as pursuing the program Newell proposed in his paper, namely, to analyze knowledge at the knowledge level. That does not mean that this line of research ignores the other goals, or that it is useless for the other perspectives. On the contrary, by formalizing the ideas which are used in existing AI systems, we get a better understanding of what these systems really do (or are supposed to do) – and this seems to be one important way to develop AI as a scientific discipline [Hobbs and Moore, 1985, p. xxi] – and it opens up the opportunity, for instance, to analyze AI systems with respect to correctness and computational complexity.

The research reported here is mostly motivated by goals of the latter perspective. This, however, is not the entire story. We are also aiming at developing the appropriate implementation techniques (at the symbol level) and demonstrate their feasibility by a running prototype. However, we will mostly ignore all issues which could be summarized under the heading of "cognitive adequacy" of the system structure.

2.2 Knowledge Representation Formalisms

While the characterization of knowledge as a competence-like notion in the last section seems to be the most plausible one, of course, the "functional role" has to be filled by a "physical structure," as Newell termed it. The *Knowledge Representation Hypothesis* tells us that this is possible.

What we need is some kind of formal language – a *KR language*[8]. Although any formal language might be used for this purpose, we had better assign meaning to expressions of such a language, in which case we will call the language a *KR formalism*.[9] A set of well-formed expressions[10] of such a KR formalism, which is intended to represent aspects of the world, will be called *knowledge base*.

Additionally, we need some kind of machinery which can make use of the expressions in the KB – a *KR system*. Such a system has to fulfill two tasks. First, it has to interpret the KB and turn it into a body of knowledge – in terms of the knowledge level – by *inferring new expressions* which are only implicit in the expressions stored in the KB. Without this ability, a KR system would be just a plain, unstructured memory.[11] We could only retrieve the expressions put into the KB previously. The second task is to provide *services to the outside world*, like e.g. TELL and ASK, which operate on the KB and make use of the inference capabilities of the KR system.

Although we cannot have a KR system without a KR formalism (or at least this is hard to conceive) and it does not seem to make much sense to talk about a KR formalism if there is no system which makes use of it, we can, of course, view them in isolation. A prerequisite is that we can talk about the *meaning* of expressions in a KR formalism without resorting to a particular system which uses the expressions.

2.2.1 Semantics of Representation Formalisms

We can, of course, manage explaining what the expressions of a KR formalism are intended to mean by giving an informal description and some examples. Perhaps, a running system can give even more insights. In fact, research in AI starts off using this experimental, engineering approach most of the time. However, staying on the informal side has several drawbacks.

One disadvantage of the informal way is that it leads to numerous arguments of the kind "... but my understanding of this example is different ..."

---

[8]Called *scheme* by Hayes [1974].

[9]I do not intend to give a broad survey of different KR formalisms here, but rather to view KR formalisms from a very abstract point of view. For an overview of particular KR formalisms, the reader should consult [Mylopoulos and Levesque, 1984] or [Barr and Feigenbaum, 1979, pp. 141–222].

[10]Hayes [1974] calls such expressions *configurations*.

[11]Note that even data base systems are more powerful by virtue of associated query languages and the employment of the closed world assumption.

Although a corresponding KR system will give a definite answer when tried on the expression, this situation reveals that we did not really understand what the system does and what expressions in the formalism mean. In scientific discourse, in particular, the lack of formal semantics is "a regrettable source of confusion and misunderstanding" [Hayes, 1974, p. 64] – and makes the comparison and analysis of different KR formalisms impossible.

Connected with this deficiency is the fact that it is impossible to say whether the KR system correctly implements the intended behavior. This might not be disturbing if a KR system is used to simulate cognitive abilities, but cannot be tolerated if a KR system is employed as a subsystem of a knowledge-based system for some application. In this case, it is mandatory to be able to predict the system's behavior. The only way to achieve that without resorting to the actual program code is to employ some sort of *formal semantics*.

There are different choices for assigning formal meaning to a KR formalism. We may, for instance, explain the meaning of a KR formalism by referring to the processes – possibly abstract ones – which operate on the expressions in the KB, as for example is done in [Shapiro and Rapaport, 1986, p. 282]:

> Arcs ... only have meaning within the system, provided by node- and path-based inference rules (which can be thought of as procedures that operate on arcs).

However, this *operational semantics* is, of course, not a very enlightening approach. It does not explain why "arcs" have to be used at all or what they stand for. Another similar approach is the "empirical semantics" described in [Reimer, 1985] and [Reimer, 1986]. Here, the well-formedness conditions for expressions in a KB and operations on them are specified with the aid of the formal specification language META-IV [Bjørner, 1980]. Although this gives us a formal and rigorous specification of the KR system, it leaves open what the expressions in the KB refer to. Both these approaches to formal semantics are *internal* in that they refer to the formalism and to the system but not to the outside world.

As has been pointed out by many researchers in knowledge representation [Hayes, 1977, McDermott, 1978, Moore, 1982, Patel-Schneider, 1987b], the only satisfying approach to assigning meaning to KR formalisms is taking seriously the ideas spelled out in Sect. 2.1.3, namely, that knowledge is about entities in the world. That means expressions of a KR formalism should derive their meaning in some way from reference to the external world; and the adequate tool for such a task is Tarskian model theory [Tarski, 1935].

The usual semantics for first-order predicate logic (see [Genesereth and Nilsson, 1987] or any standard introductory text to logic) is the canonical example of this kind of semantics. A structure is assumed, containing a set of objects, called the *domain* or *universe of discourse*, functions on and relations over this domain, plus an *interpretation function* which maps constants and variables into objects, function symbols into functions, relation symbols into relations, and propositions into truth values. Any such structure (usually called *interpretation*) satisfying a set of propositions is called a *model* of this set of propositions, and, preferably, the (aspect of the) world we intend to describe with a set of propositions should be one of all the possible models.

As a matter of fact, it is this commitment to model-theoretic semantics which makes up the essence of the *logical point of view* in knowledge representation. It is neither a claim that a particular syntax has to be used to represent knowledge, nor a consensus about a particular logic formalism, nor even a restriction to sound inference rules [Israel, 1983], but it is the idea that the meaning of a formalism has to be derived by reference to the external world – by specifying an *external semantics*.

This is not a mere philosophical position irrelevant for "real work," although a large fraction of research in knowledge representation has seemed to get along without bothering about logics or semantics.[12] On the contrary, logic proved to be quite fruitful in the development of KR formalisms and systems. For instance, the development of the NETL system [Fahlman, 1979] – a semantic network system intended to run on a massively parallel computer – which started off using an operational semantics later turned to logic in order to eliminate some serious deficiencies [Touretzky, 1986]. The same holds true for the KL-ONE system [Brachman and Schmolze, 1985], which evolved over the years from a set of loosely coupled, intuitively justified procedures [Brachman, 1979] to a formalism with a well-defined semantics (as we will see in Sections 3.1.4 and 3.2) and formally justified inference procedures. In fact, in both cases the understanding of the representation formalism was considerably strengthened by the formal semantics.

Of course, the logical point of view is not the only possible one. There are a number of good arguments challenging this standpoint (the most important papers are [Minsky, 1975] and a recent article by D. McDermott [1987]). We will, however, not go into the details of this discussion here (cf. Sect. 3.1.2).

Summarizing, the answer to one of the questions in Sect. 2.1 is that any formal language may be used as a KR formalism as long as a suitable semantics is assigned. This, of course, is not the entire story. There are also issues of expressiveness, convenience, and other criteria.

2.2.2 Adequacy Criteria

The most important criterion a KR formalism should fulfill is what McCarthy and Hayes [1969, p. 466] call *epistemological adequacy*[13]. This means it should be possible to *represent* all the aspects of the world we are interested in. This is, of course, a matter of degree, dependent on the purpose we are using the KR formalism for.

For example, a relational data base language [Date, 1981] is epistemologically adequate to represent a library catalog, but we might run into problems if we aim at representing concepts and relationships as in Sect. 1.3 with the same language. Although one can map a language as used in Fig. 1.1 (after a suitable formalization) into the language of relational data bases, it does not help very

---

[12]However, in recent years these issues appeared to be considered more important, as the papers in the Knowledge Representation sections in proceedings of AI conferences prove.

[13]Woods [1983, p. 22] calls it *expressive adequacy*.

much. The semantics of relational data base languages is totally different from the semantics of the informal concept description language. Thus, we may *store* (in an abstract sense) concept descriptions using a relational data base language, but we cannot *represent* concepts with such a language.

Although epistemological adequacy seems to be enough since anything we want to represent can be represented, different KR formalisms can offer different degrees of convenience. Michie [1982] has coined the term *human window* in order to describe this degree of convenience. KR formalisms located within the human window are those which permit to use expressions mirroring the conceptualization of the domain in order to represent something. Of course, employing Tarskian semantics helps a lot in staying inside the human window because the semantics forces us to assign meaning to expressions and sub-expressions by referring to the external world. Nevertheless, some facts may be expressed more easily and more naturally in one language than in another.[14] For example, the fact that a **Small-team** has at most 5 **members** is expressed easily in the informal concept description language in Fig. 1.1, but requires a couple of quantifiers and formulas if expressed in first-order predicate logic.

Another criterion for a KR formalism is its *heuristic adequacy*[15] [McCarthy and Hayes, 1969, p. 466] – its suitability to be used internally by a KR system to solve problems. Again, this is a matter of degree, mainly dependent on the algorithms the KR system uses. However, choosing the right formalism might enhance the performance of a system considerably. This is in particular the case if for a restricted problem domain a restricted KR formalism is chosen.

For example, first-order predicate logic is judged to be the epistemologically most adequate formalism for a wide range of representation tasks by many researchers [McCarthy, 1968, Hayes, 1977, Moore, 1982]. However, there are severe computational problems. First-order predicate logic is only semi-decidable, and, even for relatively simple cases, a theorem prover can spend a lot of time solving a problem. On the other hand, a restricted formalism can be more manageable, and problems which are hard to solve with the general formalism may turn out to be easily computable [Levesque and Brachman, 1985, p. 67]. Of course, one gives away general epistemological adequacy. However, we may aim at restoring this property by combining different formalisms – creating *hybrid representation formalisms*.

2.2.3 Hybrid Formalisms

Although it would be desirable to develop one KR formalism which meets all criteria – and in fact, some researchers are convinced that first-order predicate logic is just that formalism [Kowalski, 1980] – nowadays there seems to be a consensus that it is almost impossible to fulfill all goals simultaneously with one

---

[14]Woods [1983, p. 23] uses the term *conciseness of representation* to describe this dimension of a KR formalism.

[15]This criteria is called *computational efficiency* by Woods [1983, p. 22], and he subsumes this notion together with conciseness of representation and ease of modification under the heading *notational efficacy*.

formalism. Sometimes it is worthwhile to switch between different KR formalisms because of heuristic adequacy [Sloman, 1985], as in the hybrid system CAKE [Rich, 1982, Rich, 1985]; sometimes the limited epistemological adequacy (which may come together with high notational efficacy) may suggest the combination of different subformalisms – making up a *hybrid* KR formalism.

The informal example given in the Introduction demonstrates the latter case. The language used in Fig. 1.1 is very well-suited for the representation of terminological knowledge from the point of conciseness and heuristic adequacy but limited in its expressiveness. In order to say something definite about the world, we need an additional formalism to make assertions.

However, the mere combination of formalisms does not necessarily result in a hybrid formalism. A kind of "glue" is needed in order to constitute a hybrid formalism consisting of

- a *representational theory* (explaining what knowledge is to be represented by what formalism) and

- a *common semantics* for the overall formalism (explaining in a semantically sound manner the relationship between expressions of different subformalisms).

The representational theory should explain why there are different subformalisms, what their benefits are, and how they relate to each other. An answer should at least refer to the adequacy criteria introduced above:

- Epistemological adequacy, i.e., that the subformalisms are necessary to represent epistemologically different kinds of knowledge (e.g. analytic and synthetic knowledge).

- Heuristic adequacy, i.e., that the different subformalisms permit representation of the same knowledge in different ways for reasons of efficiency.

A necessary precondition for gluing things together is that their shapes fit, a fact which might be violated in designing a hybrid formalism, at least in the case where the subformalisms are intended to represent epistemological different kinds of knowledge. For example, if one subformalism permitted definition of terms by using time relationships but none of the other subformalisms referred to time at all, the subformalisms would be in some sense *unbalanced*. This, however, can be easily detected by inspecting the common semantics. However, there are also more subtle ways in which subformalisms can be unbalanced – a point we will return to in Sect. 4.6.

2.2.4 Formalizing a Body of Knowledge

Related to the problem of designing and implementing KR formalisms is the task of formalizing a body of knowledge, for example, the common-sense knowledge about fluids [Hayes, 1985]. It might seem that for a first attempt to formalize a new idea a very general KR formalism, the most epistemologically adequate formalism – say, first-order or higher-order predicate logic – would be a good candidate. There are some tradeoffs, though. Hobbs summarizes the issues involved as follows [Hobbs and Moore, 1985, p. xviii]:

> If only a narrow set of options is exercised in an unconstrained language, a more constrained language may be more natural and allow knowledge to be expressed more succinctly. In addition, special-purpose notations may indicate more explicitly the special-purpose deduction procedures that will use them. As Hayes admits, "idiosyncratic notations may sometimes be useful for idiosyncratic subtheories." Our concern in this volume is for facts, not notation, but sometimes getting the facts right requires notational maneuvers.

While I would admit that it might be distracting to make the move from a general to a special-purpose KR formalism too early, I also believe that the enterprise of formalizing a given domain of knowledge is not worth the effort it requires if we do not get more insights about the structure of the domain than a collection of axioms; particularly so, if no insights about the computational properties are gained.

This might sound a little overstated, and, in fact, I am not going to demand such results instantaneously, but the ultimate goal is to get the computer reason with the formalized knowledge, and this is impossible with unconstrained formalisms (as higher-order predicate logics). In order to give a positive example, the formalization of time as conducted by Allen [1983] and the analysis by others [Vilain and Kautz, 1986] represents a major leap in the right direction.

2.3 Knowledge Representation Systems

A KR system is in some sense the "materialization" of a KR formalism – it turns the semantics of the KR formalism into computations. However, KR systems do not exist in isolation. They are usually part of larger systems – of *knowledge-based systems*.

2.3.1 The Architecture of Knowledge-Based Systems

Analyzing existing knowledge-based systems, we note that large fractions of these systems do not have anything to do with "represented knowledge." For example, in [Bobrow et al., 1986] it is reported that 30-50% of the program code in expert systems is devoted to the user interface. Even if we ignore the user interface, we notice that a KR system is usually only a subsystem of a larger system which is implemented using conventional, procedural programming techniques.[16] There are many reasons for this.

---

[16]This does not mean that conventional programming languages are employed, but that the algorithmic paradigm is used in implementing the system.

First of all, it is often more efficient to express knowledge procedurally,[17] in particular if the anticipated use is obvious, rather than to use a general, declarative KR formalism. While this pays off in terms of efficiency and is often the only way to create practical systems [Hoeppner et al., 1983], it restricts the ways the knowledge can be used, and it makes modifications difficult.

Second, the theory about particular phenomena is often developed by experimenting, which may involve the formulation of this theory using procedural schemes. Third, sometimes it is hard to find a declarative representation such that it is possible to specify a clean semantics which allows the important inferences to be drawn [McDermott, 1987]. Most often, however, we will find a mixture of both kinds of expressing knowledge. Special-purpose theories are coded procedurally, but the parts which may often enough be changed and are well-understood from a formal point of view are represented declaratively.

Thus, a KR system has to offer services to the embedding knowledge-based system in some way. Furthermore, for some people – usually called *knowledge engineers* – it should be possible to manipulate the KB from the outside world[18] in order to "put knowledge into the KB." This could be done by directly manipulating data structures, by using a special KB editor, or by employing a separate knowledge acquisition system.[19] Summing up, the principal architecture of a knowledge-based system looks like Fig. 2.1 – characterizing the situation completely from a conceptual point of view, abstracting away organizational matters.

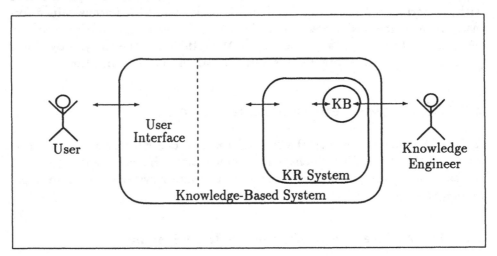

Fig. 2.1. Architecture of Knowledge-Based Systems

If a system has to perform such complex behavior as participating in a natural language dialog, a couple of capabilities are required. For instance, it is necessary to parse the input, to determine the meaning, to reason about the intentions of

---

[17]We could talk about "procedural knowledge representation" in this case. We will not do so, however. It is just programming – no more, no less.

[18]Of course, knowledge engineer and user can be the same person.

[19]This may result in embedding the knowledge-based system in the knowledge acquisition system, as it is the case in the TEIRESIAS system [Davis, 1982, p. 233].

the speaker, to determine an answer, and to verbalize this answer. Evidently, the types of knowledge required for these tasks are quite diverse; actually, different domains are modeled (syntax, morphology, world-knowledge, knowledge about the partner, etc.), and the bodies of knowledge are only loosely coupled. For this reason, it makes sense to partition the knowledge into different sub-KBs which are usually called *knowledge sources*. Moreover, due to the differing requirements for different knowledge sources, diverse KR formalisms are usually used [Hoeppner et al., 1983] – resulting in a *heterogeneous* KR formalism. This is quite different from the notion of a hybrid KR formalism as introduced above. In the case of hybrid representation formalism we require a strict connection between the subformalisms by insisting on a common semantics, while in the case of heterogeneous representation formalisms, this is not always intended.

Although these organizational issues are not trivial and many problems have to be solved in this context [Bergmann and Paeseler, 1986], we will abstract away them here, i.e., we will assume a monolithic KR system and KB as depicted in Fig. 2.1 – freeing us to analyze the problems of knowledge representation, knowledge management, and computational properties of KR systems on a more general level.

2.3.2 Services of Knowledge Representation Systems

One task a KR system has to fulfill is the transformation of symbolic expressions stored in a KB into a body of knowledge. However, a KR system is more than a static deductive calculus. A KR system has to provide services which allow accessing and maintaining the represented knowledge. This includes at least that the system is able to "assimilate new information" [Levesque and Brachman, 1985, p. 47].

Evidently, this is not enough. The world we are caught in is full of surprises, and it may turn out for a knowledge representation system that some things are different from what it believed. Usually the term *knowledge* refers to *correct belief*; therefore, by definition, a system representing knowledge cannot be wrong. Unfortunately, in reality any knowledge representation system can hold a wrong belief because somebody did not tell the truth about the state of the world, because some sensory data was inaccurate, or because something has changed in the world.[20] Sometimes there may be a more subtle reason for believing false propositions: it may be necessary to start off with some assumptions only to later discover that some of them were wrong.

Thus, besides drawing inferences and putting new knowledge into the KB, it is necessary to *modify* the KB. This is most easily achieved by directly manipulating the data structures which are used to implement the KR system; a solution used, for instance, in the frame systems FRL [Roberts and Goldstein, 1977] and KRL. There are some drawbacks to the easy way, though. Arbitrary modifications of the data structures may blow up the entire system in the worst case, and in the best case, it may lead to results which have nothing to do with

---

[20]For this reason, *belief representation* would be perhaps more appropriate, but I will follow the standard AI usage.

the semantics of the representation formalism – and then we might ask what all the fuss about semantics is good for. For this reason, it is often argued that a KR system should encapsulate the concrete implementational structures and provide only operations to the outside world which are related to the semantics of the KR formalism [Patel-Schneider, 1984, Brachman et al., 1983]). In fact, a *functional approach*, hiding the implementation and focussing on the functionality, seems to be the most preferable solution [Brachman et al., 1985, p. 532]:

> The user should know, at some level not dependent on implementation details, what questions the system is capable of answering, and what operations are permitted that allow new information to be provided to it. He needs to know how questions put to a knowledge base will be answered strictly as a function of the information it contains, and not dependent on how information is represented.

Thus, what is needed to manipulate a KB is at least a set of operations such as TELL, ASK, FORGET. In order to start off with something definite, we need, furthermore, an operation like INITKB, which yields an empty knowledge base. The important point here is that the operations should be related to the semantics of the KR formalism in a principled way.

As a matter of fact, as shown in [Levesque, 1984a] and [Brachman et al., 1985], this can be done quite elegantly on the knowledge level for most of these operations. However, FORGET presents severe conceptual problems; problems we will return to in Sect. 2.3.4.

2.3.3 Inferential Services

From a computational perspective, the capability of turning a KB into a body of knowledge is the most interesting – and the most difficult to accomplish – feature of a KR system. Given a KR formalism with an appropriate semantics and a KB containing expressions of the KR formalism, it is clear what the KB claims to be true, namely, any proposition stored in the KB. For any nontrivial KR formalism, however, there are significantly more propositions entailed than explicitly stored. For example, in the terminology given in Fig. 1.1 the concept Modern-team has been defined without reference to the concept Small-team. Nevertheless, it is obvious that the former is a specialization of the latter (see Fig. 1.2).

Precisely this task, figuring out what has been specified only implicitly, can be said to form the heart of a KR system: to perform *inferences*. In the general case, this is nontrivial, often even noncomputable. Despite this fact, it is still useful to stick to model-theoretic semantics. Even if it is possible to only partially solve the problem, at least we know what is going on: it is clear what is claimed to be true, and it is possible to characterize the *inference algorithms* supposed to compute propositions entailed by a KB according to *soundness* and *completeness*, i.e., to ensure that the inference algorithms compute only entailed propositions, and check whether an algorithm is able to compute all entailed propositions, respectively [McDermott, 1978].

If we were interested in first-order predicate logic, *resolution* [Robinson, 1965] would be the technique employed to compute propositions entailed by a KB.[21] Algorithms based on this technique are sound and complete. However, the problem of deciding whether a given proposition is true or false according to a KB is only semi-decidable. This means we only get an answer for all propositions which are entailed by a KB. Propositions unrelated to a KB, however, can result in infinite computations.

For a subsystem which is supposed to provide services to another system, it is unsatisfactory that it is impossible to predict whether the subsystem can always answer a given question in finite time. A way out could be to restrict the expressiveness – the epistemological adequacy – of the KR formalism. For instance, if only monadic predicates were allowed, the resulting calculus would be decidable. Thus, there is an obvious tradeoff between expressiveness and computational costs [Habel, 1983].

Decidability is, of course, a desirable computational property, but it is not enough. It means only that a given problem can be decided in finite time by an algorithm. This can still be more time than anyone is willing to spend waiting for an answer, say a day, a year, or longer than our sun is expected to exist. And if in the worst case such computations are exponentially time bounded, a relatively small input can easily prohibit an answer in reasonable time. A more rigid and practical measure is computational tractability [Garey and Johnson, 1979], i.e., whether it is possible to decide a given problem in time bounded polynomially by the length of the problem description.

Usually, in AI, computational complexity is not considered to be the borderline where research stops. On the contrary, it is the line where interesting research begins. E. Rich [1983, p. 104], for instance, describes AI as "an attempt to solve NP-complete problems in polynomial time,"[22] and, if so, why should we be bothered by computational complexity? Rich's characterization of AI is at least partially accurate, but the key to "solving" the hard problems is to accept approximations as solutions and, more importantly, to employ *heuristics*. Thus, if one utilized knowledge in order to solve the hard problem of applying knowledge in order to solve the hard problems, then, at least, the application of *meta-knowledge* (or meta^n-knowledge) should be easy without requiring further knowledge. Otherwise there would be an infinite regress of heuristic knowledge. Moreover, there are a number of knowledge types where application of meta-knowledge does not seem to be possible – as argued in the eloquent article of Levesque [1986] about this and related issues.

This means that computational complexity is an important issue in knowledge representation. Unfortunately, however, even very restricted formalisms, such as propositional logic, are already computationally intractable. The problem of deciding whether a given formula in propositional logic is *satisfiable*, i.e.,

---

[21]However, we will not pursue this line here. Readers interested in resolution techniques should perhaps try [Genesereth and Nilsson, 1987], which is a very readable and complete introduction to the use of logic in AI and to associated implementation techniques.

[22]Of course, Rich means intractable problems in general, not just the NP-complete ones. For instance, playing board games, which is subject to AI research, is mostly PSPACE-hard.

whether it is not always false, is *NP-complete*.[23] Two ways of dealing with this problem have been proposed by Levesque and Brachman [1987]. First, one could restrict the expressiveness of a given representation language, as exercised in that article. Second, one could accept approximations as solutions, e.g., by limiting the inferential power. In order to do this in a principled way, this limitation might be justified by an alternative, weaker semantics.

Levesque [1984b] and Patel-Schneider [1987b] pursued this second approach by employing variants of *four-valued logics* [Belnap, 1977]. Although this seems to be very promising in computational terms, a semantics for first-order predicate logic which makes entailment decidable and (almost) tractable is also very weak and thus does not support the obvious inferences one would like to draw (e.g. there are neither tautologies nor inconsistencies, and *modus ponens* is not a valid inference). This means that despite the fact that such a semantics gives a principled (model-theoretic) account to incompleteness, it is nevertheless not very useful because it is rather unintuitive. Moreover, in order to accomplish anything reasonable (pun intended), domain-specific inferences or a deductively stronger system must be used.

The main idea behind both approaches is "forging a powerful system out of tractable parts" [Levesque and Brachman, 1987, p. 89] because "as responsible computer scientists, we should not be providing a general inferential service if all we can say about it is that by and large it will work satisfactorily" [Levesque and Brachman, 1987]. In how far this goal is achievable, and what subtleties are involved in designing efficient inference algorithms will become more vivid in Chap. 4, where these issues will be discussed in the context of a concrete KR formalism.

2.3.4 Revision Services

Inferring entailed propositions is the task necessary to support ASK operations. However, what is necessary to support TELL and FORGET? Are they supposed to work on the knowledge level (i.e., on all propositions which are entailed) or simply on the set of expressions we put into the KB?

In Sect. 2.3.2, we argued in favor of the functional approach – the user should know how questions will be answered as a *function* of the information a KB contains and independently of its implementation. The easiest solution satisfying this requirement would be to realize TELL as a "store" operation and FORGET as a "delete" operation – working on the set of expressions in the KB. Both operations are well-defined and the user can predict the response of an ASK operation without being forced to know anything about the implementation. From a computational point of view, there exists only one problem. If the KR system performs *assert-time inferences*, i.e., computes and stores inferred expressions when a new expression is entered into the KB, it has to check which of the previously inferred expressions are still valid after a FORGET operation.

---

[23]This means that the problem can be solved by a polynomial time algorithm on a nondeterministic Turing Machine. However, no polynomial time algorithm is known for a realistic processor, and almost nobody believes that there is one.

While this seems to be a reasonable solution, the functional approach as described in [Levesque, 1984a] and [Brachman et al., 1985] aims for more. On carefully rereading the quotation in Sect. 2.3.2, one will discover that the result of KB operations should be a function of the information the KB contains, *not dependent on how information is represented.* In other words, the KB operations should operate on the knowledge level [Levesque and Brachman, 1986] – not on the symbol level as the solution sketched above.

A formalization of the knowledge level view could be, assuming a model-theoretic semantics, the set of all models [Levesque, 1984a]. An alternative formalization could be to use the set of all true propositions [Diettrich, 1986]. Of course, this is not an implementational model, but serves merely as an elegant abstraction describing the competence of a KR system. If we are dealing with a monotonic formalism and are only interested in TELL and ASK, everything works out fine. However, if we are interested in nonmonotonic formalisms, or if we wanted the KB to forget something, we are in trouble.[24]

The task of eliminating a theorem from an arbitrary logical theory is underconstrained, i.e., there is no unique solution. And although it is possible to analyze the nature of such operations [Alchourrón et al., 1985], it does not help us to derive a general specification for a FORGET operation in arbitrary logical theories – pragmatics have to be taken into account. This can include minimality criteria, the syntactic form of the stored propositions, the probable intentions, etc. In particular, if we have a restricted formalism and if we are able to pin down the intentions of a FORGET operation, we may be able to give an unambiguous, intuitively plausible specification of such an operation. However, we will most likely have to take into account the symbol level.

Moreover, often enough it seems appropriate to modify not the consequences of a set of expressions, but the expressions which led to the consequences in order to realize a FORGET operation. If we think, for example, of a legal code, it seems intuitively plausible to modify the code and not the consequences [Makinson, 1985], and the same holds for other applications as well [Ginsberg, 1986].

Thus, the claim made above that all operations should be performed only on the knowledge level seems to be too strong. In fact, Newell intends to describe only the potential for actions, not how knowledge gets manipulated. The notion of knowledge as viewed by Newell and used in the functional approach is a static and unstructured object [Newell, 1982, p. 101]:

> However, in terms of structure, a body of knowledge is extremely simple compared to a memory defined at lower computer system levels. There are no structural constraints to the knowledge in a body, either in capacity (i.e., the amount of knowledge) or in how the knowledge is held in the body. Indeed, there is no notion of how knowledge is held (*encoding* is a notion of the symbol level, not knowledge level). Also, there are not well-defined structural properties associated with

---

[24]See also Ullman's comment [Brodie and Mylopoulos, 1986b, p. 57] on the knowledge level view.

access and augmentation. Thus, it seems preferable to avoid calling
the body of knowledge a memory.

If we consider *actions on knowledge*, the abstraction is too coarse, as we have
seen. On the other hand, a pure symbol level account as proposed first also has
its deficiencies. Assume we told a KB that $(a \wedge b)$ is true, and, later on, try to
convince the KB that it should forget about the truth of a. Shall we ignore this
request, or shall the proposition $(a \wedge b)$ be deleted?

Another point where the pure symbol level view seems inappropriate is that
a "symbol level"-TELL operation is insensitive to its result. It does not matter
whether a TELL operation leads to an inconsistent state of the KB. However,
what one would like to have is a consistency-preserving operation which perhaps
first changes the KB so that the new expression fits in. These problems, and a
few more, will be the subject of Chap. 6.

2.4 Knowledge Base Management Systems

Some of the topics treated in this chapter may provoke the question whether
another field in computer science – data-base research – could contribute insights
and solutions to the problems described – or *vice versa*. As a matter of fact, a
quite fruitful exchange of ideas between both fields has been taking place since
approximately 1980 [Brodie and Zilles, 1980, Brodie et al., 1984, Brodie and
Mylopoulos, 1986b].

The interest of data-base researchers in AI is driven mostly by the feeling
that conventional data base management systems (DBMS) are not expressive
enough and that they do not support the kind of processing one would like to
have in order to support the user. In short, data base management systems
should become more "intelligent." Conversely, AI researchers are interested in
"scaling up" KBs, in overcoming their space limitations by adapting techniques
developed in the data-base field in order to manage large amounts of knowledge.
The common vision is the development of a new generation of software systems,
Knowledge Base Management Systems (KBMS), which are similar to DBMS, but
manage knowledge instead of data.

However, though the problems being worked on in both fields may seem similar at first sight – something is stored, accessed, and manipulated in a data base
or knowledge base – there are fundamental differences concerning requirements,
underlying assumptions, and expectations. Brodie and Mylopoulos [1986a] summarized these difference in the following way:

> Any knowledge representation language must be provided with a
> (rich) semantic theory for relating an information base to its sub-
> ject matter, while a data model requires an (effective) computational
> theory for realizing information bases on physical machines.

Of course, these are not inconsistent, but only diverging goals. There does
not seem to be a genuine problem in envisioning a system which meets both goals.

And in fact, when implementing a KR system, one tries, of course, to realize an efficient system. The measures of success and the underlying assumptions are different, though.

For instance, since the amounts of data stored in a data base usually do not fit into main memory, it is folklore in data-base research that the data has to be stored on secondary storage media. Therefore, most algorithms and techniques were developed with this assumption in mind. On the other hand, structures stored in knowledge bases are usually assumed to be stored in the main memory because otherwise the AI system would be too slow. Thus, approaches to utilize a conventional DBMS as storage machinery for a knowledge base in order to "scale up" cannot solve the problem by mapping one data-structure onto another one (as in [Härder et al., 1987]) because both requirements – speed and size – have to be met, which requires a new generation of computers as well as new data-management techniques and algorithms.[25]

Besides the management of large amounts of data, there are other advantages one gains by using a DBMS (sharing, security, recoverability, etc.). Therefore, one might argue that even though data base management systems cannot be utilized directly in KR systems, at least some important techniques may be borrowed and combined with KR technology in order to realize a KBMS. Again, one should be aware of the fact that the underlying assumptions about the application environment are fundamentally different. What is judged to be important for a data base application may be superfluous or even a handicap in an AI application [Bobrow, 1986].

In order to make this statement more vivid, let us envision a KBMS managing concepts, assertions (as sketched in the Introduction), rules, and perhaps other kinds of KR formalisms. Furthermore, let us assume that we have at hand all the operations and techniques we usually get with a full-fledged DBMS (security, concurrent access, transactions etc.). Such a system could, for example, be utilized in the development of a knowledge-based system: the developers can share the KB. However, if one member of the team changes, say, a concept definition, the effect of this change has to be propagated through the entire KB (which may take some time), and all other members of the team are suddenly faced with a new concept definition which may change the behavior of the knowledge-based system in unexpected ways. The problem is obvious: in a KB, the stored information is usually highly interconnected, and, moreover, programs may depend on a certain contents of the KB.[26] In order to avoid this problem, one could restrict updates in such a way that only one person can change the KB. However, this would limit the flexibility considerably. Thus, another solution is necessary here. For instance, the versioning method used in the LOOPS system [Bobrow and Stefik, 1981], which permits *private* updates, seems to be more appropriate.

---

[25]Moreover, as Wiederhold et al. [1987, p. 378] argue, there does not seem to be an urgent need to pursue this line of research. He believes that "for all large AI systems the amount of complex stored knowledge, by our definition, is quite modest ... ."

[26]Actually, in a data base context, a change of the data base schema, which can be seen as similar to the change of a concept definition, can, for good reasons, only be performed by a central institution.

What I am saying here is not that any exchange of ideas and techniques between data-base research and AI is doomed to failure. However, a naive approach in trying to transfer techniques based on implicit environmental and implementational assumptions or using existing software products, will probably result in inappropriate solutions. There is no ready-made technology just sitting around waiting to be integrated into a new generation of software systems. Instead, the pragmatic foundations of the techniques have to be made explicit, and implementation techniques have to be tuned to support them, perhaps using open and extensible system architectures as argued in [Carey and DeWitt, 1986].

If we set aside the ideas of implementing a KBMS in the near future and of "solving" KB problems with a DBMS, however, there are a number of important issues – practical and theoretical – which can be, or have been already, subject to research efforts in both fields.

More practical oriented approaches include

- the "enrichment" of the data-base query interface by a knowledge-based system, for instance, a natural language dialog system [Nebel and Marburger, 1982, Marburger and Nebel, 1983], which simplifies the interaction. As a matter of fact, for simple data bases, you can already buy such an interface for your personal computer [Hendrix, 1986];

- employment of a DBMS as one component of a KR system in order to store simply-structured facts as described in [Wiederhold et al., 1987, Abarbanel and Williams, 1987];

- using ideas from KR in order to develop new data models [Mylopoulos et al., 1980];

- using KR systems to support query formulation [Tou et al., 1982, Patel-Schneider et al., 1984].

From a theoretical point of view, the semantics of data models and KR formalisms, as well as the semantics of operations on data or knowledge, are a field on which the approaches are converging and fertilizing each other. Although Brodie and Mylopoulos [1986a] make a distinction between knowledge bases and data bases along the line that the former is more concerned with (external) semantics and the latter is more concerned with efficiency, efficiency is, of course, an issue in KR (a point we discussed in Sect. 2.3.3), and semantics of data models is subject to theoretical analysis in the data-base field as well [Reiter, 1984].

Brachman and Levesque [1986] propose to analyze both kinds of systems under a unifying view, which should be the knowledge level view, abstracting from implementational issues (the symbol level) and from the system engineering level (presentation and organization). The idea behind this proposal is that if we gain an understanding of a system on the knowledge level, we actually know what is going to be *represented* by the system. As was pointed out in Sect. 2.3.4, this view is too constrained if we want to do more than TELLing and ASKing. It is still useful to stick to this notion, however, because it provides a unifying view on both fields and a yardstick for describing systems, even if they depart from the knowledge level [Diettrich, 1986].

The research described here could be understood precisely in this way. The knowledge level properties of a hypothetical system are analyzed, and the computational properties are derived from this view. In addition, problems which cannot be solved solely on the knowledge level will be analyzed on this level and the solutions will be related to it.

Part II

Hybrid Representation and Reasoning

3. A Hybrid Representation Formalism

When designing a knowledge-based system, it is good practice to distinguish between different kinds of knowledge. One important kind is *terminological knowledge* – knowledge about (technical) vocabulary [Brachman and Levesque, 1982], a kind of knowledge which appears to be representable naturally by using *object-centered KR formalisms*. Factoring out terminological knowledge and devising a separate KR formalism for it makes explicit the different nature of this kind of knowledge, leads to efficient techniques for dealing with the special-purpose inferences necessary [Levesque and Brachman, 1985], and enables us to impose organizational principles on the knowledge base, which may help to maintain the overall knowledge base [Swartout and Neches, 1986]. Of course, all this implies that other KR formalisms have to be employed in order to represent more than just mere terminological knowledge. Thus, we are going for hybrid representation formalisms.

In the following, a brief historical account of object-centered knowledge representations – semantic networks and frame systems – is given,[1] including an introduction to terminological knowledge representation. Based on the intuitive understanding gained, one particular terminological representation formalism is described in detail and provided with a model-theoretic semantics. Additional to the terminological formalism, a simple assertional representation language is introduced, resulting in a hybrid KR formalism. Finally, some possible extensions are discussed.

3.1 Object-Centered Representation

The idea of organizing knowledge around objects – representing knowledge in an object-centered way – is not unique to terminological knowledge representation. It has a long history in AI. Tracing this idea back to its origin, we find *semantic networks* and *frames*. However, although the ideas developed in this context appear to be similar to the ones underlying terminological knowledge representation, there are notable differences. The most important one is that terminological formalisms focus on the representation of *definitional knowledge*.

---

[1] I will not give a complete history of research concerning semantic networks and frames. Only some influential papers and a few examples are mentioned, as far as they are relevant to the development of terminological knowledge representation. For a more complete historical account of research concerning semantic networks, the reader should consult [Sowa, 1987] or the older, but still very readable paper by Brachman [Brachman, 1979]. A concise description of research related to frames can be found in [Maida, 1987].

3.1.1 Semantic Networks

The introduction of *semantic networks* is usually attributed to Quillian [1966], although projects in machine translation and natural language understanding seem to have already used similar structures in the 1950's (e.g. [Richens, 1958], [Masterman, 1962]). Quillian aimed in his Ph.D. thesis [Quillian, 1966] (of which [Quillian, 1967] is a concise summary) at developing a "semantic memory," a data structure for storing word meanings which can be used for simulating human-like language behavior. The goal was to "constitute a theory of how human memory for semantic and other conceptual material may be formatted, organized and used" [Quillian, 1967, p. 410].

Almost all techniques later used in semantic network systems were already present. The most prominent one is the usage of *nodes* to represent conceptual entities (such as concepts and words), which are interconnected by *links* representing the conceptual relationships. Also, the idea of organizing concepts in a *concept taxonomy* can be found in his work. However, the accompanying notion of *inheritance* of properties from superconcept to subconcept nodes was not mentioned, but spelled out later [Collins and Quillian, 1970]. The general inference technique used is what has come to be called *spreading activation search*: Based on the assumption that the meaning of a concept is determined by all concepts which can be reached directly or indirectly by traversing links, two concepts are contrasted and compared by determining the set of concepts which can be reached by both concepts.

Inspired by Quillian's ideas, a number of systems were implemented employing semantic networks as the principal KR formalism, e.g. the computer-aided instruction system SCHOLAR [Carbonell, 1970], a natural language understanding system [Simmons, 1973], and a system learning concepts of physical structures from examples [Winston, 1975].

The reason for the popularity of semantic networks was probably the intuitive appeal semantic networks convey. It seems natural to organize concepts in a hierarchy connecting the concepts by different links which represent relationships, for instance, linguistic, physical, or conceptual relationships, between them: A semantic network is almost a direct representation of the "concept space." Moreover, semantic networks lend themselves to a straight-forward implementation as a list and pointer data-structure.

The intuitive appeal, however, has a severe disadvantage. One may be tempted to represent fundamentally different aspects with one and the same construct: a link between two concepts. Woods's influential paper [Woods, 1975] criticized just this tendency prevalent in almost all semantic network systems of those days. These systems usually did not distinguish between structural and assertional links, confused nodes denoting classes and nodes denoting individuals and, connected with this deficiency, were unable to differentiate between possible values and actual values. Moreover, the assertional impact of nodes were unclear – to what degree nodes imply the existence of corresponding objects in the world. Summarizing, Woods called for a semantics of semantic networks, which had been neglected in the early systems. Furthermore, Woods demanded logical adequacy of semantic networks – the ability to "precisely, formally, and unambiguously represent any particular interpretation a human listener may place on a sentence" [Woods, 1975, p. 45]. Hayes [1977] reinforced the point of demanding semantics of semantic networks by criticizing the tendency of specifying the meaning of network structures by a "pretend-it's-English" interpretation.

Later semantic network formalisms, for example, Shapiro's SNePS [Shapiro, 1979], Hendrix's partitioned semantic networks [Hendrix, 1979], and a formalism developed by Schubert et al. [1979] accounted for this criticism by extending the expressive power and by supplying semantics in form of translations to logic for some of their primitive operators.

SNePS uses a fairly nonstandard kind of logic, though. Maida and Shapiro claim that, in fact, no standard (model-theoretic) semantics can be supplied for this logic because their formalism does not obey Frege's Principle of Compositionality [Maida and Shapiro, 1982, p. 301]. Hendrix's partitioned networks, on the other hand, can be regarded as a notational variant of extended standard logic. He uses partitions to group together nodes in order to represent belief space, negation, quantifier scopes, etc. Finally, the formalism and system developed by Schubert et al. is explicitly announced to be a notational variant of first-order logic (despite the fact that they go beyond first-order logic by including modals and higher-order constructs), with the network structure used to support certain inferences.

3.1.2 Frame Systems

While semantic network researchers were struggling with expressiveness and semantics, a new idea about how knowledge should be represented and structured was launched by Minsky [1975]. He proposes organizing knowledge into chunks called *frames*. These frames are supposed to capture the essence of *stereotypical situations*, e.g. being in a living room or going out for dinner, by clustering all relevant information for these situations together. This includes information about how to use the frame, information about expectations (which may turn out to be wrong), information about what to do if expectations are not confirmed, etc. This means, in particular, that a great deal of procedurally expressed knowledge should be part of the frames. Collections of such frames are to be organized in *frame-systems* in which the frames are interconnected.

The processes working on such frame-systems are supposed to match a frame to a specific situation, to use default values to fill unspecified aspects, to recover from unsuccessful matches by trying another frame which uses information stored in the first frame, perhaps by choosing another *perspective*, which might be a transformation of the original frame, and so on.

If this brief summary of the paper sounds a little bit vague and imprecise, it correctly reproduces the general tone of the paper, as Minsky himself admits in his paper. Despite the fact that this paper was a first approach to the idea of what frames could be, Minsky explicitly argued in favor of staying flexible and nonformal. In fact, in an appendix to [Minsky, 1975], Minsky claimed that formal logic is the wrong tool for knowledge representation. Reasons include organizational matters (knowledge is distributed among independent axioms), control matters (deduction does not have a focus of interest), monotonicity of logic, and, most importantly, the notion of *consistency*. He argued that consistency is not even desirable in a knowledge base: humans can very well do without consistency.

Details which had been left out in [Minsky, 1975] were later filled in by representation systems which were inspired by Minsky's ideas – the most prominent of those are FRL [Roberts and Goldstein, 1977] and KRL [Bobrow and Winograd, 1977].

KRL was one of the most ambitious projects in this direction. It aimed at a synthesis between the positions of *declarativists* and *proceduralists* [Winograd, 1975] and addressed almost every representational problem discussed in the literature. The net result is a very complex language with an overwhelmingly rich repertoire of representational primitives and unlimited flexibility. For instance, it contains a multi-processing architecture for which the actual scheduling procedures have to be provided by the user. The same strategy was taken for the basic inference procedure – matching. The user has to provide and modify these procedures.

Though this flexibility might be seen as an advantage, it creates, of course, confusion and arbitrariness. This is even more true for the large set of representational primitives, which were never given any precise meaning, not even intuitively, as Lehnert and Wilks [1979] reported.

FRL is a more modest system sticking only to the "well-understood" features of the frame theory. A frame in FRL is a cluster of *slots*, which in turn contain *facets*, whereby some slots and facets have a standard meaning (realized by system operations), while nonstandard slots and facets must have their "meaning" provided by the user in form of LISP functions. FRL supports (as does KRL, of course) the organization of frames in hierarchies with inheritance of properties, default values, and procedural attachment, as well as a couple of retrieval operations. In order to realize a knowledge-based system, the user has to supply a large number of LISP functions in the form of attached procedures and as extensions to the basic interpreter.

As mentioned in Sect. 2.3.1, it seems unavoidable to use the conventional procedural paradigm to build a knowledge-based system, and in this context, it seems preferable to associate the knowledge representation formalism as closely as possible with the procedural part, as can be accomplished with procedural attachment. However, in the representation languages mentioned, procedural attachment can be used to manipulate the implementational data-structures without any restriction, which in light of what has been pointed out in Sect. 2.3 does not seem to be the ideal solution.

Ignoring this arbitrariness of meaning created by procedural attachment in KR systems based on frames, Hayes [1980] challenged the entire frame theory from a logical point of view. He demonstrated how important notions of the theory, such as perspectives, defaults, and perhaps even reflexive reasoning, could be reconstructed in logic – giving an answer to Minsky's polemic against logic in

[Minsky, 1975]. In particular, it becomes evident that the notion of *consistency*, which Minsky claimed to be superfluous and undesirable, is vital for any kind of reasoning. If it were not possible to detect an *inconsistent* state of knowledge, it would not be possible to pin down wrong beliefs. Finally, Hayes concludes that the main contribution of the frame theory was not on the *representational*, but on the *implementational* level.

While Hayes's analysis demonstrates neatly that even seemingly "nonlogical" ideas can be subject to logical analysis, he probably underestimated somewhat the contribution of the frame theory to the representational level. Frames are simply a good way to organize (some kinds of) knowledge.[2] For instance, the development of *object-oriented* programming languages, like Smalltalk-80 [Goldberg and Robson, 1983], LOOPS [Bobrow and Stefik, 1981], and the Flavor system [Weinreb and Moon, 1981], was heavily influenced by the frame idea. In fact, there is a strong resemblance between frames and object-oriented programming languages, as shown in [Nebel, 1985].

3.1.3 Structural Inheritance Networks

Besides providing the convenience of structuring knowledge and associating procedurally expressed knowledge via procedural attachment, frames also addressed more clearly than semantic networks the distinction between structural and other relationships, as Brachman [1979] notes while analyzing past efforts in designing semantic network systems. He points out that the underlying assumptions about representational primitives are quite diverse. In detail, Brachman identifies four different levels on which semantic networks have been used, namely:

- the *implementational level*, on which networks are viewed as data-structures, with pointers and lists as primitives.

- the *logical level*, on which logical operators and predicates are primitives, turning the semantic networks into a notational variant of (some) logic (an example is the above cited work of Hendrix [1979]).

- the *conceptual level*, which focuses on semantic (in the linguistic sense) and conceptual relationships. The primitives on this level are e.g. case relationships and primitive actions and objects (e.g. the work by Schank and others on *conceptual dependency-graphs* [Schank, 1973]).

- the *linguistic level*, on which arbitrary words and expressions are used as the primitives, and which is therefore highly language-dependent (for instance the representation system OWL [Szolovits et al., 1977]).

It is, of course, possible to analyze a given semantic network on all of these levels simultaneously. What should be avoided, however, is confusing the levels and applying operations of one level on another: In a semantic network formalism, each level should be neutral with respect to the next higher level [Brachman,

---

[2]See also [Nilsson, 1980, Chap. 9], where it is shown how to organize deduction around object-centered representations.

1979, p. 32]. For instance, the primitives on the conceptual level should not imply a commitment to any particular natural language.

Additionally, Brachman argues that one important level is missing – the *epistemological level*[3], an intermediate layer between the logical and conceptual level. On this level, *intensional* descriptions are formed and interrelated. For instance, the concept-specialization relation as well as the related notion of inheritance belong to this level.

Consequently, Brachman proposes a formalism – *structural inheritance networks* – to capture this level by using a small set of "epistemological" primitives. Main building blocks of this formalism are *concepts* which are described by their *superconcepts*, by *roles* – possible relationships to other concepts – and by *structural descriptions*, which account for relationships between roles. This means that concepts are not viewed as atomic entities, but as complex descriptions, which is a point of view leading to a more rigorous treatment of *inheritance* than usually found in semantic networks. In a structural inheritance network, not only are properties inherited, but inheritance accounts for the entire structure of a concept.

Concepts come in two flavors: *generic concepts* intended to denote classes of individuals, and *individual concepts* intended to denote individuals.[4] The former kind of concepts can in turn be divided into *defined concepts* and *primitive concepts*.[5] The meaning of defined concepts is completely determined by its description, while the meaning of primitive concepts can only partially be determined from the description. The latter kind of concepts accounts for what is called *natural kind*: concepts which cannot be exhaustively described, for instance, animal species.

Concepts can be organized in a *concept taxonomy*, as shown in Fig. 3.1. All concepts marked with an asterisk, like Plant, Animal, and Mineral, are primitive concepts. The only defined concept in this figure is Woman, which is defined by being a specialization of Female-Animal and Human. Finally, there is an individual concept Mary, depicted as an oval filled with horizontal lines, which is not a specialization, but an *individuation* – depicted by a different kind of arrow – of the generic concept Woman. Individual concepts do not denote general subclasses of the class denoted by the superconcept as usual, but singleton subclasses. Individual concepts can only be leaves in such hierarchies.[6]

Furthermore, individual concepts do not have any assertional impact but are only used to describe potential individuals. There is no implied claim that they

---

[3]The term "epistemological" might be a little bit misleading because there is no direct connection to the usual understanding of epistemology. "Structural" or "descriptional" would perhaps be more appropriate.

[4]In the following, I will use a somewhat simplified version of the notions and pictorial symbols introduced in [Brachman and Schmolze, 1985] instead of the slightly different presentation in [Brachman, 1979].

[5]Primitive concepts have also been called *starred* and *magical* concepts [Schmolze and Brachman, 1982, pp. 259–263].

[6]It is conceivable that an individual concept is subconcept of another individual concept. This would amount to a more accurate description of an individual. However, at this point [Brachman and Schmolze, 1985] is not very precise.

really exist. Thus, in order to say something definite, we would have to employ some assertional machinery – a point we will return to in Sect. 3.1.4. For the time being, however, we will neglect all issues connected with individuals and assertions.

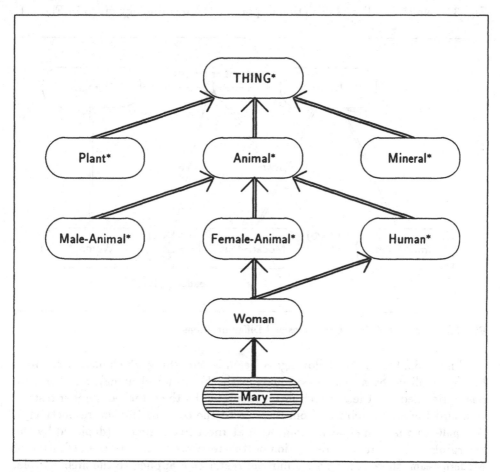

Fig. 3.1. A Simple Concept Taxonomy

An important assumption in interpreting such a structural inheritance network is that the meaning of a concept is derived only from the meaning of its superconcepts and the information associated with the concept. Thus, the meaning of Female-Animal is determined only by its primitiveness and its superconcept Animal. The fact that Woman is a subconcept of Female-Animal does not add anything to the meaning of Female-Animal.

In addition to describing concepts by means of superconcepts, we can also use roles for this process. Roles[7] can be viewed as potential relationships between individuals of the class denoted by the concept and other individuals in the world.

---

[7]In [Brachman and Schmolze, 1985], roles are further subdivided into so-called *generic role-sets*, *individual roles*, and *particular role-sets*. We will ignore this distinction here because the latter two kinds of roles appear only in the context of individual concepts.

By *restricting* and *differentiating* roles, concepts can be described. The class of individuals permitted as *role fillers* can be restricted by a *value restriction* and the number of possible role fillers may be restricted using a *number restriction*. An example of the introduction of concepts using role restrictions is shown in Fig. 3.2, which is a literal depiction of part of the terminology given in Fig. 1.1.

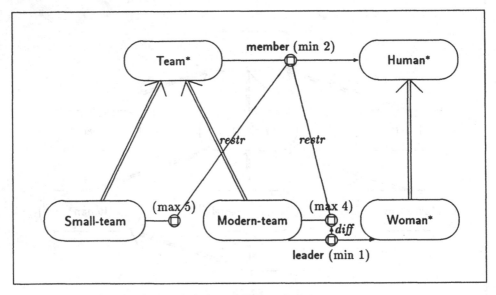

Fig. 3.2. Examples of Role Restrictions and Differentiations

Figure 3.2 tells us the following: A **Team** is something which has a role **member** (symbolized by an encircled square with the attached name), and this role has to be filled by at least two **Humans** (depicted by the attached number restriction and the arrow pointing from the role to the concept **Human**, respectively). A **Small-team** is defined as a **Team**, with at most five **members** (depicted by the *restr* link and the number restriction on the restricted role). In the definition of **Modern-team**, there is not only a number restriction applied to the **member** role, but a differentiation (symbolized by the *diff* link) of this role. The **leader** role is also restricted by number and value restrictions.

If we would now go on and combine the restrictions according to apparent inheritance rules and would rearrange the concept taxonomy such that it reflects all implicitly specified specialization relations, we would end up with Fig. 1.2. Besides the above methods of defining concepts, there are a few more which concern relationships between roles and some others which concern the individuation process, but we will ignore them here.

3.1.4 Terminological Knowledge Representation

A first implementation of structural inheritance networks was KLONE [Brachman, 1978] (the name was later changed to KL-ONE), which evolved over the years and sparked off substantial research efforts in the form of applications, theoretical work, and the development of similar systems, documented by several workshops (e.g. [Schmolze and Brachman, 1982], [Moore, 1986] and [Kobsa, 1988])).

What are the essential ideas behind KL-ONE? And what lead to the fact that (according to [Brachman and Schmolze, 1985, p.173]):

> KL-ONE has achieved a status afforded to few efforts in the brief history of Artificial Intelligence: over a significant period of time (at least six years) and over a large number of projects it has served as the foundation for some very basic research in knowledge representation, and at the same time has provided representational support in a number of implemented AI systems.

Let us first mention some points which are not responsible for the success of KL-ONE. Although KL-ONE started off as a network formalism, this is not considered to be essential. As a matter of fact, KRYPTON [Brachman et al., 1983] and KANDOR [Patel-Schneider, 1984], two descendants of KL-ONE, are described as "frame-based systems." The reason for this change of view is that structural inheritance networks appear to be very similar in structure to frames, in particular when transformed to a linear, textual notation. There is only little resemblance to the frame theory proposed by Minsky [1975], however. Patel-Schneider goes even one step further. He calls the KL-ONE-like formalism he investigates in [Patel-Schneider, 1989a] a "terminological logic."

Another nonessential in the KL-ONE paradigm is the particular set of "epistemological" primitives introduced in [Brachman, 1979] or the one given in the final description of KL-ONE [Brachman and Schmolze, 1985]. Nobody is claiming that these form the ultimate set of such primitives, necessary and sufficient to describe everything. Rather, different systems use different sets of these primitives, a fact which most often is motivated by arguments of computational complexity and requirements of the application.

The main reason behind its success is probably that KL-ONE does not attempt to give answers to every conceivable representational requirement, but that it addresses only very specific areas, namely, most prominently, how to *define* concepts. KL-ONE comes, in this respect, closer to the original idea of semantic networks as proposed by Quillian [1966] than other semantic networks, which were often designed to represent "everything." Moreover, KL-ONE leaves out all features which run counter to the notion of definition, namely *defaults* and *cancellation* of properties, i.e. ways to suppress parts of a description used to define a concept – which actually would destroy the entire idea of forming composite descriptions and defining concepts [Brachman, 1985]. This does not mean that defaults should not be represented, but only that they should not be used in the "representational kernel."

It is precisely this concentration on the representation of *definitional* knowledge which makes up the core idea of KL-ONE. The most important consequence of this is the capability to reason about the relationships between concepts based only on the description of the concept – the kind of reasoning we used in the Introduction to come to the conclusion that the concept **Modern-team** is a subconcept of **Small-team**.

While this idea was probably already present in the design of structural inheritance networks [Brachman, 1979], it was not an issue in the first papers. A first, principled approach to exploiting this kind of reasoning – we will call it *terminological reasoning* in the following – was made in the CONSUL project [Kaczmarek et al., 1983], and led to the development of a terminological reasoner, called *classifier* [Lipkis, 1982, Schmolze and Lipkis, 1983], which is able to place a new concept in the "right place" in the concept taxonomy. The classifier was used in conjunction with mapping rules to recognize natural language user requests and to redescribe them in terms of executable commands.

The development of the classifier was based on the intuitive meaning of the KL-ONE formalism, which was quite clear for a large part of the formalism. However, of course, there was the question of how much was covered and whether the classifier was correct. Attempts made to reconstruct logically the representation constructs in KL-ONE, as done in [Schmolze and Israel, 1983], revealed that reasoning by the classifier was sound, but incomplete – a topic we will return to in the next chapter. Furthermore, the reconstruction in logic shed more light on the entire formalism, showing that a number of notions were idiosyncratic (e.g. "local roles") and that others were totally obscure [Schmolze and Brachman, 1982, p. 8–17].

In essence, it resulted in a change of the view on KL-ONE spelled out in [Schmolze and Brachman, 1982, p. 8–17], [Brachman and Levesque, 1982], and [Brachman et al., 1983]. Instead of asking, "What structures should the system maintain for the user?" the interest shifted to functionality: "What exactly should the system *do* for the user?" [Brachman et al., 1983, p. 68]. Viewing KL-ONE from this angle, it can be divided into two components. First, there is a terminological component used to make definitions and to reason about the relationships between these definitions: the *TBox*. Second, there is another component to make assertions, the part we almost completely left out of our description: the *ABox*. And while the former component is very well developed in KL-ONE, the "treatment of the ABox in KL-ONE has been superficial and haphazard" [Schmolze and Brachman, 1982, p. 9]. In fact, the few things which have been written about assertions and individuality (e.g. [Schmolze and Brachman, 1982, p. 18–22, pp. 23–31] and some sections in [Brachman and Schmolze, 1985]) show that there was only a vague understanding and a large number of unresolved issues.

Taking all this into account, Brachman and Levesque proposed to complement the terminological competence of a TBox – the capability to represent terminological knowledge and to reason with it – with assertional competence of some sort [Brachman and Levesque, 1982]. We will follow this suggestion in this chapter.

3.2 The Terminological Formalism $\mathcal{TF}$

As mentioned in the last section, KL-ONE is not the only, but was simply the first system to embody the idea of terminological knowledge representation. The most prominent descendants are KRYPTON [Brachman et al., 1985] and NIKL [Moser, 1983, Schmolze, 1989a]. Additionally, a large number of projects adopted the key ideas and implemented similar systems. The following list is probably incomplete, but demonstrates the level of research activity in this area: KloneTalk [Fikes, 1982], KNET [Freeman et al., 1983], KANDOR [Patel-Schneider, 1984], BACK [von Luck et al., 1986, von Luck et al., 1987], MESON [Edelmann and Owsnicki, 1986], QUIRK [Bergmann and Gerlach, 1987], LOOM [MacGregor and Bates, 1987], K-Rep [Mays et al., 1987], SPHINX [Han et al., 1987], PROCNE [Frixione et al., 1988], TermLog [Donini and Lenzerini, 1988], KRAPFEN [D'Aloisi et al., 1988], SB-ONE [Kobsa, 1989], CLASSIC [Borgida et al., 1989]. All of these systems are inspired by the work done in the context of KL-ONE and employ as part of their system a terminological knowledge representation formalism. Although these formalisms appear to be different on the surface, the underlying notions and operations are, of course, similar. Thus, we may pick just an arbitrary one to proceed.

3.2.1 The Syntax of the Terminological Formalism

In order to have something to build on, we need a concrete representation language. Of course, we could use the graphical notation of KL-ONE or any of the textual notations used in the diverse systems, e.g. the one used in the BACK system. However, we will use a notation (which will be called $\mathcal{TF}$ in the following) similar to the one introduced in [Brachman and Levesque, 1984] because it is more concise and and more straightforward than others I know of.[8] The syntax of the formalism is given in BNF notation in Fig. 3.3.

A formal *terminology* is a sequence of *restriction declarations* and *term introductions*. For reasons of notational convenience, terminologies are sometimes also viewed as *sets* of term introductions. A structural property we would take for granted in a terminology, namely, that a term is only introduced *once*, cannot be expressed in the BNF definition but will be assumed in the following.

Following the ideas outlined in Sections 3.1.3 and 3.1.4, we have two basic kinds of *terms* – *roles* and *concepts* – which can be combined using a few *term-forming operators* resulting in new roles and concepts. A new concept can be formed by the following *concept-forming* operations:

- *Concept conjunction* by using the "and" operator. An example of the use of this operator is (and Man Student), which could be used when introducing a new atomic concept Male-student.

- *Value restriction* by using the "all" operator. An example would be (all leader Woman), stating that the leader role can only be filled with Women.

- *Number restriction* by using the "atleast" or "atmost" operator. These operators state that a role must have at least or at most a certain number of role fillers as, for instance, in (atleast 2 members).

---

[8]Reasons for not using the BACK syntax introduced in [von Luck et al., 1987] are that it is very verbose compared to the formalism introduced here.

$$
\begin{aligned}
\langle terminology \rangle \ &::= \ \{\langle term\text{-}introduction \rangle \mid \langle restriction \rangle\}^* \\
\langle term\text{-}introduction \rangle \ &::= \ \langle concept\text{-}introduction \rangle \mid \\
&\qquad \langle role\text{-}introduction \rangle \\
\langle concept\text{-}introduction \rangle \ &::= \ \langle atomic\text{-}concept \rangle \doteq \langle concept \rangle \mid \\
&\qquad \langle atomic\text{-}concept \rangle \dot{\leq} \langle concept \rangle \mid \\
&\qquad \langle atomic\text{-}concept \rangle \dot{\leq} \text{ Anything} \\
\langle role\text{-}introduction \rangle \ &::= \ \langle atomic\text{-}role \rangle \doteq \langle role \rangle \mid \\
&\qquad \langle atomic\text{-}role \rangle \dot{\leq} \langle role \rangle \mid \\
&\qquad \langle atomic\text{-}role \rangle \dot{\leq} \text{ anyrelation} \\
\langle concept \rangle \ &::= \ \langle atomic\text{-}concept \rangle \mid \\
&\qquad (\text{and } \langle concept \rangle^+) \mid \\
&\qquad (\text{all } \langle role \rangle \ \langle concept \rangle) \mid \\
&\qquad (\text{atleast } \langle number \rangle \ \langle role \rangle) \mid \\
&\qquad (\text{atmost } \langle number \rangle \ \langle role \rangle) \\
\langle role \rangle \ &::= \ \langle atomic\text{-}role \rangle \\
\langle restriction \rangle \ &::= \ (\text{disjoint } \langle atomic\text{-}concept \rangle \ \langle atomic\text{-}concept \rangle) \\[6pt]
\langle number \rangle \ &::= \ \langle non\text{-}negative\text{-}integer \rangle \\
\langle atomic\text{-}role \rangle \ &::= \ \langle identifier \rangle \\
\langle atomic\text{-}concept \rangle \ &::= \ \langle identifier \rangle
\end{aligned}
$$

Fig. 3.3. BNF Definition of $\mathcal{TF}$

Because we are interested not only in forming a variety of concept terms, but also in introducing new concepts,[9] there are two concept introduction operators. The first one " $\doteq$ " introduces a new *atomic concept* as a *defined concept* which gets the meaning of the concept on the right hand side. The second introduction operator " $\dot{\leq}$ " introduces an atomic concept as a *primitive concept*, i.e. it is more specialized than the concept on the right hand side – without saying in what sense it is more special.

A unique feature in terminological formalisms is the facility to introduce new atomic roles as well [Brachman and Schmolze, 1985, p. 185] – called *role differentiation* in Sect. 3.1.3. This permits us to represent hierarchical relationships between roles, such as the fact that **leader** is a specialization of the **member** role.

Similar to concept-forming operators, role-forming operators could be introduced, for example, *inverse roles, range restricted roles,* or *role composition.* However, because we are not mainly interested in designing a "most general ter-

---

[9]Which corresponds to creating and naming a concept node in a structural inheritance network.

minological formalism" here, we will not do so (but cf. Sect. 3.4). As it will turn out, $\mathcal{TF}$ as specified in Fig. 3.3 will give us enough puzzles to solve.[10]

In order to have a handle for introducing top-level primitive concept and roles, two predefined terms are provided: **Anything** and **anyrelation**, which are intended to denote the class of all things and all relationships, respectively. However, in order to keep things simple, these two terms may appear only as isolated terms on the right hand side of primitive introductions. The main reason to restrict the usage of **anyrelation** is that the meaning of the terms (**all anyrelation** C) and (**atleast 10 anyrelation**) is quite weird and that these terms present severe problems from an algorithmic point of view. Furthermore, since I do not see any real use for **anyrelation** and **Anything**, except for introducing top-level primitive terms, I think that this restriction is justified.

Finally, there is a disjointness operator which states that any individual belonging to the class denoted by the concept appearing as the first argument in the "disjoint" restriction cannot be a member of the class denoted by the concept appearing as the second argument. For instance, no **Man** is a **Woman**. This restriction operator does not really fit into the language because it does not *describe* a concept, but it *restricts* the interpretation of a terminology. However, I regard it as a necessary ingredient for any useful terminological formalism. For this reason, I adopted the scheme used in [Brachman et al., 1983] to state disjointness explicitly – with a certain restriction. Disjointness declarations will have an effect only if both concepts are primitive. Otherwise the declaration will be ignored. The reason for this convention is that declaring two defined concepts as disjoint is counter-intuitive. Either they are *completely* defined by the respective term introductions, and then it should follow from the definition whether they are disjoint or not, or they are not completely defined. However, in this case, they contain an undefined part and should be introduced as primitive concepts.

Using the $\mathcal{TF}$ syntax, we can reformulate our informal example used in the Introduction as shown in Fig. 3.4. Most of it is a straightforward transcription based on the intuitive meaning of $\mathcal{TF}$. There are some points to note, however. First, as suggested above, all terms left unspecified in Fig. 1.1 (e.g. **Human** and **member**) are now explicitly introduced as primitive subconcepts or primitive subroles of **Anything** or **anyrelation**, respectively.

Second, the **leader** role is now *globally* introduced as a primitive subrole of **member**, and not *locally* "inside" of a concept definition as in Fig. 1.1. This does not change the meaning of any of the concepts, but shows that roles are entities which are independent of concepts. This is in contrast to the view held

---

[10]Compared with BACK [von Luck et al., 1987, Peltason et al., 1987], $\mathcal{TF}$ contains almost all operators which are relevant for the expressiveness of the terminological formalism. *Root concepts* [von Luck et al., 1987, p. 29] and *attribute sets* [von Luck et al., 1987, p. 28] can be "simulated" within $\mathcal{TF}$ using the "disjoint" operator. The restricted form of *role-value-maps* used in BACK [von Luck et al., 1987, p. 30] and the possibility of restricting the range of primitive subroles [von Luck et al., 1987, p. 31] could be added to $\mathcal{TF}$ without any complications. The only problematical point may be the domain restriction of primitive subroles. Compared with the subset of KL-ONE investigated in [Schmolze and Israel, 1983], we miss *role-value-maps*.

Human	$\dot{\leq}$	Anything
Man	$\dot{\leq}$	Human
Woman	$\dot{\leq}$	Human
(disjoint Man Woman)		
Set	$\dot{\leq}$	Anything
member	$\dot{\leq}$	anyrelation
Team	$\dot{=}$	(and Set (all member Human) (atleast 2 member))
Small-team	$\dot{=}$	(and Team (atmost 5 member))
leader	$\dot{\leq}$	member
Modern-team	$\dot{=}$	(and Team (atmost 4 member)
		(atleast 1 leader) (all leader Woman))

Fig. 3.4. A Formal Terminology Using $\mathcal{TF}$ Syntax

in KL-ONE. This new perspective on roles, viewing them as "first-class citizens," has been called the "enlightened" view of roles in [Kaczmarek et al., 1986] and is a necessary consequence of the logical reconstruction of KL-ONE.

3.2.2 The Semantics of the Terminological Formalism

As discussed in Sect. 2.2.1, the intuitive meaning of a KR formalism should be backed up with a formal semantics, preferably with a model-theoretic semantics. One way to do this, though indirectly, is providing a translation into first-order predicate logic, perhaps employing a restricted form of lambda calculus, as exercised in [Schmolze and Israel, 1983] and [von Luck et al., 1988]. Such a solution has the advantage that we could utilize proof procedures of first-order predicate logic. For the analysis of computational properties in Chap. 4 and the exploration of different kinds of semantics in Chap. 5, however, a direct model-theoretic semantics proves to be more useful. Actually, I believe that without such a model-theoretic semantics the analysis in the next two chapters would be almost impossible.

The main idea in a model-theoretic semantics for terminological representation formalisms is that there is a set of things we are interested in – the *domain* $\mathcal{D}$ and that each concept and each role denotes a set of objects (a subset of $\mathcal{D}$) and a set of object pairs (a subset of $\mathcal{D} \times \mathcal{D}$), respectively [Brachman and Levesque, 1984]. These sets are called *extensions* of the concepts or roles. Of course, we cannot know or determine the actual extensions of any concepts or roles. However, using the relationships between terms fixed by a terminology, we can analyze the *necessary* relationships between the extensions of terms in a terminology. For example, the idea that anything which is called a Modern-team is a Small-team as well – that Modern-team is *subsumed* by Small-team – should be mirrored in a model-theoretic semantics by a set inclusion relationship between the extensions of both of these concepts, regardless of the actual extensions.

In order to formalize this idea, the notion of an *extension function* $\mathcal{E}$ will be introduced which maps terms to their extensions, respecting the intuitive rules about term-forming operators spelled out in the previous subsection. For the purpose of formally defining the extension function, we have to refer to certain subsets of $\mathcal{TF}$ defined below.

Definition 3.1 (Notation: Subsets of $\mathcal{TF}$) *We will refer to the following subsets of $\mathcal{TF}$:*

$\mathcal{N}_C$: *the set of* atomic concepts,

$\mathcal{N}_R$: *the set of* atomic roles,

$\mathcal{N}$: *the set of* atomic terms *with* $\mathcal{N} = \mathcal{N}_C \cup \mathcal{N}_R$ *and* $\mathcal{N}_C \cap \mathcal{N}_R = \emptyset$,

$\mathcal{TF}_C$: *the set of* concepts,

$\mathcal{TF}_R$: *the set of* roles,

$\mathcal{TF}_T$: *the set of* terms *with* $\mathcal{TF}_T = \mathcal{TF}_C \cup \mathcal{TF}_R$.

In the following, the letter a will be used to denote atomic terms, t and u to denote arbitrary terms, and c and r to denote concepts and roles, respectively. Furthermore, for notational convenience we will often view terminologies not as sequences but as sets. Based on these conventions, the notion of an extension function can be defined as follows.

Definition 3.2 (Extension Function) *Let $\mathcal{D}$, the domain, be any set, and let $\mathcal{E}$ be a function:*

$$\mathcal{E}: \begin{cases} \mathcal{TF}_C & \rightarrow & 2^{\mathcal{D}} \\ \mathcal{TF}_R & \rightarrow & 2^{\mathcal{D} \times \mathcal{D}}. \end{cases}$$

$\mathcal{E}$ *is an* extension function *iff*

$$\mathcal{E}[(\text{and } c_1 \ldots c_n)] = \bigcap_{i=1}^{n} \mathcal{E}[c_i] \tag{3.1}$$

$$\mathcal{E}[(\text{all } r\ c)] = \{x \in \mathcal{D} |\ \forall y : \langle x, y \rangle \in \mathcal{E}[r] \Rightarrow y \in \mathcal{E}[c]\} \tag{3.2}$$

$$\mathcal{E}[(\text{atleast } n\ r)] = \{x \in \mathcal{D} |\ \|\{y \in \mathcal{D} | \langle x, y \rangle \in \mathcal{E}[r]\}\| \geq n\} \tag{3.3}$$

$$\mathcal{E}[(\text{atmost } n\ r)] = \{x \in \mathcal{D} |\ \|\{y \in \mathcal{D} | \langle x, y \rangle \in \mathcal{E}[r]\}\| \leq n\} \tag{3.4}$$

$$\mathcal{E}[\text{Anything}] = \mathcal{D} \tag{3.5}$$

$$\mathcal{E}[\text{anyrelation}] = \mathcal{D} \times \mathcal{D}. \tag{3.6}$$

In order to formalize the effects of the term introduction operators, the possible extension functions as characterized by the above definition have to be further restricted. For instance, the introduction of **Woman** as a primitive subconcept of **Human** in Fig. 3.4 should exclude all extension functions which do not satisfy that $\mathcal{E}[\text{Woman}] \subseteq \mathcal{E}[\text{Human}]$. An extension function $\mathcal{E}$ over a domain $\mathcal{D}$ which respects all term introductions and also the "disjoint" restrictions will be called *semantic structure of a terminology*.

Definition 3.3 (Semantic Structure of a Terminology) *Let T be a terminology according to the* BNF *definition in Fig. 3.3 such that each atomic term is introduced only once. Let D and $\mathcal{E}$ be defined as above. Then $\mathcal{E}$ is called* extension *function with respect to T and $\langle D, \mathcal{E} \rangle$ is called* semantic structure *of T iff for $a \in \mathcal{N}$, $c_1, c_2 \in \mathcal{N}_C$ and primitive, and $t \in T\mathcal{F}_T$:*

$$\mathcal{E}[a] = \mathcal{E}[t] \quad \text{for all} \quad (a \doteq t) \in T \tag{3.7}$$

$$\mathcal{E}[a] \subseteq \mathcal{E}[t] \quad \text{for all} \quad (a \stackrel{.}{\leq} t) \in T \tag{3.8}$$

$$\mathcal{E}[c_1] \cap \mathcal{E}[c_2] = \emptyset \quad \text{for all} \quad (\text{disjoint } c_1 \, c_2) \in T. \tag{3.9}$$

Although everything defined so far makes perfect sense, we will put another syntactic restriction on the form of terminologies. A common intuition about terminologies is that the meaning of a concept "can be completely understood in terms of the meaning of its parts and the way these are composed" [Schmolze and Brachman, 1982, p. 11]. However, this can only be achieved if the term introductions are "well-founded," i.e. if there are no definitional cycles, such as

Human $\stackrel{.}{\leq}$ (and Mammal (all offspring Human)).

Trying to understand the meaning of Human, we will inevitably end up trying to figure what the meaning of Human could be – in other words, this term introduction runs counter to the intuition spelled out above. More generally, each *terminological cycle* as defined below violates this intuition.

Definition 3.4 (Terminological Cycle) *An atomic term a directly uses an atomic term a' in a terminology T iff the right hand side of the introduction of a mentions a'. An atomic term a_0 uses an atomic term a_n in T iff there is a chain of atomic terms $a_0, a_1, \ldots a_n$, such that a_i directly uses a_{i+1}, $0 \leq i \leq n-1$. A terminology T is said to contain a terminological cycle iff some atomic term uses itself in T.*

Since such terminological cycles are counter-intuitive and, moreover, complicate the semantics and create severe problems when designing an inference algorithm, their use is prohibited in almost all terminological representation systems. For the rest of this chapter and in the next chapter, we will follow this traditional treatment, but we will return to this problem in Chap. 5.

3.2.3 Relationships in Terminologies

Recalling our argument from the beginning of the previous subsection that *subsumption* between terms should be mirrored as a *necessary* set inclusion between extensions of terms, we can now precisely say what is meant by that.

Definition 3.5 (Subsumption in a Terminology) *A term t is subsumed by a term t' in a terminology T, written $t \preceq_T t'$, iff for every semantic structure $\langle D, \mathcal{E} \rangle$ of T it holds that $\mathcal{E}[t] \subseteq \mathcal{E}[t']$.*

Note that subsumption in a terminology is is a *transitive* and *reflexive* relation on $\mathcal{TF}_T$ because of the set-theoretic semantics.[11]

Proposition 3.1 *For any fixed terminology T and any terms t, t', and t'' :*

1. $t \preceq_T t$

2. *If $t \preceq_T t'$ and $t' \preceq_T t''$, then $t \preceq_T t''$*

With the formal definition of what is represented in a terminology we can not only say what it means that one term is subsumed by another one, but can formally define a number of other relations as well. Of course, we will not get out more than we put in. In the context of a terminology, this means we can only reason about *analytic* relationships – relationships which hold because of the way the terms are defined. For instance, whether there is a **Modern-team** in the world is not something a terminology is able to represent. Relationships and properties which can be reasoned about in terminologies are, in addition to subsumption, *equivalence*, *disjointness*, and *incoherence*. Two terms are, for instance, equivalent if they always denote the same set of objects.

Definition 3.6 (Equivalence) *Two terms t, t' are equivalent in a terminology T, written $t \approx_T t'$, iff for every semantic structure $\langle \mathcal{D}, \mathcal{E} \rangle$ of T it holds that $\mathcal{E}[t] = \mathcal{E}[t']$.*

Similarly, two terms are said to be disjoint, if it is impossible to describe anything by both terms simultaneously.

Definition 3.7 (Disjointness) *Two terms t, t' are disjoint in a terminology T iff for every semantic structure $\langle \mathcal{D}, \mathcal{E} \rangle$ of T it holds that $\mathcal{E}[t] \cap \mathcal{E}[t'] = \emptyset$.*

Finally, we will call a term incoherent if it can never be used in describing an object – if it has a necessarily empty extension.

Definition 3.8 (Incoherence) *A term t is called incoherent in a terminology T iff for every semantic structure $\langle \mathcal{D}, \mathcal{E} \rangle$ of T it holds that $\mathcal{E}[t] = \emptyset$.*

For instance, the concept term (and (atleast 1 r) (atmost 0 r)), for any role r, is an incoherent concept. According to Def. 3.2, it has a necessarily empty extension in every terminology, and will be denoted by the special atomic concept **Nothing**. Actually, disjointness and incoherency are notions which can only be applied to concepts in $\mathcal{TF}$. Roles never become incoherent and no pair of roles can be disjoint.

Obviously, the relations and properties defined above are closely related to subsumption – they can be easily reduced to it by applying the definitions above.

---

[11]Moreover, as is easy to see, the quotient set of $\mathcal{TF}_T$ w.r.t. to equivalence of terms is a *partial ordering* which forms together with the "and" operator a *semi lower lattice* on the set of concepts.

Proposition 3.2 *Let T be a terminology and t, t' two terms. Then the following relationships hold:*

1. *t and t' are equivalent in T iff $t \preceq_T t'$ and $t' \preceq_T t$,*

2. *t is incoherent in T iff $t \preceq_T$ Nothing, and*

3. *t and t' are disjoint in T iff (and $t\, t'$) $\preceq_T$ Nothing.*

Similarly, subsumption can be reduced to equivalence.

Proposition 3.3 *Given a terminology T and two term t, t':*

$$t \preceq_T t' \text{ iff } t \approx_T (\text{and } t\, t').$$

Furthermore, if we had a general concept-negation operator, it would be possible to reduce subsumption to disjointness.

3.2.4 Normal-Form Terminologies and Constructive Semantics

With the definitions in the previous two subsections, the semantics of terminological formalisms is completely specified. However, instead of stopping here, I will try to simplify matters. First, it is shown how to translate terminologies formulated using TF syntax into so-called *normal-form terminologies* which are equivalent in meaning to the original terminology, but which make symbolically explicit most of the restrictions imposed on the semantic structure of a terminology. Second, exploiting the fact that terminological cycles were excluded, it becomes possible to *construct* semantic structures instead of merely describing them.

The first of the simplifications can be accomplished by noting that the restrictions (3.8) and (3.9) on $\mathcal{E}$ in Def. 3.3 can be expressed symbolically by adding some terms to the right hand side of a term introduction. Instead of introducing a concept primitively, we can equivalently introduce it as a defined concept if the primitive part of the concept's meaning is added explicitly to the defining term. For this purpose, a new syntactic category, called *primitive component*, will be used. Primitive components are similar to atomic terms. However, they are completely undefined in the terminology. Names for these primitive components will be generated by overlining the corresponding atomic term. For instance, the introduction of Human in Fig. 3.4 could be expressed as

$$\text{Human} \doteq (\text{and Anything } \overline{\text{Human}}).$$

The introduction of primitive roles can be done in a similar way. However, a new role-forming operator is necessary for this purpose, namely, a *role conjunction* operator "androle". Employing this operator, the introduction of the **leader** role in Fig. 3.4 could be rephrased as

$$\text{leader} \doteq (\text{androle member } \overline{\text{leader}}).$$

Finally, the semantics of the disjointness restriction (3.9) could be expressed symbolically, if we had a restricted form of concept negation, namely, atomic concept-negation of primitive components. Assuming that such an operator, written "a-not", is at our disposal, the restriction that **Man** and **Woman** are disjoint concepts could be expressed by adding to one of the concept introductions the negated primitive component of the other concept, e.g.:

$$\text{Man} \; \doteq \; (\text{and Human } \overline{\text{Man}})$$
$$\text{Woman} \doteq (\text{and Human } \overline{\text{Woman}} \; (\text{a-not } \overline{\text{Man}})).$$

The resulting formalism, which will be called $\mathcal{NTF}$, is defined in Fig. 3.5.

$$
\begin{array}{rcl}
\langle terminology\rangle & ::= & \langle term\text{-}introduction\rangle^* \\
\langle term\text{-}introduction\rangle & ::= & \langle concept\text{-}introduction\rangle \mid \\
& & \langle role\text{-}introduction\rangle \\
\langle concept\text{-}introduction\rangle & ::= & \langle atomic\text{-}concept\rangle \doteq \langle concept\rangle \\
\langle role\text{-}introduction\rangle & ::= & \langle atomic\text{-}role\rangle \doteq \langle role\rangle \\
\langle concept\rangle & ::= & \langle atomic\text{-}concept\rangle \mid \\
& & \langle primitive\text{-}concept\text{-}component\rangle \mid \\
& & (\textsf{a-not} \\
& & \langle primitive\text{-}concept\text{-}component\rangle) \mid \\
& & (\textsf{and } \langle concept\rangle^+) \mid \\
& & (\textsf{all } \langle role\rangle \langle concept\rangle) \mid \\
& & (\textsf{atleast } \langle number\rangle \langle role\rangle) \mid \\
& & (\textsf{atmost } \langle number\rangle \langle role\rangle) \\
\langle role\rangle & ::= & \langle atomic\text{-}role\rangle \\
& & \langle primitive\text{-}role\text{-}component\rangle \mid \\
& & (\textsf{androle } \langle role\rangle^+) \\[1em]
\langle number\rangle & ::= & \langle non\text{-}negative\text{-}integer\rangle \\
\langle atomic\text{-}role\rangle & ::= & \langle identifier\rangle \\
\langle atomic\text{-}concept\rangle & ::= & \langle identifier\rangle \\
\langle primitive\text{-}concept\text{-}component\rangle & ::= & \langle identifier\rangle \\
\langle primitive\text{-}role\text{-}component\rangle & ::= & \langle identifier\rangle
\end{array}
$$

Fig. 3.5. BNF Definition of $\mathcal{NTF}$

Summarizing, by adding a new syntactic category – primitive components – and two term-forming operators – role conjunction and atomic concept negation – we can get rid of "$\leq$" and "disjoint". Furthermore, **Anything** and **anyrelation** can be avoided as well since top-level primitive terms can now be introduced by reference to the corresponding primitive component.

Similarly to $\mathcal{TF}$, conventions for referring to subsets of $\mathcal{NTF}$ are introduced as follows.

Definition 3.9 (Notation: Subsets of $\mathcal{NTF}$) $\mathcal{N}_C$, $\mathcal{N}_R$, and $\mathcal{N}$ are the set of atomic concepts, roles, and terms, respectively. Furthermore, the following subsets of $\mathcal{NTF}$ will be used:

$\overline{\mathcal{N}_C}$: the set of primitive concept components,

$\overline{\mathcal{N}_R}$: the set of primitive role components,

$\overline{\mathcal{N}}$: the set of primitive components with $\overline{\mathcal{N}} = \overline{\mathcal{N}_C} \cup \overline{\mathcal{N}_R}$, $\overline{\mathcal{N}_C} \cap \overline{\mathcal{N}_R} = \emptyset$, and $\mathcal{N} \cap \overline{\mathcal{N}} = \emptyset$,

$\mathcal{N}_b$: the set of base terms $= \mathcal{N} \cup \overline{\mathcal{N}}$.

$\mathcal{NTF}_C$: the set of concepts,

$\mathcal{NTF}_R$: the set of roles,

$\mathcal{NTF}_T$: the set of terms $= \mathcal{NTF}_C \cup \mathcal{NTF}_R$.

As sketched above, it is possible to transform any terminology formulated in $\mathcal{TF}$ into – what will be called – a *normal-form terminology* by employing some simple transformation rules.

Definition 3.10 (Transformation to Normal-Form Terminologies)
Let T be a terminology using $\mathcal{TF}$ syntax. Then the normal-form terminology T_N is derived from T by the following rules:

1. If $c \in \mathcal{N}_C$, then

    (a) if $(c \doteq t) \in T$, then $(c \doteq t) \in T_N$,

    (b) if $(c \mathrel{\dot{\leq}} t) \in T$, then $(c \doteq (\text{and } t\, \bar{c}\, P)) \in T_N$,

    (c) otherwise, $(c \doteq (\text{and } \bar{c}\ P)) \in T_N$,

    with P empty if $(\text{disjoint } c \ \ldots) \notin T$ and $P = (\text{a-not } c_i)\ldots(\text{a-not } c_i)$ if $(\text{disjoint } c\, c_i), \ldots, (\text{disjoint } c\, c_j) \in T$ with $c_i \ldots c_j$ primitive concepts.

2. If $r \in \mathcal{N}_R$, then

    (a) if $(r \doteq t) \in T$, then $(r \doteq t) \in T_N$,

    (b) if $(r \mathrel{\dot{\leq}} t) \in T$, then $(r \doteq (\text{androle } t\ \bar{r})) \in T_N$,

    (c) otherwise, $(r \doteq \bar{r}) \in T_N$.

3. All occurrences of Anything and anyrelation are deleted in T_N.

Analyzing the complexity of the transformation, we note that the transformation is very simple.

Proposition 3.4 *The transformation from $\mathcal{T}$ to $\mathcal{T}_N$ can be performed in linear time. The size of a normal-form terminology $\mathcal{T}_N$ derived from $\mathcal{T}$ is at most double the size of $\mathcal{T}$.*

Similarly to the definitions in the last subsection, we can now define extension functions and semantic structures for $\mathcal{NTF}$ terminologies.

Definition 3.11 ($\mathcal{NTF}$ Extension Function) *Let $\mathcal{D}$ be a set and $\mathcal{E}$ a function. $\mathcal{E}$ is a ($\mathcal{NTF}$) extension function iff*

$$\mathcal{E}[(\text{and } c_1 \ldots c_n)] = \bigcap_{i=1}^{n} \mathcal{E}[c_i] \tag{3.10}$$

$$\mathcal{E}[(\text{all } r \, c)] = \{x \in \mathcal{D} | \, \forall y : \langle x, y \rangle \in \mathcal{E}[r] \Rightarrow y \in \mathcal{E}[c]\} \tag{3.11}$$

$$\mathcal{E}[(\text{atleast } n \, r)] = \{x \in \mathcal{D} | \, \|\{y \in \mathcal{D} | \langle x, y \rangle \in \mathcal{E}[r]\}\| \geq n\} \tag{3.12}$$

$$\mathcal{E}[(\text{atmost } n \, r)] = \{x \in \mathcal{D} | \, \|\{y \in \mathcal{D} | \langle x, y \rangle \in \mathcal{E}[r]\}\| \leq n\} \tag{3.13}$$

$$\mathcal{E}[(\text{a-not } c)] = \mathcal{D} \setminus \mathcal{P}[c] \tag{3.14}$$

$$\mathcal{E}[(\text{androle } r_1 \ldots r_n)] = \bigcap_{i=1}^{n} \mathcal{E}[r_i]. \tag{3.15}$$

Definition 3.12 ($\mathcal{NTF}$ Semantic Structure) *Let $\mathcal{T}_N$ be a normal-form terminology. Then $\langle \mathcal{D}, \mathcal{E} \rangle$ is a semantic structure of $\mathcal{T}_N$ iff for $a \in \mathcal{N}, t \in \mathcal{NTF}_T$*

$$\mathcal{E}[a] = \mathcal{E}[t] \quad \text{for all} \quad (a \doteq t) \in \mathcal{T}_N. \tag{3.16}$$

Comparing these definitions with Def. 3.2 and Def. 3.3, we see that they are indeed equivalent in the sense that the resulting semantic structures for a given $\mathcal{TF}$-terminology $\mathcal{T}$ are (almost) identical to the semantic structures of a $\mathcal{NTF}$-terminology $\mathcal{T}_N$ derived from $\mathcal{T}$.

Theorem 3.1 (Equivalence of Semantic Structures) *Let $\mathcal{T}$ be a terminology, and let $\mathcal{T}_N$ be the derived normal-form terminology. Then, for any semantic structure $\langle \mathcal{D}, \mathcal{E} \rangle$ of $\mathcal{T}$ there exists a semantic structure $\langle \mathcal{D}', \mathcal{E}' \rangle$ of $\mathcal{T}_N$, and vice versa, such that for any term $t \in \mathcal{TF}_T$:*

$$\mathcal{E}[t] = \mathcal{E}'[t]. \tag{3.17}$$

Proof: Assume $\langle \mathcal{D}, \mathcal{E} \rangle$ is a semantic structure of $\mathcal{T}$. Then set $\mathcal{D}' = \mathcal{D}$, $\mathcal{E}'[\bar{a}] = \mathcal{E}[a]$, and $\mathcal{E}'[a] = \mathcal{E}[a]$ for every atomic term $a \in \mathcal{N}$. Applying the equations of Def. 3.11, $\mathcal{E}'$ can be extended to a $\mathcal{NTF}$ extension function such that Eq. (3.17) is valid. Now, since the equations in Def. 3.3 are satisfied for $\mathcal{T}$, Eq. (3.16) must be satisfied for $\mathcal{T}_N$ because

1. for defined atomic terms the equations are identical,

2. for primitive terms without a disjointness restriction, $\mathcal{E}[a] \subseteq \mathcal{E}[t]$ implies $\mathcal{E}'[a] = \mathcal{E}'[t] \cap \mathcal{E}'[\bar{a}]$,

3. for primitive terms with disjointness restrictions, $\mathcal{E}[a] \subseteq \mathcal{E}[t]$, $\mathcal{E}[a'] \subseteq \mathcal{E}[t']$ together with $\mathcal{E}[a] \cap \mathcal{E}[a'] = \emptyset$ implies $\mathcal{E}'[a] = \mathcal{E}'[t] \cap \mathcal{E}'[\overline{a}] \cap (\mathcal{D} \setminus \mathcal{E}'[\overline{a'}])$, $\mathcal{E}'[a'] = \mathcal{E}'[t'] \cap \mathcal{E}'[\overline{a'}]$.

Conversely, let us assume that $\langle \mathcal{D}', \mathcal{E}' \rangle$ is a semantic structure of $\mathcal{T}_N$. Then set $\mathcal{D} = \mathcal{D}'$, $\mathcal{E}[t] = \mathcal{E}'[t]$ for all $t \in \mathcal{TF}_T$, and apply Eq. (3.5) and Eq. (3.6). $\mathcal{E}$ is obviously a $\mathcal{TF}$ extension function that satisfies Eq. (3.17). Furthermore,

1. Eq. (3.7) is trivially satisfied,

2. Eq. (3.8) is satisfied because $\mathcal{E}'[a] = \mathcal{E}'[t] \cap \mathcal{E}'[\overline{a}]$ implies $\mathcal{E}[a] \subseteq \mathcal{E}[t]$,

3. and Eq. (3.9) is satisfied because $\mathcal{E}'[a] = \mathcal{E}'[t] \cap \mathcal{E}'[\overline{a}] \cap (\mathcal{D} \setminus \mathcal{E}'[\overline{a'}])$ and $\mathcal{E}'[a'] = \mathcal{E}'[t] \cap \mathcal{E}'[\overline{a'}]$, implies $\mathcal{E}[a] \cap \mathcal{E}[a'] = \emptyset$.

Thus, $\langle \mathcal{D}, \mathcal{E} \rangle$ is a semantic structure of $\mathcal{T}$. ∎

Since the semantic structures are identical, the subsumption relation is identical as well.

Corollary 3.1 (Equivalence of Subsumption) *Let $\mathcal{T}$ be a $\mathcal{TF}$-terminology and let $\mathcal{T}_N$ be the derived normal-form terminology. Then for any two concept or role terms $t, t' \in \mathcal{TF}_T$*

$$t \preceq_T t' \quad \textit{iff} \quad t \preceq_{T_N} t'.$$

Theorem 3.1 and Corollary 3.1 give a formal characterization of the status of primitive terms in terminological formalism – a point which was the topic of a number of discussions in the KL-ONE community. For instance, in [Schmolze and Brachman, 1982, p. 11], R. Bobrow suggested that primitive concepts should be treated in the way we did it in $\mathcal{TF}$, while Israel favored the idea that primitive concepts should have no structure at all, i.e. they should be equivalent to what I have called primitive components. The reason behind the latter proposal being that only "purely linguistic" knowledge should be represented in a terminological knowledge base, excluding statements such as "Women are Humans," which apparently express some contingent truth about our world.[12] As the theorem above shows, these two points of view are compatible with each other in the sense that a terminology containing defined and primitive concepts can be translated into one which contains only defined concepts and primitive components without changing the *relevant* semantic structure of a terminology, providing us with identical subsumption relations.

While it is more convenient to have the opportunity to introduce primitive terms as is possible in $\mathcal{TF}$, terminologies formulated using $\mathcal{NTF}$ are easier to analyze from a formal point of view. For this reason, in the following, normal-form terminologies will be the subject of investigation when the formal properties of terminologies are analyzed.

---

[12]This point of view is also held in KRYPTON [Brachman et al., 1985], where a concept is either completely defined, or it is completely undefined – i.e. there is nothing specified about a primitive concept.

One such property is the fact that it is not only possible to describe semantic structures, but that such structures can be explicitly constructed – provided the terminology is cycle-free. This will be done by assuming a *primitive assignment* – an arbitrary assignment of extensions to primitive components.

Definition 3.13 (Primitive Assignment) *A primitive assignment is any function $\mathcal{P}$ such that:*

$$\mathcal{P}: \begin{cases} \overline{\mathcal{N}_C} & \to & 2^{\mathcal{D}} \\ \overline{\mathcal{N}_R} & \to & 2^{\mathcal{D} \times \mathcal{D}}. \end{cases}$$

Based on this assignment, the extensions of all other terms can be constructed, i.e., the extension function w.r.t. to a terminology can be *defined* in terms of the primitive assignment and the semantics of the term-forming and term-introduction operators. This means we can formulate a *constructive* version of the semantics given in Definitions 3.11 and 3.12. Before we do so, however, let us define what we mean by the *level* of a term in a terminology.

Definition 3.14 (Level of a Term) *The level of a term in a terminology, written* level$(a, \mathcal{T})$*, is defined as*

$$\text{level}(t, \mathcal{T}) = \begin{cases} 0 & \text{if } t \in \mathcal{N}, \\ \max\big(\{\text{level}(a, \mathcal{T})|\ a \in \mathcal{N}_b \text{ occurring in } t\}\big) & \text{if } t \notin \mathcal{N}_b, \\ i + 1 & \text{if } (t \doteq u) \in \mathcal{T} \\ & \text{and } \text{level}(u) = i. \end{cases}$$

Theorem 3.2 (Constructive Semantics) *Let $\mathcal{T}_N$ be a cycle-free $\mathcal{NTF}$-terminology. Then any primitive assignment can be inductively extended to a unique extension function w.r.t. $\mathcal{T}_N$.*

Proof: First note that a level assignment following the definition above is well-defined for all cycle-free terminologies.

Now the extension of a base term a of level i is constructed in the following way. For $i = 0$, we set $\mathcal{E}[a] = \mathcal{P}[a]$. For $i > 0$, assume that for all base terms of level $i - 1$ the extension has been constructed. Using these extensions, compute the extension of a by applying Eq. (3.10)–(3.15) to the r.h.s. of the term introduction of a. Then Eq. (3.16) is satisfied for the introduction of a. Moreover, $\mathcal{E}[a]$ cannot conflict with the extension of any other atomic term of the same or lower level. Since this holds for all levels, the construction never leads to a conflict and, thus, defines an extension function w.r.t. to $\mathcal{T}_N$. ∎

Intuitively, this theorem tells us that terminologies are never inconsistent, even if they contain incoherent concepts, because it is always possible to generate semantic structures by starting with an arbitrary primitive assignment.

3.2.5 Abstracting from Term Introductions

In analyzing the proof above, one may note that the facility of introducing terms is not crucial for the (formal) expressiveness of the language. Term introductions are something like *macro definitions*, and we can do very well without them. In particular, it is possible to reduce *subsumption in a terminology* to *subsumption between terms*.

In order to see this, note that the extension of a concept or role s does not change if a subterm t of s is replaced by another term t', provided that $t \approx_T t'$. Since it holds that any atomic term in a normal-form terminology T_N is equivalent to its defining term in T_N, it is possible to replace any atomic term by its defining term. Furthermore, since we assumed that terminologies do not contain any terminological cycles, the repeated replacement of atomic terms by their defining terms results in terms which contain only primitive components and no atomic terms (henceforth p-terms). Formally, let us define a function EXP which recursively replaces all atomic terms in an expression by their definitions:

$$
\text{EXP}(t, T_N) \overset{\text{def}}{=} \begin{cases} \text{EXP}(u, T_N) & \text{if } t \in \mathcal{N} \text{ and } (t \doteq u) \in T_N, \\ (op\ \text{EXP}(t_1)\ \dots\ \text{EXP}(t_n)) & \text{if } t = (op\ t_1\ \dots\ t_n), \\ t & \text{otherwise.} \end{cases}
$$

By using similar arguments as in the proof of Theorem 3.2, it is easy to see that EXP always terminates, provided that T_N is cycle-free. Moreover, by the comments made above, it should be clear that EXP is *extension-preserving*, i.e., EXP does not change the meaning of a term in a terminology.

Proposition 3.5 *Let T_N be a cycle-free normal-form terminology, and let t be an arbitrary $\mathcal{NTF}_T$ term. Then for any semantic structure $\langle D, \mathcal{E} \rangle$ of T_N:*

$$
\mathcal{E}[t] = \mathcal{E}[\text{EXP}(t, T_N)].
$$

In a sense, EXP realizes something similar to what is usually called *inheritance* in semantic networks. Substituting the defining term t of an atomic concept a for the appearance of the atom a in a top-level "**and**" term amounts to adding the restrictions mentioned in the definition of a to this "**and**" term – to "inherit" the restrictions from a. However, EXP does more. It also performs "inheritance" for all concepts mentioned in the value restrictions.

The most interesting point about EXP is that it allows us to *abstract* from a terminology when determining subsumption. Since the p-terms generated by EXP contain no atomic terms, the semantic structure of the terminology is irrelevant for their extensions, and by that, for subsumption between p-terms. In order to capture this formally, let us denote the *empty terminology* – the terminology which contains no term introductions – by $\emptyset$. Since subsumption in the empty terminology plays a prominent role in the following, a special name is invented for it.

Definition 3.15 (Term-Subsumption) *Let $t, t' \in \mathcal{NTF}_T$. If $t \preceq_\emptyset t'$, we will also write $t \preceq t'$ and call $\preceq$ term-subsumption.*

Theorem 3.3 (Reduction to Term-Subsumption) *Given a cycle-free terminology $\mathcal{T}$, for all terms t and t':*

$$t \preceq_{\mathcal{T}} t' \quad \textit{iff} \quad \text{EXP}(t, \mathcal{T}_N) \preceq \text{EXP}(t', \mathcal{T}_N).$$

Proof: First of all, we know by Corollary 3.1 that $t \preceq_{\mathcal{T}} t'$ implies $t \preceq_{\mathcal{T}_N} t'$. Furthermore, because of Prop. 3.5 and the fact that any semantic structure of $\mathcal{T}_N$ is also a semantic structure of $\emptyset$, the "only if" direction follows.

For the "if" direction assume that $t \preceq_{\mathcal{T}_N} t'$, but $\text{EXP}(t, \mathcal{T}_N) \not\preceq \text{EXP}(t', \mathcal{T}_N)$, i.e., there exists a semantic structure $\langle \mathcal{D}, \mathcal{E} \rangle$ of $\emptyset$ such that $\mathcal{E}[\text{EXP}(t, \mathcal{T}_N)] \not\subseteq \mathcal{E}[\text{EXP}(t', \mathcal{T}_N)]$. Taking the primitive assignment $\mathcal{P}$ of $\mathcal{E}$ (the restriction of $\mathcal{E}$ to primitive terms), we know by Theorem 3.2 that there must be an extension function $\mathcal{E}'$ w.r.t. $\mathcal{T}_N$ that extends $\mathcal{P}$. Furthermore, since the extension of the two p-terms must be the same in $\langle \mathcal{D}, \mathcal{E} \rangle$ and $\langle \mathcal{D}, \mathcal{E}' \rangle$, the above assumption cannot be right. Finally, since subsumption in a terminology $\mathcal{T}$ and its derived normal-form terminology $\mathcal{T}_N$ is equivalent, the "if" direction holds, as well. ∎

This theorem shows that for a formal analysis of terminological representation formalisms it suffices to analyze the *underlying term-forming formalism*. In particular, it demonstrates that *restrictions* imposed on semantic structures can be equivalently formulated by extending the vocabulary and *describing* the structures. For instance, the disjointness restriction on primitive concepts can be expressed by using atomic negation. From an algorithmic point of view, it shows that determination of subsumption in an arbitrary terminology can be reduced to determination of subsumption in the empty terminology, to term-subsumption.

3.2.6 The Significance of Term Introductions

Although for the purpose of analyzing the formal properties of subsumption it is possible to abstract completely from terminologies, as we have seen above, the facility of introducing terms is, of course, crucial for a terminological formalism if it should be used in a *representation system*. First of all, the atomic parts in p-terms are artificially constructed entities – namely, the undefined parts of a concept – entities we are usually not interested in. Second, from a point of notational convenience, the ability to introduce "abbreviations" and to specify restrictions at the most general concept is important for any knowledge representation language which is aimed at describing conceptual entities. Finally, when we use a terminology in an AI system, we usually "attach" a certain pragmatic property to atomic terms.

There is a particular mode of reasoning – *classification-based reasoning* [Kaczmarek et al., 1986] – which makes use of the fact that there is a difference between atomic concepts explicitly introduced and concepts which are constructible. This kind of reasoning uses a concept introduction as something like a "conceptual coat rack" [Woods, 1983] in the following way. A new concept term c which evolved during the processing in the system is compared with all atomic concepts in a terminology, and the set of concepts most accurately describing c – the set of *immediate subsumers* of c is returned. These may then be used in order to trigger some action, as in the CONSUL system [Kaczmarek et al., 1983], to select a plan, as in the EES system [Neches et al., 1985], or to select the most appropriate lexeme for a given concept to be verbalized, as in the JANUS system [Sondheimer and Nebel, 1986]. Formally, we may define *immediate subsumption* between atomic terms as follows.

Definition 3.16 (Immediate Subsumption) *Let T be a terminology with $\mathcal{N}$ being the set of atomic terms introduced in T. Then, a concept term $c \in T\mathcal{F}_C$ is immediately subsumed by an atomic concept term $a \in \mathcal{N}_C$ in T, written $c \lhd_T a$, iff*

$$c \preceq_T a \text{ and } \forall b \in \mathcal{N}_C: \text{ If } c \preceq_T b \text{ then } (a \approx_T b \text{ or } b \not\preceq_T a).$$

However, in [Brachman et al., 1983], it is argued that the capability to distinguish between concepts which have been *explicitly introduced* and those which could be *constructed* is not part of the functionality of a terminological reasoner. On the contrary, relying on the fact that there is something special about introduced concepts is judged as drawing "unwarranted inferences."

This point of view, though possible to hold, rules out most of the applications of terminological reasoners, as is admitted in [Brachman et al., 1983]. For example, the PSI-KLONE parser [Webber and Bobrow, 1980], the CONSUL system [Kaczmarek et al., 1983], and the RABBIT information retrieval system [Tou et al., 1982] all rely on the distinction between introduced and constructible concepts (see p. 417 in the revised version of [Brachman et al., 1983]). The same holds for the natural language access system to expert systems XTRA [Allgayer and Reddig, 1986], an attempt to represent knowledge about drugs and their effects for use in an information retrieval system [Schmiedel et al., 1986], applications in representing design knowledge [Peltason, 1987], and an information retrieval application for TTL circuits [Corella, 1986]. All of these systems make inferences in one way or another based on the presence or absence of concepts. There seems to be an "assertion ... that the domain includes a certain second-order entity (a 'kind'), represented by the concept" (p. 417 in the revised version of [Brachman et al., 1983]).

If we reconsider what a *terminological* representation system should do for us, we may come to the conclusion that it is indeed essential that such a reasoner is able to represent the second-order property that a particular concept is of interest to the user. As a matter of fact, if we think of a natural language generation system, we expect that such a system can "verbalize" a particular state of affairs using the vocabulary we provided. In other words, it should be capable of accessing the concepts explicitly introduced. This is, of course, an unwarranted inference in the sense that the model-theoretic semantics as specified in Definitions 3.2 and 3.3 cannot tell the difference between introduced atomic concepts and unintroduced concepts. Moreover, it is also nonmonotonic in the sense that new concept introductions may invalidate immediate subsumption relationships. However, as we have seen in Def. 3.16, there is no real problem in defining this notion, even though it is second-order.[13]

---

[13]This does not cause any formal problems, however. We quantify only over a *finite* set of

Summing up, when we analyze the formal properties of terminologies with respect to subsumption and related relations, we can and should abstract from the facility of introducing terms and the ability to distinguish between atomic and nonatomic concepts. Demanding, however, that this abstraction should be carried over to a representation system seems to be too strong – it would make such a representation system useless in most cases.

3.3 The Assertional Formalism $\mathcal{AF}$

Sometimes, it is enough to have a terminological formalism such as described above. For example, Corella [1986] implemented a TTL-device catalog system which is able to answer questions like "List the edge-triggered flip-flops" using only the terminological subsystem of the hybrid representation system KANDOR [Patel-Schneider, 1984]. Of course, Corella had to adopt the view spelled out above – that the introduction of a concept has a second-order assertional impact. But this seemed more acceptable than to view specifications of TTL-devices as individuals in the world. In particular, it makes it possible to give concise answers by returning abstract characterizations instead of enumerating all device identifications matching a specification.

Often, however, an application requires that we can say something about objects in the world. In a presentation planning system as described in [Arens et al., 1988]), for instance, the objects to be presented to the user have to be represented in the system. In a computer configuration application, as described in [Owsnicki-Klewe, 1988], individual components have to be represented.

As mentioned already, assertional capabilities were only very poorly developed in KL-ONE. In order to assert something, an individual concept had first to be created, which then could be related to a *nexus* – a proxy of a real-world object – using a *description wire*. The problem with this approach was that the semantics of individual concepts and nexuses were never fully worked out, and, thus, appeared to be rather obscure and useless in the end [Schmolze and Brachman, 1982, pp. 23–31].

Accounting for this deficiency, KRYPTON [Brachman et al., 1985] combines a terminological representation system – a TBox – with a full-fledged theorem prover for first-order logic [Stickel, 1985] as its assertional component, i.e. as its ABox. Although such an ABox seems to be optimal because of its assertional competence, its expressive power [Brachman and Levesque, 1982], there are some problems. First, there are some constructs in terminological formalisms which do not fit quite so well into the framework of first-order logic, in particular general number-restrictions [Pigman, 1984a, p. 24]. For this reason, the terminological formalism employed in KRYPTON is not very elaborate. Second, a switch has to be provided "to limit how long the system should try a proof before giving up" because the inferential power of the ABox can easily lead to unreasonably long proofs [Pigman, 1984a, p. 22]. All in all, KRYPTON can be regarded as an interesting experiment in combining knowledge representation and theorem proving

concepts.

techniques. However, it was not used for any application and probably never will be because it "is very large and cumbersome and is 'sort of unusable in its current state,'" as Brachman put it [Moore, 1986, p. 7]. Another, more recent effort aiming into the same direction and addressing some of the problems mentioned is the LLILOG formalism [Pletat and von Luck, 1989], which integrates a rich terminological formalism and first-order predicate logic with some extensions for the modularization of the knowledge base.

A more modest approach is the KL-TWO system [Vilain, 1985] using NIKL [Moser, 1983] as the TBox and PENNI – a version of RUP [McAllester, 1982] – as its ABox. RUP is a reason-maintenance system (see Sect. 6.6.3) supporting reasoning in variable-free predicate logic with equality, i.e. the system does not only support knowledge base revision in the ABox in a principled way, but is more efficient than KRYPTON because of its limited expressiveness. However, there are short-comings as well. The TBox, called NIKL and the ABox do not match very well. There are a couple of constructs in NIKL which do not have the expected effects on the ABox, most prominently, the number restriction. Cardinalities of sets are not handled in RUP because different constants do not denote different objects, and even though it would be theoretically possible to express such facts by a set of negated equations, the implemented system cannot control or use such information for (hybrid) reasoning. And it is not only this point where reasoning is incomplete. There are a large number of other "inferential gaps," and it is hard to tell what the system will infer and what it will miss. Although this might seem to be a serious defect, it does often not matter too much, particularly so, when missing inferences will not result in malfunctions and only a small number of options are exercised, as it was the case when applying KL-TWO in a natural language generation system [Nebel and Sondheimer, 1986], turning first-order predicate logic statements into English sentences using the NIGEL sentence generator [Mann and Matthiessen, 1983].

While in the two cases mentioned existing assertional reasoners were employed in creating a hybrid system, there is another class of hybrid systems using special-purpose ABoxes for dedicated applications. QUARK [Poesio, 1988a], for instance, the ABox for QUIRK [Bergmann and Gerlach, 1987] was designed with a natural language dialog application in mind. For this reason, it supports the representation of time [Poesio, 1988b], belief contexts, and employs a style of representation suggested by J. Hobbs [1985], called *ontological promiscuity*. However, the main effort has been put in designing a formalism for storing the desired facts with less effort devoted to inferences.

Contrasting this approach, there are a number of systems which could be characterized as expressively limited, but computationally efficient and inferentially almost complete as we will see Sect. 4.2. Examples are KANDOR [Patel-Schneider, 1984], MESON [Edelmann and Owsnicki, 1986], CLASSIC [Borgida et al., 1989], and BACK [Nebel and von Luck, 1988]. All these systems use an expressively limited TBox – employing a formalism very similar to $\mathcal{TF}$– and an ABox which is similar in expressive power to a relational database, an approach we will follow here.

3.3.1 Syntax and Semantics of $\mathcal{AF}$

The syntax of the assertional formalism, which we will call $\mathcal{AF}$, is given in Fig. 3.6. A *world description* is a sequence of *object* and *relation descriptions*.

$$\begin{aligned}
\langle \textit{world-description} \rangle \quad &::= \quad (\langle \textit{object-description} \rangle \mid \langle \textit{relation-description} \rangle)^* \\
\langle \textit{object-description} \rangle \quad &::= \quad (\langle \textit{atomic-concept} \rangle \; \langle \textit{object} \rangle) \\
\langle \textit{relation-description} \rangle \quad &::= \quad (\langle \textit{atomic-role} \rangle \; \langle \textit{object} \rangle \; \langle \textit{object} \rangle) \mid \\
&\qquad\quad (\langle \textit{atomic-role} \rangle \; \langle \textit{object} \rangle \; (\textbf{atleast} \; \langle \textit{number} \rangle)) \mid \\
&\qquad\quad (\langle \textit{atomic-role} \rangle \; \langle \textit{object} \rangle \; (\textbf{atmost} \; \langle \textit{number} \rangle))
\end{aligned}$$

Fig. 3.6. BNF Definition of $\mathcal{AF}$

With an *object description* we can assert that a certain object belongs to the extension of an atomic concept – that the object is an *instance* of the concept. With a *relation description* we are able to assert that an object has certain *role fillers* of a certain role or that a role is filled with a certain number of role fillers without identifying them.

In order to give an example, Fig. 3.7 displays a world description using concepts and roles from the "team" terminology. This small example demonstrates that even though $\mathcal{AF}$ is a rather restricted formalism, there are some interesting inferences one can draw if the world description is interpreted in combination with a terminology. For instance, we can conclude that MARY must be an instance of Woman because she is the leader of the team. Moreover, we see that all members of TEAM-A are known.

```
(Modern-team   TEAM-A)
(Man           DICK)
(Human         MARY)
(member        TEAM-A DICK)
(member        TEAM-A HARRY)
(leader        TEAM-A MARY)
(member        TEAM-A (atmost 3))
```

Fig. 3.7. A Formal World Description Using $\mathcal{AF}$ Syntax

Although the meaning of $\mathcal{AF}$ appears to be obvious, some points should be made explicit. For example, nothing has been said so far about whether different object names are assumed to denote different individuals in the world or whether only the explicitly given descriptions hold and nothing else – two properties of world descriptions usually assumed in the database world. The first is called the *unique name assumption* (UNA), the second *closed world assumption* (CWA) [Reiter, 1984].

In the context of a KR system, the closed world assumption is not very realistic in conceiving a system which is incrementally creating an image of its environment – a partial description of the world. Most likely, it will never reach a state of a complete description of the world, and it even seems not very desirable to attempt that. For example, if we assume a concept **Human** with a role **parent**, then we would have to specify the role fillers of this role for any individual which is a **Human**. And if these role fillers are **Humans** themselves, the role fillers would have to be specified until we reach the first **Humans** – in face of the fact that all this may be rather superfluous. Most likely, we are only interested in describing at most one or two generations and not the entire race.

The unique name assumption seems to be more natural. In fact, without it we could not reason about cardinalities and completeness of descriptions – a capability which seems desirable, in particular, if the number restrictions in $\mathcal{TF}$ and the limited, numeric quantifiers in $\mathcal{AF}$ should be more than mere comments. Note that in the example above, I already made this assumption when inferring that all members of the **TEAM-A** are known.

Summarizing, $\mathcal{AF}$ allows stating nondisjunctive, variable-free, positive propositions about the world, including a limited form of numeric quantification over role fillers, and employing the UNA but not the CWA. Although this means that $\mathcal{AF}$ is not very expressive, it suffices for supporting applications such as information retrieval systems similar to ARGON [Patel-Schneider et al., 1984], and is able to support computer configuration tasks as described in [Owsnicki-Klewe, 1988].

Before we now go on and investigate the combined representational power of our TBox and ABox, we will specify the meaning of $\mathcal{AF}$ formally and independently of $\mathcal{TF}$ by saying what a model of a world description is supposed to be.

Definition 3.17 (Model of a World Description) *Let* $\mathcal{D}$*, the* domain*, be an arbitrary set. Let* $\mathcal{N_O}, \mathcal{N_C}, \mathcal{N_R}$ *be sets of objects, atomic concepts, and atomic roles, respectively. Let* $\mathcal{I}$*, the* interpretation function*, be a function*

$$\mathcal{I}: \begin{cases} \mathcal{N_O} & \to & \mathcal{D} \\ \mathcal{N_C} & \to & 2^{\mathcal{D}} \\ \mathcal{N_R} & \to & 2^{\mathcal{D} \times \mathcal{D}}. \end{cases}$$

being injective on $\mathcal{N_O}$*. A pair* $\mathcal{M} = \langle \mathcal{D}, \mathcal{I} \rangle$*, called* interpretation*, satisfies a description* δ*, written* $\models_{\mathcal{M}} \delta$*, under the following conditions:*

$$\models_{\mathcal{M}} (c\,o) \quad \text{iff} \quad \mathcal{I}[o] \in \mathcal{I}[c]$$
$$\models_{\mathcal{M}} (r\,o\,p) \quad \text{iff} \quad \langle \mathcal{I}[o], \mathcal{I}[p] \rangle \in \mathcal{I}[r]$$
$$\models_{\mathcal{M}} (r\,o\,(\text{atleast}\,n)) \quad \text{iff} \quad \|\{\langle \mathcal{I}[o], x \rangle \in \mathcal{I}[r]\}\| \geq n$$
$$\models_{\mathcal{M}} (r\,o\,(\text{atmost}\,n)) \quad \text{iff} \quad \|\{\langle \mathcal{I}[o], x \rangle \in \mathcal{I}[r]\}\| \leq n.$$

An interpretation is a model *of a world description* $\mathcal{W}$*, written* $\models_{\mathcal{M}} \mathcal{W}$ *iff it satisfies all descriptions in* $\mathcal{W}$*.*

It is now easy to say what it means that some description is *entailed* by a world description, written $\mathcal{W} \models \delta$, namely, any description which is satisfied by all models of the world description. This means in particular, that a world description without any model, an *inconsistent* world description, entails everything (expressible in $\mathcal{AF}$).

3.3.2 Hybrid Entailment and Subsumption

Interpreting a terminology and a world description in combination means that we have to somehow relate the models of a world description and the semantic structure of a terminology. While we may view the semantic structure of a terminology as possible structures induced by the way we have organized our vocabulary, world descriptions are partial descriptions of how the world actually is supposed to be. However, such partial descriptions should, of course, respect the relationships laid down in a terminology. Respecting a terminology means, for a world description, that the models we really intend to have are simultaneously semantic structures of a terminology.

Definition 3.18 (Models Respecting a Terminology) *A model $\langle \mathcal{D}, \mathcal{I} \rangle$ of a world description $\mathcal{W}$ is said to* respect the terminology $\mathcal{T}$ *iff there is a semantic structure $\langle \mathcal{D}, \mathcal{E} \rangle$ of $\mathcal{T}$ such that the restrictions of $\mathcal{I}$ and $\mathcal{E}$ to atomic concepts and roles, $\mathcal{I}|_{\mathcal{N}}$ and $\mathcal{E}|_{\mathcal{N}}$, are identical, i.e. $\mathcal{I}|_{\mathcal{N}} = \mathcal{E}|_{\mathcal{N}}$.*

Using the set of models respecting a terminology, we can say which descriptions are entailed by both a world descriptions and a terminology, as is spelled out in the next definition.

Definition 3.19 (Hybrid Entailment) *Let $\mathcal{W}$ be a world description and $\mathcal{T}$ be a terminology. Then we say an object or relation description δ is* hybridly entailed *by $\mathcal{W}$ and $\mathcal{T}$ iff all models of $\mathcal{W}$ respecting $\mathcal{T}$ satisfy δ, written $\mathcal{W} \models^{\mathcal{T}} \delta$.*

Since this definition is quite abstract, it might be worthwhile to make things a little bit more concrete and characterize possible classes of entailment relationships. First, there is the obvious class induced by the subsumption relationships. That is, if we have an object description $(c\,o)$ and there is another concept b in $\mathcal{T}$ such that $c \preceq_{\mathcal{T}} b$, then we know immediately that $(b\,o)$. The same holds for roles, of course.

However, it can get more complicated. As an example take Fig. 3.7 and assume that instead of (Modern-team TEAM-A) we have (Team TEAM-A). Taking the by now familiar "team" terminology from Fig. 3.4 into account, we see that (Small-team TEAM-A) is entailed because of the number restriction on the member role. Furthermore, HARRY must be a Human because all members of Teams are.

If we look on the interaction between $\mathcal{TF}$ and $\mathcal{AF}$ from the other side, i.e. whether a world description can influence the relationships induced by the semantic structure of a terminology, we see that this kind of interaction is much simpler. Except for the case that the world description is inconsistent w.r.t. a terminology, i.e. there are no models respecting the terminology, the relationships between term extensions are not changed. In order to put that formally, let us define what we mean by *semantic structures respecting a world* and *hybrid subsumption*.

Definition 3.20 (Hybrid Subsumption) *A semantic structure $\langle D, \mathcal{E} \rangle$ of a terminology is said to respect a world description W iff there is a model $\langle D, \mathcal{I} \rangle$ of W such that $\mathcal{E}|_N = \mathcal{I}|_N$. Furthermore, a term t is hybridly subsumed by t' in T and W, written $t \preceq_T^W t'$, iff for all semantic structures $\langle D, \mathcal{E} \rangle$ of T that respect W it holds that $\mathcal{E}[t] \subseteq \mathcal{E}[t']$.*

Hybrid subsumption is, however, identical with normal subsumption in a terminology (except for world descriptions that are inconsistent w.r.t. a terminology).

Proposition 3.6 *For any terminology T and any world description W such that there exists a model of W respecting T, it holds for all $t, t' \in T\mathcal{F}_T$:*

$$t \preceq_T t' \quad iff \quad t \preceq_T^W t'.$$

Proof: The "only if" direction is obvious. For the other direction let us assume that there are only semantic structures $\langle D, \mathcal{E} \rangle$ of T respecting W such that $\mathcal{E}[t] \subseteq \mathcal{E}[t']$, but at least one semantic structure $\langle D', \mathcal{E}' \rangle$ of T with $\mathcal{E}'[t] \not\subseteq \mathcal{E}'[t']$. Fix one semantic structure respecting W $\langle D_0, \mathcal{E}_0 \rangle$ with $\langle D_0, \mathcal{I}_0 \rangle$ the corresponding model of W. Now we can construct a new model $\langle D^*, \mathcal{I}^* \rangle$ respecting T with $D^* = D_0 \uplus D'$ and $\mathcal{I}^* = \mathcal{I} \uplus \mathcal{E}'|_N$ and a semantic structure $\langle D^*, \mathcal{E}^* \rangle = \langle D^*, (\mathcal{E}_0 \uplus \mathcal{E}') \rangle$, which obviously respects W. However, in this semantic structure the assumption $\mathcal{E}^*[t] \subseteq \mathcal{E}^*[t']$ does not hold. Thus, the assumption must be wrong. ∎

Summing up, $\mathcal{AF}$ is not only very limited in its expressiveness, but it also guarantees a limited form of interaction between both formalisms. When reasoning with the hybrid formalism we can be sure that necessary set-inclusion relationships between concept extensions can be completely decided in the terminology. Technically speaking, $T\mathcal{F}/\mathcal{AF}$ is a *conservative extension* of $T\mathcal{F}$. This is in contrast to such formalisms as KRYPTON [Brachman et al., 1985], where the interactions are much more complex – a fact leading to quite complex proof procedures.

3.4 Possible Extensions of the Formalisms

There may be the question of why the particular formalisms presented here have been chosen. Are they somehow special? And which other options do we have? The main reason behind choosing $\mathcal{AF}$ and $T\mathcal{F}$ is that they are idealizations of the formalisms used in the BACK system, a system in whose development I have participated over the last few years. As we will see in the next chapter, the formalism is not special in the sense that it is possible to specify a complete and tractable inference algorithm. However, this is a property it shares with almost all other formalisms in this family. Despite this fact, though, the formalism is *balanced* in the sense that all obvious inferences are drawn and that no construct is ignored by the inference algorithms (see also Sect. 4.6). Nevertheless, it might be interesting to get an idea how the formalisms could be extended and how it relates to other, similar formalisms.

3.4.1 Extending the Terminological Formalism

As mentioned in Sect. 3.2.1, there are a variety of term-forming operators which could be added to $\mathcal{TF}$.[14] We sketched already some of the conceivable role-forming operators which can be found in some terminological representation systems. *Inverse roles* ("inv") are just the inverse relation a role stands for. For instance, a **begetter** role could be defined as being the inverse role of the **off-spring** role. *Composite roles* ("comp") are role chains formed by composing roles, much like relations can be composed. As an example, a **grandchild** role could be defined by composing the **child** role with itself. *Range restricted roles* ("range") are formed by specifying a restriction on the range of a role, such as defining **daughter** to be an **offspring** with a range restriction of **Women**. Finally, one could add operators for the disjunction ("orrole") and complement of roles ("notrole"), or even for the transitive closure of roles ("trans"), as was done in the almost universal "terminological logic" $\mathcal{U}$ Patel-Schneider presented in [Patel-Schneider, 1987a] – which in a sense gives the upper bound for the expressiveness of any terminological representation language.

Coming to concept-forming operators, there are only a few which have been spared. Besides the obvious extension of using concept-complement ("not") and concept-disjunction operators ("or"), there are two operators which state relationships between role fillers of different roles. The first one, the so-called *role-value-map* ("rvm"), can be used to restrict the role-filler set of one role to being a subset of another role-filler set. For instance, assuming that a **Biography** is defined as something with a **author** role and a **subject** role, an **Autobiography** could be defined by specifying that the role-filler set of both of these roles are identical. The other operator, the *structural description* ("sd") is more complex. It can be used to specify the existence of another object such that some role-filler sets of that object are related to role-filler sets of the original object.

Other proposals for extending terminological formalisms are not aimed at enhancing the expressive power by including more term-forming operators, but by permitting other primitives than roles and concepts. One such extension, already sketched in Sect. 3.2.1, is to allow for attribute values in the formalism. Values such as **male** and **female**, which in our setting are either concepts or objects, are seen as constant values, but are usable in the process of defining concepts. In BACK, for instance, sets of attribute values can be used to define *attribute sets* – concepts defined by their extensions – which may then be used in value restrictions [von Luck et al., 1987]. In KANDOR, domain objects, strings, and integers

---

[14]A more formal description of the term-forming operators described here can be found in Appendix A.

can be used in a concept definition. However, none of these extensions enhance the principal expressive power. They are simply convenient, but may also be realized by using only term-forming operators, as long as the associated theories are not imported as well.

A more radical proposal to extend terminological formalisms was made by Schefe [1987]. He criticized the object-centered view terminological formalisms imply. For instance, in the definition of the **Team** concept we were forced to assume that there are *objects* which are **Teams** and somehow loosely connected by the member relation to other *objects*, which are **Humans**. Schefe argued that this is an "inadequate representation," because there is no distinction between objects which really exist in the world and objects which exist only by virtue of a collection of other objects. Accounting for this deficiency, he proposed to include sets and n-ary relations as special kinds of term-forming operators.

However, if the distinction between "system aggregations" (as it is called in [Schefe, 1987]) and atomic objects is Schefe's only concern, there would be the solution to use disjointness restrictions to express this. In fact, these fundamental distinctions are usually represented in a prominent place; namely, in the basic ontological part of a terminological knowledge base which is shared across different applications. An example of this is the "Upper Structure" [Mann et al., 1985] developed for the JANUS system.

It is probably the notational inconvenience associated with the fact that any *n*-ary relation has to be expressed as a unary predicate plus *n* binary relations that bothered Schefe. Schmolze [1989b] addresses this issue by his system NARY[KANDOR], which is an extension of KANDOR supporting *n*-ary relations. While such an extension seems to a good idea at first sight – because of the notational convenience and some extra inferences concerning identity of individuals – it also has some drawbacks. In particular, it is not possible to define subconcepts by adding extra roles and restrictions on them not mentioned at the superconcept. Furthermore, from a philosophical point of view, it is often more convenient to conceive relations as objects, for example when representing sentence-meanings [Davidson, 1967]. Thus, it seems arguable whether such an extension is really useful.

3.4.2 Attributive Descriptions

Taking a broader perspective, we note that there are a number of other formalisms closely related to terminological formalisms (or, more accurately, to the underlying term-forming formalisms), for instance, *feature terms* [Kasper and Rounds, 1986] – used in unification grammars – and ψ-terms as introduced by Aït-Kaci [1986]. All of these formalisms aim at *describing* sets of objects by specifying restrictions on *attributes* the objects may have, similar to terminological formalisms – a fact leading to the characterization of all of these formalisms as *attributive concept description* formalisms [Nebel and Smolka, 1989].

Although feature terms and ψ-terms were not provided with a general model-theoretic semantics originally, a reconstruction of these formalisms in a more general setting as *feature logic* by Smolka [1989b], including a model-theoretic semantics, revealed that there is indeed only one simple difference between them and terminological formalisms. In feature logic, *features* – which correspond to *roles* in terminological formalisms – are assumed to be functional. This means, the interpretation of any *feature* is not a relation, as in terminological languages, but a function. For this reason, there is also less emphasis on defining features, but they are usually assumed to be primitive. However, the counter-part to *role-value-maps*, called *agreement* in feature logic, is usually heavily exploited.

Despite this similarity between terminological formalisms and feature logic, it turns out that the *computational services* provided by terminological representation systems and unification-based parsing systems are quite different. In the former kind of systems we are usually interested in relationships between concepts (e.g., subsumption and disjointness), while in the latter kind of systems constraints in a domain of so-called feature graphs are solved (see also [Nebel and Smolka, 1989]). Nevertheless, it is possible to apply theoretical results achieved in one approach to the other because of the same underlying model-theoretic semantics. For instance, Schmidt-Schauß' [1989] undecidability result for subsumption in term-forming languages containing *role-value-maps* shows that the move from single-valued features to multi-valued features in a feature logic would be extremely expensive. Conversely, it is possible to apply the quasi-linear algorithm developed for the unification of feature terms containing *agreements* (i.e., role-value maps over single-valued roles) in terminological representation systems, as done, for example, in the CLASSIC system [Borgida et al., 1989].

3.4.3 Extending the Assertional Formalism

Considering how to extend $\mathcal{AF}$, we note that there are a large number of options. For instance, KRYPTON and KL-TWO employ assertional formalisms which are considerably more expressive than $\mathcal{AF}$. However, as already mentioned, with that comes also the problem of controlling the amount of reasoning in KRYPTON and the problem of unprincipled inferential gaps in KL-TWO.

The ABox of BACK was designed to be slightly more powerful than in $\mathcal{AF}$ allowing special kinds of disjunctions and local closed world assumption on role fillers [von Luck, 1986]. In applications, however, this additional expressive power did not seem to be of great value – which was a reason to restrict the expressiveness at this point because the processing is considerably simplified and because it opens up the opportunity to use a relational DBMS to store assertions [Peltason et al., 1989].

Patel-Schneider [1987a, 1987b] explored an inferentially very weak version of first-order predicate logic to be used as an ABox for which a complete inference algorithm would be tractable, provided some conditions on the structures of the formulas are met. As already pointed out in Sect. 2.3.3, such an approach does guarantee completeness, but almost no interesting inferences can be achieved.

A better solution is perhaps to leave the ABox as it is and to add new "Boxes" as also suggested in [Brachman and Levesque, 1987, pp. 36ff]. Recalling the arguments from Sect. 2.2.3, it seems to be worthwhile to devise special-purpose KR formalisms for different representational needs.

One such box could be a "universal box," a place where universal, but nondefinitional knowledge could be represented. This includes, for instance, universal implications like "every featherless biped is a human." Such an extension has been already incorporated into LOOM [MacGregor and Bates, 1987] and MESON [Owsnicki-Klewe, 1988]. The "procedural" nature of such rules has been formally characterized by Schild [1989].

Following this line, there are a number of other extensions which are conceivable. For example, a box for representing default knowledge, another one for representing time, etc. The important point is that the formalisms have to be combined in a sensible way in order to make up a hybrid formalism and to allow for sound inferences – a task which requires some substantial research effort [Frisch, 1988].

4. Reasoning in the Formalism

Knowing what a knowledge representation formalism is supposed to mean is a necessary prerequisite for any serious attempt of representing knowledge. However, although the semantics of a representation formalism tells us what is entailed by a given knowledge base, it does not give us a hint how to derive implicit facts. If we want a computer to reason with the representation formalism, we need *inference algorithms* which compute entailed facts.

We will start off by describing an algorithm for testing *term-subsumption*, which is an extension of the algorithm presented in [Schmolze and Israel, 1983]. Similar to that algorithm, our own is *efficient* and *sound* but *incomplete*, i.e., it misses certain subsumption relationships. Although this sounds distressing, there is unfortunately no easy way to achieve completeness. Subsumption in $\mathcal{NTF}_T$, though decidable, is a very hard problem – a *co-NP-hard* one, as will be shown in Sect. 4.2. Interestingly, this result also applies to another terminological reasoner which has been conjectured to be complete and tractable, namely, the KANDOR system [Patel-Schneider, 1984]. Instead of specifying a complete algorithm, it will be argued that sometimes it may be better to live with an efficient but incomplete reasoner which uncovers all obvious subsumption relationships.

As we have seen in Sect. 3.2.5, subsumption in a terminology can be easily reduced to term-subsumption. Thus, when knowing a way to compute (incomplete) term-subsumption, subsumption in a terminology can be computed (incompletely), as well. However, there is the question of whether the computational complexity of term-subsumption carries over to subsumption in a terminology. As it turns out, this is not the case. In Sect. 4.3 we will see that subsumption in a terminology is computationally much harder than term-subsumption – theoretically. However, it seems to be the case that the worst-case behavior occurs only seldomly in practice.

Subsumption is the basic terminological relation on which all other ones can be based, as has been shown in Sect. 3.2.2. If we want to build a practical system, however, it does not suffice to check subsumption on demand. It is necessary to compute subsumption in advance for reasons of pragmatics and efficiency. The common technique to deal with this topic is called *classification* – an issue we will deal with in Sect. 4.4.

After that, we will tackle the problem of hybrid inferences in Sect. 4.5, concentrating on the problem of checking whether an object is an instance of a concept. In analyzing this problem, it turns out that most systems described in the literature missed an important class of inferences. As in the case of subsumption, it pays to compute these relationships in advance – using a technique called *realization*. Furthermore, it will be shown that although the basic inference algorithm – subsumption – is incomplete, realization is complete under certain conditions.

Finally, in Sect. 4.6, we will evaluate the inference algorithms in the light of the claims we made in Chap. 2 and come to the conclusion that because of the balanced expressiveness of the formalisms, the inference capabilities are balanced as well.

4.1 Computing Term-Subsumption

In determining subsumption between two concepts c and c' in a terminology, the relation between the extensions of the two concepts is symbolically evaluated. This amounts to

1. transforming (the relevant part of) a terminology into the corresponding normal-form terminology (as described in Sect. 3.2.4) and expanding terms into p-terms (as specified in Sect. 3.2.5),

2. propagating constraints and recognizing inconsistencies, and

3. comparing structurally the resulting expressions.

Determining subsumption between roles follows the same line. However, it is considerably easier because roles are very simply structured in $\mathcal{TF}$.

In this section, we will abstract from step 1 above and consider subsumption between p-terms only. For reasons of simplicity, primitive components will not be overlined. Rather all names will be assumed to denote primitive components. Moreover, we will often talk about concepts and roles where we actually mean p-concepts and p-roles.

Adopting this perspective, two points should be noted, however. First, when we apply an algorithm developed for subsumption determination between p-terms to the problem of subsumption determination between terms in a terminology, we have to assure that EXP does not create expressions which are "too large" (a point we will return to in Sect. 4.3). Second, we should be aware of the fact that the equivalence between subsumption in a terminology and subsumption over p-terms depends on a syntactical property of the terminology – it must not contain any terminological cycles. If a terminology contains a cycle, EXP may go into an infinite loop – which gives us another argument against terminological cycles.

4.1.1 An Algorithm for Subsumption Detection

Following the ideas sketched out above, we shall now specify an algorithm intended to check subsumption between p-terms.[1]

---

[1]The following formal description of the TSUB algorithm resembles to a large extent the algorithm used in the BACK classifier [von Luck et al., 1987, pp. 70–79].

Algorithm 4.1 (TSUB) TSUB is a function defined as follows:

$$\text{TSUB}: (\mathcal{NTF}_C{}^2 \cup \mathcal{NTF}_R{}^2) \rightarrow \{true, false\}$$
$$\text{TSUB}(t, u) \mapsto \text{COMPARE}(\text{NORM}(t), \text{NORM}(u))$$

with NORM, and COMPARE as defined below.

NORM transforms an arbitrary p-term into a *normalized p-term*. Such a normalized p-term contains no "and" expression embedded in another "and" expression (and the same holds for "androle" expressions), value restrictions for the same role are collected, and incoherent subexpressions are detected and marked as such.

Algorithm 4.2 (NORM) NORM is defined as:

$$\text{NORM}: \mathcal{NTF}_T \rightarrow \mathcal{NTF}_T$$

The input expression is transformed by rules (N1)–(N8) given below. These transformations are applied to the input expression and all its subexpressions, taking into account the commutativity of the "and" operator, until no further transformations are applicable.

(N1) If an "androle" expression is part of another "androle" expression, it is spliced into the surrounding expression, i.e.,

$$(\text{androle} \ldots (\text{androle } r_i \ldots r_j) \ldots) \mapsto (\text{androle} \ldots r_i \ldots r_j \ldots)$$

(N2) If an "and" expression is part of another "and" expression, it is spliced into the surrounding expression, i.e.,

$$(\text{and} \ldots (\text{and } c_i \ldots c_j) \ldots) \mapsto (\text{and} \ldots c_i \ldots c_j \ldots)$$

(N3) All value restrictions which are not "and" expressions are converted into "and" expressions, i.e., if $c \neq (\text{and} \ldots)$,

$$(\text{all } r\ c) \mapsto (\text{all } r\ (\text{and } c))$$

(N4) If an "and" expression contains two "all" restrictions on the same role, the value restrictions are combined, i.e.,

$$(\text{and} \ldots (\text{all } r\ (\text{and } c_1 \ldots c_i)) \ldots (\text{all } r\ (\text{and } c_{i+1} \ldots c_n)) \ldots)$$
$$\mapsto (\text{and} \ldots (\text{all } r\ (\text{and } c_1 \ldots c_i\ c_{i+1} \ldots c_n)) \ldots)$$

(N5) If an "and" expression contains a primitive components and its negation then the "and" expression is replaced by the special concept **Nothing**, i.e.,

$$(\text{and} \ldots c \ldots (\text{a-not } c) \ldots) \mapsto \textbf{Nothing}$$

(N6) If an "and" expression contains "atleast" and "atmost" restrictions with conflicting number restrictions, then the "and" expression is replaced by the special concept **Nothing**. More formally, if $\text{TSUB}(r_1, r_2)$ and $n_1 < n_2$, then

$$(\text{and} \ldots (\text{atmost } n_1 \, r_1) \ldots (\text{atleast } n_2 \, r_2) \ldots) \mapsto \textbf{Nothing}$$

(N7) If an "and" expression contains a value restriction identical to **Nothing** on a role and an "atleast" restriction on a subrole of that role, then the entire "and" expression is replaced by **Nothing**, i.e., if $\text{TSUB}(r_1, r_2)$ and $n_2 > 0$, then

$$(\text{and} \ldots (\text{all } r_1 \, \textbf{Nothing}) \ldots (\text{atleast } n_2 \, r_2) \ldots) \mapsto \textbf{Nothing}$$

(N8) Value restrictions of **Nothing** are replaced by an "atmost" restriction on the same role with the number 0, i.e.,

$$(\text{all } r \, \textbf{Nothing}) \mapsto (\text{atmost } 0 \, r)$$

Obviously, all transformations performed by NORM are extension-preserving.

Proposition 4.1 *For all p-terms $t \in \mathcal{NTF}_T$ and all extension functions $\mathcal{E}$:*

$$\mathcal{E}[t] \;=\; \mathcal{E}[\text{NORM}(t)]$$

Based on the result of NORM, COMPARE compares the resulting expressions structurally.

Algorithm 4.3 (COMPARE) COMPARE is defined as:

$$\text{COMPARE:} (\mathcal{NTF}_C{}^2 \cup \mathcal{NTF}_R{}^2) \rightarrow \{true, false\}$$

COMPARE(t, u) computes its results by the following rules:

(C1) If $u = \textbf{Nothing}$
 then return *true*.

(C2) If $t = (\text{and } t_1 \ldots t_n)$ or $t = (\text{androle } t_1 \ldots t_n)$
 then test COMPARE(t_i, u) for all $i : 1 \leq i \leq n$.

(C3) If t is a positive or negated primitive component, then

    (a) if u is a positive or negated primitive component
        then test $t = u$.

    (b) if $u = (\text{and } u_1 \ldots u_n)$ or $u = (\text{androle } u_1 \ldots u_n)$
        then test $t = u_i$ for some $i : 1 \leq i \leq n$.

    (c) return *false* otherwise.

(C4) If $t = (\text{all } r_t \, c_t)$, then

(a) if $u = ($all $r_u\ c_u)$

then test COMPARE$(c_t, c_u) \wedge$ COMPARE(r_u, r_t).

(b) if $u = ($atmost $0\ r_u)$

then test COMPARE(r_u, r_t).

(c) if $u = ($and $u_1 \ldots u_n)$

then test COMPARE(t, u_i) for some $i : 1 \leq i \leq n$.

(d) return *false* otherwise.

(C5) If $t = ($atleast $n_t\ r_t)$, then

(a) if $u = ($atleast $n_u\ r_u)$

then test COMPARE$(r_t, r_u) \wedge n_t \leq n_u$.

(b) if $u = ($and $u_1 \ldots u_n)$

then test COMPARE(t, u_i) for some $i : 1 \leq i \leq n$.

(c) return *false* otherwise.

(C6) If $t = ($atmost $n_t\ r_t)$, then

(a) if $u = ($atmost $n_u\ r_u)$

then test COMPARE$(r_u, r_t) \wedge n_t \geq n_u$.

(b) if $u = ($and $u_1 \ldots u_n)$

then test COMPARE(t, u_i) for some $i : 1 \leq i \leq n$.

(c) return *false* otherwise.

For most of the rules in the COMPARE algorithm, it should be obvious that COMPARE returns *true* only if t subsumes u according to Def. 3.15, i.e. that COMPARE is sound.

Proposition 4.2 *For any two p-terms, t and u it holds that:*

$$\text{COMPARE}(t, u) \quad only\ if \quad u \preceq t \tag{4.1}$$

Proof: Assume that COMPARE$(t, u) = true$, i.e., all of the tests applied to t and u and their corresponding subexpressions returned true. Then $\mathcal{E}[t] \supseteq \mathcal{E}[u]$ for all extension functions $\mathcal{E}$ according to Def. 3.11, hence $u \preceq t$. This is obvious for (C1) and can be shown by straightforward structural induction for the other rules. The only nonobvious cases are (C4a), (C4b), and (C6a). In order to see that (C4a) is a sound rule note that for all extension function $\mathcal{E}$, it holds that

$$\mathcal{E}[c_t] \supseteq \mathcal{E}[c_u] \wedge \mathcal{E}[r_t] \subseteq \mathcal{E}[r_u] \Rightarrow \mathcal{E}[(\text{all } r_t\ c_t)] \supseteq \mathcal{E}[(\text{all } r_t\ c_u)] \supseteq \mathcal{E}[(\text{all } r_u\ c_u)].$$

Furthermore, (C4b) is sound because of the above observation and

$$(\text{atmost } r\ 0) \approx_\emptyset (\text{all } r\ \text{Nothing}).$$

Finally, (C6a) is sound because

$$n_t \geq n_u \wedge \mathcal{E}[r_t] \subseteq \mathcal{E}[r_u] \Rightarrow \mathcal{E}[(\text{atmost } n_t\ r_t)] \supseteq \mathcal{E}[(\text{atmost } n_u\ r_t)] \supseteq \mathcal{E}[(\text{atmost } n_u\ r_u)]$$

for every extension function $\mathcal{E}$. ■

4.1.2 Properties of the Algorithm

Comparing TSUB with the algorithm described in [Schmolze and Israel, 1983], we note that TSUB detects and handles concept descriptions which are obviously incoherent ((N5)–(N8), (C1), and the second test in (C4)) – a point completely ignored in [Schmolze and Israel, 1983]. As is easy to see, TSUB is sound with respect to the subsumption relation.

Theorem 4.1 (Soundness of TSUB) *For any two p-terms, t and u it holds that:*

$$\text{TSUB}(t, u) \quad only\ if \quad u \preceq t \tag{4.2}$$

Proof: Immediate by Prop. 4.1 and Prop. 4.2. ∎

From the specification of the algorithm it is easy to see that TSUB is well-behaved in the sense that the subset of the subsumption relation computed is *reflexive* and *transitive*. This means that although we do not know (yet) whether TSUB detects all subsumption relationships, the subset it computes has similar properties as the subsumption relation (see Prop. 3.1).

Proposition 4.3 *For all $t, u, v \in \mathcal{NTF}_T$, it holds that:*

1. $\text{TSUB}(t, t)$

2. if $\text{TSUB}(t, u)$ *and* $\text{TSUB}(u, v)$, *then* $\text{TSUB}(t, v)$.

Additionally, TSUB always returns a result, i.e., it terminates on all p-terms. Instead of proving this here, a stronger result will be proven, namely, that TSUB has polynomial time complexity.

Theorem 4.2 (Complexity of TSUB) *Let t and u be two p-terms and let $|t|$ denote the length of t. Then TSUB runs in $O((|t| + |u|)^2)$ time on t and u.*[2]

Proof: If the arguments of TSUB are p-roles, then NORM needs only one scan for each input expression. Hence, the time to execute NORM on roles is $O(|t| + |u|)$. The running time of COMPARE on roles is determined by (C1), (C2), and (C3). If we assume that both arguments are "androle" expressions, then

1. (C2) leads to $|t|$ recursive calls of COMPARE with a primitive component as the first argument and an "androle" expression as the second argument.

2. (C3b) leads to $|u|$ recursive calls of COMPARE with both arguments as positive or negated primitive components.

3. (C3a) can be executed in constant time.

---

[2]Actually, it is possible do to better than that. Employing sophisticated implementation techniques for locating role restrictions and primitive components in a p-term can reduce the complexity. We will be satisfied with the polynomial complexity here, however.

Hence, COMPARE, and by that TSUB, can be executed in $O(|t| \times |u|)$ time if both arguments are roles.

In the case when the arguments are concepts, the analysis is more complex. First, we give an approximation for the running time of NORM. (N1), (N2), (N3), and (N8) require $O(|t| + |u|)$ comparison and substitution steps each. (N4) and (N5) require $O(|t|^2 + |u|^2)$ comparisons each. (N6) and (N7) require that we check every pair of "atmost/atleast" or "all/atleast" restrictions, respectively. Assume that there are n and m number and value restrictions in t and u, respectively. Then $O(n^2 + m^2)$ TSUB calls with the respective role expressions are necessary. Let t_i be the ith subexpression in t and u_j be the jth subexpression in u. Then the overall time to execute (N6) and (N7) is

$$O((\sum_{i=1}^{n} \sum_{j=1}^{n} |t_i| \times |t_j|) + (\sum_{j=1}^{m} \sum_{j=1}^{m} |u_i| \times |u_j|)) \leq O(|t|^2 + |u|^2)$$

Hence, the time to execute NORM on concept expressions is in the worst case linearly proportional to $(|t|^2 + |u|^2)$.

Finally, the running time of COMPARE for concept expressions has to be determined, which will be done by induction over the depth of nested "all" expressions.

Assume first that we do not have any "all" expressions. Without loss of generality, we will assume that both t and u are "and" expressions having n and m subexpressions. Similar to the analysis of the execution time of COMPARE on roles, we have:

1. (C2) leads to n recursive calls of COMPARE with an "and" expression as its second parameter and an expression which is not an "and" expression as its first parameter.

2. Depending on the type of the first parameter, (C1), (C3), (C5), or (C6) applies. If the second parameter is not Nothing, (C3), (C5), or (C6) leads to m recursive calls of COMPARE with parameters which are not "and" expressions.

3. Depending on the type of the parameters, either direct comparisons (C3a) are performed requiring constant time, or role subsumption tests are necessary ((C5a) and (C6a)), which require $O(|t_i| \times |u_j|)$ time.

Summing up, the execution time of COMPARE on concepts without "all" expressions is

$$O(\sum_{i=1}^{n} \sum_{j=1}^{m} |t_i| \times |u_j|) = O((\sum_{i=1}^{n} |t_i|) \times (\sum_{j=1}^{m} |u_j|))$$
$$= O(|t| \times |u|)$$

Now assume that COMPARE runs in $O(|t| \times |u|)$ time for expressions with a nesting depth of k for "all" expressions. Then the same holds for expressions with a nesting depth of $k + 1$ because of an argument about the running time similar to the one we made for the subsumption of roles in "atleast" and "atmost" expressions.

Combining the approximations for the different steps and cases leads to the stated time complexity $O((|t| + |u|)^2)$. ■

Although TSUB is more extensive than the algorithm presented in [Schmolze and Israel, 1983] in that it checks for obviously incoherent concepts, it is nevertheless incomplete. For instance, if we consider the two p-terms below, we see that TSUB misses the subsumption relation between them:

> (and (all r A)
>   (all (androle r q) B))

> (all (androle r q) (and A B))

It can be inferred that the "all" restriction of the role (androle r q) in the first concept expression is (and A B), but COMPARE and NORM ignore this fact. Actually, this defect could be repaired by performing inheritance of value restrictions for subroles in NORM. However, this would affect the computational complexity – NORM might create expressions which are not bounded linearly by the length of the input expressions!

In any case, there are more severe reasons for the incompleteness of TSUB – reasons which have to do with interactions of number restrictions between subroles which have disjoint value restrictions. Consider, for example, the two following concept expressions:

> (atleast 3 r)

> (and (all (androle r p) A)
>   (all (androle r q) (a-not A))
>   (atleast 2 (androle r p))
>   (atleast 2 (androle r q)))

Here, we can infer from the disjointness of the value restrictions of the roles (androle r p) and (androle r q) that there must be at least 4 role-filler for role r in the second concept expression, and for this reason the second concept expression is subsumed by the first one. COMPARE misses this fact, however. This means that a complete subsumption algorithm has to take the disjointness of restrictions on subroles into account, otherwise it would miss certain subsumption relationships.

We therefore have to take care of pairs of disjoint value restrictions (if we are going for a complete algorithm). This still seems to be manageable in polynomial time, because there are "only" $O((|t| + |u|)^2)$ such pairs. Taking a second look at the problem, however, we detect that there are even more complex cases, as exemplified by the next three concept expressions:

> (and (all (androle r q) A)
>   (atleast 1 (androle r q)))

```
(and (all (androle r p) (a-not A))
     (atleast 1 (androle r p)))
```

```
(atmost 1 r)
```

The concepts above are not pairwise disjoint. The conjunction of the three concepts, however, is an incoherent concept. Assuming that these descriptions serve as arguments to "all" restrictions of subroles, the computation of the actual "atleast" restrictions for the superrole becomes even more complicated. In the general case, the subsets of subroles leading to incoherent "all" restrictions have to be determined and then the "atleast" restriction for the superrole has to be computed by a minimization process.[3] However, instead of continuing the reflection about how to repair the algorithm by trying to account for "missed inferences," it seems more promising to analyze subsumption from a more general point of view.

4.2 Analysis of the Term-Subsumption Problem

Abstracting from the algorithm presented in the previous section, we will investigate the computational properties of the subsumption problem. What are the computational costs implied by this problem?

4.2.1 Decidability of Subsumption in $\mathcal{NTF}_T$

The common opinion in research concerning terminological knowledge representation was that subsumption determination is decidable for most, if not all, "reasonable" term-forming formalisms. Recently, however, it turned out that this is wrong.

Schild [1988] shows that a sublanguage of the "universal terminological logic" $\mathcal{U}$ presented in [Patel-Schneider, 1987a] suffices to describe the behavior of any Turing Machine. This sublanguage, called $\mathcal{R}$, contains only the role-forming operators *role-conjunction* ("androle"), *role-negation* ("notrole"), *role-composition* ("comp"), and the special self-role – the *identity role*.[4] While Schild's result finally answers the question raised by Patel-Schneider [1987a] of whether $\mathcal{U}$ is decidable or not, it has no immediate consequences. The role-negation operator was never considered a reasonable operator for any term-forming formalism. However, the undecidability result for $\mathcal{R}$ is a first hint that terminological reasoning is more difficult than believed and that the combination of other term-forming operators may lead to a similar result.

As a matter of fact, Patel-Schneider [1989b] shows, using some of the techniques of Schild's proof, that a subset of the term-forming formalism underlying NIKL [Moser, 1983] is undecidable with respect to subsumption. In addition to

---

[3]Note that these problems are independent from the restricted "a-not" operator. Even without it, it would be possible to force disjointness on role-fillers by using conflicting number restrictions.

[4]For the syntax and semantics of these operators see Appendix A.

the concept-forming operators in $\mathcal{NTF}_T$, Patel-Schneider uses the role-forming operator *range-restricted role* ("range") and the concept-forming operator role-value-map ("rvm") applied to composed roles. In this language, subsumption can be reduced to the Post's Correspondence Problem, which is known to be undecidable.

Independently from Schild and Patel-Schneider, Schmidt-Schauß [1989] proves that the generalization of feature logic to term-forming formalisms – by generalizing features to roles – leads to undecidability of subsumption. As a side-effect, he proves that an an even smaller subset of NIKL (and also KL-ONE) is undecidable. Only concept conjunction, value restriction, and role-value-maps stating the identity of role-filler sets are necessary to achieve undecidability.

Compared with the three languages for which undecidability of subsumption has been proven, $\mathcal{NTF}_T$ appears to be quite simple and, hence, probably decidable. However, instead of relying on mere intuition, we will give some formal arguments to justify this claim.

For roles, subsumption is trivially decidable. For concepts, it is the case that a concept definition can impose only very simple structures on a domain – concept definitions say something only about a *finite local context* of the domain elements which belong to the extensions of the concepts. As we will see, it is always possible to find a semantic structure of a certain finite size, given an arbitrary semantic structure, without destroying an important property, namely, *non-inclusion of concept-extensions*. Based on that, it is easy to see that it suffices to inspect only a certain *finite number of semantic structures with finite domains*. Provided it can be shown that one concept extension is a subset of another one in all these finite semantic structures, it must be a subset in all semantic structures. Otherwise, we would have a contradiction. In order to prove this claim, let us first define what we mean by a *non-inclusion situation*.

Definition 4.1 (Non-Inclusion Situation) *Let c_{in} and c_{out} be two p-concepts and $\mathcal{D}$, $\mathcal{P}$, $\mathcal{E}$ as defined in Sect. 3.2.4 Furthermore, assume $d \in \mathcal{D}$. Then $(c_{in}, c_{out}, \mathcal{D}, \mathcal{P}, \mathcal{E}, d)$ is called a non-inclusion situation iff $d \in \mathcal{E}[c_{in}]$ and $d \notin \mathcal{E}[c_{out}]$.*

Starting off with arbitrary non-inclusion situations, we will identify step by step non-inclusion situations which are simpler and smaller, aiming for non-inclusion situations which contain a domain of bounded size. The first simplification is aimed at restricting the length of role chains in the semantic structure to a number dependent on the concepts we consider. For this purpose, let us define what we mean by the relevant role-chain length of a concept.

Definition 4.2 (Relevant Role-Chain Length of a Concept)
The relevant role-chain length of a p-concept c is the maximum nesting depth of "all" expressions plus one, written as $\text{rlength}(c)$.

Definition 4.3 (Notation: Relation Composition) *The composition of two relations R, S, written $R \circ S$, is a relation, such that*

$$\langle x, y \rangle \in R \circ S \text{ iff } \exists z : \langle x, z \rangle \in R \wedge \langle z, y \rangle \in S$$

Lemma 4.1 *Let* $(c_{in}, c_{out}, \mathcal{D}, \mathcal{P}, \mathcal{E}, d)$ *be a non-inclusion situation and assume that* $\overline{\mathcal{N}_C}$ *and* $\overline{\mathcal{N}_R}$ *are the sets of primitive concept and role components used in* c_{in} *and* c_{out}. *Furthermore, let* $l = \max(\text{rlength}(c_{in}), \text{rlength}(c_{out}))$. *Then there exists a non-inclusion situation* $(c_{in}, c_{out}, \mathcal{D}', \mathcal{P}', \mathcal{E}', d)$ *such that:*

$$\forall e \in \mathcal{D}' : \langle d, e \rangle \in (\mathcal{E}'[r_1] \circ \ldots \circ \mathcal{E}'[r_i]), r_1, \ldots, r_i \in \mathcal{NTF}_R, 0 \leq i \leq l \qquad (4.3)$$

Proof: Define $\mathcal{D}'$ as

$$\mathcal{D}' = \{x \in \mathcal{D} | \langle d, x \rangle \in (\mathcal{P}[rp_1] \circ \ldots \circ \mathcal{P}[rp_i]), 0 \leq i \leq l, rp_1, \ldots rp_i \in \overline{\mathcal{N}_R}\}$$

Define $\mathcal{P}'$ for all primitive concept components $cp \in \overline{\mathcal{N}_C}$ as

$$\mathcal{P}'[cp] = \mathcal{P}[cp] \cap \mathcal{D}'$$

and for all primitive role components $rp \in \overline{\mathcal{N}_R}$ as

$$\mathcal{P}'[rp] = \{\langle x, y \rangle \in \mathcal{P}[rp] | \langle d, x \rangle \in (\mathcal{P}[rp_1] \circ \ldots \circ \mathcal{P}[rp_i])\}$$

with $0 \leq i \leq l-1$ and $rp_1, \ldots rp_i \in \overline{\mathcal{N}_R}$. Use $\mathcal{P}'$ to create a new extension function $\mathcal{E}'$ on the domain $\mathcal{D}'$. Then for the domain element $d \in \mathcal{D}'$, we have $d \in \mathcal{E}'[c_{in}]$ and $d \notin \mathcal{E}'[c_{out}]$ because we have removed only elements and pairs which do not contribute to the determination of whether d belongs to the extension of c_{in} and c_{out} according to the rules in Def. 3.11. Moreover, because of the way we constructed $\mathcal{P}'$, (4.3) holds as well. ∎

A visualization of the effect of the transformation in Lemma 4.1 is given in Figure 4.1, where nodes stand for domain elements and edges represent role-relationships (without specifying primitive assignments).

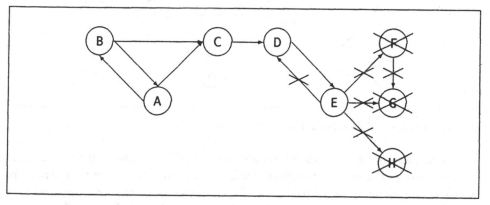

Fig. 4.1. Role-Chain Length Pruning

Assuming a maximum relevant role-chain length of 3 and the domain element A as the one which should stay in the extension of c_{in} and should not become part of the extension of c_{out}, then the domain elements F, G, and H, as well as the pairs $\langle E, D \rangle$, $\langle E, F \rangle$, $\langle E, G \rangle$, $\langle E, H \rangle$, and $\langle F, G \rangle$ can be deleted. This simplifies the semantic structure considerably, but it may be still too large and too structured. As a next step, *assertional cycles* such as $(\langle A, B \rangle, \langle B, A \rangle)$ are removed by "unfolding" them.

Definition 4.4 (Assertional Cycle) *Assume* $\mathcal{D}$, $\mathcal{P}$ *over* $\overline{\mathcal{N}_C} \cup \overline{\mathcal{N}_R}$, *and* $\mathcal{E}$ *as above. Then* $\langle \mathcal{D}, \mathcal{E} \rangle$ *contains an* assertional cycle *iff there is a domain element* $e \in \mathcal{D}$ *and a nonempty chain of role expressions* $r_1, \ldots, r_n \in \mathcal{NTF}_R$ *such that*

$$\langle e, e \rangle \in (\mathcal{E}[r_1] \circ \ldots \circ \mathcal{E}[r_n])$$

Lemma 4.2 *Let* $(c_{in}, c_{out}, \mathcal{D}, \mathcal{P}, \mathcal{E}, d)$ *be a non-inclusion situation. Then there exists a non-inclusion situation* $(c_{in}, c_{out}, \mathcal{D}', \mathcal{P}', \mathcal{E}', d)$ *such that* $\langle \mathcal{D}', \mathcal{E}' \rangle$ *contains no assertional cycle.*

Proof Sketch: Let $l = \max(\mathrm{rlength}(c_{in}), \mathrm{rlength}(c_{out}))$. Applying Lemma 4.1, we know that there exists a non-inclusion situation such that (4.3) holds. However, there can be chains of role relationships between two elements e, f which are longer than l because of assertional cycles.

From Def. 3.11, we know that only chains of length l are relevant for the determination of the inclusion in concept extensions. Additionally, we know that *identity* of elements comes only into play for "atleast" and "atmost" restrictions. This means that assertional cycles can be "unfolded" by copying elements and pairs with their respective primitive assignments to a length of l. This does not change any instance relationships for the element d, i.e., we know that a noninclusion situation with the desired property exists. ∎

Applying this transformation to Figure 4.1 results in a semantic structure as visualized by Figure 4.2.

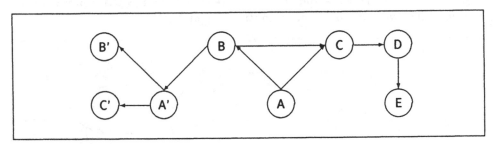

Fig. 4.2. Unfolding of Assertional Cycles

Such semantic structures correspond to (possibly infinite) directed, acyclic graphs. Evidently, we can transform such an semantic structure to a structure which corresponds to a directed tree by "splitting" shared elements, such as C in Figure 4.2, and copying the rest of the structure. Again, this has no effect on the instance relationships of the domain element d in our non-inclusion situation.

Lemma 4.3 *Let* $(c_{in}, c_{out}, \mathcal{D}, \mathcal{P}, \mathcal{E}, d)$ *be a non-inclusion situation. Then there exists a non-inclusion situation* $(c_{in}, c_{out}, \mathcal{D}', \mathcal{P}', \mathcal{E}', d)$ *such that for any two different lists of role expressions* $r_{1_1}, \ldots, r_{n_1}$, $r_{1_2}, \ldots, r_{n_2}$ *with* $n_1, n_2 > 0$:

$$\forall x, y \in \mathcal{D}' : \langle d, x \rangle \in (\mathcal{E}'[r_{1_1}] \circ \ldots \circ \mathcal{E}'[r_{n_1}]) \wedge \quad (4.4)$$
$$\langle d, y \rangle \in (\mathcal{E}'[r_{1_2}] \circ \ldots \circ \mathcal{E}'[r_{n_2}]) \Rightarrow x \neq y$$

Proof Sketch: Applying Lemma 4.1 and Lemma 4.2, we know that there is a non-inclusion situation with a semantic structure which corresponds to a directed, acyclic graph with all paths of finite length. If this semantic structure violates (4.4), then there must exist an extension function $\mathcal{E}'$ which satisfies (4.4) because of similar arguments as used in the proof of Lemma 4.2. ∎

Applying the above transformations to Figure 4.2 yields Figure 4.3.

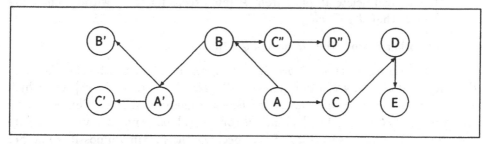

Fig. 4.3. Splitting of Shared Elements

The three lemmas above tell us that we can reduce an arbitrary semantic structure to a semantic structure which corresponds to a directed tree of finite depth without changing the non-inclusion relationship between the extensions of concepts. However, the tree-like semantic structure can still be arbitrarily, even infinitely large. There could be an element in the domain which is connected to infinitely many other domain elements by role-relationships. However, only a finite number of them are relevant for the non-inclusion situation.

Definition 4.5 (Relevant Breadth of a Concept)
The relevant breadth of a p-concept c is the sum of all numbers used in number-restriction expressions plus one multiplied by $\|\overline{\mathcal{N}_R}\|$, written rbreadth(c).

Lemma 4.4 *Let $(c_{in}, c_{out}, \mathcal{D}, \mathcal{P}, \mathcal{E}, d)$ be a non-inclusion situation, and let $b = \max(\text{rbreadth}(c_{in}), \text{rbreadth}(c_{out}))$. Let R be the set of different p-roles used in c_{in} and c_{out}. Then there exists a non-inclusion situation $(c_{in}, c_{out}, \mathcal{D}', \mathcal{P}', \mathcal{E}', d)$ such that:*

$$\forall x \in \mathcal{D}' : \| \bigcup_{r \in R} \{y \in \mathcal{D}' \mid \langle x, y \rangle \in \mathcal{E}'[r]\} \| \le b \qquad (4.5)$$

Proof: Let $(c_{in}, c_{out}, \mathcal{D}^*, \mathcal{P}^*, \mathcal{E}^*, d)$ be a non-inclusion situation identified by Lemma 4.3. Assume that $\mathcal{P}^*$ is minimal with respect to roles, i.e., for all pairs in the primitive assignment of a primitive role component rp: $\langle x, y \rangle \in \mathcal{P}^*[rp]$ if and only if for some p-role $r \in R$ with $r \preceq rp$ we have $\langle x, y \rangle \in \mathcal{E}^*[r]$.

Now assume that (4.5) does not hold. Let us first consider the case that d is responsible for this fact, i.e., d has more than b role fillers. This means there must be some primitive role component rp with

$$\| \{x \in \mathcal{D}' \mid \langle d, x \rangle \in \mathcal{P}^*[rp]\} \| > \frac{b}{\|\overline{\mathcal{N}_R}\|} \qquad (4.6)$$

There can be three different reasons for the fact that $d \notin \mathcal{E}^*[c_{out}]$, namely

1. c_{out} contains an "atmost" expression on a role r with $r \preceq rp$. In this case, we can delete all pairs $\langle d, x \rangle \in \mathcal{P}^*[rp]$ except for $b/\|\overline{\mathcal{N}_R}\|$ pairs without changing the fact that $d \notin \mathcal{E}^*[c_{out}]$. This is so because the maximum number of an "atmost" restriction is less than $b/\|\overline{\mathcal{N}_R}\|$

2. c_{out} contains an "all" expression on a role r with $r \preceq rp$ with a value restriction of cr, and there is an element e with $\langle d, e \rangle \in \mathcal{E}^*[r]$ but $e \notin \mathcal{E}^*[cr]$. Here we can delete all pairs from $\mathcal{P}^*[rp]$ except for $\langle d, e \rangle$ without changing the fact that $d \notin \mathcal{E}^*[c_{out}]$.

3. Any other reason why we have $d \notin \mathcal{E}^*[c_{out}]$.

Then there exists another primitive assignment $\mathcal{P}'$ and extension function $\mathcal{E}'$ which contains only $b/\|\overline{\mathcal{N}_R}\|$ pairs of all pairs $\langle d, x \rangle$ from $\mathcal{P}^*[rp]$ and which also contains the pairs mentioned in the case analysis above. This semantic structure preserves $d \notin \mathcal{E}'[c_{out}]$ because it contains all pairs necessary to invalidate $d \in \mathcal{E}'[c_{out}]$. It also preserves $d \in \mathcal{E}'[c_{in}]$ because the maximum possible number of "atleast" restrictions (added up over subroles) is $b/\|\overline{\mathcal{N}_R}\| - 1$. If there are still other atomic roles with more than $b/\|\overline{\mathcal{N}_R}\|$ role-fillers, we apply the entire procedure again. Finally, we delete all elements from $\mathcal{D}^*$ which cannot be reached by role-chains from d, resulting in $\mathcal{D}'$.

This results in

$$b \geq \sum_{rp \in \overline{\mathcal{N}_R}} \|\{x \in \mathcal{D}' \mid \langle d, x \rangle \in \mathcal{P}'[rp]\}\|$$

$$\geq \| \bigcup_{rp \in \overline{\mathcal{N}_R}} \{x \in \mathcal{D}' \mid \langle d, x \rangle \in \mathcal{P}'[rp]\}\|$$

$$\geq \| \bigcup_{r \in R} \{x \in \mathcal{D}' \mid \langle d, x \rangle \in \mathcal{E}'[r]\}\|$$

which is the desired property for d.

Now consider the case that for some element e with $\langle d, e \rangle \in \mathcal{E}'[r]$, e has more than b role-fillers. If e satisfies every "all" restriction in c_{out} on r and superroles of r, then we may obviously delete all but b role-fillers following the same strategy as above. If e is responsible for the fact that $d \notin \mathcal{E}'[c_{out}]$ because it violates some "all" restrictions, then the same case analysis as above applies and some role-fillers have to be marked as non-deletable, but the same strategy can be applied leading to at most b fillers. The procedure can be applied recursively along role-chains. Thus, there exists a non-inclusion situation with the property desired. ∎

Taking all the above results together, it is always possible to find a semantic structure of a certain finite size depending on the terms under consideration such that non-inclusion of concept extensions is preserved.

Definition 4.6 (Relevant Size of a Concept) *The* relevant size *of a p-concept c is defined as:*

$$\mathrm{rsize}(c) \stackrel{\mathrm{def}}{=} \mathrm{rbreadth}(c)^{\mathrm{rlength}(c)+1}$$

Using this definition, we can summarize all the above lemmas:

Lemma 4.5 *Let* $(c_{in}, c_{out}, \mathcal{D}, \mathcal{P}, \mathcal{E}, d)$ *be an arbitrary non-inclusion situation, and let* $s = \max(\text{rsize}(c_{in}), \text{rsize}(c_{out}))$. *Then there exists another non-inclusion situation* $(c_{in}, c_{out}, \mathcal{D}', \mathcal{P}', \mathcal{E}', d)$ *such that* $\|\mathcal{D}'\| \leq s$.

Proof: Follows immediately from Lemmas 4.1–4.4 and the fact that a tree of depth d with a maximum degree of b has less than b^{d+1} nodes (for $b > 1$). ∎

This enables us to prove the desired statement:

Theorem 4.3 *Term-subsumption in* $\mathcal{NTF}_T$ *is decidable.*

Proof: For roles, the theorem is trivial. Hence, let us focus on concepts. Let us assume two p-concepts c_1, c_2, and let $s = \max(\text{rsize}(c_1), \text{rsize}(c_2))$. Now $c_1 \preceq c_2$ can be decided by checking whether $\mathcal{E}[c_1] \subseteq \mathcal{E}[c_2]$ for all semantic structures $\langle \mathcal{D}, \mathcal{E} \rangle$ generated by $\mathcal{P}$, with $\|\mathcal{D}\| \leq s$, of which we have only a finite number. If the extension of c_1 is a subset of the extension of c_2 in all of these finite semantic structures, then this holds for all semantic structures because otherwise Lemma 4.5 would be contradicted. ∎

Because subsumption in a terminology is reducible to term-subsumption (Theorem 3.3), the following corollary is immediate.

Corollary 4.1 *Subsumption in cycle-free* $\mathcal{TF}$ *terminologies is decidable.*

4.2.2 Computational Complexity of Subsumption in $\mathcal{NTF}_T$

Having shown that subsumption in $\mathcal{NTF}_T$ is decidable does not imply that it is a trivial problem. As we have seen in the proof, extensions of a concept affect a number of elements exponentially proportional to the size of a concept in the general case. Moreover, there seems to be no easy way to avoid some combinatorial analysis. The examples given in the end of Sect. 4.1.2 demonstrate that we have to identify incoherent sets of value-restrictions and minimize the respective "atleast" restrictions, which seems to be feasible only by testing different combinations if we cannot find a more clever way.

As it turns out, it is indeed impossible to avoid a combinatorial analysis. Subsumption in $\mathcal{NTF}_T$ is a *co-NP-hard* problem[5] [Nebel, 1988]. In order to prove this, the complement of a known NP-complete problem is transformed into a special-case subsumption problem, namely,

$$c \stackrel{?}{\preceq} (\text{atleast } 3 \text{ r})$$

with c a p-concept containing a set of "atleast" restrictions on subroles of r. The transformation is performed such that a solution to the special-case subsumption problem also applies to the co-NP-complete problem.

A natural candidate for the proof is the problem of *set splitting*, also known as *hypergraph-2-colorability*.

---

[5]A problem is *co-NP-hard* if the complementary problem is NP-hard, i.e. if the complementary problem is at least as hard as a NP-complete problem.

Definition 4.7 (Set Splitting Problem) *Given a collection C of subsets of a finite set S, is there a partition of S into two subsets S_1 and S_2 – a set splitting – such that no subset in C is entirely contained in either S_1 or S_2?*

The following theorem is taken from [Garey and Johnson, 1979, p. 221]. The proof is published in [Lovasz, 1973].

Theorem 4.4 *The set-splitting problem is NP-complete.*

Now we will show how to reduce the complement of set-splitting to subsumption in $\mathcal{NTF}_T$.

Lemma 4.6 *Given an instance of the set-splitting problem, it is possible to generate a p-concept c_{split} such that*

$$c_{split} \preceq (\text{atleast } 3 \text{ r})$$

if and only if there is no set-splitting.

Proof: Given an instance of the *set splitting* problem with

$$S = \{s_1, s_2, \ldots, s_n\}$$
$$C = \{C_1, C_2, \ldots, C_m\}$$

with each C_i having the form

$$C_i = \{s_{f(i,1)}, s_{f(i,2)}, \ldots, s_{f(i,\|C_i\|)}\}$$

and letting g be a function such that

$$g(i,j) = \begin{cases} k & \text{if } s_j \in C_i \text{ and } f(i,k) = j \\ 0 & \text{otherwise} \end{cases}$$

then c_{split} has the form:

$$
\begin{aligned}
c_{split} = (\text{and } &(\text{atleast } 1 \text{ (androle r } p_1)) \\
&(\text{all (androle r } p_1) \ \pi(s_1)) \\
&(\text{atleast } 1 \text{ (androle r } p_2)) \\
&(\text{all (androle r } p_2) \ \pi(s_2)) \\
&\qquad\vdots \\
&(\text{atleast } 1 \text{ (androle r } p_n)) \\
&(\text{all (androle r } p_n) \ \pi(s_n)))
\end{aligned}
$$

The transformation function π is now specified in such a way that for each set C_i, the conjunction of all $\pi(s_{f(i,k)})$, $1 < k < \|C_i\|$, forms an incoherent concept. This means the corresponding subroles cannot be filled with the same element. On the other hand, each subset of the subroles with the property that the corresponding subset of S does not contain a set C_i can have the same role-filler. For this purpose, we assume m different roles q_i corresponding to the sets C_i, and $n \times m$ roles $t_{i,j}$ and concepts $d_{i,j}$ which encode the appearance of an element s_j in C_i:

$$\pi(s_j) = (\text{and } (\text{atmost } \|C_1\| - 1 \ q_1)$$
$$(\text{atleast } 1 \ (\text{androle } q_1 \ t_{1,g(1,j)}))$$
$$(\text{all } (\text{androle } q_1 \ t_{1,g(1,j)}) \ d_{1,g(1,j)})$$

$$\vdots$$

$$(\text{atmost } \|C_m\| - 1 \ q_m)$$
$$(\text{atleast } 1 \ (\text{androle } q_m \ t_{m,g(m,j)}))$$
$$(\text{all } (\text{androle } q_m \ t_{m,g(m,j)}) \ d_{m,g(m,j)}))$$

Now the $d_{i,j}$ are specified such that the conjunctions of $d_{i,j}$ and $d_{i,k}$ for all pairs of different j and k, $j \neq 0$, $k \neq 0$, are incoherent, employing another set of roles u_i corresponding to the C_i's:[6]

$$d_{i,0} = (\text{atleast } 0 \ u_i)$$
$$d_{i,k} = (\text{and } (\text{atleast } k \ u_i) \ (\text{atmost } k \ u_i)), 1 \leq k \leq \|C_i\|$$

This means that a conjunction of $\pi(s_j)$'s is incoherent if and only if for some role q_i, we have more than $\|C_i\| - 1$ different "atleast" restrictions on subroles of q_i, i.e., on roles such as (androle q_i $t_{j,k}$).

The entire construction leads to the following result: If role r of concept c_{split} can be filled with two (or less) role-fillers, then there is a set splitting. On the other hand, if more than two role-fillers are necessary, then there cannot be a set splitting. This means that the special subsumption problem given above can be used to solve the complement of the *set splitting* problem. ∎

Because the construction of c_{split} in the proof of the above lemma can be performed in time polynomially proportional to the size of the problem description, and because subsumption solves the complement of the original NP-complete problem, it is evident that subsumption in $\mathcal{NTF}_T$ is co-NP-hard.[7] However, we can make the point even stronger.

When a problem involving numbers (in our case the "atleast" and "atmost" restrictions) has been proven to be (co-)NP-hard, there might still be the possibility that the problem is tractable in a weak sense – solvable by an algorithm with *pseudo-polynomial* complexity [Garey and Johnson, 1979, pp. 91–92]. A problem has pseudo-polynomial complexity if it can be solved in time polynomially proportional to the numbers appearing in the problem description. The well-known *knapsack* problem, for instance, has this property. In our case, however, even this possibility of weak tractability can be ruled out because in the transformation all numbers are bounded by the length of the problem description of the original problem (the cardinalities of the C_i's).

Theorem 4.5 *Subsumption in $\mathcal{NTF}_T$ is co-NP-hard in the strong sense.*

---

[6]We could, of course, use the "a-not" operator instead. However, the construction shows that even without restricted concept-negation the desired result can be achieved.

[7]It is not obvious whether the problem is co-NP-complete or not because in the general case the relevant size of concept extensions is exponential in the size of the concepts.

Evidently, this result does not only apply to $\mathcal{NTF}_T$, but to all term-forming formalisms containing $\mathcal{NTF}_T$ as a subset, e.g. the subset of KL-ONE described in [Schmolze and Israel, 1983]. Moreover, it applies to all languages which can express the same relationships as the ones used in the proof. In analyzing the transformation, we may note that the full expressive power of $\mathcal{NTF}_T$ was not used. For top-level roles, only "atleast" and "atmost" restrictions were needed. For subroles, only the "atleast" and "all" operators were used, and only for describing that the superroles are filled with at least a certain number of role-fillers of a certain concept.

In particular, the term-forming formalism used in KANDOR [Patel-Schneider, 1984] can be characterized in this sense since it contains, besides the concept-forming operators of $\mathcal{NTF}_T$, a special three-argument "c-atleast" operator with the meaning that there are at least a specified number of role-fillers for the given role of a particular concept. Formally, this operator has the following semantics:

$$\mathcal{E}[(\text{c-atleast } n \ r \ c)] \stackrel{\text{def}}{=} \{x \in \mathcal{D}| \ \|\{y \in \mathcal{D}|\langle x,y\rangle \in \mathcal{E}[r]\} \cap \mathcal{E}[c]\| \geq n\} \qquad (4.7)$$

This concept-forming operator can obviously be substituted for the use of "atleast" and "all" on subroles of a certain role in the proof above – which leads to the following corollary:

Corollary 4.2 *Subsumption in* KANDOR *is co-NP-hard in the strong sense.*

Thus, the conjecture of tractability for complete subsumption determination in KANDOR in [Patel-Schneider, 1984, p. 16] does not hold. Even the weaker conjecture in [Patel-Schneider, 1986, p. 345], where a pseudo-polynomial complexity is conjectured, is wrong. As it turns out, the algorithm implemented in KANDOR is an *incomplete* one. It fails to detect subsumption relationships when confronted with concepts similar to the ones used in the proof.

4.2.3 Living with an Incomplete Reasoner

Levesque and Brachman [1984, 1987] show that another term-forming formalism, called $\mathcal{FL}$, has the same property as $\mathcal{NTF}_T$ – subsumption determination is co-NP-hard. $\mathcal{FL}$ contains the concept-forming operators "and," "all," and "some." The two former operators are the same as in $\mathcal{NTF}_T$, while the "some" operator corresponds to (atleast 1 ...) in $\mathcal{NTF}_T$. Additionally, there is a role-forming operator "range" – *range-restricted role* – creating a role by restricting its range, which turns out to be quite powerful. With the "range" operator, subsumption is co-NP-hard – without it, it is polynomial. Together with Theorem 4.5 and Corollary 4.2, this demonstrates that any term-forming formalism with a reasonable expressive power implies the intractability of complete subsumption.

This sounds rather disturbing, but terminological formalisms are undoubtedly a very useful class of knowledge representation formalisms. Furthermore, we know that almost all representation formalisms used in Artificial Intelligence are intractable or even undecidable. Therefore, in practical systems, tractable but incomplete algorithms are often used, for example, in the reason maintenance system RUP [McAllester, 1982], in Allen's temporal reasoner [Allen, 1983], in the terminological representation system NIKL [Kaczmarek et al., 1986], and in the set reasoning facility SERF [Wellman and Simmons, 1988].

If, however, completeness is a goal one cannot dispense with, expressive power has to be severely restricted. In our case, one solution would be to sacrifice all operators that state relationships between roles, i.e., primitive subrole introduction – a solution chosen, for instance, by the designers of the MESON system [Edelmann and Owsnicki, 1986].

Another way out of this dilemma, pursued by Patel-Schneider [1989a], could be to use a different semantics based on a four-valued logic, for which a complete and tractable subsumption algorithm even for very expressive term-forming formalisms can be specified. This solution provides a sound algorithm for standard semantics and gives a precise account – a model theoretic one – of incompleteness with respect to standard semantics. This meets all the demands for a representation formalism D. McDermott [1978] required. However, this solution has, because of the weak semantics, the disadvantage that a lot of inferences cannot be drawn even though they might be "obvious." These missed inferences are of the "nonstructural" kind, involving reasoning similar to *tertium non datur* and *modus ponens*. In particular, incoherent concepts cannot be detected.

We are thus confronted with a tradeoff between weak semantics with a complete subsumption algorithm, which misses a lot of inferences we intuitively would take for granted, and, on the other hand, strong semantics and an incomplete algorithm, which might miss inferences we never expected but which are implied by the semantics. From a pragmatic point of view, it seems more worthwhile to choose the latter alternative sometimes, for example, in natural language generation [Sondheimer and Nebel, 1986]. Even though it is possible that we will miss an inference granted by the semantics – although this is not very likely in the normal case – it would not result in a disaster. The same seems to be true for other applications as well. The inferences which are computed can then only be characterized by an axiomatic or procedural account. Nevertheless, we will follow this more pragmatically oriented way.

In conclusion, it is, of course, an unsatisfying (and surprising) state of affairs that the deductive power of a mechanized (i.e., tractable) reasoner cannot be described cleanly by means of model theoretic semantics without either tolerating incompleteness or ignoring some intuitively "obvious" inferences.

4.3 Subsumption in Terminologies Revisited

Equipped with an efficient (but incomplete) term-subsumption algorithm, it seems reasonable to expect that the original problem, namely, *subsumption in a terminology*, can be solved efficiently, as well. Actually, this seems to be a hidden assumption in all research concerning terminological reasoning. When computational complexity of a terminological representation system is analyzed, then this is done only for term-subsumption. For instance, Brachman et al. [1985, p. 533] justify the design of the terminological formalism used in KRYP-

TON partly by arguments of computational complexity of term-subsumption. The range operator mentioned above was omitted because it leads to intractability of term-subsumption.

Similarly, the tractability proofs or claims about KANDOR [Patel-Schneider, 1984], CLASSIC [Borgida et al., 1989], and the four-valued terminological formalism developed by Patel-Schneider [1989a] are – implicitly or explicitly – relative to term-subsumption. However, since in terminological representation systems we are not interested in term-subsumption but in subsumption between concepts defined in a terminology, the reduction from subsumption in a terminology to term-subsumption deserves some attention.

4.3.1 The Complexity of the Reduction to Term-Subsumption

Although the reduction to term-subsumption is conceptually simple, it can be computationally expensive. The function EXP defined in Sect. 3.2.5 can lead to expressions which are not polynomially bounded by the size of a terminology. Consider, for example, the somewhat weird terminology in Figure 4.4.

$$C_1 \doteq (\text{and } (\text{all } r_1\ C_0)\ (\text{all } r_2\ C_0) \ldots (\text{all } r_m\ C_0))$$
$$C_2 \doteq (\text{and } (\text{all } r_1\ C_1)\ (\text{all } r_2\ C_1) \ldots (\text{all } r_m\ C_1))$$
$$\vdots$$
$$C_n \doteq (\text{and } (\text{all } r_1\ C_{n-1})\ (\text{all } r_2\ C_{n-1}) \ldots (\text{all } r_m\ C_{n-1}))$$

Fig. 4.4. A Pathological Terminology Leading to an Exponential Explosion

This terminology has a length of $O(n \times m)$. If we apply EXP to C_n, we see that the resulting p-concept would have a length of $O(m^n)$. This means that the running time of, for instance, $\text{TSUB}(\text{EXP}(C_n, \mathcal{T}_N), \text{EXP}(C_n, \mathcal{T}_N))$ is exponential in the size of $\mathcal{T}_N$.

This situation seems to resemble the problem in first-order term-unification, where the string representation of a unified term can be exponential in the size of the original terms. Thus, one might hope that techniques similar to the ones used to design linear unification algorithms [Paterson and Wegman, 1978, Martelli and Montanari, 1982] could be helpful. Unfortunately, this hope turns out to be unjustified. Subsumption in a terminology is *inherently intractable*. Even for a minimal terminological formalism that contains only " $\doteq$," "and," and "all," subsumption is already co-NP-complete, as we will see below (see also [Nebel, 1989c]).

4.3.2 Complexity of Subsumption in Terminologies

The claim above will be proved by reducing the co-NP-complete problem of deciding whether two *nondeterministic finite state automatons that accept finite languages* are equivalent to equivalence of concepts in a terminology (see Def. 3.6).

Since equivalence can be reduced to subsumption in linear time (Prop. 3.2), co-NP-hardness of subsumption follows. Additionally, we will show that subsumption in our minimal terminological formalism, which will be called $\mathcal{MINI}$, is in co-NP and, hence, subsumption is co-NP-complete.

For $\mathcal{MINI}$, we assume all the definitions made in Sect. 3.2.4 with the appropriate restrictions to the language under consideration. Since $\mathcal{MINI}$ does not contain disjointness restrictions and primitive introductions, all $\mathcal{MINI}$ terminologies are already in normal form. All roles and all atomic concept not defined in the terminology will be considered as primitive components.

First of all, a simple transformation from $\mathcal{MINI}$-concepts to sets of $\mathcal{MINI}$-concepts, called *unfolding*, is defined.

Definition 4.8 (Concept Unfolding) UNFOLD *is a function from concept terms to sets of concept terms:*

$$\text{UNFOLD}(\text{and } c_1 \ldots c_n) = \bigcup_{i=1}^{n} \text{UNFOLD}(c_i)$$

$$\text{UNFOLD}(\text{all } r\ c) = \{(\text{all } r\ d) | d \in \text{UNFOLD}(c)\}$$

$$\text{UNFOLD}(a) = \{a\} \text{ otherwise.}$$

The expanded and unfolded form of a concept $\text{UNFOLD}(\text{EXP}(c, \mathcal{T}))$ is called *completely unfolded* concept, written $\text{CUNFOLD}(c, \mathcal{T})$.

Proposition 4.4 *Let $\mathcal{T}$ be a cycle-free $\mathcal{MINI}$-terminology and let c be a concept term. Furthermore, if $S = \{c_1, \ldots, c_n\}$ is a set of concept terms, then let $(\text{and } S)$ denote the concept term $(\text{and } c_1 \ldots c_n)$. Then for all semantic structures of $\mathcal{T}$:*

$$\mathcal{E}[c] = \mathcal{E}[(\text{and CUNFOLD}(c, \mathcal{T}))]$$

A concept term of the form "$(\text{all } r_1\ (\text{all } r_2\ (\ldots (\text{all } r_n\ a))))$," a a primitive concept component, will be called *linear concept*, written $(\text{all } p\ a)$ with $p = (r_1, r_2, \ldots r_n)$. For $n = 0$, i.e. $p = ()$, the convention $(\text{all } p\ a) = a$ will be adopted.

Using the completely unfolded form of a concept, equivalence of concepts in a terminology can be decided using a simple syntactic criterion, namely, set equivalence of completely unfolded concepts.

Lemma 4.7 *Let $\mathcal{T}$ be a cycle-free $\mathcal{MINI}$-terminology, and let c, c' be two concept terms. Then*

$$c \approx_{\mathcal{T}} c' \quad \text{iff} \quad \text{CUNFOLD}(c, \mathcal{T}) = \text{CUNFOLD}(c', \mathcal{T})$$

Proof: The "if" direction follows immediately from Prop. 4.4.

For the converse direction note that all elements of a completely unfolded concept are linear concepts. Assume that $(\text{all } p\ a) \in \text{CUNFOLD}(c, \mathcal{T})$ and that $(\text{all } p\ a) \notin \text{CUNFOLD}(c', \mathcal{T})$. Now we construct a primitive assignment such that the corresponding extension function w.r.t. $\mathcal{T}$ has the property that for a particular element $d_0 \in \mathcal{D}$, we have $d_0 \notin \mathcal{E}[c]$ but $d_0 \in \mathcal{E}[c']$.

Let $p = (r_1, r_2, \ldots r_n)$. Then set $\mathcal{D} = \{d_0, d_1, d_2, \ldots d_n\}$. Set $\mathcal{P}[b] = \mathcal{D}$ for all primitive concept components $b \in \overline{N_C}$ except for a. Set $\mathcal{P}[a] = \mathcal{D} \setminus \{d_n\}$. Set $\mathcal{P}[r_i] = \{\langle d_{i-1}, d_i \rangle\}$ for all roles $r_i, 1 \leq i \leq n$. Constructing a semantic structure using Theorem 3.2 leads then to $d_0 \notin \mathcal{E}[(\text{all } p\ a)]$ because $d_n \notin \mathcal{E}[a]$. Furthermore, since $(\text{all } p\ a) \in \mathrm{CUNFOLD}(c, \mathcal{T})$, d_0 cannot be in the extension of $(\text{and } \mathrm{CUNFOLD}(c, \mathcal{T}))$. Hence, by Prop. 4.4, $d_0 \notin \mathcal{E}[c]$.

On the other hand, $d_0 \in \mathcal{E}[(\text{all } p'\ a')]$ for all $p' \neq p$ or $a' \neq a$. This is easily seen when one considers the fact that $d \in \mathcal{E}[(\text{all } r\ c)]$ if there is no $x \in \mathcal{D}$ with $\langle d, x \rangle \in \mathcal{E}[r]$. Thus, we have $d_0 \in \mathcal{E}[c']$ and by that and the above arguments, it follows that $c \not\approx_{\mathcal{T}} c'$. ∎

Now, we will show that equivalence of automatons can be reduced to concept equivalence. The automatons we will consider are defined next.

Definition 4.9 (Nondeterministic Finite State Automaton) A

nondeterministic finite state automaton *(NDFA) is a tuple* $\mathcal{A} = (\Sigma, \mathcal{Q}, \delta, q_0, \mathcal{F})$ *where* Σ *is a set of* input symbols *(denoted by* s*),* $\mathcal{Q}$ *is a set of* states *(denoted by* q*),* δ *is a total function from* $\Sigma \times \mathcal{Q}$ *to* $2^{\mathcal{Q}}$*,* $q_0 \in \mathcal{Q}$ *is the* initial state, *and* $\mathcal{F} \subseteq \mathcal{Q}$ *is the set of* final or accepting states.
A state $q' \in \mathcal{Q}$ *is* reachable *from another state* q *by a word* $w = s_1 s_2 \ldots s_n$ *iff there exists a sequence of states* $q_1, q_2, \ldots q_{n+1}$ *with* $q = q_1$*,* $q' = q_{n+1}$*, and* $q_{i+1} \in \delta(q_i, s_i), 1 \leq i \leq n$*. The set of words* w *such that some final state* $q' \in \mathcal{F}$ *is reachable from* q_0 *by* w *is called the* language accepted by $\mathcal{A}$ *and denoted by* $\mathcal{L}(\mathcal{A})$.

The reader might have noticed that we consider only "ε-free" NDFAs. However, this does not affect generality. Furthermore, the definition is the same as the one given in [Garey and Johnson, 1979, p. 265], from which the following theorem is taken.

Theorem 4.6 *Let* $\mathcal{A}^1$ *and* $\mathcal{A}^2$ *be two NDFAs. Then the decision whether* $\mathcal{L}(\mathcal{A}^1) \neq \mathcal{L}(\mathcal{A}^2)$ *is PSPACE-complete in the general case and NP-complete if the accepted languages are finite.*

We are interested in the special case that the automatons accept finite languages because such automatons can be easily transformed into cycle-free automatons. In order to do so, redundancies are removed. A state $q \in \mathcal{Q}$ is said to be *redundant* iff q is not reachable from q_0 by any word, or if q cannot reach a final state by any word. A NDFA is *nonredundant* iff it does not contain redundant states. Furthermore, a NDFA is *acyclic* iff no state can reach itself by a nonempty word.

Proposition 4.5 *For any NDFA* $\mathcal{A}$ *an equivalent nonredundant NDFA* $\mathcal{A}'$ *can be identified in polynomial time.*

Proof: It is possible to mark all states reachable from q_0 in polynomial time. Similarly, all states that can reach a final state can be marked in polynomial time.

Taking the intersection of the two sets of marked states results in the set of all nonredundant states. Restricting the automaton to this set results obviously in an equivalent automaton that is nonredundant. ∎

Since a language of a NDFA cannot be infinite if the NDFA does not contain a cycle over nonredundant states, and since every cycle using nonredundant states leads to an infinite language, the next proposition is immediate.

Proposition 4.6 *Let $\mathcal{A}$ be an nonredundant NDFA. Then $\mathcal{L}(\mathcal{A})$ is finite if and only if $\mathcal{A}$ is acyclic.*

Thus, it suffices to consider acyclic, nonredundant NDFAs (ANDFAs) in the following, for which a translation to terminologies is given. Actually, ANDFAs are *seen* as cycle-free terminologies. Given two ANDFAs $\{\mathcal{A}^i = (\Sigma, \mathcal{Q}^i, \delta^i, q_0^i, \mathcal{F}^i)\}_{i=1,2}$ with $\mathcal{Q}^1 \cap \mathcal{Q}^2 = \emptyset$, a terminology $\mathcal{T}_{\mathcal{A}}$ is constructed in the following way:

$$
\begin{aligned}
\mathcal{N}_R &= \Sigma \\
\mathcal{N}_C &= \mathcal{Q}^1 \cup \mathcal{Q}^2 \\
\overline{\mathcal{N}_C} &= \{\mathsf{F}\} \\
(q \doteq (\text{and } S_q)) &\in \mathcal{T}_{\mathcal{A}}.
\end{aligned}
$$

with

$$
S_q = \{(\text{all } s\ q')|\ q' \in \delta^i(q, s), i = 1, 2\} \cup \{\mathsf{F}|\ q \in \mathcal{F}^1 \cup \mathcal{F}^2\}
$$

Note that $\mathcal{T}_{\mathcal{A}}$ is indeed a legal, cycle-free $\mathcal{MINI}$-terminology. Every atomic concept q has a nonempty definition because the ANDFAs are nonredundant. For this reason, q is either a final state, which implies $\mathsf{F} \in S_q$, or there is another state q' reachable from q by s, and then we have (all $s\ q'$) $\in S_q$, or both. Furthermore, $\mathcal{T}_{\mathcal{A}}$ is cycle-free because ANDFAs are acyclic.

Lemma 4.8 *Let $\mathcal{T}_{\mathcal{A}}$ be a terminology generated from two ANDFAs $\{\mathcal{A}^1, \mathcal{A}^2\}$. Then*

$$
w \in \mathcal{L}(\mathcal{A}^i) \quad \textit{iff} \quad (\text{all } w\ \mathsf{F}) \in \text{CUNFOLD}(q_0^i, \mathcal{T}_{\mathcal{A}}).
$$

Proof: Assume that $w = s_1 s_2 \ldots s_n$ is accepted by $\mathcal{A}^i$. Then there is a sequence of states $q_0, q_1, \ldots q_n$ with $q_0 = q_0^i$, $q_n \in \mathcal{F}^i$, and $q_{j+1} \in \delta^i(q_j, s_{j+1})$, for $0 \leq j \leq n-1$. Because of the way $\mathcal{T}_{\mathcal{A}}$ was constructed and by induction over the length of w, it follows that (all $(s_{j+1}, s_{j+2}, \ldots s_n)\ \mathsf{F}$) $\in \text{CUNFOLD}(q_j, \mathcal{T}_{\mathcal{A}})$, with $q_0 = q_0^i$, for $0 \leq j \leq n-1$. For this reason (all $(s_1, s_2, \ldots s_n)\ \mathsf{F}$) $\in \text{CUNFOLD}(q_0^i, \mathcal{T}_{\mathcal{A}})$.

Conversely, assume that (all $w\ \mathsf{F}$) $\in \text{CUNFOLD}(q_0^i, \mathcal{T}_{\mathcal{A}})$. Then, because of the way $\mathcal{T}_{\mathcal{A}}$ was set up and by induction over the length of w, a state $q \in \mathcal{F}^i$ is reachable from q_0^i by w in $\mathcal{A}^i$, that is, $w \in \mathcal{L}(\mathcal{A}^i)$. ∎

Now, the reduction from automaton equivalence to concept equivalence is almost immediate.

Lemma 4.9 *Concept equivalence in $\mathcal{MINI}$-terminologies is co-NP-hard.*

Proof: By Lemma 4.8 and Lemma 4.7, it is immediate that

$$q_0^1 \approx_T q_0^2 \quad \text{iff} \quad \mathcal{L}(\mathcal{A}^1) = \mathcal{L}(\mathcal{A}^2)$$

Furthermore, since any NDFA can be transformed into an equivalent nonredundant NDFA in polynomial time (Prop. 4.5), since nonredundant NDFAs that accept finite languages are acyclic (Prop. 4.6), and since T_A can be constructed in time linear in the size of the ANDFAs, by Theorem 4.6 we know that nonequivalence of concepts in $\mathcal{MINI}$-terminologies is NP-hard. Thus, equivalence is co-NP-hard. ∎

Using Lemma 4.7, it is also easy to see that concept equivalence in $\mathcal{MINI}$-terminologies is in co-NP.

Lemma 4.10 *Concept equivalence in $\mathcal{MINI}$-terminologies is in co-NP.*

Proof: Nonequivalence of concepts can be decided by guessing a linear concept and checking whether this linear concept is an element of one of the completely unfolded concepts and not in the other completely unfolded concept. The guess is obviously polynomially bounded. The test can also be performed in polynomial time by computing only this part of the completely unfolded concept which is relevant, i.e., expansion and unfolding proceeds along the role-chain of the guessed linear concept. Thus, nonequivalence is in NP, and equivalence is in co-NP. ∎

Summarizing these results, we get the next theorem.

Theorem 4.7 *Concept equivalence in $\mathcal{MINI}$-terminologies is co-NP-complete.*

Since equivalence and subsumption are reducible to each other in linear time (see Prop. 3.2 and Prop 3.3), the corollary is immediate.

Corollary 4.3 *Subsumption in $\mathcal{MINI}$-terminologies is co-NP-complete.*

4.3.3 Efficiency of Subsumption in Practice

The above result means that the goal of "forging a powerful system out of tractable parts" [Levesque and Brachman, 1987, p. 89] cannot be achieved in the area of terminological representation systems. KRYPTON [Brachman et al., 1985] MESON [Edelmann and Owsnicki, 1986], CLASSIC [Borgida et al., 1989], and Patel-Schneider's [1989a] specification of a terminological system using a four-valued semantics, although tractable with respect to term-subsumption, are worst-case intractable with respect to subsumption in a terminology.

However, this fact has not been noticed for a long time. The reason for this is probably that worst cases show up in practice with a very low frequency. In this respect and with regard to the structure of the problem, our result is very similar to a result about the complexity of type inference in *core* ML, which had been believed to be linear. Only recently, it has been shown [Kanellakis and Mitchell, 1989] that the problem is PSPACE-hard.

Looking for an explanation of why subsumption in terminologies is usually well-behaved, one notes that the the *maximum level of an atomic term* in a terminology (see Def. 3.14) – the *depth* of a terminology – leads to the combinatorial explosion. Let us denote the depth of a terminology by depth($\mathcal{T}$).

Assuming that $|(a \doteq t)|$ denotes the size of a concept introduction and that $\|M\|$ denotes the cardinality of the set M, the following parameters are important:

$$
\begin{aligned}
n &= \text{depth}(\mathcal{T}), \\
m &= \max\big(\{|(a \doteq t)| \,\big|\, (a \doteq t) \in \mathcal{T}\}\big), \\
s &= m \times \|\mathcal{T}\|.
\end{aligned}
$$

Now, it is easy to see that the size of expressions EXP($c, \mathcal{T}$) is at most $O(m^n)$. Thus, in all cases such that $n \leq \log_m s$, which is a reasonable assumption, the expanded concept descriptions have a size of $O(s)$. In these cases, a polynomial term-subsumption algorithm guarantees polynomial subsumption determination in the terminology.

The interesting point about this observation is that sometimes complete algorithms are feasible although the problem in general is intractable, namely, if the worst cases do only seldomly occur in practice. Furthermore, although this strategy works probably only for a very limited number of intractable problems (e.g., subsumption in $\mathcal{MINI}$ and type inference in *core* ML) without considerable problems, often there is no freedom regarding expressiveness or semantics (as discussed in the previous section). Changing the rules of the game can lead to uselessness of a representation formalism.[8] For instance, unification grammars rely heavily on disjunctive feature terms[9] in order to represent ambiguity of natural language expressions. Although reasoning with such disjunctive feature terms is worst-case intractable, nobody wants to give them up—they are simply necessary for the particular kind of problem one wants to solve. The challenge then is to identify the structure of normal cases and to design algorithms that deal with these normal cases [Kasper, 1987, Dörre and Eisele, 1989]—which are informally characterized by the fact that humans can deal with them effortlessly.

Summarizing, after discovering that a representation formalism leads to intractable reasoning problems, it may be worthwhile to analyze how the representation formalism is *used*. If it turns out, that the cases occurring in practice can be handled by a polynomial algorithm, although reasoning in general is intractable (see also [Levesque, 1988]), then it seems better to support these normal

---

[8]This is a point also noted by Doyle and Patil [1989] about the restricted language approach in terminological knowledge representation.

[9]Similarities and differences between concept terms and feature terms have been discussed in Section 3.4.2.

cases than to restrict the language or to weaken the semantics. Actually, it may be interesting to reevaluate the intractability results for term-subsumption in light of this observation.

4.4 Classification

As we saw in Sect. 3.2.2, all properties and relationships in a terminology can be reduced to subsumption – perhaps taking into account the set of explicitly introduced atomic terms in order to determine immediate subsumers (see Sect. 3.2.6). Thus, we are done with specifying a subsumption algorithm – in principle. However, there are a number of reasons to go beyond subsumption which have to do with pragmatics and efficiency considerations.

4.4.1 Assert-Time versus Query-Time Inferences

While it is possible to implement a knowledge representation system by storing all explicitly given propositions (in our case, term introductions) and drawing inferences (in our case, determining subsumption relationships) only on demand at *query time*, other strategies are possible. For instance, it may pay to cache computed results in order to avoid recomputations. A more radical solution is to precompute a large number of all possible inferences when a proposition is entered into the system – to perform inferences at *assert time* in order to allow for quicker responses at query time. Actually, this strategy may not only reduce the response time for single queries, but may lead to a net efficiency improvement when the time needed for query-time and assert-time inferences is summed up [Rollinger, 1980].

In order to speed up responses, almost all terminological representation systems follow the strategy of computing the most important inferences at assert time. The most important inference is what was called *immediate subsumption* in Sect. 3.2.6 – determining the immediate subsumers of a new term. This is needed, for example, to implement classification-based reasoning as sketched in Sect. 3.2.6. Without any caching or assert-time inferences, the determination of immediate subsumers could be implemented by determining the set of all subsumers filtering out all those concepts for which an intermediate concept can be found, which requires $O(n^2)$ TSUB operations, n being the number of introduced concepts. If, however, a terminology is processed in advance and the immediate subsumption relation between all atomic terms – the *concept taxonomy* and the *role taxonomy* – is precomputed, then the determination of immediate subsumers for a new term can be done by virtually inserting the concept into the concept taxonomy, which amounts to inserting an element into a partial order. The worst case complexity for such an operation is $O(n)$, with an average case complexity which is much better.

Having the immediate subsumption relation, it is also possible to determine subsumption between atomic concepts by simply traversing the graph instead of expanding, normalizing, and comparing concept expressions.[10]

Furthermore, precomputation of subsumption (or immediate subsumption) can avoid recomputations when determining subsumption. In order to see the importance of this fact, note that although straightforward subsumption determination in the terminology displayed in Fig. 4.4 requires exponential time, it is possible to do better than that. The exponential explosion is unnecessary and can be avoided if TSUB works by caching intermediate results from the bottom up.

Summarizing, to speed up responses for often-used queries types and to avoid expensive recomputations, it is worthwhile to compute some of the relationships in a terminology in advance.

Finally, there are also pragmatic reasons to precompute the immediate subsumption relation. If terminological knowledge about a domain is represented, the knowledge engineer responsible for representing this knowledge usually has a vague idea how the terms relate to each other. If the representation system is able to compute these relationships when a new term is entered (or after an entire terminology has been entered), then a visualization of these relationships can greatly increase the comprehensibility of a terminology and provides the knowledge engineer with an opportunity to check his intuitions about the domain with the computed concept taxonomy [Kindermann and Quantz, 1988].

4.4.2 A Classification Algorithm

The technique to deal with the problems described above is called *classification* [Lipkis, 1982, Schmolze and Lipkis, 1983]. In essence, it amounts to maintaining directed acyclic graphs reflecting the immediate subsumption relationships between concepts and between roles – the role taxonomy and the concept taxonomy – by placing each new term at the "right place" in one of the graphs. Examples for concept taxonomies are Figure 1.2 and 3.1. Inserting a new role in a role taxonomy is a trivial task in $\mathcal{TF}$. Inserting a concept in a concept taxonomy requires some effort, however. The details are given below.

Algorithm 4.4 (CLASSIFY) Assume a *concept taxonomy* represented as a directed, acyclic graph reflecting the immediate subsumption relationships as computed by TSUB. Then a *concept* is inserted into the taxonomy by carrying out the following steps:

(Cl1) The defining expression is converted into an expressions containing a top-level "and" expression without embedded "and" expressions, and all atomic concept in this top-level "and" expression are expanded by replacing defined concepts by their normal-form defining expressions. We do not expand any value restrictions or roles, however.

(Cl2) The resulting concept expression is transformed according to the rules of NORM.

---

[10]It also may pay to precompute the subsumption relation – the reflexive, transitive closure of the immediate subsumption relation. This is done, for example, in LOOM [MacGregor, 1988b].

(Cl3) If a value restriction is a nonatomic concept, then an *anonymous atomic concept* is created with the original value restriction as its defining expression.

(Cl4) The anonymous concepts generated in step (Cl3) and the atomic value restrictions of the concept are classified, i.e., CLASSIFY is applied recursively.

(Cl5) The taxonomy is traversed in order to find the place where the new concept belongs – below all immediate subsumers and above all immediate subsumees. Comparisons with concepts already in the taxonomy follow the rules of COMPARE, except that subsumption between value restrictions and roles is determined by using the taxonomy instead of calling COMPARE recursively.

(Cl6) Finally, the concept is inserted at the place determined in step (Cl5). If the new concept is equivalent to a concept already in the taxonomy, this means that both are to be merged into one concept.

This informal sketch of an algorithm captures the essence of classification, but there are some details which have to be worked out. First, there are some problems with anonymous concepts generated in step (Cl3). If we generated anonymous atomic concepts for all nonatomic value restriction and classified them regardless of whether they are literally equivalent (ignoring the order of subexpressions in "and" expressions), we may end up classifying a large number of concepts which are equivalent. In fact, it is easy to construct a terminology similar to Figure 4.4 where all value restrictions are nonatomic, thus leading to exponentially many classification operations. The solution is to compare the defining expression of an anonymous concept with the defining expression of all already introduced anonymous concepts (ignoring the order of subexpressions in "and" expressions) before invoking classification.

The second problem with generated anonymous concepts is that if they are inserted into the taxonomy, we may blur the distinction between explicitly introduced concepts and constructible ones. Thus, anonymous concepts should be treated in a special way in order to make them distinguishable from introduced concepts, e.g. by marking them.[11]

Finally, there is the problem of traversing the taxonomy to find the place where to insert a new concept c in an efficient way. The most simple-minded strategy would compare the new concept with all concepts already in the terminology, resulting in $2n$ comparisons (n being the number of concepts already in the taxonomy). A better solution is, of course, starting at the most general concept Anything, descending downwards, and stopping when a concept x is found such that x subsumes c, but all immediate subsumees of x do not subsume c. Clearly, x is one of the new immediate subsumers of c.

---

[11]Most terminological representation systems, however, do not care whether a concept is introduced by the user or created for internal usage by the classifier. This leads to the question of what the semantic status of the immediate subsumption relation reflected by the concept taxonomy is.

In order to find the set of immediate subsumees of c, it does not suffice to search in the subtaxonomies of the immediate subsumers of c, but rather it is necessary to start from the leaves and to search upwards, trying to find concepts y which are subsumed by c such that all immediate subsumers of y are not subsumed by c.

Although the worst case complexity (in terms of subsumption tests) is still $O(n)$, the average case can be expected to be much better. It is possible to utilize even more optimizations in order to reduce the number of necessary TSUB operations so that in most cases only a small percentage of all concepts in a taxonomy have to be checked [MacGregor, 1988a]. However, we will not delve deeper into this issue.

4.4.3 Worst Cases in Classification

Although, the worst-case computational costs of the classification algorithm are, of course, the same as for straightforward subsumption determination, it is difficult to find a terminology which blows up the classification algorithm. In order to give an impression what such a beast might look like, Fig. 4.5 gives a worst-case example.[12]

$$
\begin{aligned}
C_0 &\doteq (\text{and } (\text{all } r_1\ C_1)\ (\text{all } r_2\ (\text{and } C_1\ C_2)))\\
C_1 &\doteq (\text{and } (\text{all } r_1\ C_2)\ (\text{all } r_2\ (\text{and } C_2\ C_4)))\\
&\ \vdots\\
C_i &\doteq \begin{cases} (\text{and } (\text{all } r_1\ C_{i+1})\ (\text{all } r_2\ (\text{and } C_{i+1}\ C_{2i}))) & \text{if } 2i \le n,\\ (\text{and } (\text{all } r_1\ C_{i+1})\ (\text{all } r_2\ C_{i+1})) & \text{otherwise.} \end{cases}\\
&\ \vdots\\
C_n &\doteq \text{Primitive}
\end{aligned}
$$

Fig. 4.5. A Worst-Case Terminology for Classification

If a classification algorithm as described in the previous subsection is confronted with the terminology in Fig. 4.5, it has to generate exponentially many anonymous concepts. However, this terminology does not look very natural. More generally, it is the case that all terminologies I have seen so far are well-behaved in the sense that the classifier is not forced to introduce a large number of anonymous concepts. Furthermore, a similar approximation as the one given in Sect. 4.3.3 applies to classification. Let

$$
\begin{aligned}
a &= \|\mathcal{T}\|,\\
r &= \|\mathcal{N}_R\|,
\end{aligned}
$$

---

[12]Note that this example can even blow up classifiers which are deliberately designed to be incomplete in their reasoning, e.g. NIKL [Kaczmarek et al., 1986], BACK [von Luck et al., 1987], LOOM [MacGregor and Bates, 1987], and SB-ONE [Kobsa, 1989]. The only requirement is that the equivalence $(\text{and } (\text{all } r\ c)\ (\text{all } r\ c')) \approx_{\mathcal{T}} (\text{all } r\ (\text{and } c\ c'))$ is handled completely.

$$l = \max\big(\{\mathrm{rlength}(\mathrm{EXP}(a, \mathcal{T}))\big| \, a \in \mathcal{N}_C, \}\big),$$

then in the worst case $O(a \times r^l)$ anonymous concepts are generated. That means that under the plausible assumption that $l \leq \log_r a$, "only" $O(a^2)$ new atomic concepts are generated. This means that if we use classification instead of EXP and TSUB, the requirements for polynomial subsumption determination are less strict. It is not the depth of a terminology, but the maximum relevant role-chain length that appears as the exponent.

4.5 Hybrid Inferences

If we have a hybrid formalism, we not only need inference algorithms for the separate subformalisms, but also have to account for the connection between both formalisms. In our case, we have already described what inference algorithms for $\mathcal{TF}$ look like. Inferences for $\mathcal{AF}$ viewed in isolation are almost trivial. What is interesting, however, is how to infer hybridly entailed propositions as defined in Sect. 3.3.2 – how to perform *hybrid inferences*.

In this section we will concentrate on how to compute whether a given object necessarily belongs to the extension of a concept – whether the object is an *instance* of the concept. As we will see, there are reasons similar to the ones discussed above for performing assert-time inferences. In order to detect inconsistent world descriptions and for reasons of efficiency, it is worthwhile to determine at assert-time the set of concepts which describe an object most accurately. Moreover, we will show that this can be done completely, provided the world description is "detailed" enough.

4.5.1 Testing Instance Relationships

One basic inference task in a system employing a hybrid representation formalism as described in the previous chapter is to test whether a given object o is an instance of a concept c. In terms of Sect. 3.3.2 this means to test whether the object description $(c\,o)$, c an atomic concept, is hybridly entailed by a terminology $\mathcal{T}$ and a world description $\mathcal{W}$.

The simplest case is that the world description $\mathcal{W}$ contains an object description $(d\,o)$ such that $d \preceq_{\mathcal{T}} c$. We then immediately know that $(c\,o)$ holds. However, even if we do not find such an object description, it is still possible that the object o is an instance of c. For example, if there are two object descriptions of o in $\mathcal{W}$ such that the conjunction of the respective atomic concepts is subsumed by c, then $(c\,o)$ is, of course, entailed. Moreover, role-fillers of o for some role – i.e., relation descriptions having o as their first argument – may also be taken into account in order to determine whether o belongs necessarily the extension of c. Summarizing these ideas, an *instance testing* algorithm which tests whether an object is an instance of a concept relative to a terminology and a world description could be sketched as follows.

Algorithm 4.5 (CINST) Let $\mathcal{N}_O$ be the set of objects, and $\mathcal{N}_C$ the set of atomic concepts used in a world description. Then CINST is defined as:

$$\text{CINST}: \mathcal{N}_C \times \mathcal{TF} \times \mathcal{N}_O \times \mathcal{AF} \to \{true, false\}$$

CINST computes whether the object o is an instance of the concept c relative to a world description $\mathcal{W}$ and a terminology $\mathcal{T}$ by carrying out the following steps:

(I1) Collect all object descriptions of the form $(x_i\ o)$ from $\mathcal{W}$, set $x =$ (and $x_1 \ldots x_n$), and test $\text{TSUB}(\text{EXP}(c, \mathcal{T}), \text{EXP}(x, \mathcal{T}))$. If this test succeeds, return *true*.

(I2) If the test failed because a positive or negated primitive component which is part of c is missing from x, then return *false*.

(I3) If the test failed because an "**atmost**" restriction on a role r is too large or missing from x, then collect all relation descriptions $(r_i o(\textbf{atmost} n_i))$ from $\mathcal{W}$ such that $r \preceq_{\mathcal{T}} r_i$, add them to x, and test again for subsumption. If the test fails for the same reason, return *false*. Otherwise continue.

(I4) If the test failed because an "**atleast**" number on a role r restriction is too small or missing from x, count the role-fillers for r and subroles of r, collect all relation descriptions of the form $(r_i\ o\ (\textbf{atleast } n_i))$ from $\mathcal{W}$ with $r_i \preceq_{\mathcal{T}} r$, add them to x, and test again for subsumption. If the test fails for the same reason, return *false*. Otherwise continue.

(I5) If the test failed because of a missing subsumption relationship between value restrictions on a role r, then check whether all role-fillers of object o for role r are *known* (by counting the role-fillers and checking the number against relevant "**atmost**" restrictions). If they are, try to show that all role-fillers are instances of the value restriction concept mentioned in c by invoking the *instance test* recursively. Otherwise return *false*.

Note that we assumed that the subsumption algorithm as described in Sect. 4.1.1 has to be extended in a way such that it returns the part of a concept expression for which subsumption has not been established. Otherwise, we would have been forced to collect all available information for an object beforehand, which would be very inefficient.

All the tests in the algorithm above test for the instance relationships by applying the concept definitions as "recognition schemata" – a method also used in the implementations of the hybrid representation systems KANDOR and KL-TWO [Vilain, 1983, Vilain, 1985]. As can be verified easily by applying the definitions in Chap. 3, this method leads to sound inferences.

However, the "recognition" mode of testing does not take all of the "propositional force" of a world description into account. A relation description of the form $(r\ q\ o)$ asserts something not only about the object q but also about the object o – a point neglected in KANDOR and the KL-TWO version described in the literature.[13] Given that q is an instance of concept c, the object o must be

---

[13]This deficiency has since been removed from KL-TWO [Vilain, 1987].

an instance of the value-restriction concept of role r mentioned in the concept definition of c – a fact verifiable by checking the definitions in Chap. 3.

This fact could be utilized by adding the following step to the algorithm described above:

(I6) Assume that we have to check whether the object o is in the extension of concept c. Assume further that the algorithm above was able to verify that o could be in the extension of c, provided that we can show that some positive or negated primitive components, value and number restrictions could be proven to hold as well. Let us call this "rest"-concept b. Then we set up a subgoal of trying to show that q is in the extension of (all r b) for an object q such that the relation description $(r\ q\ o)$ is in $\mathcal{W}$.

In order to make this kind of reasoning clearer, let us analyze a small example. Assuming again our "team" terminology, let us try to test whether MARY as described in Figure 3.7 in Sect. 3.3.1 is a Woman. The object description (Human MARY) does not help very much. There are also no relation descriptions having MARY has its first argument. However, MARY is a role-filler for the leader role of TEAM-A. Thus, if we can show that TEAM-A is in the extension of (all leader Woman), MARY would indeed by a Woman. As it turns out, TEAM-A is a Modern-team, a concept which is subsumed by the previous concept expression, and, thus, we are done.

As should be obvious, this kind of reasoning is very complex. It can involve very long chains of objects connected by relation descriptions. However, fortunately, the length of these chains is bounded. As should be evident, (I5) should be called recursively at most l times, l being the relevant role-chain length of the concept we test. Similarly, (I6) should be called only m times, m being the length of the maximum relevant role-chain length of all concepts in a terminology.

4.5.2 Realization = Propagation + Abstraction + Classification

As in the case of subsumption determination, there are good reasons to use assert-time inferences for the determination of instance relationships. First, it enables us to detect at the earliest possible time. Second, if we are interested in *retrieving* all objects which satisfy a certain description, it would be an advantage if we already knew the set of *most specific concepts* for every object – the MSC.

More specifically, if a hybrid representation system is used as a kernel of an information retrieval system, such as ARGON [Patel-Schneider et al., 1984], the individual objects are indexed by the MSC, i.e., lists of instances of every atomic concepts are maintained. Queries in such an information retrieval system are just concept expressions (or logical expressions using concepts) which get classified into the concept taxonomy. Using the *immediate subsumers* of the query concept, a set of *candidate objects* which may be instances of the query concept can then be retrieved by looking up the lists of objects stored at those immediate subsumers of the query concept. The set of immediate subsumees can be used to determine the set of all objects which are known to be instances of the query concept. Only the objects lying in the set-difference of those two sets have to be tested to see whether they are instances of the query concepts. Such an approach to information retrieval has the advantage of having a flexible and uniform language for data definition (the terminology) and queries (the query concept expression). Furthermore, indexing is done very naturally in a semantic way.

Although the computation of MSCs could be implemented by applying the instance recognition algorithm (incl. (I6)) described in the previous subsection for all possible pairs of atomic concepts and objects, there are clearly more efficient ways. First, step (I6) can be performed in a forward-chaining manner by propagating value-restriction constraints to role-fillers. This avoids recomputation of (I6) for an object with more than one role-filler. Additionally, it allows checking whether the symbolic restrictions expressed as value-restrictions are really satisfied by the role-fillers. Second, the most specialized concept expression describing an object can be maintained incrementally for every object. For this purpose, we need the notion of a *generalization* of two concepts, which is defined below.

Definition 4.10 (Generalization of Concepts) *The generalization of two normalized p-concepts c_1, c_2, written $\text{gen}(c_1, c_2)$, is defined as c_1 if $c_2 =$ Nothing, as c_2 if $c_1 =$ Nothing, or otherwise as an "and" expression containing the following subexpressions:*

- *all positive and negated primitive concept components appearing in both c_1 and c_2.*

- *restrictions of the form (atleast $n\,r$), if in both c_1 and c_2 there are "atleast" restrictions on r. Let m_i be the maximum of all "atleast" restrictions on r in c_i. Then n is set to $\min(m_1, m_2)$.*

- *restrictions of the form (atmost $n\,r$) , if in both c_1 and c_2 there are "atmost" restrictions on r. Let m_i be the minimum of all "atmost" restrictions on r in c_i. Then n is set to $\max(m_1, m_2)$.*

- *restrictions of the form (all $r\,v$) for all roles r such that "all" restrictions on r appear in both c_1 and c_2. The concept v is defined recursively as the generalization of the value restrictions in the original expressions.*

The general technique for determining MSCs, which is very similar to classification, is called *realization* – a term coined by Mark [1982]. A realization algorithm similar to the one implemented in the BACK system could be described as follows (see also [Nebel and von Luck, 1988]).

Algorithm 4.6 (REALIZE) Assume a terminology $\mathcal{T}$ and a world description $\mathcal{W}$. Assume further that for each object in the world description an *abstraction* is maintained which is the "most specialized concept expression" the object is an instance of. If a new world description $\mathcal{W}'$ is generated by adding a new object or relation description δ to $\mathcal{W}$, then:

(R1) If $\delta = (r\,o\,p)$, then take all object descriptions of o, look up the value restrictions (computed by the classification algorithm) for r and any superroles in the concepts used to describe o, and *propagate* the value restrictions to p by adding the value restrictions as an "internal" object description on p.

If $\delta = (c\,o)$, then *propagate* all computed value restrictions mentioned in c on a role r or one of its superroles to all objects p if the relation description $(r\,o\,p)$ is in the world description of $\mathcal{W}$.

If such a propagation leads to new internal object descriptions, then apply (R1) recursively.

(R2) If a new object description $(c\,o)$ or a new relation description $(r\,o\ldots)$ has been entered or if a role-filler of object o for some role has been assigned a new *abstraction*, then compute a new *abstraction* for o. This abstraction is built[14] by taking the conjunction of

- all concepts mentioned in object descriptions of o, entered or generated in step (R1),

- "atleast" restrictions for all roles r for which there are relation-descriptions of the form $(s\,o\ldots)$ or $(s\,o\,(\text{atleast}\ldots))$ with $s \preceq_{\mathcal{T}} r$, by counting distinct role fillers and using explicit "atleast" relation-descriptions.

- "atmost" restrictions for all roles r for which there are relation-descriptions of the form $(t\,o\,(\text{atmost}\ldots))$ with $r \preceq_{\mathcal{T}} t$.

- "all" restrictions for all roles r for which *all* role-fillers are known. This can be checked by counting the role-fillers for r and its sub-roles and comparing this number with the relevant "atmost" restrictions computed above or derived from object descriptions of o. The value restrictions are *generalizations* of the abstractions of the role-fillers for the role r and its subroles. "all" restrictions which are nested deeper than the maximum relevant role-chain length of all concepts in $\mathcal{T}$ can be omitted.

(R3) Finally, the abstractions created in step (R2) are *classified* into the concept taxonomy. The immediate subsumers of the abstractions form the new MSCs.

Comparing this forward chaining inference algorithm with the backward-chaining algorithm in the Sect. 4.5.1, we note that step (R1) corresponds to step (I6) (the step omitted in KANDOR and KL-TWO) and (R2) corresponds to (I1)–(I5). (R3) comprises all the subsumption tests in (I1)–(I6). However, REALIZE does more than CINST. By propagating value restrictions in step (R1)

---

[14]Actually, the process of building an abstraction can be thought of as two separate steps. The first one – *completion* – computes all consequences derived from role-relationships, i.e., subrole declarations and role-value-maps, while the second one creates the concept expression [Nebel and von Luck, 1987].

and using them to build the abstraction in step (R2), the classification step (R3) is able to detect inconsistent world descriptions – a point neglected in CINST.

Furthermore, in contrast to CINST, the realization algorithm does not require any extension of the basic inference algorithms for subsumption and classification, but realization can make use of these algorithms by calling CLASSIFY as a subroutine. From a conceptual point of view, this sounds quite elegant. However, as pointed out by MacGregor [1988a], this kind of processing is unfeasible for terminological formalisms containing role-value-maps and range-restricted roles. The abstractions generated in step (R2) are much too fine-grained in this case. Instead of always creating a complete abstraction, MacGregor proposes building an initial abstraction and testing whether role-fillers are instances of value-restrictions on demand. Such a mix of backward and forward-chaining inference techniques avoids the pitfall of creating too fine-grained abstractions and is more efficient than a pure forward-chaining inference algorithm such as the one described above. However, we will not pursue this issue further, but rather analyze the general properties of the realization algorithm described above.

From the structure of the algorithm, it should be clear that realization can be computationally expensive. In step (R1), propagation can proceed along role-chains which are as long as the relevant role-chain length of the atomic concept used in the object description. Furthermore, all role-fillers for the respective role and its subroles are subject to the propagation of value restrictions. Thus, the input of one object description may affect a number of other objects proportional to the number of role-fillers for a role at one object to the power of the relevant role-chain length of the atomic concept used in the object description. In step (R2), we have to compute new abstractions for all objects which received a value restriction concept by propagation. Recursively, all objects which have role-fillers that got a new abstraction have to be treated in the same way – a process which may in the worst case proceed along role-chains which are as long as the maximum relevant role-chain length of all introduced concepts in a terminology. Finally, in step (R3), the CLASSIFY procedure has to be applied for all objects with new abstractions.

Summing up, the cost of the realization algorithm is dominated by steps (R1) and (R2). If we denote the maximum number of role-fillers in the world description of one object for all roles with n, the maximum number of objects which "share" a role-filler with m, and the maximum relevant role-chain length of all concepts in the terminology with l, then the worst case complexity is $O(n^l \times m^l)$ classification steps.

In practical applications, however, this theoretical worst-case behavior does not seem to play a role. First, the relevant role-chain length of concepts and the number of role-fillers are usually small. Second, there are a number of natural optimizations which speed up the realization process considerably:

- If a value restriction is propagated to a role-filler and the propagated value-restriction is already subsumed by the abstraction of the role-filler, further propagations are not necessary.

- If a role-filler of some object gets a new abstraction, the abstraction for the object has to be recomputed only if *all* role-fillers for the corresponding role are known.

- It is not necessary to completely recompute abstractions, but it suffices to add the new parts conjunctively to the old abstraction. For this reason, classification does not need to start at **Anything**. It can use the old set of most specialized concepts, the old MSC, as a starting point when determining the right place in the concept taxonomy.

- Abstractions do not need full classification. It is enough to compute the set of immediate subsumers if we are interested in the MSC only. This also means that we do not need to insert the abstraction into the concept taxonomy. It suffices to maintain the MSC.

Moreover, if no assertional cycles are present in the world description and if no object can be reached by two different role-chains from another object, then the number of recomputations of an abstraction is bounded by the number of objects in the world description. This means that although realization is exponential with respect to the complexity of the concept (the size of the p-concept) used in the object description, it is (almost) linearly proportional to the size of the world description.

As regards soundness and completeness, it should be obvious from the arguments made above that steps (R1)–(R3) are sound. Completeness, on the other hand, is a goal we already gave up in Sect. 4.2.2 when we discovered that complete subsumption is too expensive. However, it might be interesting to get an idea of how complete or incomplete realization is.

The first thing we note is that realization inherits the incompleteness of classification and subsumption. This means that if a object description $(c\,o)$ is part of a world description and $c \preceq_T d$, but TSUB misses this relationship, then realization will not discover that o is an instance of d. Moreover, realization itself adds new sources of incompleteness. The abstraction in step (R2) may ignore some information which is important, as is exemplified in Figure 4.6.

Assuming again our "team" terminology, the object description (Woman MARY) follows from the world description in Figure 4.6 because MARY is the only member which *could be* a Woman and thus is the required leader of the Modern-team. All other members are Men and, for this reason, are not qualified for the leader position. However, the abstraction process does not do any reasoning by case and thus does not fill the leader role with MARY. Hence, there is no way to detect that MARY is a Woman. However, this kind of reasoning was left out on purpose because it leads to exponential explosions if a number of such cases have to be analyzed. Similar to subsumption, where no reasoning by case is done and only structural relationships and easily detectable incoherencies are dealt with, only these properties are computed in realization so as to avoid *puzzle mode reasoning* [Levesque, 1988].

Nevertheless, although we miss the fact that MARY is a Woman and the leader of TEAM-A, this fact is implicit in the world description and will be detected if

```
(Modern-team TEAM-A)
(Man        TOM)
(Man        DICK)
(Human      MARY)
(member     Modern-team TOM)
(member     Modern-team DICK)
(member     Modern-team MARY)
(member     Modern-team (atmost 3))


⊨^T (Woman MARY) ?
```

Fig. 4.6. A Hybrid Inference Ignored by the Realization Algorithm

we add more information to the world description. If the object description (Man MARY) and the relation description (leader TEAM-A MARY) are added to the world description in Figure 4.6, then, by the propagation of value restrictions in step (R1), MARY would be asserted to be a Woman, and would thus be an impossible object, being a Woman and a Man at the same time. Generalizing this example, one could expect that the more specific we are in the world description, the more complete the realization algorithm will be – perhaps leading to a limiting case where REALIZE completely infers all entailed propositions.

4.5.3 Model-Based Terminological Reasoning

The reason why instance recognition and subsumption is very hard, even in a simple hybrid formalism like $\mathcal{TF}/\mathcal{AF}$, is that we always have to take into account all possible models and all possible semantic structures. If we focus on only a single model, things are suddenly very simple. Consider a finite semantic structure $\langle \mathcal{D}, \mathcal{E} \rangle$ of a terminology $\mathcal{T}$ and a generating primitive assignment $\mathcal{P}$. Then for every $d \in \mathcal{D}$ and every concept c it is easy to determine whether $d \in \mathcal{E}[c]$ by considering only $\mathcal{D}$ and $\mathcal{P}$. Such a procedure – which we will call *instance test on a model* – can be specified as follows.

Algorithm 4.7 (MINST) Let $\langle \mathcal{D}, \mathcal{E} \rangle$ be a finite semantic structure of a normal-form terminology $\mathcal{T}_N$. Let $\mathcal{P}$ be the corresponding primitive assignment. Then the test whether an object $d \in \mathcal{D}$ is an instance of the concept c in the semantic structure $\langle \mathcal{D}, \mathcal{E} \rangle$ proceeds as follows:

(M1) If c is an atomic concept, test whether d is an element of EXP(c) by calling MINST recursively.

(M2) If c is a primitive concept component, then check whether $d \in \mathcal{P}[c]$.

(M3) If $c = (\text{a-not } p)$, then check $d \notin \mathcal{P}[p]$.

(M4) If $c = (\text{and } c_1 \ldots c_n)$, then test whether d is an instance of all c_i's by applying MINST recursively.

(M5) If $c = (\text{all } r \; v)$, then check for all objects x such that $\langle d, x \rangle \in \mathcal{E}[r]$ whether x is an instance of v by applying the test recursively, where $\mathcal{E}[r]$ is easily computed by taking the intersection of the extensions of all primitive role components in r.

(M6) If $c = (\text{atleast } n \; r)$, then check $\|\{\langle d, x \rangle | \; \langle d, x \rangle \in \mathcal{E}[r]\}\| \geq n$.

(M7) If $c = (\text{atmost } n \; r)$, then check $\|\{\langle d, x \rangle | \; \langle d, x \rangle \in \mathcal{E}[r]\}\| \leq n$.

Inspecting Def. 3.11, it is easy to see that MINST is an algorithmic realization of the equations for the extension function on concepts. We left out the part on roles here because they are trivial.

Instead of MINST as described above, an equivalent procedure, based on *abstractions* of objects as described in Sect. 4.5.2 and on the TSUB algorithm as described in Sect. 4.1.1, is also conceivable. For this purpose, let us formally define what we mean by an *abstraction* of a domain object.

Definition 4.11 (Abstraction of a Domain Object) *Let $\langle \mathcal{D}, \mathcal{E} \rangle$ be a finite semantic structure of a terminology $\mathcal{T}$ and $\mathcal{P}$ be a corresponding primitive assignment. Then an abstraction of degree 0 of a domain object d, written $\text{abs}^0(d, \mathcal{D}, \mathcal{P})$, is a normalized p-concept of the following form:*

$$
\begin{aligned}
(\text{and} \quad & p_1 \ldots p_l \\
& (\text{a-not } q_1) \ldots (\text{a-not } q_m) \\
& (\text{atleast } k_1 \; r_1) \ldots (\text{atleast } k_n \; r_n) \\
& (\text{atmost } k_1 \; r_1) \ldots (\text{atmost } k_n \; r_n))
\end{aligned}
$$

with p_i primitive concept components such that $d \in \mathcal{P}[p_i]$, $1 \leq i \leq l$, q_i primitive components such that $d \notin \mathcal{P}[q_i]$, $1 \leq i \leq m$,[15] and r_i p-roles corresponding to all atomic roles used in $\mathcal{T}$, and k_i the number of role-fillers of d for the roles r_i, $1 \leq i \leq n$.

An abstraction of degree n, written $\text{abs}^n(d, \mathcal{D}, \mathcal{P})$, has the form:

$$(\text{and } \text{abs}^0(d, \mathcal{D}, \mathcal{P}) \; (\text{all } r_1 \; gen_1) \ldots (\text{all } r_m \; gen_m))$$

with $gen_i, 1 \leq i \leq m$ being generalizations (as defined in Def. 4.10) of $\text{abs}^{n-1}(e, \mathcal{D}, \mathcal{P})$ for all e such that $\langle d, e \rangle \in \mathcal{E}[r_i]$.

Because of the way the abstraction of an object d is constructed, it is evident that d is always an instance of the abstraction, as spelled out in the next proposition.

Proposition 4.7 *Let $\langle \mathcal{D}, \mathcal{E} \rangle$ be a finite semantic structure of a terminology $\mathcal{T}$ with a corresponding primitive assignment $\mathcal{P}$. Then it holds for any n that*

$$d \in \mathcal{E}[\text{abs}^n(d, \mathcal{D}, \mathcal{P})]$$

---

[15] Actually, it suffice to collect negated primitive components for primitive components used as disjointness markers.

More generally, an abstraction of a lower degree always subsumes an abstraction of a higher degree for the same object, and because increasing the degree amounts to adding more restrictions to the concept expression, subsumption between abstractions of different degrees for the same object is always detected by TSUB.

Proposition 4.8 *Let $\langle D, \mathcal{E} \rangle$ be a finite semantic structure of a terminology T with a corresponding primitive assignment P. Then it holds for any n and m with $n \geq m$ that*

$$\text{TSUB}(\text{abs}^m(d, D, P), \text{abs}^n(d, D, P))$$

Since abstractions of domain objects specify restrictions on all roles exhaustively, a generalization of two abstractions contains enough structure so that the generalization is subsumed by an arbitrary concept if and only if the two abstractions are subsumed by the concept. Furthermore, TSUB always detects such subsumption relationships!

Lemma 4.11 *Let $\langle D, \mathcal{E} \rangle$ be a finite semantic structure of a terminology T with a corresponding primitive assignment P. Let $d, e \in D$, and let $a_1 = \text{abs}^n(d, D, P)$ and $a_2 = \text{abs}^n(e, D, P), n \geq 0$. Then for any concept c*

$$\text{TSUB}(\text{EXP}(c, T), a_1) \wedge \text{TSUB}(\text{EXP}(c, T), a_2) \text{ iff } \text{TSUB}(\text{EXP}(c, T), \text{gen}(a_1, a_2))$$

Proof: Assuming that TSUB returns that c subsumes the generalization of a_1 and a_2, then, of course, it returns true for the subsumption tests between c and a_1 and c and a_2 because the a_is have stronger restrictions on all roles than the generalization.

For the other direction, we will use induction on n. Let us first assume that a_1 and a_2 are abstractions of degree 0. Then in order to have TSUB to return true, the tests in (C3), (C5), and (C6) have to be successful. Because the generalization of a_1 and a_2 contains all those positive and negated primitive components which have been tested in step (C3), and conforms to the number restrictions for all roles r which have number restrictions in c, the generalization of abstractions of degree 0 will be detected to be subsumed by the TSUB algorithm.

Now let us assume that the lemma holds for all abstractions of degree k. Let a_1 and a_2 be two abstractions of degree $k + 1$ and assume that TSUB detects that both are subsumed by c. That means in particular that value restrictions on any role r in c subsume all value restrictions on the role r in both a_1 and a_2 and that TSUB has detected this. Because of the induction hypothesis, the value restriction of any role r in c subsumes the generalization of the value restriction on r in both a_1 and a_2. Thus, taking into account the definition of the generalization, c subsumes the generalization of a_1 and a_2. ∎

Using this lemma, we can prove that abstraction and incomplete subsumption are sufficient to test for instance relationships in one model, i.e., they are equivalent to MINST as specified in the beginning of this section.

Theorem 4.8 *Let $\langle \mathcal{D}, \mathcal{E} \rangle$ be a finite semantic structure of a terminology $\mathcal{T}$ with a corresponding primitive assignment $\mathcal{P}$. Let c be a concept with* rlength($\text{EXP}(c, \mathcal{T})$) $= n$. *Then*

$$\text{TSUB}(\text{EXP}(c, \mathcal{T}), \text{abs}^{n-1}(d, \mathcal{D}, \mathcal{P})) \quad \textit{iff} \quad d \in \mathcal{E}[c]$$

Proof: If TSUB detects that c subsumes the abstraction of d, then d must evidently be an instance of c because of Prop. 4.7 and the soundness of TSUB.

For the other direction, we will use induction over the relevant role-chain length of c. Assume rlength($\text{EXP}(c, \mathcal{T})$) $= 1$. Now, if d is an instance of c, then MINST must have been successful on the normalized p-concept, i.e., all positive and negated primitive components in the normalized p-concept of c are satisfied and all number restrictions on roles are satisfied. Consider now $\text{abs}^0(d, \mathcal{D}, \mathcal{P})$. It contains all positive and negated primitive components p and (a-not q) such that $d \in \mathcal{P}[p]$ and $d \notin \mathcal{P}[q]$, respectively. That means all of the tests in the first subcase of (C3) in the COMPARE algorithm will succeed. Moreover, all tests concerning "atleast" restrictions on a role r (first subcase of (C5)) will succeed because the abstraction of d contains a number restriction on r which is at least as strong as the one in c. And the same holds for "atmost" restriction because of the same argument.

Now assume the lemma holds for all concepts with a relevant role-chain length of k. Assume further we have a concept c with rlength($\text{EXP}(c, \mathcal{T})$) $= k+1$ such that $d \in \mathcal{E}[c]$. Because of the arguments made above, the tests (C3), (C5), and (C6) succeed. Moreover, we know that the value restrictions on any role r in c subsume the abstractions of all role-fillers e for role r of object d, and TSUB detects this subsumption relationship because of the induction hypothesis. Because of Lemma 4.11 test (C4) will also succeed. ∎

Another view of the fact that abstraction and incomplete subsumption suffice to realize an instance test on models is that the TSUB algorithm is a complete algorithm if the second parameter is an abstraction of some object in some semantic structure.

Corollary 4.4 *Let $\langle \mathcal{D}, \mathcal{E} \rangle$ be a finite semantic structure of a terminology $\mathcal{T}$ with a corresponding primitive assignment $\mathcal{P}$. Let c be a concept, and let $a_n = \text{abs}^n(d, \mathcal{D}, \mathcal{P})$ for some $d \in \mathcal{D}$ and some natural number $n \geq$ rlength($\text{EXP}(c, \mathcal{T})$)$- 1$. Then*

$$\text{TSUB}(\text{EXP}(c, \mathcal{T}), a_n) \quad \textit{iff} \quad a_n \preceq \text{EXP}(c, \mathcal{T})$$

Proof: Because TSUB is sound, the right hand side follows from the left hand side.

For the other direction, assume that c subsumes a_n, but TSUB misses this fact. Let $m = $ rlength($\text{EXP}(c, \mathcal{T})$).

If $m - 1 = n$, then the we have the following relationships in the semantic structure $\langle \mathcal{D}, \mathcal{E} \rangle$ mentioned in the theorem: $d \in \mathcal{E}[a_n] \subseteq \mathcal{E}[c]$. This, however, leads to an immediate contradiction by Theorem 4.8.

If $m - 1 < n$, then there exists another abstraction a_{m-1} of degree $m - 1$ such that $d \in \mathcal{E}[a_n] \subseteq \mathcal{E}[a_{m-1}] \subseteq \mathcal{E}[c]$. Since we have $\text{TSUB}(a_{m-1}, a_n)$ by Prop. 4.8, $\text{TSUB}(\text{EXP}(c, \mathcal{T}), a_{m-1})$ by Theorem 4.8, and $\text{TSUB}(\text{EXP}(c, \mathcal{T}), a_n)$ because of Prop. 4.3, we again have a contradiction. ∎

4.5.4 Model-Based Reasoning as the Limiting Case of Realization

Although the results above sound quite interesting, they do not apply directly to our case. In general, a world description has a large number of models respecting a terminology. Thus, hybrid reasoning in general cannot be based on a single model. However, it may be possible to give a characterization when we can base our reasoning on one model. Trying to do this, let us focus on world descriptions which are quite explicit about role relationships – world descriptions we will call *role-closed*.

Definition 4.12 (Role-Closed World Description)
A world-description $\mathcal{W}$ is a role-closed w.r.t. a set of atomic roles R iff for every atomic role $r \in R$ and every two objects o, p appearing in $\mathcal{W}$, the world description either contains a relation description $(r \ o \ p)$ or the addition of such a relation description eliminates all possible models of $\mathcal{W}$.

This definition implies that a role-closed world description is either inconsistent, or we have for every object o and every role $r \in R$ a relation description of the form $(r \ o \ (\text{atmost } n))$, with n being the number of role fillers of o for role r. That means our description is quite explicit. Interpreting such a world description using a terminology, the only propositions which do not follow immediately from the world description alone are object descriptions. In order to compute those, let us first define what we mean by a *generalized world description*.

Definition 4.13 (Generalized World Description)
A generalized world description $\mathcal{W}$ is a world description which uses not only atomic concepts in object descriptions, but also arbitrary concept expressions. The definitions for models and models respecting a terminology, as well as hybrid entailment are to be extended in the obvious way by considering not only atomic roles and concepts but also arbitrary term expressions.

Based on this definition, role-closed world descriptions will be transformed to equivalent generalized world description where only primitive concept components are used in object descriptions.

Definition 4.14 (Value Restriction Propagation) *Let $\mathcal{W}$ be a generalized world description and $\mathcal{T}$ be a terminology. Let $\text{prop}_\mathcal{T}$ be a function transforming an arbitrary $\mathcal{W}$ into $\mathcal{W}'$ by applying the following rules:*

1. *For all object descriptions $(c \ o)$, let $x = \text{NORM}(\text{EXP}(c, \mathcal{T}))$.*
2. *Remove $(c \ o)$ from $\mathcal{W}$.*

3. *Add $(c_i\, o)$ for every positive or negated primitive component c_i appearing as a subexpression in the top-level "and" expression of x.*

4. *Add $(r_i\, o\, (\text{atmost}\, n_i))$ for every $(\text{atmost}\, r_i\, n_i)$ appearing in the top-level "and" expression of x.*

5. *Add $(r_i\, o\, (\text{atleast}\, n_i))$ for every $(\text{atleast}\, r_i\, n_i)$ appearing in the top-level "and" expression of x.*

6. *Add $(v_i\, p)$ for every object p with $(s\, o\, p)$ in $\mathcal{W}$ and $(\text{all}\, r_i\, v_i)$ is a subexpression of the top-level "and" expression of x with $s \preceq_T r_i$.*

This definition is obviously the formal counterpart of the propagation step (R1) in REALIZE. Unlike in (R1), however, the original object description is deleted. In general, this would amount to a loss of information. However, in world descriptions which are role-closed w.r.t. the atomic roles used in a terminology, nothing is lost.

Lemma 4.12 *Let $\mathcal{W}$ be a generalized world description which is role-closed w.r.t. the atomic roles used in a terminology T. Then it holds that*

$$\mathcal{W} \models^T \delta \quad \text{iff} \quad \text{prop}_T(\mathcal{W}) \models^T \delta$$

Proof: Inspecting the equations of Def. 3.11, we see that all the transformations in Def. 4.14 never lead to the elimination of models respecting a terminology regardless of whether the world description is role-closed or not. That means we have $\mathcal{W} \models^T \delta$ *if* $\text{prop}_T(\mathcal{W}) \models^T \delta$.

For the other direction, assume the world description is role-closed w.r.t. the atomic roles used in T. Although the original object description $(c\, o)$ is deleted, we see by inspecting the equations in Def. 3.11 that all semantic structures of T which are models of $\mathcal{W}'$ must have o as an instance of c. Thus, for world descriptions role-closed w.r.t. the set of atomic roles used in T, the other direction is valid as well. ∎

If we take an arbitrary role-closed world description and apply the propagation function as often as the maximum relevant role-chain length of all concepts in the terminology under consideration, then we obviously get a generalized world description such that only primitive concept components are used in object descriptions. Such a world description is very similar to a primitive assignment $\mathcal{P}$ as defined in Def. 3.13. Inspecting such a world description, it is possible to determine easily whether it is consistent w.r.t. the terminology.

Lemma 4.13 *Let $\mathcal{W}$ be a world description which is role-closed w.r.t. the atomic roles used in a terminology T. Let l be the maximum relevant role-chain length of all concepts defined in T, and set $\mathcal{W}' = \text{prop}_T^l(\mathcal{W})$. Then $\mathcal{W}'$ has a model respecting T iff in $\mathcal{W}'$*

1. *there are no pairs of object descriptions $(p\, o)$, $((\text{a-not}\, p)\, o)$,*

2. *there are no pairs of relation descriptions* $(s \, o \, (\text{atleast } n))$, $(r \, o \, (\text{atmost } m))$, *with* $m > n$ *and* $s \preceq_T r$, *and*

3. *there are no relation descriptions* $(s \, o \, p)$, *if* W' *does not contain* $(r \, o \, p)$ *with* $s \preceq_T r$.

Proof: From Lemma 4.12, we know that the models of W and W' (w.r.t. atomic terms) respecting T are the same. Furthermore, we know that a violation of conditions 1 and 2 leads to the fact that there cannot be any model respecting T. If condition 3 is violated, then we get the same result since $(r \, o \, p)$ is entailed by all models respecting T, but this violates the "atmost" relation-description on r being in W' because W' is role-closed w.r.t. T.

For the other direction, assume that all of the conditions mentioned in the lemma are satisfied. Because *prop* is applied l times, the resulting generalized world description W' contains only object descriptions with positive or negated primitive concept components. Using these and the relation description as a starting point, a semantic structure of T could be created by applying the equations in Def. 3.11. Thus, W' has a model respecting T, and because of Lemma 4.12, W has a model respecting T. ∎

Applying this result to REALIZE, it is evident that REALIZE would detect all inconsistencies in this case. However, this is not the entire story. Role-closed world descriptions do not only allow for detection of inconsistencies, but also permit the derivation of all entailed propositions because they have *canonical models*, which can be computed easily.

Definition 4.15 (Canonical Model) *A model of a world description* W *respecting a terminology* $\mathcal{M} = \langle \mathcal{D}, \mathcal{I} \rangle$ *is a* canonical model *iff for all descriptions* δ:

$$\models_{\mathcal{M}} \delta \quad \text{iff} \quad W \models^T \delta$$

As should be obvious, most of the models of a world description are not canonical, and often enough there is even none. For instance, the world description in Figure 4.6 does not have such a model. In order to characterize such models, let us define the notion of a model ordering.

Definition 4.16 (Model Ordering) *Let* W *be a world description,* T *a terminology,* $\mathcal{N}_O$ *a set of objects,* $\mathcal{N}_R$ *a set of atomic roles, and* $\mathcal{N}_C$ *a set of atomic concepts. A model of a world description* $\langle \mathcal{D}, \mathcal{I} \rangle$ *respecting* T *is contained in another model* $\langle \mathcal{D}', \mathcal{I}' \rangle$ *respecting* T, *written* $\langle \mathcal{D}, \mathcal{I} \rangle \sqsubseteq \langle \mathcal{D}', \mathcal{I}' \rangle$ *iff there is an injective function* h *such that:*

1. $h : \mathcal{D} \rightarrow \mathcal{D}'$

2. $h(\mathcal{I}[o]) = \mathcal{I}'[o] \quad \forall o \in \mathcal{N}_O$

3. $\{ h(x) \in \mathcal{D}' \mid x \in \mathcal{I}[c] \} \subseteq \mathcal{I}'[c] \quad \forall c \in \mathcal{N}_C$

4. $\{ \langle h(x), h(y) \rangle \in \mathcal{D} \times \mathcal{D} \mid \langle x, y \rangle \in \mathcal{I}[r] \} \subseteq \mathcal{I}'[r] \quad \forall r \in \mathcal{N}_R$

Definition 4.17 (Unique Minimal Model) *A model $\langle \mathcal{D}, \mathcal{I} \rangle$ is a minimal model of $\mathcal{W}$ respecting $\mathcal{T}$ iff for all other models $\langle \mathcal{D}', \mathcal{I}' \rangle$ we have either $\langle \mathcal{D}, \mathcal{I} \rangle \sqsubseteq \langle \mathcal{D}', \mathcal{I}' \rangle$ or $\langle \mathcal{D}', \mathcal{I}' \rangle \not\sqsubseteq \langle \mathcal{D}, \mathcal{I} \rangle$. It is a unique minimal model (modulo renaming) iff it is minimal and for all other minimal models $\langle \mathcal{D}', \mathcal{I}' \rangle$ it holds that $\langle \mathcal{D}, \mathcal{I} \rangle \sqsubseteq \langle \mathcal{D}', \mathcal{I}' \rangle$.*

Although unique minimal models are not canonical models, the converse holds. Since a canonical model satisfies all descriptions entailed by a world description, it evidently has a minimal domain and minimal extensions of concepts and roles. The converse relationship does not hold because a model $\langle \mathcal{D}', \mathcal{I}' \rangle$ including a unique minimal model $\langle \mathcal{D}, \mathcal{I} \rangle$ may support more role-relationships, leading to the fact that some relation descriptions using "atmost" are satisfied in $\langle \mathcal{D}, \mathcal{I} \rangle$, but not in $\langle \mathcal{D}', \mathcal{I}' \rangle$.

Lemma 4.14 *A unique minimal model $\langle \mathcal{D}, \mathcal{I} \rangle$ of $\mathcal{W}$ respecting $\mathcal{T}$ is a canonical model iff for any model $\langle \mathcal{D}', \mathcal{I}' \rangle$:*

$$\forall o, p \in \mathcal{N}_O, r \in \mathcal{N}_R : \langle \mathcal{I}'[o], \mathcal{I}'[p] \rangle \in \mathcal{I}'[r] \Rightarrow \langle \mathcal{I}[o], \mathcal{I}[p] \rangle \in \mathcal{I}[r] \qquad (4.8)$$

Proof: Since a unique minimal model satisfies object descriptions and relation descriptions of the form $(c\,o)$ and $(r\,o\,(\text{atleast } n))$, if and only if they are entailed, the only problematic point are the relation descriptions using "atmost" restrictions. Condition (4.8), however, guarantees that satisfaction in $\langle \mathcal{D}, \mathcal{I} \rangle$ implies entailment. ∎

Theorem 4.9 *Let $\mathcal{W}$ be a world description which is role-closed w.r.t. the atomic roles appearing in $\mathcal{T}$. Let l be the maximum relevant role-chain length in $\mathcal{T}$. Let $\mathcal{N}_C$, $\mathcal{N}_R$, and $\mathcal{N}_O$ be the sets of atomic concepts, atomic roles and objects appearing in $\mathcal{T}$ and $\mathcal{W}$. Then $\mathcal{W}$ has a canonical model constructible from $\text{prop}_\mathcal{T}^l(\mathcal{W})$, or $\mathcal{W}$ is inconsistent.*

Proof: If $\mathcal{W}'$, and thus $\mathcal{W}$, is not inconsistent, define a partial model $\langle \mathcal{D}', \mathcal{I}' \rangle$ by the following rules:

$$\mathcal{D}' \overset{\text{def}}{=} \{o|\ o \text{ is an object in } \mathcal{W}'\}$$
$$\mathcal{I}'[o] \overset{\text{def}}{=} o\ \forall o \in \mathcal{D}'$$
$$\mathcal{I}'[r] \overset{\text{def}}{=} \{\langle o, p \rangle|\ (r\,o\,p) \text{ appears in } \mathcal{W}'\}$$
$$\mathcal{I}'[c] \overset{\text{def}}{=} \{o|\ (c\,o) \text{ appears in } \mathcal{W}' \text{ and } c \in \overline{\mathcal{N}_C}\}$$

Use this partial model as a primitive assignment for the normal-form terminology $\mathcal{T}_N$ and create a complete model which assigns values to $\mathcal{I}'$ for all possible concept expressions by applying the equations in Def. 3.11. This model respects $\mathcal{T}$ because of the way it is constructed. Moreover, it is a unique minimal one w.r.t. $\mathcal{N}_C$, $\mathcal{N}_R$ and $\mathcal{N}_O$, since it covers only the objects and role-relationships mentioned in $\mathcal{W}'$, and the concepts are constructed deterministically from these and the primitive assignments. $\mathcal{I}'$ is also a canonical model, because condition (4.8) is satisfied by the role-completeness restriction. ∎

This characterization of role-closed world descriptions shows that they are similar to what Levesque [1986] has called *vivid* knowledge bases – a kind of representation permitting tractable inference algorithms because they are canonical models of themselves. Although this is not the case with role-closed world descriptions, they can be mapped to a vivid representation by applying *prop*. Combining this result and Theorem 4.8, we see that REALIZE is a complete inference algorithm for role-closed world descriptions.

Theorem 4.10 *Let $\mathcal{W}$ be a world description role-closed w.r.t. the atomic roles used in a terminology $\mathcal{T}$. Then*

1. *$\mathcal{W}$ is inconsistent w.r.t. $\mathcal{T}$ iff some abstraction computed by REALIZE is Nothing– the concept with a necessarily empty extension.*

2. *$\mathcal{W} \models^{\mathcal{T}} (c\,o)$ iff $\mathcal{W}$ is inconsistent with respect to $\mathcal{T}$ or the abstraction a of o computed by REALIZE is subsumed by c and it holds that $\mathrm{TSUB}(\mathrm{EXP}(c, \mathcal{T}), a)$.*

Proof: Proposition 1 holds because of Lemma 4.13 and the way REALIZE computes abstractions.

Proposition 2 holds because of the following arguments. If $\mathcal{W}$ is inconsistent w.r.t. $\mathcal{T}$, everything is entailed. Thus, let us assume that $\mathcal{W}$ is consistent w.r.t. $\mathcal{T}$. By Theorem 4.9 we know that there is a canonical model which can be easily constructed from $prop'_{\mathcal{T}}$. Moreover, this construction uses a subset of the transformations of the of the REALIZE algorithm. Thus, since we showed in Theorem 4.8 that reasoning of REALIZE on a single model is complete, the proposition follows. ∎

4.6 Evaluation of the Inference Capabilities

From the analysis of the inferential capabilities of REALIZE in the previous section, two important conclusions can be drawn. First, it shows that REALIZE converges towards completeness with the limiting case of role-closed world descriptions resulting in a complete inference algorithm – REALIZE is *conditionally complete*. This characterizes the algorithm much better than the mere statement that it is sound – which in the extreme case could mean that it does nothing at all. Moreover, it shows that the algorithm is not only more complete than the hybrid inference algorithms used in KL-TWO and KANDOR, but also that it is of a different quality.

Second, in information retrieval applications such as ARGON, where it seems to be crucial that inference algorithms are complete (as argued in [Patel-Schneider, 1984]), completeness can be guaranteed for world descriptions of a certain form. Although we have proven this only for the formalisms $\mathcal{TF}/\mathcal{AF}$, it seems possible to extend the result to formalisms such as the one used in KAN-DOR – the representation kernel of ARGON. Classification of a query-concept (as described in the beginning of Sect. 4.5.2) would still miss some subsumption relationship. However, by Theorem 4.10, we would be able to retrieve *all* instances of the query-concept.

In general, it can be said that when we sacrifice completeness, we should not do so arbitrarily. On the contrary, we should be very careful in deciding which kinds of inferences we support and which ones we ignore. Otherwise, there may be situations where one subformalism allows expressing something which obviously should have some impact on another subformalism according to the common semantics, but the system does not realize this because its reasoning is incomplete in this aspect. This "black hole" might be there because the inferred propositions cannot be expressed or because one subformalism is not heuristically adequate for this aspect. In any case, the subformalisms of the system appear to be unbalanced. Although the term *balancedness* is a little bit vague, it can be captured by the following *principle of balancedness in hybrid representation systems*:

> If a representation construct in a subformalism of a hybrid formalism suggests that its usage has some impact on knowledge represented in another subformalism (according to the common semantics), then this should be realized by the system.

An example for a system with unbalanced subformalisms is KL-TWO [Vilain, 1985]: While it is possible to define concepts with a very rich terminological language, only a fraction of it is used for hybrid reasoning. In particular, the number restrictions used in the terminological component has only a very limited impact on the assertional component because the latter is not heuristically adequate to deal with cardinalities (as discussed in Sect. 3.3).

In contrast to KL-TWO, the described abstract system, which resembles the BACK system to a large extent, is designed to allow for balanced inference capabilities. Any construct in the terminological language has some impact on the assertional formalism and vice versa and although the inference capabilities are incomplete, at least they are balanced in their ignorance. Furthermore, any expression used in one subformalism which should have an impact according to the semantics will eventually have this effect when more assertions are added to the world description.

5. Terminological Cycles

As noted in Sect. 3.2.2, terminological cycles (see Def. 3.4) are counter-intuitive. Furthermore, as pointed out in Sect. 4.1.1, terminological cycles may result in an infinite recursion of the subsumption algorithm. For these reasons, we demanded that terminologies be cycle-free. Skimming through the relevant literature reveals that this treatment of terminological cycles is common in research concerning terminological formalisms:

- "we should be careful to avoid circular definitions" [Brachman et al., 1985, p. 534]

- "In the first mode, if the classifier discovers a cycle, it simply declares the concept classified and warns the user about the existence of a cycle." [Kaczmarek et al., 1986, p. 982]

- "Loom has taken an opposite position – cyclic definitions are illegal in Loom." [MacGregor and Bates, 1987, p. 6]

- "Two properties that must be met by any set of definitions in this [terminological] logic are that all definitions in the set must be unique and that there be no circular definitions." [Patel-Schneider, 1987a, p. 100]

- "Independent of the user's intention, the cyclic definition first does not seem to do any harm within the network. Considering the classification process, however, it becomes obvious that the subsumption relation between both concepts cannot be determined, the classifier will go astray." [von Luck et al., 1987, p. 69]

There are two reasons for not following this lead [Nebel, 1989b]. First, terminological cycles can be useful. Some terms can be introduced only by using a terminological cycle. Second, when we envision a system which views a terminological knowledge base as an abstract object which has to be changed, a point of view we will take in Chap. 7, it would be rather arbitrary to permit only operations which do not result in terminological cycles. In fact, it would be quite difficult to express such a restriction in an abstract specification and to explain it to a user.

In the next section, we will analyze why terminological cycles could be useful and what kind of intuitive semantics is implied. These ideas will then be used in Sect. 5.2 to judge how much a formal semantics can capture.

As it turns out, the style of semantics introduced in Chap. 3 – which will be called *descriptive semantics* – seems to come closest to the intuitive understanding of terminological cycles. Therefore, we will adopt this style of semantics and analyze the formal meaning of terminological cycles in Sect. 5.3 using the descriptive semantics. Finally, in Sect. 5.4, we will discuss how to extend the basic inference algorithms described in Chap. 4.

5.1 The Intuitions Behind Terminological Cycles

Basically, there are two kinds of terminological cycles – one which is obviously meaningful and another one which violates the requirement that concept hierarchies should not contain cycles. The latter kind of terminological cycles is exemplified by Fig. 5.1.

Human	$\dot{\leq}$	Anything
Man	$\dot{=}$	(and Human Male-human)
Male-human	$\dot{=}$	(and Human Man)

Fig. 5.1. Circular Definition of Man and Male-human

Man is introduced by using Male-human as a component in an "and" expression, suggesting that Man is a specialization of Male-Human. In turn, Male-human is introduced by using Man as a component in an "and" expression, suggesting that Male-Human is a specialization of Man. This is obviously a modeling-error.

We might simply prohibit the use of such concept introductions. However, if we view a terminological knowledge base as an abstract object on which some modification operations can be carried out, we have to take special care to detect such situations and reject operations intended to introduce cycles. This makes the specification of such a system complicated and clumsy. Therefore, if the semantics of the representation language could give us a sensible answer as to what such "definitions" could possibly mean, this would be much more elegant.

Besides the meaningless kind of cycles, there are cycles which are obviously meaningful and which often appear when modeling a domain. What kind of intuition is implied by these cycles will be the subject of the next subsections.

5.1.1 Recursively Defined Finite Object Structures

Usually, if we define something, we do not refer to the term which is to be defined. One exception is a *recursive* definition. In recursive definitions, the term defined is used in the definition, informally speaking, with the hope that any time the definition is applied, the objects denoted get simpler until we reach a final state which does not require further application of the definition. For example, a binary tree can be defined elegantly in this way. Using $\mathcal{TF}$, we might be tempted to describe a binary tree as in Fig. 5.2.

branch $\overset{.}{\leq}$ anyrelation
Tree $\overset{.}{\leq}$ (all branch Tree)
Binary-tree $\overset{.}{=}$ (and Tree (atmost 2 branch) (all branch Binary-tree))

Fig. 5.2. Recursive Definition of Binary-tree

This concept definition looks perfectly reasonable and has a clear intuitive semantics. Apparently, something like binary trees are denoted by the concept definition. Object structures which could be part of the extension of Binary-tree are displayed in Fig. 5.3.

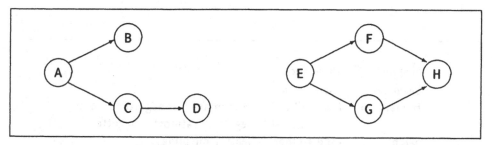

Fig. 5.3. Some Object Structures Satisfying the Definition of Binary-tree

Let us assume that all circles in Fig. 5.3 are Tree objects and that the arrows represent branch relationships between those objects. Then we can infer that objects B and D are Binary-trees since they do not have any role-fillers. For this reason, C and thus A are Binary-trees, as well. By the same line of reasoning, we can conclude that E, F, G, and H are Binary-trees. Thus, our definition does not denote what we intended but something similar, namely, directed acyclic graphs (DAGs) with degree two. Note, however, that this result depends on the assumption that E, F, and G are Trees, but because Tree is a primitive concept, we are not forced to assume that. This means that if the concept Tree indeed denotes only trees, then Binary-tree denotes only trees with degree two. In any case, in this example, we are aiming for recursively defined, noncyclic, finite object structures.

5.1.2 Infinite Object Structures

There are, of course, other situations where one would like to refer back to the term one is defining but which cannot be categorized as describing recursively defined finite structures. In order to motivate such definitions, let us consider Fig. 5.4.

There are two things in this terminology which appear to be unnatural. First, the value restriction on the offspring role is set in the definition of Parent, in spite of the fact that it "belongs" to Human. Stating it the other way around, is it conceivable that there is a Human who has a Non-human offspring? And if so,

```
offspring  ≤·  anyrelation
Human      ≤   Anything
Parent     ≐   (and Human (atleast 1 offspring) (all offspring Human))
```

Fig. 5.4. Humans and Parents

would that amount to excluding her or him from the class of **Parents**? Second, it seems to be impossible to state that **Humans** have exactly two **begetters** which are **Humans**. In order to account for this – and ignoring any of the interesting science fiction literature on this subject – we may define **Human** and **Parents** as in Fig. 5.5.

```
offspring  ≤·  anyrelation
begetter   ≤·  anyrelation
Human      ≐   (and (all offspring Human) (all begetter Human)
                    (atleast 2 begetter) (atmost 2 begetter))
parent     ≐   (and Human (atleast 1 offspring))
```

Fig. 5.5. Definition of Human and Parent Using Cycles

In this terminology, I have included not only the necessary condition that offsprings of **Humans** are **Humans** but have also added another necessary condition, namely, that a **Human** must have two **begetters** who are themselves **Humans**. This kind of concept introduction might raise the question of the origin of human beings. Because of space limitations, however, we will not discuss this subject further. For a common sense view of the world, at least, the definition seems reasonable. I have even dared to go one step further: I think there is reason to believe that the conditions on **Human** are sufficient! This sounds a little strange at first but can be defended by the argument that an entity can be recognized as a **Human** when the entity has two **begetters** which are known to be **Humans**.

Obviously, this time we used the circular concept introduction to denote something different than in the last example. In Fig. 5.5 we have an infinite structure in mind – an infinite chain connected by the **begetter** and **offspring** relationships as shown in Fig. 5.6 (the **begetter** relationship is depicted by a solid arrow, the **offspring** relationship by a dashed one). However, as in the **Binary-tree** examples, there are structures possible which satisfy the structural conditions in the definition but which are not intended. For instance, there may be objects which are not offsprings of their **begetters**. Even worse, one could think of objects which are their own **begetters**. Such strange semantic structures could be eliminated only with a more powerful terminological language.

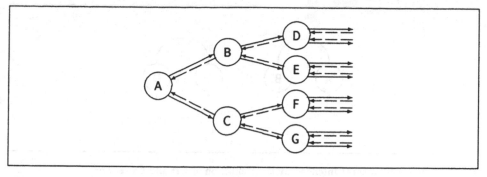

Fig. 5.6. Object Structures Intended by the Definition of Human

5.1.3 Circular Object Structures

A third kind of circular concept introductions stresses the idea that it may be impossible to define a concept by referring to already defined terms, but possible to define two concepts by referring each to the other. In other words, we are aiming at describing cyclic object structures.

sub-part	$\dot{\leq}$	anyrelation
engine-part	$\dot{\leq}$	sub-part
is-part-of	$\dot{\leq}$	anyrelation
is-engine-part-of	$\dot{\leq}$	is-part-of
Vehicle	$\dot{\leq}$	Anything
Engine	$\dot{\leq}$	Anything
Car	$\doteq$	(and Vehicle
		(all engine-part Car-engine)
		(atleast 1 engine-part))
Car-engine	$\doteq$	(and Engine
		(all is-engine-part-of Car)
		(atleast 1 is-engine-part-of))

Fig. 5.7. Circular Definition of Car and Car-engine

This idea is exemplified in Fig. 5.7 by the introductions of Car and Car-engine. The intended object structures are depicted in Fig. 5.8. Note, however, that object structures are conceivable which do not follow this pattern, e.g. infinite chains of Car objects and Car-engine objects connected by the appropriate relationships.

I know that if I really insisted that this example is reasonable and has to be part of any knowledge engineer's basic skills in modeling terminological knowledge, then I probably would loose some credibility. Therefore, I will defend this kind of terminological modeling only with a pragmatic argument.

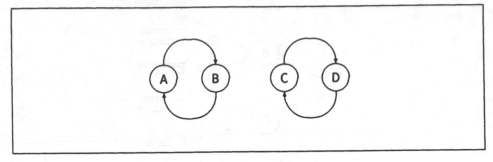

Fig. 5.8. Object Structures Intended by the Definition of Car and Car-engine

Although concept introductions such as those in Fig. 5.7 are not really "well-founded," they can be exploited by the realization process (as described in Sect. 4.5.2). Thus, in some sense such cycles convey meaning. For instance, if it is known that A is a Car and a role filler of the engine-part role for A is B, then we can conclude that B must be a Car-engine. Obviously, this game also works the other way around. Thus, this kind of cycle permits a special and interesting mode of hybrid reasoning.

5.1.4 Primitiveness and Instance Recognition

One may argue that introducing all the concepts in the last three subsections *primitively* would be in some sense "cleaner" because some sort of "base" for the definition is provided. However, even if we insisted on introducing all the above concepts as primitive concepts, the cycles would not vanish. We would still have to explain what they mean and how a knowledge representation system should handle them. And, in this context, it appears to be arbitrary to restrict an explanation to primitive concepts.

Furthermore, with defined concepts, instance recognition in the realization process is a little bit more powerful. For example, the introduction of Human in Fig. 5.5 as a defined concept allows us to recognize any entity with only Human offsprings and with two begetters who are Humans as an instance of Human. This obvious inference would not be sanctioned if Human were a primitive concept. Finally, I believe that a *sufficient* condition for a Human is that their begetters are Humans.

Two things, however, have to be investigated in this context. Are we really getting only sensible inferences, i.e., are unexpected, counter-intuitive conclusions excluded? Before we can answer this question, we have to explain what the (formal) semantics of such terms are. Next, knowing what can be derived and implementing the inferences are two different things. Therefore, the second problem we are faced with is: What are the algorithms for implementing the semantics correctly? All these problems will be investigated in the following sections.

5.2 Semantics of Terminological Cycles

As already pointed out in Sect. 3.2.2, the *constructive semantics* introduced by Theorem 3.2 gives up on terminological cycles because the "level" function on terms is not well-defined. This means that we cannot extend a primitive assignment to a unique extension function w.r.t. the terminology.

For example, if we try to construct an extension for the term Binary-tree in Fig. 5.2, we get the following defining expression for $\mathcal{E}$ at the point Binary-tree:

$$\mathcal{E}[\text{Binary-tree}] = \mathcal{P}[\overline{\text{Tree}}] \cap \tag{5.1}$$
$$\{x \in \mathcal{D} \mid \|\{y \in \mathcal{D} \mid \langle x, y \rangle \in \mathcal{P}[\overline{\text{branch}}]\}\| \leq 2\} \cap$$
$$\{x \in \mathcal{D} \mid \forall y : \langle x, y \rangle \in \mathcal{P}[\overline{\text{branch}}] \Rightarrow y \in \mathcal{E}[\text{Binary-tree}]\}$$

In order to determine a value for $\mathcal{E}[\text{Binary-tree}]$, we could choose different methods. One way would be to keep inserting the right hand expression for the term $\mathcal{E}[\text{Binary-tree}]$ into the right hand side until we are dead – perhaps giving our children directions how to proceed. A more promising way out would be to view the definition of the extension as an equation we have to solve. However, can we be sure that there is always a solution? Furthermore, what should we do if there is more than one solution?

Basically, there are two ways out of this dilemma. Either we accept all solutions as valid semantic structures, i.e., we adopt the view inherent in the nonconstructive definition of semantic structures in Def. 3.12, or we select a particular semantic structure. The latter approach can be realized by employing some sort of *fixed point semantics*, as is done in the semantics for programming languages [Stoy, 1977]. The main idea behind such an approach is that we view definitions as above as an attempt to solve the following equation:

$$x = f(x) \tag{5.2}$$

This means we are interested in points where the function f maps the argument to itself – the *fixed points* of f. In programming language semantics, we are usually interested in the *least fixed point* because in the space of functions the least fixed point is the partial function giving results for terminating computations and being undefined for endless computations. In our case, the least fixed point amounts to something similar. It is the least semantic structure w.r.t. a given primitive assignment $\mathcal{P}$, i.e., a subset of all possible semantic structures w.r.t. $\mathcal{P}$.

Applied to our example (5.1), we would look for the least fixed point of $f_{\text{Binary-tree}}$, if this function is defined as:

$$f_{\text{Binary-tree}} : 2^{\mathcal{D}} \rightarrow 2^{\mathcal{D}}$$
$$f_{\text{Binary-tree}}(X) \mapsto \mathcal{P}[\overline{\text{Tree}}] \cap$$
$$\{x \in \mathcal{D} \mid \|\{y \in \mathcal{D} \mid \langle x, y \rangle \in \mathcal{P}[\overline{\text{branch}}]\}\| \leq 2\} \cap$$
$$\{x \in \mathcal{D} \mid \forall y : \langle x, y \rangle \in \mathcal{P}[\overline{\text{branch}}] \Rightarrow y \in X\}$$

Assuming that the least fixed point always exists and that the function *fix* is a
function yielding the least fixed points of functions, then the extension of Binary-
tree could be defined as:

$$\mathcal{E}[\text{Binary-tree}] \stackrel{\text{def}}{=} \text{fix}(f_{\text{Binary-tree}}) \qquad (5.3)$$

5.2.1 Lattices and Fixed Points

In order to apply the technique sketched above, we need some prerequisites. We
have to make sure that a least fixed point exists, and we should have an idea what
it looks like. For these reasons, let us briefly recall some basic facts about the
theory of fixed points (leaving out any proofs). For a more complete treatment,
the reader is referred to [Stoy, 1977, Chap. 6], for instance.

Assuming familiarity with the notions of *partial orderings* (we will denote by
$\sqsubseteq$), *lower* and *upper bounds* (written as $a \sqsubseteq X$ and $X \sqsubseteq a$), *greatest lower* and
least upper bounds (written as $\sqcap X$ and $\sqcup X$), let us recall what we mean by a
lattice:

Definition 5.1 (Lattice) *A partially ordered set D is a lattice iff for any finite,
nonempty set $X \subseteq D$:*
$$\sqcap X \in D \quad and \quad \sqcup X \in D$$

Notice that the definition of lattice does not say that *every* subset must have
a greatest lower bound and a least upper bound. Nothing has been said about
empty and infinite sets so far.

Definition 5.2 (Complete Lattice) *A lattice D is a complete lattice iff every
subset of D has a greatest lower bound and a least upper bound.*

Actually, as can be shown, it suffices to have either least upper bounds or
greatest lower bounds. The other direction can be derived easily. Moreover, the
definition of complete lattices implies that there is a greatest and a least element
in D. The greatest element, written $\top$ (pronounced *top*) is equal to $\sqcup D$ and
$\sqcap \emptyset$. The least element $\bot$ (pronounced *bottom*) is equal to $\sqcap D$ and $\sqcup \emptyset$.

Now let us turn to functions on lattices specifying necessary and sufficient
conditions for the existence of least fixed points.

Definition 5.3 (Monotonic Function) *Let D and D' be two partially ordered
set. Then the function $f: D \to D'$ is monotonic iff*

$$\forall a, b \in D : a \sqsubseteq b \Rightarrow f(a) \sqsubseteq f(b)$$

Although monotonicity on complete lattices is enough to guarantee the existence of a least fixed point, as we will see below in Theorem 5.1, it does not
suffice to derive an explicit formula describing it. There are additional conditions
required for this purpose, namely, that the function is *continuous*. To define this
notion, we first have to say what we mean by a *directed set*.

Definition 5.4 (Directed Set) *A set X is directed iff every finite subset of X has an upper bound in X, i.e.*

$$\forall S \subseteq X, S \text{ finite} : \exists x \in X : S \sqsubseteq x$$

Definition 5.5 (Continuous Function) *Let D and D' be two complete lattices. Then a function $f \colon D \to D'$ is continuous iff for all directed sets $X \subseteq D$*

$$f(\bigsqcup X) = \bigsqcup \{f(x) \mid x \in X\}$$

With all these definitions, we can finally specify when a fixed point exists and what it looks like, following [Tarski, 1955].

Theorem 5.1 *Let D be a complete lattice, and let f be a monotonic function from D to D; then*

1. *f has at least one fixed point in D;*

2. *the set of fixed points of f is a complete lattice;*

3. *if f is continuous, then its least fixed point $\mathrm{fix}(f)$ is:*

$$\mathrm{fix}(f) = \bigsqcup_{i=0}^{\infty} f^i(\bot)$$

5.2.2 Fixed Point Semantics

Using Theorem 5.1, we could now try to determine the least fixed point of $f_{\text{Binary-tree}}$. However, this procedure of defining the extension function $\mathcal{E}$ for particular points is not a general solution. Terminological cycles can involve more than one concept, as the concepts Car and Car-engine in Fig. 5.7 demonstrate. This means we have to determine the least fixed point for a system of functional equations.

In order to start this adventure, let us introduce the notion of a *valuation function* $\mathcal{V}$. By that we mean any function from concepts to subsets of a domain $\mathcal{D}$ and from roles to subsets of $\mathcal{D} \times \mathcal{D}$, i.e.

$$\mathcal{V} \colon \begin{cases} \mathcal{NTF}_C & \to \quad 2^{\mathcal{D}} \\ \mathcal{NTF}_R & \to \quad 2^{\mathcal{D} \times \mathcal{D}} \end{cases}$$

The set of all such valuation functions will be denoted by Υ.

Next, we will define a *completion function* Γ which takes a valuation $\mathcal{V}$ and computes a new valuation $\mathcal{V}'$ based on a given primitive assignment. The value for each point of $\mathcal{V}'$ is determined by applying the equations in Def. 3.11 and 3.12.

Definition 5.6 (Completion Function) *Let $\mathcal{T}$, $\mathcal{T}_N$, $\mathcal{D}$, and $\mathcal{P}$ be defined as in Sect. 3.2.4. Then the completion function Γ is a mapping from valuations to* *valuations, mapping $\mathcal{V}$ to $\mathcal{V}'$ using the following rules:*

$$\mathcal{V}'[a] \overset{\text{def}}{=} \mathcal{V}[t] \ if \ (a \doteq t) \in \mathcal{T}_N \tag{5.4}$$

$$\mathcal{V}'[a] \overset{\text{def}}{=} \mathcal{P}[a] \ if \ a \in \mathcal{N} \tag{5.5}$$

$$\mathcal{V}'[(a\text{-not } c)] \overset{\text{def}}{=} \mathcal{D} \setminus \mathcal{P}[c] \tag{5.6}$$

$$\mathcal{V}'[(\text{and } c_1 \ldots c_n)] \overset{\text{def}}{=} \bigcap_{i=1}^{n} \mathcal{V}[c_i] \tag{5.7}$$

$$\mathcal{V}'[(\text{all } r \ c)] \overset{\text{def}}{=} \{x \in \mathcal{D} | \ \forall y : \langle x, y \rangle \in \mathcal{V}[r] \Rightarrow y \in \mathcal{V}[c]\} \tag{5.8}$$

$$\mathcal{V}'[(\text{atleast } n \ r)] \overset{\text{def}}{=} \{x \in \mathcal{D} | \ \|\{y \in \mathcal{D} | \langle x, y \rangle \in \mathcal{V}[r]\}\| \geq n\} \tag{5.9}$$

$$\mathcal{V}'[(\text{atmost } n \ r)] \overset{\text{def}}{=} \{x \in \mathcal{D} | \ \|\{y \in \mathcal{D} | \langle x, y \rangle \in \mathcal{V}[r]\}\| \leq n\} \tag{5.10}$$

$$\mathcal{V}'[(\text{androle } r_1 \ldots r_n)] \overset{\text{def}}{=} \bigcap_{i=1}^{n} \mathcal{V}[r_i] \tag{5.11}$$

A fixed point of Γ is then a valuation function $\mathcal{V}$ such that $\mathcal{V} = \Gamma(\mathcal{V})$, i.e., applying the equations in Def. 5.6 does not change anything in the valuation. Interpreting such "stable" valuations as extension functions, we see that the system of equations generated by a terminology is satisfied. The least such fixed point w.r.t. a given primitive assignment would then be an extension function which is included in all other possible extension functions w.r.t. to this primitive assignment. We have to make sure, however, that the least fixed point always exists.

First of all, it should be evident that Υ forms a complete lattice if we define $\sqsubseteq$ in the following way:

$$\mathcal{V} \sqsubseteq \mathcal{V}' \overset{\text{def}}{\Leftrightarrow} \forall x \in \mathcal{NTF}_T : \mathcal{V}[x] \subseteq \mathcal{V}'[x] \tag{5.12}$$

Set intersection and set union on corresponding values are the greatest lower bounds and least upper bounds. The bottom element is the valuation yielding the empty set for all arguments, and the top element is the valuation returning the entire domain $\mathcal{D}$ for every concept and $\mathcal{D} \times \mathcal{D}$ for every role. Thus, one prerequisite is met. Γ is a function on complete lattices.

Unfortunately, Γ is not monotonic. In order to demonstrate this, let us assume the terminology of Fig. 5.2. Furthermore, we choose the following values for $\mathcal{D}$ and $\mathcal{P}$:

$$\mathcal{D} = \{a, b, c, d\}$$
$$\mathcal{P}[\overline{\text{branch}}] = \{\langle a, b \rangle, \langle a, c \rangle, \langle a, d \rangle\}$$

Now assume two valuations $\mathcal{V}$ and $\mathcal{V}'$ with all values being $\emptyset$, except:

$$\mathcal{V}[(\text{atmost } 2 \ \overline{\text{branch}})] = \{a, b, c, d\}$$
$$\mathcal{V}[\overline{\text{branch}}] = \{\langle a, b \rangle, \langle a, c \rangle\}$$
$$\mathcal{V}'[(\text{atmost } 2 \ \overline{\text{branch}})] = \{a, b, c, d\}$$
$$\mathcal{V}'[\overline{\text{branch}}] = \{\langle a, b \rangle, \langle a, c \rangle, \langle a, d \rangle\}$$

Thus, we have $\mathcal{V} \sqsubseteq \mathcal{V}'$. As can be seen easily, we also have $\Gamma(\mathcal{V}) \not\sqsubseteq \Gamma(\mathcal{V}')$. The reason is that by rule (5.10) in Def. 5.6, the object a is excluded from $\Gamma(\mathcal{V}')[(\text{atmost } 2 \ \overline{\text{branch}})]$ while it can stay in $\Gamma(\mathcal{V})[(\text{atmost } 2 \ \overline{\text{branch}})]$. In general, a new role-relationship can invalidate the membership of an object in a concept valuation. Using this observation, we can easily construct a terminology such that Γ does not have a least fixed point (by employing circular role introductions).

Instead of giving up at this point, let us reconsider Def. 5.6. It is evident that valuations for roles are independent from valuations for concepts. Thus, Γ can determine new valuations for roles even if rules (5.6)–(5.10) are ignored. Moreover, the remaining rules lead to a monotonic behavior of Γ. Therefore, in order to get monotonic functions, we may choose the solution of first determining the least fixed point of a role completion function Γ_R and then using that to determine the least fixed point of a concept completion function Γ_C relative to the least fixed point of Γ_R. This still has the intuitive appeal that we get only least extensions of roles and least extensions of concepts relative to the least role extension. However, this demonstrates that we are in trouble if role extensions depend on concept extensions, as would be the case with the "range" operator. If a terminological cycle involves a role and a concept, then the two-step determination of least fixed points will not work.

For this purpose, let us split the valuation function into two parts, a concept valuation $\mathcal{V}_R$ and a role valuation $\mathcal{V}_C$ with

$$\mathcal{V}_R : \mathcal{NTF}_R \ \rightarrow \ \mathcal{D} \times \mathcal{D}$$
$$\mathcal{V}_C : \mathcal{NTF}_C \ \rightarrow \ \mathcal{D}$$
$$\mathcal{V} \ = \ \mathcal{V}_R \cup \mathcal{V}_C$$

The respective sets of valuation functions are denoted by Υ_R and Υ_C, which obviously form complete lattices again. The bottom elements will be denoted by $\bot_{\Upsilon_R}$ and $\bot_{\Upsilon_C}$.

Definition 5.7 (Role and Concept Completion Functions)

Assume all sets and functions as introduced in Def. 5.6. Then the role completion function Γ_R *is a function:*

$$\Gamma_R : \Upsilon_C \rightarrow [\Upsilon_R \ \rightarrow \ \Upsilon_R]$$
$$\Gamma_R(\mathcal{V}_C)(\mathcal{V}_R) \ \mapsto \ \Gamma(\mathcal{V}_C \cup \mathcal{V}_R) \ \textit{restricted to roles}$$

Similarly, the concept completion function Γ_C is defined as:

$$\Gamma_C : \Upsilon_R \rightarrow [\Upsilon_C \ \rightarrow \ \Upsilon_C]$$
$$\Gamma_C(\mathcal{V}_R)(\mathcal{V}_C) \ \mapsto \ \Gamma(\mathcal{V}_C \cup \mathcal{V}_R) \ \textit{restricted to concepts}$$

These functions have the properties desired. $\Gamma_R(\mathcal{V}_C)$ and $\Gamma_C(\mathcal{V}_R)$ are monotonic for any fixed $\mathcal{V}_C$ and $\mathcal{V}_R$ on the respective domains Υ_R and Υ_C. Moreover, the functions are continuous if we assume that all role-filler sets are finite—which can be done without changing any relevant subsumption relationships (see Lemma 4.4).

Proof: The monotonicity of both functions can be easily verified by checking the rules in Def. 5.6.

Thus, let us prove continuity. Let us first show that $\Gamma_R(\mathcal{V}_C)$ is continuous on Υ_R for any $\mathcal{V}_C$. This means we have to show that any *directed set* $\Phi \subseteq \Upsilon_R$ satisfies the equation:

$$\Gamma_R(\mathcal{V}_C)(\bigsqcup \Phi) \;=\; \bigsqcup\{\Gamma_R(\mathcal{V}_C)(\phi)\,|\,\phi \in \Phi\} \qquad (5.13)$$

Because of monotonicity we have

$$\Gamma_R(\mathcal{V}_C)(\bigsqcup \Phi) \;\sqsupseteq\; \bigsqcup\{\Gamma_R(\mathcal{V}_C)(\phi)\,|\,\phi \in \Phi\} \qquad (5.14)$$

In order to show the other direction, let us assume the contrary, i.e.

$$\Gamma_R(\mathcal{V}_C)(\bigsqcup \Phi) \;\not\sqsubseteq\; \bigsqcup\{\Gamma_R(\mathcal{V}_C)(\phi)\,|\,\phi \in \Phi\} \qquad (5.15)$$

This means for the two role valuation functions

$$\mathcal{V}_R \;=\; \Gamma_R(\mathcal{V}_C)(\bigsqcup \Phi)$$
$$\mathcal{V}'_R \;=\; \bigsqcup\{\Gamma_R(\mathcal{V}_C)(\phi)\,|\,\phi \in \Phi\}$$

there is at least one role r such that $\langle x, y \rangle \in \mathcal{V}_R[r]$ but $\langle x, y \rangle \notin \mathcal{V}'_R[r]$. However, the reason for $\langle x, y \rangle$ being an element of $\mathcal{V}_R[r]$ is that there are a finite number of roles r_i such that $\langle x, y \rangle \in (\bigsqcup \Phi)[r_i]$ and the rules (5.4), (5.5), and (5.11). This, however, means that there is a finite subset $\{\phi_j\} \subseteq \Phi$ such that $\langle x, y \rangle \in \phi_j[r_i]$. Now, since Φ is a directed set, we know that there is an element $\phi' \in \Phi$ such that $\phi' \sqsupseteq \{\phi_j\}$, i.e., we have $\langle x, y \rangle \in \phi'[r_i]$ for all r_i. By that, however, we know that $\langle x, y \rangle \in \Gamma_R(\mathcal{V}_C)(\phi')[r]$ and thus $\langle x, y \rangle \in \mathcal{V}'_R[r]$, which is a contradiction of our assumption (5.15). Hence (5.13) holds, and $\Gamma_R(\mathcal{V}_C)$ is continuous on Υ_R for any $\mathcal{V}_C$.

Obviously, the same line of arguments can be used to show that $\Gamma_C(\mathcal{V}_R)$ is continuous on Υ_C for any fixed $\mathcal{V}_R$. ∎

Following the ideas spelled out above, we may obtain a least fixed point semantic structure of a terminology by a two-step process, as spelled out in the next definition.

Definition 5.8 (Least Fixed Point Semantic Structure) *Let $\mathcal{T}$ be a terminology, $\mathcal{T}_N$ the derived normal-form terminology, $\mathcal{D}$ a set, and $\mathcal{P}$ the primitive assignment. Then the* least fixed point extension function $\mathcal{E}_l$ *is defined as:*

$$\mathcal{E}_l \;\stackrel{\text{def}}{=}\; \text{fix}(\Gamma_R(\bot_{\Upsilon_C})) \cup \text{fix}(\Gamma_C(\text{fix}(\Gamma_R(\bot_{\Upsilon_C}))))$$

The pair $\langle \mathcal{D}, \mathcal{E}_l \rangle$ is the least fixed point semantic structure *of $\mathcal{T}$.*

The notion of *subsumption* employing a fixed point semantics is, of course, the same as before (see Def. 3.5) – except that we now refer to all *least fixed point semantic structure* of a terminology. The question of whether we carried over the intuitive appeal of the constructive semantics is answered by the following proposition.

Proposition 5.1 *For any terminology T without terminological cycles, subsumption w.r.t. constructive semantics is equivalent to subsumption w.r.t. least fixed point semantics.*

Proof: In a cycle-free terminology for any domain $\mathcal{D}$ and primitive assignment $\mathcal{P}$, there is only one fixed point for the completion function, which can be shown by induction over the depth of terminologies. Because of the similarity of the equations in Def. 3.11 and 5.6 and the definition of $\mathcal{E}_l$, we have $\mathcal{E}_l = \mathcal{E}$ for identical $\mathcal{D}$ and $\mathcal{P}$. Thus, subsumption is identical. ∎

The question remains what the fixed point semantics does to our examples presented in the last section. As the next observation shows, the concept **Binary-tree** from Sect. 5.1.1 is handled in the way expected.

Definition 5.9 (Notation: Transitive Closure of a Relation) *Let R be a binary relation. Then the* transitive closure *of R, written R^+, is the smallest relation such that*

$$\langle x, y \rangle \in R^+ \text{ iff } \langle x, y \rangle \in R \vee \exists z : \langle x, z \rangle \in R \wedge \langle z, y \rangle \in R^+$$

Observation 5.1 *Assuming a terminology as in Fig. 5.2, no least fixed point extension of* **Binary-tree** *contains objects with circular role-chains, i.e., for all objects $x \in \mathcal{E}_l[\text{Binary-tree}]$:*

$$\langle x, x \rangle \notin (\mathcal{E}_l[\text{branch}])^+$$

Proof: Assume there is an $x \in \mathcal{D}$ such that $\langle x, x \rangle \in (\mathcal{E}_l[\text{branch}])^+$. By induction over the construction of the least fixed point, x is in not in any finite approximation of the least fixed point extension **Binary-tree**. Hence, x is not in any least fixed point extension of **Binary-tree**. ∎

However, we can of course get an object structure similar to the left structure in Fig. 5.3, i.e., a directed, acyclic graph. This means we get almost the structure we expect. Furthermore, if we defined a **Ternary-tree** similar to a **Binary-tree**, except that the number in the **atmost** clause is changed to 3 and the "all" restriction is changed to **Ternary-tree**, then we would get a subsumption relationship between **Binary-tree** and **Ternary-tree**. Although this sounds satisfying, there is a big surprise when it comes to concepts like **Human**, **Car** and **Car-engine** defined in Sect. 5.1.

Observation 5.2 *Assuming a terminology as defined in Fig. 5.5, the least fixed point extension of* **Human** *is empty for any $\mathcal{D}$ and $\mathcal{P}$. The same holds for the extension of* **Car** *in the terminology of Fig. 5.7.*

Proof: Every finite approximation of the least fixed point extensions of the concepts mentioned is empty. Hence, the extensions are empty. ∎

We could take this observation either as a deep truth we would not have detected if we were not interested in terminological cycles or, taking a more

pragmatic view, as an indication that the least fixed point does not capture our
intuitive understanding of what a terminological cycle means.

In order to get around this problem, we could look for another fixed point.
Because our completion functions are monotonic on complete lattices and, therefore, the fixed points form complete lattices as well, we can, for example, consider
the *greatest* fixed point as the "right" solution. Let us denote extension functions
defined in this way by $\mathcal{E}_g$. Obviously, these fixed points share the property of
being equivalent to the semantic structures of the constructive semantics in the
non-circular case – because if there is only one fixed point, it is the least and
the greatest one. However, this semantics also leads to some counter-intuitive
results as the following observations demonstrate.

Observation 5.3 *Assuming the terminology of Fig. 5.2, under a greatest fixed
point semantics, there are semantic structures which contain objects x such that*

$$x \in \mathcal{E}_g[\text{Binary-tree}] \text{ and } \langle x, x \rangle \in (\mathcal{E}_g[\text{branch}])^+$$

Proof: Obviously, such structures can be part of a fixed point for appropriate $\mathcal{D}$
and primitive assignment. Thus, if such structures are part of some fixed points,
they are necessarily in the greatest fixed point. ∎

That means that a greatest fixed point semantics permits semantic structures
other than those considered in our intuitive analysis in Sect. 5.1.1. However, this
is not a big surprise because we intended to consider other kinds of semantic
structures in order to get at least an approximate model for Humans. While
we now get non-empty extensions for Humans, there is another surprise when
Centaurs come into play as in Fig. 5.9.

$$
\begin{array}{rcl}
\text{begetter} & \dot{\leq} & \text{anyrelation} \\
\text{Human} & \dot{=} & \text{(and (atleast 2 begetter) (atmost 2 begetter)} \\
& & \quad \text{(all begetter Human))} \\
\text{Horse} & \dot{=} & \text{(and (atleast 2 begetter) (atmost 2 begetter)} \\
& & \quad \text{(all begetter Horse))} \\
\text{Centaur} & \dot{=} & \text{(and Human Horse)}
\end{array}
$$

Fig. 5.9. Humans, Horses and Centaurs

Observation 5.4 *Assuming a terminology as in Fig. 5.9, under a greatest fixed
point semantics, the extension of* Human *is always the same as the extension of*
Horse *and thus identical to the extension of* Centaur.

Proof: Let us assume a greatest fixed point extension function $\mathcal{E}_g$ with
$\mathcal{E}_g[\text{Human}] \neq \mathcal{E}_g[\text{Horse}]$. This however means that there is another extension
function which is greater, which is a contradiction. ∎

The conclusion we can draw from these observations is that if we are to adopt a greatest fixed point semantics, we had better introduce any circular concept primitively because otherwise the extensions would be far too large. This, however, violates the intuitions we spelled out in Sect. 5.1.4 and limits the recognition capabilities.

5.2.3 Descriptive Semantics

A different way to assign semantics to a terminology is to abandon the notion of *construction*: Why did we insist on building up unique extensions for a given set $\mathcal{D}$ and a given primitive assignment $\mathcal{P}$? Getting rid of this idea, we may view terminologies as *describing* possible worlds in which we can apply the introduced terms, as we did originally (see Def. 3.12). Instead of constructing extensions by starting with a domain and a primitive assignment, we consider all those semantic structures which are *admissible* with respect to the system of set equations generated by the normal-form terminology. This means in terms of the last subsection that we consider *all* fixed points of Γ as possible extension functions. This style of semantics will be called *descriptive semantics*.

Comparing subsumption w.r.t. to descriptive semantics with subsumption w.r.t. to fixed point semantics yields the next proposition.

Proposition 5.2 *Subsumption with respect to descriptive semantics is weaker than subsumption with respect to a least or greatest fixed point semantics.*

Proof: Note first that for any domain and primitive assignment, the fixed point extension functions $\mathcal{E}_l$ and $\mathcal{E}_g$ determined by least or greatest fixed points of $\Gamma_R(\mathcal{V}_C)$ and $\Gamma_C(\mathcal{V}_R)$ are admissible extension functions in the sense of Def. 3.12. On the other hand, not all extension functions $\mathcal{E}$ in the sense of Def. 3.12 correspond to least or greatest fixed points. Thus, subsumption w.r.t. descriptive semantics implies subsumption w.r.t. fixed point semantics, but not the other way around. ∎

Turning this rather abstract characterization of the relationship between the two notions of subsumption into an example, let us reconsider the terminology from Fig. 5.9 describing Humans, Horses and Centaurs.

Observation 5.5 *Assuming a terminology as in Fig. 5.9, under a descriptive semantics, the extension of the concept Human is not necessarily the same as the extension of Horse.*

Proof: We will give an example to demonstrate that.

$$\mathcal{D} \;=\; \mathbb{R}$$
$$\mathcal{E}[\text{begetter}] \;=\; \{\langle x,y\rangle|\; \exists n \in \mathbb{N} : x = a_0 + \sum_{i=1}^{n} a_i \wedge y = x + a_{n+1} \wedge$$
$$a_0 \in \mathbb{N} \wedge (a_i = 2^{-i} \vee a_i = -2^{-i})\}$$

$$\mathcal{E}[\mathsf{Human}] = \{x \mid \exists n \in \mathbb{N} : x = 1 + \sum_{i=1}^{n} a_i \wedge (a_i = 2^{-i} \vee a_i = -2^{-i})\}$$

$$\mathcal{E}[\mathsf{Horse}] = \{x \mid \exists n \in \mathbb{N} : x = 3 + \sum_{i=1}^{n} a_i \wedge (a_i = 2^{-i} \vee a_i = -2^{-i})\}$$

Obviously, $\mathcal{E}$ is an admissible extension function in the sense of Def. 3.12 and $\mathcal{E}[\mathsf{human}] \neq \mathcal{E}[\mathsf{horse}]$. ∎

We may see this result in a positive light because it matches our intuitions spelled out in Sect. 5.1.4, or in a negative light because it shows that a **Ternary-tree** as mentioned in the last subsection *does not* subsume a **Binary-tree** in this semantics. However, turning to hybrid reasoning (as described in Sect. 4.5), we see that any object which is recognized as a **Binary-tree** by using only **branch** relation descriptions and **Tree** object descriptions will be recognized as a **Ternary-tree** as well.

5.2.4 Evaluating the Semantics

Instead of a unique answer to the question we posed in this section, namely, what terminological cycles mean if we apply formal semantics, we now have four. While all kinds of semantics agree on the meaning of cycle-free terminologies, they take different tacks when cycles are present:

1. Constructive semantics tells us nothing about terminological cycles. They are simply ill-defined.

2. Least fixed point semantics tells us that concepts which permit a "base," i.e., concepts without an "atleast" restriction, are reasonable. However, requiring that all **Humans** have two **Humans** as their **begetters** is an "empty" definition. It leads to a necessarily empty extension.

3. Greatest fixed point semantics does not insist on the non-existence of **Humans**. However, it views all structurally similar concepts, for example, **Human** and **Horse** in Fig. 5.9, as identical.

4. Descriptive semantics does not merge **Human** and **Horse** in Fig. 5.9. However, this also means that **Ternary-tree** does not subsume **Binary-tree**. For this reason, it seems that *concept names* get more significance in this kind of semantics than in the other kinds of semantics.

Therefore, the question is what kind of semantics should we believe in? Of course, it is not a question of believing but a question of convenience and intention. What inferences do we expect, and what worlds do we intend to model?

In Sect. 5.1, we spelled out the intuitions about circular concepts. As it turns out, no single style of assigning semantics matches these intuitions. Furthermore, taking each example on its own, there is no semantics which matches the intuition behind it because our terminological language is too weak. Even more expressive terminological languages such as NIKL are not powerful enough to prohibit

Binary-trees from becoming DAGs or to prohibit Humans from becoming their own begetters.

Since the question of which semantics matches the intuition cannot be answered, we may ask which kind of semantics *covers* the intuition best. The only semantics which covers our intuitions is the descriptive one – all extensions we expect *can* be extensions. However, we have to give up subsumption relationships one would expect between data-type like structures. This, however, is not a serious defect because we never intended to specify data-types and to reason with them. On the contrary, what is an essential property for formal specification in programming languages might not be adequate for knowledge representation. In knowledge representation, we do not *specify* entities but *describe* them.

While the descriptive semantics seems to be the most preferable one, there are still some deficiencies. First, it is a "loose semantics." In contrast to the constructive and the least fixed point semantics, it does not give hints about how to construct models but only characterizes them in a very abstract manner. This makes it hard to prove properties about cycles. Second, although the descriptive semantics seems to meet our intuitions about recognizing members of species (e.g. Humans), the corresponding admissible semantic structures do not reflect our intuitions. The extension of the concept Human, for instance, contains either infinitely many objects connected by an infinite chain of begetter relationships, or it is "based" on objects which are circularly connected, e.g., "Adam has two begetters, namely Eve and himself, and Eve has two begetters, namely Adam and herself".

A third argument against the descriptive semantics could be that names seem to play more significant role than in the other styles of semantics. However, names already play an important role, at least in the case of primitive concepts. Two structurally equivalent primitive concepts do not necessarily have the same extension. Circularly introduced concepts are, in a sense, similar to primitive ones – there is a subtle difference, though (see Sections 5.3.3 and 5.3.5).

Comparing the descriptive semantics with the other styles of semantics we introduced, we may recognize a weak analogy to a recent debate in the philosophy of science [Brown, 1986, p. 275]:

> A major theme of recent philosophy of science has been the rejection of the empiricist thesis that, with the exception of terms which play a purely formal role, the language of science derives its meaning from some, possibly quite indirect, correlation with experience. The alternative that has been proposed is that meaning is internal to each conceptual system, that terms derive their meaning from the role they play in a language, and that something akin to "meaning" flows from conceptual framework to experience.

If we interpret the primitive components as something like "empirical evidence" we employ to recognize entities belonging to a certain category – and there does not seem to be another intuitive interpretation – then the constructive semantics represents the "empiricist" point of view very well. Both kinds of fixed point semantics can be taken as a generalization of this view because they take structure into account – the least fixed point semantics formalizing the view of recursive definition, and the greatest fixed point semantics formalizing the notion of structural equivalence. Only the descriptive semantics admits that there is more than experience (primitive components) and structure. The application of a term to an object depends partly on *a priori* knowledge about the object which cannot be derived solely from empirical data.

5.3 Consequences of the Descriptive Semantics

While only some plausible examples of terminological cycles were analyzed above, in this section we will try to investigate them in a more principled way. This will be done by using the descriptive semantics because it seems to be the semantics which fits best.

Obviously, there are different kinds of cycles: circular role introductions, circular concept introductions using the concept components, as in the Man/Male-human example of Fig. 5.1, and circular concept introductions using value restrictions, as in the Human example of Fig. 5.5. In order to make it easier to state something about cycles, let us first introduce some notation.

Definition 5.10 (Notation: Usage Relation) *If an atomic term a_i directly uses an atomic term a_u, i.e., a_u appears on the right hand side of the introduction of a_i, we will write $a_i \hookrightarrow a_u$. If a_i uses a_u, then we write $a_i \overset{+}{\hookrightarrow} a_u$.*

5.3.1 Circular Roles

Let us start with the most meaningless and simplest case, with roles introduced circularly – which we will call *component circular roles*. First, let us define formally what we mean by that.

Definition 5.11 (Component Circular Roles) *Let T be a terminology. Then we say that a role r is* component-circular *iff $r \overset{+}{\hookrightarrow} r$ in T. A set of atomic roles $R \subseteq \mathcal{N}_R$ is a set of mutually component-circular roles iff $\forall r, r' \in R \Rightarrow r \overset{+}{\hookrightarrow} r'$.*

Because role introductions in TF are very simple – only one role name is permitted on the right hand side of a role introduction – there is not much meaning in this kind of terminological cycles. Independent of whether the roles of a set of mutually circular roles were introduced as primitive or as defined roles, they are all equivalent. Assume a set of introductions as below:

$$
\begin{array}{llll}
r_1 & \doteq & r_2 & \qquad \mathcal{E}[r_1] = \mathcal{E}[r_2] \\
r_2 & \overset{.}{\leq} & r_3 & \qquad \mathcal{E}[r_2] = \mathcal{E}[r_3] \cap \mathcal{P}[\overline{r_2}] \\
& \vdots & & \qquad\qquad \vdots \\
r_n & \doteq & r_1 & \qquad \mathcal{E}[r_n] = \mathcal{E}[r_1]
\end{array}
$$

Then we can immediately derive $\forall i, j : 1 \leq i, j \leq n \Rightarrow \mathcal{E}[r_i] = \mathcal{E}[r_j]$. Moreover, it seems plausible that we can eliminate such cycles without changing the meaning of the terminology. In order to formalize what we mean by "eliminating something without changing the meaning," let us first define what we mean by saying that one terminology is a *conservative extension* of another one.

Definition 5.12 (Conservative Extension) *Let T and T' be two terminologies and N and N' the respective sets of atomic terms and primitive components. We say T' is a conservative extension of T, written $T \subseteq T'$, iff $N \subseteq N'$ and for any D and any extension function $\mathcal{E}'$ w.r.t. T', there is an extension function $\mathcal{E}$ w.r.t. T and vice versa such that $\forall a \in N : \Rightarrow \mathcal{E}[a] = \mathcal{E}'[a]$.*

The meaning of this definition is obvious. It means that if we ignore the extensions of the extra terms in T' (probably only introduced because of technical reasons), we get identical extensions for all terms. To give an example, any normal-form terminology T_N is a conservative extension of the original terminology T. With this notion, we can say what we mean by eliminating role cycles.

Proposition 5.3 *Let T be a terminology containing circular roles. Then there is another terminology T' such that $T \subseteq T'$, and T' contains no circular roles.*

Proof: Note that the extensions of roles in one set of mutually circular roles are all the same and that the only other restriction is that they have to be subsets of the primitive assignments for primitive components mentioned. For this reason, the characteristic of the extensions is not changed by the following transformation: First, all concept introductions and role introductions for noncircular roles are copied to T'. Second, for any set of mutually circular roles R_i in T, a new role s_i is introduced in T' as "$s_i \leq$ anyrelation." Third, any role $r_{i,j}$ in R_i is introduced as "$r_{i,j} \doteq s_i$." ∎

Thus, circular role introductions do not add anything interesting to our language. We may eliminate them without affecting the rest of the terminology.

5.3.2 Component-Circular Concepts

With concept introductions, the situation seems to be more complex. We have at least two different kinds of terminological cycles – cycles occurring because an atomic concept is used as a component in an "and" expression (not inside an "all" restriction) and cycles occurring because an atomic concept is mentioned in an "all" restriction.

Definition 5.13 (Notation: Kinds of Usage) *Let T be a terminology and c_i and c_u two atomic concepts. Then we say c_i uses c_u as a direct component iff c_u appears at the right hand side of the introduction of c_i outside of the scope of any "all" expressions, written $c_i \overset{and}{\hookrightarrow} c_u$. If c_i uses c_u, and c_u appears inside of an "all" expression, we say c_i uses c_u in a value restriction, written $c_i \overset{all}{\hookrightarrow} c_u$. The relations $\overset{and+}{\hookrightarrow}$ and $\overset{all+}{\hookrightarrow}$ are the transitive closures of the above relations.*

As usual, we will start with the simple case, with cycles appearing by using an atomic concept as a component in a concept introduction.

Definition 5.14 (Component Circular Concepts) *An atomic concept c is component-circular iff $c \overset{\text{and+}}{\hookrightarrow} c$. A set of atomic concepts $C \subseteq \mathcal{N}_C$ is a set of mutually component-circular concepts iff $\forall x, y \in C \Rightarrow x \overset{\text{and+}}{\hookrightarrow} y$.*

At first sight, component-circular concepts appear to be very similar to circular roles. However, while role introductions are very simple, this is not the case with concept introductions. Concept introductions permit situations in which an atomic concept participates in more than one cycle and perhaps even in different kinds of cycles.

Let us first analyze what it means that an atomic concept participates in more than one cycle induced by the relation $\overset{\text{and}}{\hookrightarrow}$. We would have something like:

$$c \overset{\text{and}}{\hookrightarrow} c_{1,1} \quad c_{1,1} \overset{\text{and}}{\hookrightarrow} c_{1,2} \quad \cdots \quad c_{1,n_1-1} \overset{\text{and}}{\hookrightarrow} c_{1,n_1} \quad c_{1,n_1} \overset{\text{and}}{\hookrightarrow} c$$
$$c \overset{\text{and}}{\hookrightarrow} c_{2,1} \quad c_{2,1} \overset{\text{and}}{\hookrightarrow} c_{2,2} \quad \cdots \quad c_{2,n_2-1} \overset{\text{and}}{\hookrightarrow} c_{2,n_2} \quad c_{2,n_2} \overset{\text{and}}{\hookrightarrow} c$$
$$\vdots$$

Obviously, all atomic concepts above belong to one unique set of mutually component-circular concepts because for all of them we have $c_i \overset{\text{and+}}{\hookrightarrow} c_j$. Thus, multiple, overlapping cycles do not add anything new. Moreover, it does not matter whether the concepts in a set of mutually component-circular concepts participate in other kinds of terminological cycles. Component-circular concepts can be eliminated in a way similar to the way component-circular roles can.

Proposition 5.4 *Let T be a terminology containing component-circular concepts. Then there is another terminology T' such that $T \subseteq T'$, and T' contains no component-circular concepts.*

Proof Sketch: Obviously, the extensions of all atomic concepts in a set of mutually component-circular concepts have to be identical. Moreover, the extensions of these atomic concepts have to obey the restrictions spelled out by the non-component-circular parts of the concept introductions. These are the only restrictions, and thus we may apply a similar construction of a new terminology as in the proof above without changing the extension characteristics. ∎

This means component-circular concepts are as useless as circular roles are. Neither of them adds anything to the expressiveness. We can eliminate both without affecting the rest of the terminology. Therefore, we will ignore them in the following and assume that the terminologies we consider do not contain such cycles.

5.3.3 Restriction-Circular Concepts

The interesting species of terminological cycles is the one generated by using a atomic concept in a value restriction, as the examples in Sect. 5.1 demonstrate. These cycles add something to the expressive power. Obviously, they allow putting restrictions on semantic structures which cannot be expressed by cycle-free terminologies.

The first interesting problem which comes up in this context is: What does a cycle generated by combinations of the relations $\overset{\text{and}+}{\hookrightarrow}$ and $\overset{\text{all}+}{\hookrightarrow}$ amount to? In the examples of Sect. 5.2, we only analyzed cycles generated by $\overset{\text{all}+}{\hookrightarrow}$. However, there are, of course, cycles conceivable which are generated by a combination of both usage relations as, for instance, Fig. 5.10 shows.

branch	$\overset{.}{\leq}$	anyrelation
Tree	$\overset{.}{\leq}$	(all branch Tree)
3-2-tree	$\doteq$	(and Tree (atmost 3 branch) (all branch Binary-tree))
Binary-tree	$\doteq$	(and 3-2-tree (atmost 2 branch))

Fig. 5.10. General Restriction-Circular Concepts

As a matter of fact, these kinds of cycles seem to be similar to cycles created by using only the relation $\overset{\text{all}+}{\hookrightarrow}$. It seems plausible that we would be able to reduce such general cycles to cycles using only the relation $\overset{\text{all}+}{\hookrightarrow}$.

Definition 5.15 (Restriction Circular Concepts) *Let T be a terminology without component-circular concepts. Let $\overset{*}{\hookrightarrow}$ be the transitive, reflexive closure of $\hookrightarrow$. We say that the atomic concept c is a general restriction-circular concept iff $c(\overset{*}{\hookrightarrow} \circ \overset{\text{all}}{\hookrightarrow} \circ \overset{*}{\hookrightarrow})c$. We say that c is a simple restriction-circular concept iff $(c\overset{\text{all}+}{\hookrightarrow}c)$ and not $\left(c(\overset{*}{\hookrightarrow} \circ \overset{\text{and}}{\hookrightarrow} \circ \overset{*}{\hookrightarrow})c\right)$.*

Proposition 5.5 *If T is a terminology containing general restriction-circular concepts which are not simple restriction-circular, then there is another terminology T' such that $T \subseteq T'$, and T' contains only simple restriction-circular concepts.*

Proof: T' can be constructed in a stepwise manner, eliminating one $\overset{\text{and}}{\hookrightarrow}$ relationship in each step. Assume that T_i contains an atomic concept c which is general restriction-circular but not simple restriction-circular. Then there are two atomic concepts c_1 and c_2 such that $c\overset{*}{\hookrightarrow}c_1$, $c_1\overset{\text{and}}{\hookrightarrow}c_2$, and $c_2\overset{*}{\hookrightarrow}c$. A new terminology T_{i+1} can be constructed such that $T_i \subseteq T_{i+1}$ and $c_1\overset{\text{and}}{\not\hookrightarrow}c_2$ in the following way:

1. If c_2 is introduced as "$c_2 \overset{.}{\leq} def_{c_2}$" in T_i, then a new atomic concept c_{p_2} is introduced in T_{i+1} as "$c_{p_2} \overset{.}{\leq}$ Anything." C_2 is introduced as "$c_2 \doteq$ (and def_{c_2} c_{p_2})." This operation evidently does not affect the characteristics of the extensions.

2. Thus, we may assume that c_2 is a defined concept. Changing the introduction of c_1 by replacing each occurrence of c_2 in c_1 by the definition of c_2 obviously does not change the characteristics of the extensions.

This transformation does not affect the extensions and eliminates one relationship of the $\overset{\text{and}}{\hookleftarrow}$ relation. Furthermore, since we assumed that there are no component-circular concepts, the transformations will lead to the result desired after a finite number of steps. ∎

5.3.4 Semantic and Syntactic Cycles

If we could now prove that simple restriction-circular concepts could be eliminated, as well, terminological cycles would no longer be a problem. However, this attempt is apparently doomed to failure. Otherwise we would not have had so many problems with Binary-trees and Humans in Sect. 5.2.

In order to shed more light on such concepts, let us analyze their semantic properties. If we have $c \overset{\text{all}+}{\hookrightarrow} c$, then we can identify at least one chain of atomic concepts such that $c_0 \overset{\text{all}}{\hookrightarrow} c_1 \overset{\text{all}}{\hookrightarrow} \ldots c_n$ with $c = c_0 = c_n$.[1] Corresponding to this concept chain, a *role chain* $r_1, r_2, \ldots, r_m$ can be found such that the concepts c_i are used in "all" restrictions[2] of these roles in the introductions of the concepts c_{i-1}. We will call the concept c *restriction-circular over* $r_1, r_2, \ldots, r_m$ (and perhaps over other role chains as well).

The evident property of any element x in the extension of c is that if we follow the role chain, we come to another object y which is in the extension of c as well – or there is no such role-chain in the semantic structure. This, however, does not suffice to characterize restriction-circular concepts. There are also some non-circular concepts having this property, e.g. a concept with an (atmost 0 r_1) restriction. What makes restriction-circular concepts special is that there are some semantic structures where we can follow the role chain arbitrarily often and still find objects which belong to the concept extension of c. This alone also does not constitute a distinguishing semantic criterion for restriction-circular concepts because we can have similar extensions in cycle-free terminologies – by accident. However, taking both properties simultaneously describes very well what is special about restriction-circular concepts.

Definition 5.16 (Notation: Iterated Composition) *Let R be a relation $R \subseteq D \times D$. Then by R^n we mean the composition of R with itself n times, i.e.,*

$$R^n \overset{\text{def}}{=} \underbrace{R \circ \ldots \circ R}_{n}$$

Definition 5.17 (Semantically Circular Concepts) *Let $\mathcal{T}$ be a terminology. Then the atomic concept c is* semantically circular over the role chain

---

[1] There can be more than one such chain, of course.

[2] Note that "all" restrictions can be nested. In this case, we will take all nested roles in the obvious order.

$r_1, \ldots, r_m$ *iff for any semantic structure* $\langle \mathcal{D}, \mathcal{E} \rangle$ *it holds that*

$$\forall\, x, y : x \in \mathcal{E}[c] \wedge \langle x, y \rangle \in (\mathcal{E}[r_1] \circ \ldots \circ \mathcal{E}[r_m]) \Rightarrow y \in \mathcal{E}[c]$$

and for any $n \in \mathbb{N}$ *there are* $\mathcal{D}$ *and* $\mathcal{E}$ *such that*

$$\exists\, x, y : x \in \mathcal{E}[c] \wedge \langle x, y \rangle \in (\mathcal{E}[r_1] \circ \ldots \circ \mathcal{E}[r_m])^n$$

Although we started off to find a unique property of restriction-circular concepts, it turns out that the notions of semantically circular and restriction-circular do not coincide. We may have restriction-circular concepts which are not semantically circular and vice versa. For example, the concepts D and E are not restriction circular, but they are semantically circular – because they *use* restriction-circular concepts. Conversely, the concept A in Fig. 5.11 is restriction-circular, but not semantically circular. Although from a syntactic point of view there is a circularity, it does not lead to cycles in the semantic structure because the role r – the role A is restriction-circular over – cannot have any role-fillers.

$$A \doteq (\text{and (all } r \text{ A) (atmost 0 } r))$$

$$
\begin{aligned}
B &\doteq (\text{all } r \text{ B}) \\
C &\doteq (\text{all } r \text{ C}) \\
D &\doteq (\text{and B C}) \\
E &\doteq (\text{all } r \text{ B})
\end{aligned}
$$

Fig. 5.11. Syntactic and Semantic Cycles

The conditions under which a restriction-circular concept is not semantically circular or vice versa can, of course, be qualified. The first case occurs when a concept is restriction-circular over a role chain $r_1, \ldots, r_m$ but is *length-restricted* over this role chain, as in the case of concept A in Fig. 5.11.

Definition 5.18 (Length-Restricted Concepts) *Let* $\mathcal{T}$ *be a terminology. A concept c is* length restricted *over a role chain* $r_1, \ldots, r_m$ *iff there exists some* $n \in \mathbb{N}$ *such that for any domain* $\mathcal{D}$ *and any extension function* $\mathcal{E}$:

$$\neg(\exists\, x, y : x \in \mathcal{E}[c] \wedge \langle x, y \rangle \in (\mathcal{E}[r_1] \circ \ldots \circ \mathcal{E}[r_m])^n)$$

Proposition 5.6 *Any restriction-circular concept (over role chains R_i) which is not length-restricted (over all R_i) is a semantically circular concept. Conversely, any semantically circular concept is either a restriction-circular concept or uses such a concept.*

Proof: The first proposition follows directly from the definitions. The second proposition is also evident because an atomic concept c which is neither restriction-circular nor uses such a concept cannot be semantically circular. ∎

Although this characterizes cycles completely from a semantic and syntactic point of view in $\mathcal{TF}$, the question is how much expressivity we added to the language. Apparently, we lost the property that concepts say something only about a finite, local context – a property we used in order to prove that subsumption in $\mathcal{TF}$ is decidable. With cycles we can have extensions such that infinitely many domain objects are relevant for the decision of whether a given object is in the extension of a concept or not. Hence, it may be the case that if cycles are added to the language, subsumption is not longer decidable. However, as we will see in the next subsection, we can always find semantic structures with a finite domain which are "indistinguishable" from infinite semantic structures with respect to given concepts.

5.3.5 Finite, Cyclic Semantic Structures

Although restriction-circular concepts may have infinite extensions such that infinitely many objects are relevant for the determination of whether an object is in the extension of a concept, it is nevertheless possible to create a finite semantic structure such that the extension of the concept is nonempty. The key idea in this construction is based on the fact that for the determination of whether an object is part of a concept extension it does not make a difference whether there is an infinite chain of objects or an assertional cycle. Assuming, for instance, a simple restriction-circular concept, such as

$$C \doteq (\text{and } (\text{all } r \text{ } C) \text{ } (\text{atleast } 1 \text{ } r))$$

then an object x_0 will be in $\mathcal{E}[C]$ if there is an infinite chain

$$\langle x_0, x_1 \rangle, \langle x_1, x_2 \rangle, \ldots \langle x_i, x_{i+1} \rangle, \ldots$$

with $x_j \in \mathcal{E}[C]$ and $\langle x_j, x_{j+1} \rangle \in \mathcal{E}[r]$. However, if we simply have $x_0 \in \mathcal{E}[C]$ and $\langle x_0, x_0 \rangle \in \mathcal{E}[r]$, then $\mathcal{E}$ would be an admissible extension function, and $\mathcal{E}[C]$ is nonempty, as well. In a sense, the definition of C does not distinguish between these two extensions. Based on this idea, we will show that we can always find a finite admissible semantic structure of a terminology – containing a finite cyclic object structure – such that the extension of a given concept is nonempty.

In order to keep things simple, this claim will be proven first for a sublanguage of $\mathcal{TF}$ which does not contain role introductions – a language we will call $\mathcal{TF}^-$. This means every role in $\mathcal{TF}^-$ is a primitive subrole of **anyrelation**, and all role extensions are independent of each other.

Lemma 5.1 *Let $\mathcal{T}$ be a terminology using $\mathcal{TF}^-$ syntax and assume that $\mathcal{T}$ contains terminological cycles. Then, for any concept c which is not incoherent, there is an admissible semantic structure $\langle \mathcal{D}, \mathcal{E} \rangle$ of $\mathcal{T}$ such that $\mathcal{E}[c] \neq \emptyset$ and $\mathcal{D}$ is finite and bounded in size by the structure of the terminology.*

Proof: Let $\mathcal{T}_N$ be the normal-form terminology corresponding to $\mathcal{T}$, and let $\mathcal{T}'$ be a conservative extension of $\mathcal{T}_N$ such that all value restrictions are atomic concepts and there are no component-circular concepts.

If c is not restriction-circular and does not use such a concept, then the proof is obvious. In the case when c is restriction-circular or uses such a concept, apply the following extension-preserving *expansion transformation* to c:

1. Replace all atomic concepts not appearing in "all" expressions by their respective normal-form definitions as long as there are atomic concepts which are not embedded in "all" expressions and apply NORM to the resulting expression, which leads to an expression of the form

$$(\text{and } p_1 \ldots p_l \, (\text{all } r_1 \, (\text{and } c_{1,1} \ldots c_{1,m_1})) \ldots (\text{all } r_n \ldots))$$

   with p_i positive or negated primitive concept components and $c_{j,k}$ atomic concepts.

2. Check each value restriction in the resulting expression whether it appeared previously in the expansion process (ignoring the order in the "and" expression). If this is the case, do not expand this expression further.

3. Otherwise remember this value restriction, and apply the expansion process recursively to it.

Since we have only a finite number of finite cycles in T', this process always terminates. The resulting concept, which is equivalent to c in T', will be denoted by c_{exp}. All nonexpanded value restrictions in c_{exp} will be called *terminal value restrictions,*, and the atomic concepts used in terminal value restrictions will be called *t-concepts*. Furthermore, we will refer to chains of roles formed by immediately embedded "all" expressions, starting at the top-level and extending to terminal value restrictions, as *t-chains*. Furthermore, we will say that a role-chain $r_{1,1} \ldots r_{1,k}$ is a *proper prefix* of a role-chain $r_{2,1} \ldots r_{2,l}$ iff $k < l$ and $r_{1,i} = r_{2,i}$, for all $1 \leq i \leq k$.

Assuming that the t-concepts are new primitive concept components, the relevant breadth and size of the expanded concept is computed, $b = \text{rbreadth}(c_{exp})$ and $s = \text{rsize}(c_{exp})$, which evidently depends on the structure of the terminology. In order to prove the lemma, let us assume that there are only admissible semantic structures of T' with domains larger than $s \times b$ such that the extension of c is nonempty. Choose one such semantic structure $\langle \mathcal{D}, \mathcal{E} \rangle$ of T' with a corresponding primitive assignment $\mathcal{P}$ and an element d such that $d \in \mathcal{E}[c]$, and thus $d \in \mathcal{E}[c_{exp}]$.

Extend $\mathcal{P}$ to $\mathcal{P}^*$ by using the values from $\mathcal{E}$ for the t-concepts, generate a new extension function $\mathcal{E}^*$ defined on expressions containing only primitive components and t-concepts, and apply Lemma 4.5 to identify a semantic structure $\langle \mathcal{D}', \mathcal{E}' \rangle$ of size s (or smaller) with a generating primitive assignment $\mathcal{P}'$ such that $d \in \mathcal{E}'[c_{exp}]$. Remember, that the semantic structure corresponds to a tree. Now copy $\langle \mathcal{D}', \mathcal{E}' \rangle$ and $\mathcal{P}'$ b times, naming the copies $\mathcal{E}^i$, $x^i \in \mathcal{D}^i$, and $\mathcal{P}^i$, $1 \leq i \leq b$, and create a new semantic structure by taking the disjoint union of these copies, i.e.,

$$\langle \mathcal{D}'', \mathcal{E}'' \rangle \stackrel{\text{def}}{=} \biguplus_{i=1}^{b} \langle \mathcal{D}^i, \mathcal{E}^i \rangle$$

for which we have $d^i \in \mathcal{E}^i[c_{exp}]$.

Let (all r (and $c_1 \ldots c_q$)) be one of the terminal value restrictions with $r_1, \ldots r_p, r$ the corresponding t-chain. Now we have two cases. First, there may not exist an element $y \in \mathcal{D}'$ such that $\langle d, y \rangle \in \mathcal{E}'[r_1] \circ \ldots \circ \mathcal{E}'[r_p] \circ \mathcal{E}'[r]$. Then d can be in the extension of c_{exp} in a semantic structure of T' even if there are no role-fillers for this t-chain. Second, it may be the case that there are some objects reachable from d using the t-chain, which will be denoted by $\{y_{k,j}\}$. The objects, the $y_{k,j}$s are role-fillers of for role r, will be denoted by $\{x_k\}$.

Obviously, it holds that $\{y_{k,j}\} \subseteq \mathcal{P}'[c_i]$, $1 \leq i \leq q$. Otherwise the original semantic structure would not have supported $d \in \mathcal{E}[c_{exp}]$. Since we stopped expanding the terminal value restriction because it appeared previously in the expansion process, there is at least one object z in $\mathcal{D}'$ which is in the extension of (and $c_1 \ldots c_q$) and is reachable from d by a proper prefix of the t-chain. This element and all those which can be characterized in the same way are in the extension of the terminal value restriction because we copied these elements to the expanded primitive assignment. If we could satisfy all terminal value restrictions, the assumption that all t-concepts are primitive components could be dropped, without removing z and all similar elements from the extension of the terminal value restriction.

In order to achieve this, delete all pairs $\langle x_k^i, y_{j,k}^i \rangle$ from $\mathcal{P}^i[r]$ and $\mathcal{E}^i[r]$, and all elements $y_{j,k}^i$ from $\mathcal{D}^i$, $\mathcal{E}^i[x]$, $\mathcal{P}^i[x]$, and insert into $\mathcal{P}^i[r]$ and $\mathcal{E}^i[r]$ the following role-relationships: $\langle x_k^i, z^j \rangle$, $0 \leq i \leq b$, $1 \leq j \leq m$. After having done this for all terminal value restrictions, call the new structure $\langle \mathcal{D}''', \mathcal{E}''' \rangle$ and create a new primitive assignment $\mathcal{P}'''$ by copying everything from $\mathcal{P}''$ except for the t-concepts.

Although $\langle \mathcal{D}''', \mathcal{E}''' \rangle$ is not an admissible semantic structure for T' w.r.t. $\mathcal{P}'''$, it can be used to generate one by applying the completion function Γ under the assumption that the extension of all undefined terms in $\mathcal{E}'''$ is empty. Such an application of Γ never leads to a removal of an element of $\mathcal{E}[c_i]$ for any t-concept c_i since the created assertional cycle corresponds to the definitional cycle explicated during the expansion process. Thus, there exists an admissible semantic structure of T' bounded by $s \times b$ such that $\mathcal{E}[c_{exp}]$ is nonempty, and, evidently, this holds for T and c as well. ∎

This gives us a strong indication that subsumption is decidable. However, in order to give a complete proof, we have to use the technique applied in Lemma 4.5 – and we have to guarantee that the identified non-inclusion situation contains a semantic structure of the original terminology.

Lemma 5.2 *Let T be a terminology using $\mathcal{TF}^-$ syntax and assume that T contains terminological cycles. Then, for any semantic structure $\langle \mathcal{D}, \mathcal{E} \rangle$ of T such that $d \in \mathcal{E}[c_{in}]$ and $d \notin \mathcal{E}[c_{out}]$, we can identify another semantic structure $\langle \mathcal{D}', \mathcal{E}' \rangle$ of T, $\mathcal{D}'$ bounded in size by the structure of T, with the same relationships.*

Proof: Similar to the technique used above, the *expansion process* described in the proof of Lemma 5.1 is applied to c_{in} and c_{out}. If there is a t-chain R in the expanded expression of c_{in} such that R is a proper prefix of a t-chain R' in the expanded expression of c_{out}, or vice versa, then the expansion process is applied to the terminal value expression of the shorter t-chain. Furthermore, if a t-chain T in one concept is a proper prefix of or identical with a chain T' in the other concept, such that T' starts at the top-level and ends at a value restriction which contains only primitive components, the expansion process is applied to the terminal value restriction at T. This is done until no t-chain is a proper prefix of any chain in the other concept. Since there are only a finite number of cycles and all cycles are of finite length, this process terminates. The resulting two expressions will be denoted by $c_{e,i}$ and $c_{e,o}$.

Now we apply the same technique as in the proof of the previous lemma, i.e., we start to construct an admissible extension by pretending that the remaining atomic concepts are primitive components, applying Lemma 4.5, and taking the disjoint union of $\max(\text{rbreadth}(c_{e,i}), \text{rbreadth}(c_{e,o}))$ copies of the semantic structures.

Finally, we create assertional cycles. This time we have to take care, however, to construct cycles for two concepts simultaneously preserving the non-inclusion situation. Basically, there are three cases. First, $c_{e,o}$ contains a t-chain not appearing in $c_{e,i}$. Then we may simply delete all objects reachable from d using this t-chain from the primitive assignment of the t-concepts. Second, $c_{e,i}$ contains a t-chain not occurring in $c_{e,i}$. Then we create a cycle as in Lemma 5.1. Third, if there are identical t-chains in both $c_{e,i}$ and $c_{e,o}$, then we also create an assertional cycle using $c_{e,i}$. However, if the terminal value restriction in $c_{e,o}$ contains some t-concepts not occurring in the terminal value restriction of $c_{e,i}$, and some objects reachable from d by the t-chain are not in the extension of these t-concepts, we have to guarantee that the selected elements z^j have the same property. This can be achieved by deleting the objects z^j from all primitive assignments to t-concepts which do not occur in the terminal value restriction of $c_{e,i}$ without changing the instance relationships for d.

Applying Γ obviously creates an admissible semantic structure of $\mathcal{T}$ such that there is the non-inclusion situation desired. ■

Corollary 5.1 *Subsumption in $\mathcal{TF}^-$ is decidable, even if there are terminological cycles.*

Proof: Using the same arguments as in Theorem 4.3, Lemma 5.2 is enough to guarantee decidability. ■

In trying to generalize this result to $\mathcal{TF}$, we note that we made use of the fact that all role extensions are independent in $\mathcal{TF}^-$ – a property we do not have in $\mathcal{TF}$. However, this turns out not to be crucial.

Theorem 5.3 *Subsumption in $\mathcal{TF}$ is decidable, even if there are terminological cycles.*

Proof: We will use the same construction as for $\mathcal{TF}^-$. However, instead of expanding along role-chains, we will expand value restrictions on roles which are interdependent in *parallel*. Since the combination of cycles leads to finite cycles again, the expansion of concepts according to the rules spelled out in the proof of Lemma 5.2 will always terminate as well. Additionally, it is obviously possible to construct the appropriate assertional cycles such that an arbitrary non-inclusion situation is transformed into a finite one with a domain bounded in size by the structure of the terminology. ∎

5.4 Reasoning with Terminological Cycles

The proofs in the last section already gave hints how to reason with terminological cycles. For $\mathcal{TF}^-$, we even could derive a complete subsumption algorithm from the proof of Lemma 5.2. After the expansion according to the rules spelled out in the proof of Lemma 5.2, application of CSUB results in a complete subsumption determination with respect to the descriptive semantics. The reason for the completeness lies in the facts that CSUB is complete for $\mathcal{TF}^-$ without cycles.[3] In adding cycles, rules for the comparison of terminal value restrictions on identical t-chains have to be added. However, these are easy. If the concept c is tested whether it subsumes c', and this test succeeds except for a terminal value restriction on one t-chain, then it subsumes c' *iff* the set of t-concepts in the terminal value restriction in c is a subset of those in c'. Otherwise, we can create a semantic structure such that some object is in the extension of c' but not in the extension of c by using an assertional cycle.

In the case of $\mathcal{TF}$, however, we gave up the hope for completeness anyway. Thus, the question is how far we should go in supporting the detection of subsumption relationships between restriction-circular concepts. The simplest strategy would be to consider all simple restriction-circular concepts as primitive concepts, using only roles which are not used in cycles for subsumption determination. This is the strategy used in the NIKL system. However, this would mean that we would not detect that the two concepts B and E in Fig. 5.11 are equivalent, although they are defined by *literally equivalent* expressions. Moreover, we would not be able to *recognize* Binary-trees and Humans if we employed such a subsumption algorithm in the realization process described in Sect. 4.5.2.

A better way is, of course, to adopt the strategy which leads to completeness for $\mathcal{TF}^-$, namely, to expand circular concepts until a cycle is detected, adjusting the depth of expansion between the concepts to be compared. This would uncover at least such obvious subsumption relationships as those between B and E in Fig. 5.11.

Thinking about how to integrate such an algorithm into the framework of classification, we see that a classification algorithm has to be considerably modified in order to account for cycles. We cannot simply create anonymous concepts for every value restriction and classify them, but we can only partially classify value restrictions of restriction-circular concepts. If all concepts have been entered into the concept hierarchy, however, we can try to find more subsumers for

---

[3]I do not provide a proof for this claim, but it be can easily shown using the proof technique used in [Levesque and Brachman, 1987].

all concepts participating in the cycle, and may stop if there is no change after we tried to find more subsumers for all concepts participating in a cycle.[4]

Finally, there is the question of how to deal with terminological cycles in the realization process. First of all, it should be clear that restriction-circular concepts cannot be completely expanded into number restrictions on roles and primitive components. The propagation step (R1) has to stop as soon as a value restriction which is already part of the description of a role-filler is propagated in order to achieve termination. Note that this termination condition is a special case of a possible optimization mentioned in Sect. 4.5.2. Steps (R2) and (R3) are not critical, except that the classification of abstractions containing restriction-circular concepts may be more expensive than the classification of noncircular concepts. This means that the realization process is already equipped to deal with restriction-circular concepts. Moreover, it should be obvious that the realization process recognizes objects as **Humans** if they have two **begetters** which are described as **Humans** and all its **offsprings** are **Humans** – supposing the terminology of Fig. 5.5. Furthermore, noncircular, finite **Binary-trees** as defined in Fig. 5.2 would be recognized by the realization process. Finally, if a world description is role-closed, realization is complete – a claim we will not prove here, though.

We will close this section with a reflection about how general the extension of terminological languages by cycles as exercised in this chapter is. From a semantic point of view, there is, of course, no problem. The critical point is the complexity of the inference algorithms. We have shown that for $\mathcal{TF}$ the addition of cycles does not destroy the decidability property of subsumption. The computational complexity is increased somewhat because the expansion of concepts leads to larger expressions. However, is this true for any conceivable terminological language?

Although it is difficult to make a general statement concerning this issue, it is obvious that all languages which cannot distinguish between assertional cycles and infinite chains of objects of the same type permit the extensions of terminological cycles without crossing the boundary to undecidable subsumption. If, however, a language allows us to state restrictions concerning role-chains, decidability of subsumption is endangered. Smolka [1989a] showed that even in feature logic agreements (i.e., role-value maps over functional roles) and cycles result in undecidability.

Applying this result to our case, we know that $\mathcal{TF}$, enriched by role-value-maps, would buy us undecidability if we allowed for cycles. However, as already mentioned in Sect. 4.2.1, role-value-maps alone lead to undecidability, even without terminological cycles. However, without role-value-maps or anything similar able to state "long-range" restrictions, it seems very likely that terminological cycles do not result in the undecidability of subsumption.

---

[4]This is also the strategy Lipkis proposes for handling terminological cycles in the KL-ONE classifier [Lipkis, 1982, p. 134] – a fact, which shows that Lipkis also had the *descriptive semantics* in mind when he thought about how to resolve terminological cycles. However, to my knowledge, this proposal has never been implemented in KL-ONE.

Part III

Revision

6. Belief Revision

In the previous three chapters, the discussion of representation and reasoning was based on the assumption that the knowledge base under consideration is more or less static. Actually, in discussing inferences, we allowed for monotonic growth of the knowledge base, but we never considered the possibility that a fact or definition has to be retracted or modified once entered.

Precisely this topic will be the subject of the present chapter. However, we will not try to develop a solution for the revision of terminological knowledge bases, but will take a more general view on the problem of revision, which will be used as a yardstick for the solutions to terminological revision in the next chapter. Sect. 6.1 introduces a (nonexhaustive) list of problems which are all subsumed under the general heading *belief revision*. Following this list, the ideas behind the different approaches to belief revision are analyzed and compared in Sections 6.2–6.6. In particular, the comparison between the revision of *closed theories* (which can be regarded as a formalization of the knowledge-level view on knowledge bases) and the revision of *finite theory bases* (which can be interpreted as the symbol-level perspective on knowledge bases) in Sect. 6.3 leads to an interesting result (Theorem 6.3) which gives a partial answer to the questions posed in Sect. 2.3.4. The revision of a KB viewed on the symbol level can be interpreted as a revision of the KB using the knowledge-level perspective but taking into account an additional relevance metric on propositions – the *epistemic relevance* of propositions.

Moreover, it turns out that it is not necessary to incorporate any notion of *reason maintenance* into a theoretical framework of belief revision, contrary to the opinion most authors seem to have. That does not mean that reason maintenance is superfluous, but that it is simply an implementational, symbol-level notion – a topic we will study in Sect. 6.6. Some *data-dependency network maintenance* algorithms are presented, and so-called *reason maintenance systems* are described.

6.1 Problems in Belief Revision

Belief revision is a field covering topics which are seemingly unrelated at first sight: theories about the *dynamics of epistemic states* of rational agents, *analysis of counterfactuals, diagnosis from first principles, data base updates, nonmonotonic reasoning, dependency-directed backtracking*, and so on [Doyle and London, 1980]. The underlying common theme is that a *logical theory* cannot be seen as static object, but that it is necessary to modify a theory according to some requirements and evaluate the consequences of the modification.

This theme is obvious when we try to analyze the dynamics of epistemic states, provided we view epistemic states of a rational agent as *closed logical theory*. A rational agent may learn something new about the world, may abandon an old belief, or may get information contradicting his old beliefs. Under the premise that the epistemic state of an agent – the agent's current beliefs – is formalized as a closed logical theory, we have to figure out what a theory might look like which takes into account the changed beliefs [Gärdenfors, 1988]. One immediate requirement is that the new theory should differ *minimally* from the original one. However, this is precisely the main problem. What is a reasonable metric for comparing different theories?

As it turns out, the theory of the dynamics of epistemic states shares its basic idea with the analysis of the meaning of *counterfactuals* and *conditionals*. These are sentences of the form:

If Kohl were not chancellor, the economic situation would be better.

Using classical logical analysis, the phrase "If ... then ... " could be formalized as a *material implication* – and we would conclude that this sentence is true simply because its antecedent is false. However, following the argument that the world-wide economic situation has much more impact on the national economy than the chancellor does, we may deny the sentence above. Following this lead, philosophers tried to pin down the truth conditions behind such sentences. In his seminal paper [Stalnaker, 1968], Stalnaker came up with a theory of conditionals explaining the truth conditions for conditional sentences in terms of a "nearest" possible world. A conditional sentence is true if in the "nearest" possible world in which the antecedent is true, the consequent turns out to be true as well. Later on, this idea was modified by Lewis [1973], who argued that it is more reasonable to consider a *set* of most similar possible worlds instead of a single one.[1] In any case, this leaves us again with a problem of measurement, namely, of determining the "distance" between possible worlds. In fact, it is the same problem as determining a new epistemic state which differs minimally from the old one when the epistemic input contradicts old beliefs.[2]

Following the thread laid out above, we may ask what *counterfactuals* or the *dynamics of epistemic states* have in common with *diagnosis from first principles*. As Ginsberg [1986] shows, there is a rather obvious connection. When a technical system is formalized as a logical theory describing the interconnections and the expected behavior of the components of such a system, a failure in such a system would amount to an inconsistency between the system description and the observational data. Diagnosing the failure can then be rephrased as finding

---

[1]We will not delve into these details. However, the underlying reason for considering sets of possible worlds instead of single possible worlds is that in the latter case the law of the "counterfactual excluded middle" is valid, which does not seem very reasonable.

[2]With the difference that logical theories usually correspond to sets of possible worlds, while one possible world corresponds to a *complete theory* – a theory in which each proposition is either true or false, but never undetermined.

a theory which is consistent with the observations but otherwise most similar to the original description of the system. The difference between the original theory and the new one is then the diagnosis – describing which original assumptions cannot be satisfied. As shown by Ginsberg in his paper and amplified by Reiter [1987], we may view diagnosis alternatively as a special instance of nonmonotonic reasoning, which can be formalized to a certain extent by default theories [Reiter, 1980], a point we will return to in Sect. 6.5. For this reason, it is obvious that implementation techniques developed in the context of nonmonotonic reasoning and belief revision fit well into the entire framework, in particular *reason-maintenance systems* (RMS)[3] and associated techniques, such as *dependency-directed backtracking*.

In order to complete the explanation for the list given in the beginning of this section, only the reason for the inclusion of *data base updates* has to be given. First, it might seem that what has been said so far has nothing to do with data base updates at all. Data base updates are usually unique operations on sets of tuples, and there is no question of what has to be done when a tuple should be inserted, deleted, or modified – except that data base integrity has to be maintained. If, however, we allow for *exceptions*, as discussed in [Borgida, 1985], or for *incomplete* data bases, we meet problems very much alike the ones discussed above. In order to analyze these problems, we have to view data bases as logical theories (which are then called *logical data bases*) and are faced with the problem of changing these theories minimally if an update should be performed [Fagin et al., 1983, Fagin et al., 1986]. However, as we will see in Sect. 6.4, it is possible to have another opinion about this matter.

6.2 The Logic of Theory Change

Most closely related to the idea of changing a knowledge base on the knowledge level, as discussed in Sect. 2.3.4, is the research by Alchourrón, Gärdenfors, and Makinson [Alchourrón and Makinson, 1982, Alchourrón et al., 1985, Makinson, 1985, Gärdenfors, 1988][4], some of whose main results will be presented in this section. The intention of this work is to find a characterization of the process of changing logical theories which are closed with respect to a logical *consequence operation*. Gärdenfors [1988] even tries to build an entire theory of the *dynamics of epistemic states* on the notion of closed logical theories.

For the following discussion, we will assume a logical language $\mathcal{L}$ containing propositions and the standard sentential connectives ($\neg$, $\vee$, $\wedge$, $\Leftarrow$, $\Leftrightarrow$), which can be used to form new propositions. The *consequence operation* mentioned above shall be a function named Cn, mapping sets of propositions to sets of propositions with the following properties [Alchourrón et al., 1985]. For any sets

---

[3]Not very surprisingly, in the context of diagnosis from first principles, we find a RMS: de Kleer's ATMS [de Kleer and Williams, 1987].

[4][Gärdenfors, 1988] contains almost all of the results of the papers written by Alchourrón, Gärdenfors, and Makinson.

A, B of propositions it shall hold that:

$$A \subseteq Cn(A) \quad (inclusion) \tag{6.1}$$
$$Cn(A) = Cn(Cn(A)) \quad (iteration) \tag{6.2}$$
$$Cn(A) \subseteq Cn(B) \text{ whenever } A \subseteq B \quad (monotonicity) \tag{6.3}$$

Furthermore, we will assume that Cn includes tautological implication, that Cn is compact, i.e., $x \in Cn(A')$ for some finite subset A' of A whenever $x \in Cn(A)$, and, finally, that Cn satisfies the rule of *introduction of disjunction in the premise*, i.e., if $x \in Cn(A \cup \{y\})$ and $x \in Cn(A \cup \{z\})$ then $x \in Cn(A \cup \{(y \vee z)\})$.

A set of propositions A closed with respect to Cn (i.e., $A = Cn(A)$) is called a *closed theory* or *theory* for short. A set of propositions B generating a theory A (i.e., $A = Cn(B)$) is called its *base*.

6.2.1 Expansion, Contraction, and Revision

Analyzing potential operations which change closed theories, we note that *theory expansion*, i.e., adding a proposition x to a given theory A (written $A + x$) is well-defined and unique. It amounts to creating the set-union of A and $\{x\}$ and closing the set with respect to Cn. Actually, as can be easily derived from the properties of the consequence operation, it does not make a difference whether we add the new proposition to the theory A or to a base B of A, i.e.,

$$Cn(B) + x \overset{\text{def}}{=} Cn(Cn(B) \cup \{x\}) = Cn(B \cup \{x\}) \tag{6.4}$$

Other theory change operations are more problematical. *Theory contraction*, i.e., removing a proposition x from a theory A (written $A \div x$), and *theory revision*, i.e., adding a proposition x to a theory A under the requirement that the resulting theory shall be consistent and closed under logical consequence (written $A \dotplus x$),[5] cannot be expressed as simple set operations, and they have no obvious, unique result, either. Of course, when applying such operations, we would like to change the original theory *minimally*. But even this constraint does not lead to a unique result. When trying to remove a proposition x from a closed theory A, there are usually many *maximal* subsets of A which fail to imply x. The same holds for revision if we define it using equation (6.5), which is called the *Levi Identity* after I. Levi [1977]:

$$A \dotplus x \overset{\text{def}}{=} Cn((A \div \neg x) \cup \{x\}) \tag{6.5}$$

Now one may give up and conclude that theory revision and contraction is outside of the scope of logical analysis and largely dependent on pragmatics. Although this is almost correct, it is possible to say a little more about the processes. In the work of Alchourrón, Gärdenfors, and Makinson, the problem

---

[5]Note that we referred to the general process of modifying a KB as *revision*, where in the context of theory change operation only the introduction of a propositions under the requirement of consistency preservation is called *revision*. To avoid confusion, we will use the terms *knowledge base revision* and *theory revision* when ambiguities are possible.

of finding intuitive plausible theory-change operations is approached by formulating postulates on possible change operations and testing candidates against them. Even stronger, Gärdenfors argues that these rationality postulates, which have come to be called to be the "Gärdenfors Postulates," are the only *logical* constraints on such operations. Any other requirement has to be *extra-logical* [Gärdenfors, 1988, Sect. 3.3]. One set of these postulates describing contraction operations[6] can be given as follows (A a theory, x, y propositions):

($\dot{-}$1) $A \dot{-} x$ *is a theory* (*closure*);

($\dot{-}$2) $A \dot{-} x \subseteq A$ (*inclusion*);

($\dot{-}$3) *If* $x \notin A$, *then* $A \dot{-} x = A$ (*vacuity*);

($\dot{-}$4) *If* $x \notin Cn(\emptyset)$, *then* $x \notin A \dot{-} x$ (*success*);

($\dot{-}$5) *If* $Cn(x) = Cn(y)$, *then* $A \dot{-} x = A \dot{-} y$ (*preservation*);

($\dot{-}$6) $A \subseteq Cn((A \dot{-} x) \cup \{x\})$ (*recovery*);

($\dot{-}$7) $(A \dot{-} x) \cap (A \dot{-} y) \subseteq A \dot{-} (x \wedge y)$;

($\dot{-}$8) *If* $x \notin A \dot{-} (x \wedge y)$, *then* $A \dot{-} (x \wedge y) \subseteq A \dot{-} x$.

Most of these postulates are quite straightforward and intuitively plausible. The *closure* postulate tells us that we always get a theory when applying $\dot{-}$. The *inclusion* postulate assures that when a proposition is removed, nothing previously unknown can enter into the theory, setting an upper bound for any possible contraction operation. Postulate ($\dot{-}$3) takes care of one of the limiting cases, namely, that the proposition to be removed is not part of the theory, while the next postulate ($\dot{-}$4) describes the effect of the other cases: if the proposition to be removed is not a logically valid one, then the contraction operation will effectively remove it. The *preservation* postulate assures that the syntactical form of the proposition to be removed will not effect the resulting theory: any two propositions which are logically equivalent shall lead to the same result. Finally, the *recovery* postulate describes the lower bound of any contraction operation: the contracted theory should contain enough information to recover all propositions deleted. Note that the properties of Cn together with ($\dot{-}$6) and ($\dot{-}$2) lead to the following conditional equation:

$$If \ x \in A \ then \ A = Cn((A \dot{-} x) \cup \{x\}) \tag{6.6}$$

The two postulates ($\dot{-}$7) and ($\dot{-}$8) are less obvious and not as basic as the former ones – a reason for calling them "supplementary postulates." ($\dot{-}$7) states that retracting a conjunction should remove less information than retracting both conjuncts individually in parallel, with ($\dot{-}$8) its conditional converse. Although

---

[6]A similar set of postulates can be given for theory revision, which can be proven to be equivalent using the Levi Identity (6.5). Here, we will regard contraction as the basic operation and consider revision only as a derived operation, following the arguments in [Makinson, 1985].

this does not sound like a strong restriction, not all conceivable contraction operations satisfy it.[7]

6.2.2 Full Meet Contraction

Trying to construct contraction functions, a first idea could be to take into account all possible outcomes of removing a proposition, and, since we do not have a measure of what is a better solution, to choose the intersection of the outcomes as the result of the contraction operation. Because we do not want to give up more than necessary, we will consider only the family of *maximal* subsets of a theory not implying a given proposition. Let us denote the family of maximal subsets of a theory A not implying x by $A \downarrow x$ (pronounced "A less x"), defined as:

$$A \downarrow x \stackrel{\text{def}}{=} \{B \subseteq A \mid x \notin Cn(B) \text{ and } \forall B' : B \subset B' \subseteq A \text{ then } x \in Cn(B')\} \quad (6.7)$$

It can be easily verified that $A \downarrow x$ is nonempty if and only if x is not a valid proposition. Following the arguments above, a contraction operation $\dot{-}$ could then be defined as:[8]

$$A \dot{-} x \stackrel{\text{def}}{=} \begin{cases} \bigcap(A \downarrow x) & \text{if } x \notin Cn(\emptyset) \\ A & \text{otherwise} \end{cases} \quad (6.8)$$

As is easy to see, this operation, called *full meet contraction*, satisfies $(\dot{-}1)$–$(\dot{-}5)$. As we will see, it also satisfies $(\dot{-}6)$ – in a very strange way, though. The information left in a contracted theory is really minimal, as shown by the following theorem (Observation 2.1 in [Alchourrón and Makinson, 1982] and Theorem 3 in [Fagin et al., 1983]):

Theorem 6.1 (Full Meet Contraction) *If $\dot{-}$ is a full meet contraction operation as defined by equation (6.8), then for $x \in A$ and $x \notin Cn(\emptyset)$:*

$$A \dot{-} x = A \cap Cn(\{\neg x\}) \quad (6.9)$$

Proof: First, we will consider the case when $y \in A$ and $y \in Cn(\{\neg x\})$. Now assume that $y \notin A \dot{-} x$. That means that there is a set $K' \in A \downarrow x$ such that $y \notin K'$. Because of the maximality condition on all such sets, we know that $x \in Cn(K' \cup \{y\})$. Using contraposition on our premise $y \in Cn(\{\neg x\})$, we get $x \in Cn(\{\neg y\})$ and hence $x \in Cn(K' \cup \{\neg y\})$. Together with the previous result and the introduction of disjunctions in premises, we have $x \in Cn(K' \cup \{(y \lor \neg y)\}) = Cn(K')$ and a contradiction.

---

[7]The main reason Gärdenfors includes them is to apply the theory of theory revision to the analysis of *counterfactuals*. For this analysis, these postulates are quite useful. In particular, they lead to a relation between revised theories similar to a principle for selecting neighboring possible worlds Stalnaker [1968] postulated.

[8]Note that the maximality of the elements of $A \downarrow x$ implies that the elements are closed theories. Moreover, any intersection of closed theories is itself a closed theory

For the converse case $y \in A$ and $y \notin Cn(\{\neg x\})$, we know by contraposition that $x \notin Cn(\{\neg y\})$ and hence $x \notin Cn(\{(x \vee \neg y)\})$. Because of the maximality of the sets in $A \downarrow x$, there are at least two sets K', K'' with $y \in K'$ and $(x \vee \neg y) \in K''$, but there can be no set which includes both because $x \in Cn(\{y, (x \vee \neg y)\})$, and thus $y \notin \cap(A \downarrow x)$. ∎

This means that when retracting x from A with a full meet contraction operation, we are left with only the propositions of A which are already consequences of $\neg x$. Carrying this result over to theory revision we have: If $\neg x \in A$ and $\neg x \notin Cn(\emptyset)$ then $A \dotplus x = Cn(\{x\})$, which is probably not what one would like. Despite this fact, the recovery postulate is satisfied. This is trivial for the two limiting cases when $x \in Cn(\emptyset)$ or $x \notin A$, and becomes obvious for the other cases when substituting the right hand side of equation (6.9) for $A \dotdiv x$ in ($\dotdiv$6), which leads to:

$$A \subseteq Cn((A \cap Cn(\{\neg x\})) \cup \{x\}) \tag{6.10}$$

Now, because for any $y \in A$ we know that $(y \vee \neg x) \in Cn(\{\neg x\})$ and that this together with x implies y, the right hand side of (6.10) is clearly a superset of the left hand side. Furthermore, using (6.9), it can be easily derived that ($\dotdiv$7) (it can even be strengthened to equality) and ($\dotdiv$8) hold as well.

6.2.3 Maxichoice Contraction

One conclusion one may draw from the observations above could be that the given postulates are too weak – because they obviously allow for rather useless theory change operations. More generally, one may argue that the idea of changing closed theories is on the wrong track, as done in [Fagin et al., 1983]. Instead, however, full meet contraction could be regarded as a kind of lower bound any contraction operation has to obey. This lead is followed in [Alchourrón and Makinson, 1982], where an operation called *maxichoice contraction* is analyzed. This contraction operation is defined using a *choice function* γ which picks one element of $A \downarrow x$ which is used as the result of the contraction:

$$A \dotdiv x \overset{\text{def}}{=} \begin{cases} \gamma(A \downarrow x) & \text{if } x \notin Cn(\emptyset) \\ A & \text{otherwise} \end{cases} \tag{6.11}$$

Evidently, maxichoice contraction satisfies the postulates ($\dotdiv$1)–($\dotdiv$6) – the latter because a single element of $A \downarrow x$ is always larger than $\cap(A \downarrow x)$. The "supplementary postulates," however, are only satisfied if the choice function γ adheres to an additional constraint. There has to be some partial ordering $\leq$ of 2^A such that the choice function always selects one of the largest elements (w.r.t. $\leq$):

$$\forall x \in A: \forall B \in (A \downarrow x): B \leq \gamma(A \downarrow x) \tag{6.12}$$

If this is the case, it is possible to derive some other neat properties which seem to be plausible for rational belief revision [Alchourrón and Makinson, 1982]. However, we will not go into these details here.

Despite this positive result, there is a serious drawback. While full meet contraction leaves us with theories which are too small, the other extreme – maxichoice contraction – usually creates theories far too large, as shown by the next theorem [Alchourrón and Makinson, 1982]:

Theorem 6.2 (Maxichoice Contraction) *If* $\div$ *is a maxichoice contraction operation as defined by (6.11), then for* $x \in A$:

$$\text{For any proposition } y : (x \vee y) \in A \div x \text{ or } (x \vee \neg y) \in A \div x \qquad (6.13)$$

Proof: Note that with $x \in A$ we always have $\{(x \vee y), (x \vee \neg y)\} \subseteq A$ for all propositions y. In the limiting case when x is a logical tautology, i.e., $x \in Cn(\emptyset)$, (6.13) holds because $A = A \div x$.

For the principal case when $x \in A$ and $x \notin Cn(\emptyset)$, let us assume contrary to (6.13) that $(x \vee \neg y) \notin A \div x$ and $(x \vee y) \notin A \div x$. Since $A \div x \in (A \downarrow x)$, we know that $x \in Cn((A \div x) \cup \{(x \vee \neg y)\})$ and $x \in Cn((A \div x) \cup \{(x \vee y)\})$. Hence, we have $x \in Cn((A \div x) \cup \{\neg y\})$ and $x \in Cn((A \div x) \cup \{y\})$ and thus $x \in (A \div x)$, which is a contradiction. ∎

Therefore, when revising a theory using maxichoice contraction, we see by applying the Levi Identity (6.5) that in the case when $\neg x \in A$ and $\neg x \notin Cn(\emptyset)$, we would end up with a revised theory $A \dotplus x$ such that either $y \in A \dotplus x$ or $\neg y \in A \dotplus x$ for *all* propositions y. In other words, by revising an arbitrary theory in this way, we would all of a sudden get a *complete theory*,[9] i.e., we would "learn" something new not connected with the proposition we inserted! Obviously, this is a property which runs counter to any possible intuition of revising a set of beliefs, a body of legal regulations, or whatsoever.

6.2.4 Partial Meet Contraction

Since full meet contraction results in theories too small to be useful, and maxichoice contraction produces theories too large to be plausible, it might be worthwhile to study the middle ground – *partial meet contraction* [Alchourrón et al., 1985]. Again, we will assume a choice function γ – this time selecting a subset of $A \downarrow x$ instead of a singleton, as above. Partial meet contraction is then defined as the intersection over the sets in this subset:

$$A \div x \stackrel{\text{def}}{=} \begin{cases} \bigcap \gamma(A \downarrow x) & \text{if } x \notin Cn(\emptyset) \\ A & \text{otherwise} \end{cases} \qquad (6.14)$$

Using the arguments given above, it is easy to see that partial meet contraction satisfies all the basic postulates $(\div 1)$–$(\div 6)$.[10] In order to also satisfy the supplementary postulates, again a relation $\leq$ over 2^A must be employed;

---

[9]Interpreting such complete theories epistemically, Gärdenfors [1988, Sect. 3.3] calls them belief states of *besserwissers*.

[10]Actually, the converse also holds: any contraction operation satisfying $(\div 1)$–$(\div 6)$ is a partial meet contraction [Alchourrón et al., 1985].

however, this time we do not require it to be a partial ordering. It has to satisfy only the following *marking off* identity – only "best" elements are chosen by γ for all $x \notin Cn(\emptyset)$:

$$\gamma(A \downarrow x) = \{B \in (A \downarrow x) | \forall B' \in (A \downarrow x) : B' \leq B\} \qquad (6.15)$$

In [Alchourrón et al., 1985], possible constraints on the relation $\leq$ and their consequences for the corresponding contraction and revision functions are analyzed, resulting in a complex web of relationships we are not interested in here. The main results are that (6.15) alone suffices to achieve ($\dot{-}7$), in which case the choice function is called *relational choice function*. If (6.15) holds and the relation is even transitive, the choice function is called *transitively relational*, and ($\dot{-}8$) is satisfied as well.

The interesting point in this game is how to arrive at a relation over 2^A. Gärdenfors and Makinson introduce in [Gärdenfors, 1988, Sect. 4.6] and [Gärdenfors and Makinson, 1988] the notion of *epistemic entrenchment* of propositions, which has the intuitive meaning that the more epistemically entrenched a proposition is, the harder it will be to get rid of it during contraction operations. After presenting some postulates for epistemic entrenchment functions, Gärdenfors relates such functions to contraction operations and shows that any partial meet contraction employing a transitive relation $\leq$ can be used to generate an entrenchment function and vice versa. The underlying idea of epistemic entrenchment is that although all believed or accepted propositions are equally certain, some of them have greater informative or explanatory value than others. In particular, Gärdenfors [1988, Sect. 4.7] argues that the change of paradigms in science [Kuhn, 1970] could be explained as a change of epistemic entrenchment. A paradigm change is not so much a change in the theory – theories change continually – but a change in what propositions are considered important. Thus, the main outcome of a paradigm change is a different future evolution of the theory.

6.3 Changes of Finite Theory Bases

Although the results presented in the previous section sound interesting and seem to provide some insights into the problem of belief revision, it seems arguable whether the approach could be used in a computational context, as in AI or in the data base world. First of all, closed theories cannot be dealt with directly in a computational context because they are too large. At least, if we deal with them, we would like to have a finite representation (i.e., a finite axiomatization), and there seems to be no obvious way to derive a finite representation from a revised or contracted theory in the general case.

Second, it seems to be preferable for pragmatic reasons to modify finite theory bases, or for short *finite bases*, instead of closed theories. Propositions in finite bases usually represent something like facts, observations, rules, laws, etc., and when we are forced to change the theory we would like to stay as close as possible to the original formulation of the finite base. In particular, when it becomes necessary to give up a proposition in the finite base, we would like to throw away the consequences of the retracted proposition as well. For instance, let a be the proposition "it is raining," let b be the proposition "John is wearing a hat," and let us assume we have the base $B = \{a, a \Rightarrow b\}$, i.e., "it is raining" and "John wears his hat when it is raining." That means that from B we can infer that "John is wearing a hat." Now, when we learn that it is not raining, then together with a we would like to get rid of b. This, however, cannot be easily accomplished by the approach described in Sect. 6.2. On the contrary, since the theory of the *dynamics of epistemic states* formalizes the idea of keeping as much of the old propositions (in the closed theory) as possible, it seems likely that b will be among the propositions in the contracted theory since it does not contradict $\neg a$. Gärdenfors [1988, Sect. 3.5] puts it in the following way:

> However, belief sets cannot be used to express that some beliefs may be *reasons* for other beliefs. (This deficiency was one of the motivations behind Doyle's TMS ...). And intuitively, when we compare degrees of similarity between different epistemic states, we want the structure of reasons or justifications to count as well.

6.3.1 Logical Data Bases and Diagnosis

Due to the reasons above, revision and contraction operations for applications as counterfactual reasoning in diagnosis from first principles [Ginsberg, 1986] and data base updates [Fagin et al., 1983, Fagin et al., 1986] are performed not on closed theories, but on finite bases. In both applications, the basic contraction operation on a finite base B with respect to a proposition x determines the family of maximal subsets of B not implying x, i.e., in terms of the previous section: $B \downarrow x$ (applying $\downarrow$ to finite bases instead of theories). Then, any proposition y which is in the logical closure of *all* elements of $B \downarrow x$ is considered to be in the logical closure of the contracted base. If we denote the the contraction operation on theory bases as $\sim$, a *base contraction* operation could be defined as:

$$B \sim x \stackrel{\text{def}}{=} \begin{cases} \bigcap_{C \in (B \downarrow x)} Cn(C) & \text{if } x \notin Cn(\emptyset) \\ Cn(B) & \text{otherwise} \end{cases} \qquad (6.16)$$

Applied to our example above, $\{a, a \Rightarrow b\} \sim a$ leads to the intended result $Cn(\{a \Rightarrow b\})$. Although this is a satisfying result, there are a few open questions:

- Does $\sim$ satisfy the Gärdenfors Postulates?

- How does base contraction relate to the contraction of closed theories?

- How should we represent a contracted base?

Evidently, the postulates $(\dot{-}1)$–$(\dot{-}5)$ are satisfied by $\sim$ if the postulates are adapted to base changes (at some places Cn must be added). However, $(\dot{-}6)$ does not hold in general. Consider, for instance,

$$\{a, a \Rightarrow b\} \sim b = Cn(\{a \vee (a \Rightarrow b)\}) \qquad (6.17)$$

which after the addition of b is weaker than the original theory. The reason is obvious: $\sim$ is not a partial meet contraction on closed theories, i.e., in general, we do *not* have

$$B \sim x \supseteq Cn(B) \cap Cn(\neg x) \tag{6.18}$$

This could be taken as evidence that, despite the fact that the underlying ideas are similar, theory contraction and base contraction are quite different. However, after some reflection and playing around with the formulas, the situation appears to be totally different.

First of all, we might ask what will happen if we add $Cn(B) \cap Cn(\neg x)$ to the right side of the definition of $\sim$. Thus, let us define a new contraction operation $\approx$ as:

$$B \approx x \stackrel{\text{def}}{=} \begin{cases} Cn((\bigcap_{C \in (B \downarrow x)} Cn(C)) \cup (Cn(B) \cap Cn(\neg x))) & \text{if } x \notin Cn(\emptyset) \\ Cn(B) & \text{otherwise} \end{cases} \tag{6.19}$$

It is easy to see that a base revision operation $\tilde{+}$ defined using the Levi Identity (6.5) leads to the same results regardless of whether $\sim$ or $\approx$ is employed. This is evident for the limiting case $\neg x \in Cn(\emptyset)$, which leads to an inconsistent theory. It becomes obvious for the other cases when applying (6.16) and (6.19):

$$\begin{aligned} B \tilde{+} x &\stackrel{\text{def}}{=} Cn((B \approx \neg x) \cup \{x\}) \tag{6.20} \\ &= Cn((\bigcap_{C \in (B \downarrow \neg x)} Cn(C)) \cup (Cn(B) \cap Cn(\{x\})) \cup \{x\}) \\ &= Cn((\bigcap_{C \in (B \downarrow \neg x)} Cn(C)) \cup \{x\}) \\ &= Cn((B \sim \neg x) \cup \{x\}) \end{aligned}$$

Thus, $\sim$ and $\approx$ are *revision-equivalent* operations [Makinson, 1987]. This justifies the usage of $\sim$ in contexts where we are mainly interested in revisions – as is the case with counterfactual reasoning or diagnosis from first principles. When, however, contraction and revision are considered as equally important – as in the context of updating logical data bases, where we want to add new information as well as to delete outdated information – then we had better use $\approx$. Otherwise, more information is lost than intended. In particular, we would be unable to undo a contraction operation.

6.3.2 Base Contraction is a Partial Meet Contraction

Before we now go on trying to verify that the "supplementary" postulates are satisfied by $\approx$, we will try to establish a connection between base contraction and theory contraction. In [Ginsberg, 1986], as well as in [Fagin et al., 1983], some thoughts are devoted to the issue of modifying closed theories. In [Fagin et al., 1983], however, these considerations are quickly dropped after proving a theorem similar to Theorem 6.1 – syntactic considerations seem necessary when modifying theories. Ginsberg [1986] comes to the same conclusion, however, he at least tries to relate his approach to the modification of closed theories. He proposes using a multi-valued logic in which reason maintenance information is encoded as truth-values (for a similar approach cf. [Martins and Shapiro, 1986]). Thus, Ginsberg accounts for the inability of closed theories to express reasons for beliefs discussed in the beginning of this section. This proposal does seem to lead to the desired results, i.e., changes of closed theories (in the reason maintenance style logic) are identical to changes of finite bases. However, I have to admit that I am not really fond of encoding meta-theoretical facts (derivations) as truth-values. Moreover, this approach does not shed too much light onto the relation between modifications of closed theories and modifications of finite bases.

In trying to establish a relation between base contraction and contraction of closed theories, the notion of *epistemic entrenchment* as sketched in the end of the previous subsection might be of help. Unfortunately, however, it is not possible to specify the degree of entrenchment without considering the logical force of propositions. In particular, Gärdenfors and Makinson [1988] postulate that if $y \in Cn(\{x\})$, then y is at least as epistemically entrenched as x. In other words, the consequence of a proposition is at least as entrenched as the proposition itself. The rationale behind this postulate has been already spelled out in the beginning of this section, namely, that when we have to give up something, we should try to minimize the loss. If we have to choose among a proposition x and its consequence y, we had better give up x alone instead of y and its *generating* proposition x! In a nutshell, epistemic entrenchment runs counter to the idea of reason maintenance.

Setting the reason maintenance problem aside for a while, we will try to analyze the other interesting aspect of base contraction – the syntactical aspect. In contracting bases, we try to preserve as much as possible of the original formulation of the base. Interpreting this in terms of closed theories, we could say that the propositions in the base are regarded as somehow more *relevant* – they have a higher degree of what we will call *epistemic relevance* than propositions which are not in the base but only implied by it. Following this idea, we clearly would like to minimize the loss of *epistemically relevant* propositions.

Formally, given a base B, we may define a choice function γ_B which selects just the elements of $(Cn(B) \downarrow x)$ containing maximal subsets of relevant propositions – maximal subsets of B not implying x:

$$\gamma_B(Cn(B) \downarrow x) \overset{\text{def}}{=} \{C \in (Cn(B) \downarrow x) | \forall \ C' \in (Cn(B) \downarrow x): \quad (6.21)$$
$$C' \cap B \not\supset C \cap B\}$$

Using this choice function, we can define a partial meet contraction on closed theories $Cn(B)$:

$$Cn(B) \dotminus x \overset{\text{def}}{=} \begin{cases} \bigcap \gamma_B(Cn(B) \downarrow x) & \text{if } x \notin Cn(\emptyset) \\ Cn(B) & \text{otherwise} \end{cases} \quad (6.22)$$

The interesting point about $\dotminus$ as defined above is that its results are the same as $\sim$, provided the same base is used.

Theorem 6.3 (Equivalence of Base and Partial Meet Contraction)

Let B be a finite base, $\dot{-}$ be a partial meet contraction on closed theories as defined in equation (6.22), and $\sim$ a base contraction operation as defined in equation (6.19). Then

$$Cn(B) \dot{-} x = B \sim x \qquad (6.23)$$

Proof: For the limiting cases when $x \notin Cn(B)$ or $x \in Cn(\emptyset)$ the result is immediate. Thus let us assume $x \in Cn(B)$ and $x \notin Cn(\emptyset)$.

First, we will show that for any $x \in Cn(B)$ and any set $S \subseteq B$ with $x \notin Cn(S)$ the following equation holds:

$$\bigcap \{C \in (Cn(B) \downarrow x) | S \subseteq C\} = Cn(S \cup (Cn(B) \cap Cn(\{\neg x\}))) \qquad (6.24)$$

It is clear that in (6.24) the right hand side (RHS) is a subset of the left hand side (LHS) because, first, the LHS is larger than $\bigcap(Cn(B) \downarrow x)$ and thus by Theorem 6.1 larger than $Cn(B) \cap Cn(\{\neg x\})$ and because, second, the LHS includes the set S. Since the LHS is a closed theory (see page 8), it must be a closed theory including S and $Cn(B) \cap Cn(\{\neg x\})$.

It remains to be shown that *all* propositions of the left hand side are also propositions of the right hand side in (6.24). Let us assume the contrary, i.e., there is a y such that $y \in$ LHS and $y \notin$ RHS. Using set theory and the properties of Cn, we can transform the RHS to $Cn(S \cup \{\neg x\}) \cap Cn(B)$. Since $y \in Cn(B)$, our assumptions lead to $y \notin Cn(S \cup \{\neg x\})$ and, in particular, to $y \notin Cn(\{\neg x\})$. Using this, we can derive $x \notin Cn(\{(x \vee \neg y)\})$, following the same line of arguments as in the proof of Theorem 6.1. By that and the observation that $y \notin Cn(S)$, we can conclude that $x \notin Cn(S \cup \{(x \vee \neg y)\})$. Since adding y to this set would lead to the derivation of x, there must be a set $S' \supseteq S \cup \{(x \vee \neg y)\}$ with $y \notin S'$ and $S' \in (Cn(B) \downarrow x)$, which means that y cannot be a member of all sets in $Cn(B) \downarrow x$ which contain S, and we have a contradiction.

Using equation (6.24) and the argument that γ_B plays the role of selecting sets $C \in (Cn(B) \downarrow x)$ which contain *maximal* subsets of B not implying x, we know:

$$\begin{aligned} \bigcap \gamma_B(Cn(B) \downarrow x) &= Cn((\bigcap_{C \in (B \downarrow x)} Cn(C)) \cup (Cn(B) \cap Cn(\{\neg x\}))) \\ &= B \sim x \end{aligned}$$

∎

6.3.3 Epistemic Relevance and Reason Maintenance

Although we started off with the conjecture that base contraction and theory contraction are quite different operations, Theorem 6.3 shows that the former is only a special case of the latter. Moreover, it demonstrates that the intuitive idea of modifying bases in [Fagin et al., 1983] and [Ginsberg, 1986], which seemed somehow arbitrary, can be cleanly reconstructed as an operation on closed theories. Applying this result to the discussion in Sect. 2.3.4, we see that modifications of a knowledge-level KB do not make much sense (taking into account Theorem 6.1). In order to modify such knowledge-level KB, more knowledge than is captured by the abstraction of logical closure is necessary. We have to decide which propositions are important, on which propositions our "body of knowledge" is based. The symbol-level, the theory base, may just be taken as the set of important propositions.

Actually, it is not necessary to refer to a theory base. The only important point is that we decide which propositions are *epistemically relevant*. In the case when we only distinguish between two degrees of epistemic relevance (relevant and irrelevant), a theory base can just be used to *encode* such an assignment of epistemic relevance. However, we can, of course, abstract from any symbolic representation and can regard the epistemic relevance of proposition as just another piece of knowledge.

Another interesting point about base contraction is that from a theoretical point of view *reason maintenance* is simply a by-product of base contraction and revision. Taking our example from the beginning of this section:

$$\{a, a \Rightarrow b\} \sim a = Cn(\{a \Rightarrow b\})$$

we see that base contraction removes the consequences of retracted propositions. Contrary to the assumptions of Gärdenfors and Ginsberg, it is not necessary to put the reasons for beliefs or derivations of propositions into belief sets. Partial meet contraction takes care of these things by itself, if we provide the "right" choice function. What really counts is the *epistemic relevance* of propositions.

Apart from these general considerations, there are a few details of the contraction operation defined in equation (6.22), and hence of $\sim$, which still need some investigation. First, there is the question of whether this kind of contraction satisfies the "supplementary" postulates and, second, how *epistemic relevance* relates to *epistemic entrenchment*.

Concerning the postulates, it is easy to see that there is a relation $\leq_B$ over $2^{Cn(B)}$ such that the *marking off* identity (6.15) holds:

$$X \leq_B Y \overset{\text{def}}{\Leftrightarrow} X \cap B \not\supseteq Y \cap B \tag{6.25}$$

This means that γ_B is a *relational choice function*, and by that, ($\dot{-}7$) is satisfied (see page 159). Additionally, it is evident that $\leq_B$ is not transitive. For instance, let $B = \{a, b, c\}$. Then we have $\{a, b\} \leq_B \{c\}$, and $\{c\} \leq_B \{a\}$, but $\{a, b\} \not\leq_B \{a\}$! This means we cannot expect that ($\dot{-}8$) holds in general.[11] In order to give an example where ($\dot{-}8$) does indeed not hold, let us assume the following base

$$B = \{a, b \wedge c, a \wedge b \wedge d, a \wedge d\}$$

Then it holds that

$$(a \wedge c) \notin (B \sim ((a \wedge c) \wedge (b \wedge d)))$$

---

[11]In order to achieve that, we would have to put more into γ_B than a set-inclusion relation restricted to the base. However, as pointed out by Ginsberg [1986] in a similar context, it seems questionable whether this is really necessary from a practical point of view.

$$a \in (B \sim ((a \wedge c) \wedge (b \wedge d)))$$
$$a \notin (B \sim (a \wedge c))$$

That means

$$(B \sim ((a \wedge c) \wedge (b \wedge d))) \not\subseteq (B \sim (a \wedge c))$$

Comparing the notion of *epistemic entrenchment* as introduced by Gärdenfors and Makinson with *epistemic relevance* as introduced above, we see that these two notions definitely do not coincide. The former respects the logical force of propositions and is strictly connected to contraction operations. For instance, in [Gärdenfors and Makinson, 1988], a principle is derived from the postulates about degrees of *epistemic entrenchment*, which reads translated to our notation:

$$y \in A \div x \text{ iff } (x \vee \neg y) <_\eta (x \vee y) \text{ or } y \in Cn(\emptyset) \qquad (6.26)$$

where $a <_\eta b$ means "a is epistemically less entrenched than b." Clearly, our notion of *epistemic relevance* does not allow deriving this principle. *Epistemic relevance* simply marks propositions which are considered somehow as crucial, regardless of how the propositions logically or in the course of contractions are related to others.

An obvious generalization of the construction given is to use a more fine-grained measure of *epistemic relevance*. We might not only distinguish between propositions which are in the base and those which are not, but may assign multiple degrees of relevance to propositions to distinguish between simple facts and integrity rules in a logical data base, the latter more relevant than the former. In fact, this is done in [Ginsberg, 1986] and in [Fagin et al., 1983], although, only on the theory base level, of course. With the reconstruction of base contraction as a special case of theory contraction, we are in a position to explain this assignment of priorities to propositions as a generalization of the more basic notion of *epistemic relevance*.

Let us assume a function ρ_n which assigns integers between 0 and n to all propositions in a logical language $\mathcal{L}$:

$$\rho_n : \mathcal{L} \rightarrow \{0, 1, 2, \ldots, n\} \qquad (6.27)$$

with the intuitive meaning that if x and y are propositions of a theory A and if $\rho_n(x) < \rho_n(y)$, then y is *epistemically more relevant* than x. Based on this function, we can define a kind of "prioritized set inclusion" on sets of propositions. Let

$$\rho_n^{-1}(i) \stackrel{\text{def}}{=} \begin{cases} \{x \in \mathcal{L} \mid \rho_n(x) = i\} & \text{for } 0 \leq i \leq n \\ \emptyset & \text{otherwise} \end{cases} \qquad (6.28)$$

then $\supset_{\rho_n}$, a prioritized set-inclusion operator with respect to the assignment of *epistemic relevance* ρ_n, can be defined as:

$$X \supset_{\rho_n} Y \stackrel{\text{def}}{\Leftrightarrow} \exists i \geq 0 : X \cap \rho_n^{-1}(i) \supset Y \cap \rho_n^{-1}(i) \wedge \qquad (6.29)$$
$$\forall j > i : X \cap \rho_n^{-1}(j) = Y \cap \rho_n^{-1}(j)$$

It should now be evident from the discussion in the previous section that it is possible to define a choice function γ_{ρ_n} similar to γ_B. This function would not only try to maximize the loss of one set of relevant propositions, but it would do so in a prioritized way. Namely, if a proposition x to be removed from a theory A is not implied by the set of most relevant proposition $A \cap \rho_n^{-1}(n)$, then this set will be in the contracted theory. Moreover, it is easy to verify that a choice function defined in this way is again *relational*, and thus the postulates $(\div 1)$–$(\div 7)$ are satisfied. We will not dive deeper into these issues at this point, however. For the rest of this section, we will be satisfied with the base contraction operation defined by equation 6.22.

As a last point, we should note that not only the *epistemic relevance* or any other measure is important when changing a theory, but also the pragmatics of the contraction or revision operation has to be taken into account. Assume, for instance, somebody tells you that "Kim is John's wife." From that it is, of course, valid to conclude that "Kim is a woman." Now, if you later learn that "Kim divorced John," there is no reason to give up the belief that "Kim is a woman," although the original propositions has become invalid. If, however, the speaker corrects the statement by saying: "Oh, it isn't Kim but Joan who is married to John," the belief in Kim being a female may become arguable.

6.3.4 Representational and Computational Issues

A point we have neglected so far is how a contracted base could be represented by a finite axiomatization. In the definition of the base contraction functions the result was a closed theory. What we want, however, is a finite representation of this result. Using the properties of Cn, a finite representation can be easily derived:

$$
\begin{aligned}
B \sim x &= Cn((\bigcap_{C \in (B \downarrow x)} Cn(C)) \cup (Cn(B) \cap Cn(\{\neg c\}))) \\
&= Cn((\bigvee_{C \in (B \downarrow x)} C) \wedge (B \vee \neg x)) \\
&= Cn((\bigvee_{C \in (B \downarrow x)} C \wedge \neg x) \vee B)
\end{aligned}
$$

Thus, assuming B is finite, $B \sim x$ can be represented by a finite disjunction. A less obvious point is what should be considered as the new set of propositions in the base. This is not a problem for counterfactual reasoning or diagnosis from first principles as described in [Ginsberg, 1986] and [Reiter, 1987] because only *one* revision operation is needed to give the desired result. Updating logical data bases, however, requires that an arbitrarily long sequence of deletions and insertions (read: contractions and revisions) can be dealt with, and in this case, we do not want to view a changed theory as just *one* proposition – the one proposition serving as an argument to Cn above. Otherwise, the next contraction would wipe out everything!

One solution is to collect all common propositions from the maximal subsets of $B \downarrow x$ and create disjunctions for the others. Another way could be to view a changed theory as a collection of *alternative* theories, an approach analyzed in [Fagin et al., 1986]. There it is proposed to use a *flock* of theory bases to represent a changed base. Logically, it does not make a difference whether the first solution or the second one is used. In either case, it is evident that, without applying simplifications, the base may grow exponentially with the number of change operations. However, the interesting point about flocks is that a change operation is applied to all elements of a flock individually, which leads to a new set of alternative theories. Thus, we are never forced to create disjunctions of propositions in the base after a change operation since the disjunctions are implicitly represented by the flock. As shown in [Fagin et al., 1986], sequences of theory base change operations lead to different results depending on whether the flocks approach or the solution sketched first is employed, and it is argued that flocks are more reasonably behaved than simple theory bases under change operations.

After the discussion in the previous subsection, it should be evident that the underlying problem in finding a reasonable representation of a changed theory base is how to determine the new set of *epistemically relevant* propositions, or, if we are dealing with more than two degrees of relevance, how to distribute the relevance after a theory change operation. In other words, we have to solve the problem of revising degrees of *epistemic relevance*, which had been invented to solve the belief revision in the first place. Although it is an interesting problem, we will not seek a solution here because the problem turns out not to be relevant for the problem of terminological revision.

Turning finally to computational issues, we note that in the general case – in the case when we use first-order predicate logic – we are lost. Consistency, the problem to be solved when $(B \downarrow x)$ is computed, is undecidable in first-order predicate logic. However, this does not mean that belief revision is completely useless for practical purposes. When restricted formalisms are considered, the situation is more feasible. In the context of logical data bases as well as in diagnosis from first principles [Reiter, 1987], the formulas are restricted, and thus the general undecidability is not relevant in these cases. The problem is still very difficult, though. Even in propositional logic it is NP-complete. With clever implementation techniques, however, one might reduce the time to such an extent that reasonably large theory bases could be handled. Another way out may be to reduce the expressiveness even more or to employ incomplete inference algorithms.

6.4 Model-Theoretic Updates

While in Sections 6.2 and 6.3 we focused on propositions and tried to minimize the loss of propositions considered to be important, another perspective on the update problem is possible. Instead of the logical closure, the models of a theory can be modified (which in turn can then be described by a set of propositions, hopefully). Two such approaches will be briefly sketched in this section.

6.4.1 Minimal Pertubation of Models

In [Dalal, 1988], the problem of revising a knowledge base is viewed from a model-theoretic point of view. Despite this difference, the underlying assumption of *minimally changing* a knowledge base is the same as in the previous two sections. In this case, the *models* of the theories will minimally differ. If we consider only propositional logic as in [Dalal, 1988], this notion can be easily formalized.

Let A be the *atomic* propositions – the *atoms* – and let M an *interpretation*, i.e., a *truth-value assignment* to all *atoms*. An interpretation M is a *model* of a set of formulas B, if all formulas in B evaluate to *true*, given the truth-value assignment M, written $\models_M B$. All such models of a set of propositions are denoted by $\mathrm{mod}(B)$. A distance measure between models, which we will call *pertubation distance*, can be defined by referring to the number of *changed* truth-values. For instance, given the two models[12] $M_1 = \{a : \mathsf{T}, b : \mathsf{F}\}$ and $M_2 = \{a : \mathsf{F}, b : \mathsf{F}\}$, the pertubation distance is one, in symbols: $\Delta(M_1, M_2) = 1$. Using this measure, a function can be defined which generates pertubed models. Let M be a model, then

$$g(n, M) \stackrel{\mathrm{def}}{=} \{M_x | \Delta(M_x, M) \leq n\} \tag{6.30}$$

If we now generalize g to sets of models in the obvious way by creating the set-union of all pertubations, a *model-theoretic revision* operation can be defined, denoted by $\stackrel{m}{+}$. Let B be a set of propositions and x be a proposition to be added. Then $\stackrel{m}{+}$ can be defined indirectly:

$$\mathrm{mod}(B \stackrel{m}{+} x) \stackrel{\mathrm{def}}{=} \begin{cases} g(i, \mathrm{mod}(B)) \cap \mathrm{mod}(\{x\}) & \textit{for the least } i \textit{ with} \\ & \textit{nonempty result} \\ \emptyset & \textit{if there is no such } i \end{cases} \tag{6.31}$$

As can be shown, this revision operation satisfies all the Gärdenfors Postulates for theory revision [Dalal, 1988]. Thus, applying the *Gärdenfors identity* [Makinson, 1985, p. 352]

$$A \dot{-} x = (A \dot{+} \neg x) \cap A \tag{6.32}$$

it is possible to generate a contraction operation which satisfies all the postulates for contraction, even ($\dot{-}8$). Although this an interesting and encouraging result, we still have to figure out how a revised knowledge base could be represented symbolically. Using results from Weber [1987], Dalal shows that revisions of models which are characterized by finite bases can be carried out by a simple symbolic transformation of the theory base. However, similar to the solutions we investigated in Sect. 6.3, consistency checks have to be performed (i.e., the approach is NP-complete in the propositional case), and the theory base grows exponentially with the number of revision operations if no simplifications are applied.

---

[12]Without loss of generality, we will assume that A is finite.

Comparing this model-theoretic approach to belief revision with the solution presented in Sect. 6.3, an immediate advantage is that model-theoretic changes are independent of the syntactic form of the knowledge base – which actually was the reason to investigate this kind of revision in the first place. For this reason, it is not necessary to worry about *epistemic relevance* or any other preference measure. However, what is regarded as an advantage by some people may be considered as a shortcoming by others. The model-theoretic approach is not as flexible as the solution presented in Sect. 6.3. It does not account for different degrees of *epistemic relevance*, but focuses only on minimal changes of truth-values of atoms. Thus, reason maintenance is a notion neglected in this approach. Taking, for instance, our example from Sect. 6.3 $\{a, a \Rightarrow b\}$ (which is logically equivalent to $\{a, b\}$), it is evident that a model-theoretic contraction of the proposition a would *not* remove b. A minimal pertubation would only change the truth-value of a.

Besides the independence from symbolic representation, Dalal [1988] conjectures in that the model-theoretic approach to revision "retains more old knowledge" than the proposals by Ginsberg [1986] and Fagin et al. [1983] we analyzed in the previous section. Putting it formally, Dalal conjectures that

$$(B \overset{\sim}{+} x) \cap Cn(B) \subseteq (B \overset{m}{+} x) \cap Cn(B) \text{ for any } B \text{ and } x \qquad (6.33)$$

From the discussion of revision and contraction operations in the previous sections, it should have become obvious that such a claim is very probably wrong. Different revision (or contraction) operations are, in most cases, not comparable along the dimension of set-inclusion. In order to make this statement more vivid, let us analyze a small example. Assuming

$$C = \{a \Leftrightarrow b, b \Leftrightarrow c\}$$

we get

$$C \overset{\sim}{+} \neg(b \Leftrightarrow c) = Cn(\{a \Leftrightarrow b, \neg(b \Leftrightarrow c)\})$$

If we try to revise C with respect to $\neg(b \Leftrightarrow c)$ using $\overset{m}{+}$, we first have to apply the pertubation function g to $mod(C)$:

$$
\begin{aligned}
g(1, \text{mod}(C)) &= g(1, \{\{a:\mathsf{T}, b:\mathsf{T}, c:\mathsf{T}\}, \{a:\mathsf{F}, b:\mathsf{F}, c:\mathsf{F}\}\}) \\
&= \left\{ \begin{array}{l}
\{a:\mathsf{T}, b:\mathsf{T}, c:\mathsf{T}\}, \{a:\mathsf{F}, b:\mathsf{F}, c:\mathsf{F}\}, \\
\{a:\mathsf{F}, b:\mathsf{T}, c:\mathsf{T}\}, \{a:\mathsf{T}, b:\mathsf{F}, c:\mathsf{F}\}, \\
\{a:\mathsf{T}, b:\mathsf{F}, c:\mathsf{T}\}, \{a:\mathsf{F}, b:\mathsf{T}, c:\mathsf{F}\}, \\
\{a:\mathsf{T}, b:\mathsf{T}, c:\mathsf{F}\}, \{a:\mathsf{F}, b:\mathsf{F}, c:\mathsf{T}\}
\end{array} \right\}
\end{aligned}
$$

which permits a nonempty intersection with $mod(\neg(b \Leftrightarrow c))$, namely:

$$g(1, \text{mod}(C)) \cap \text{mod}(\neg(a \Leftrightarrow b)) = \left\{ \begin{array}{l} \{a:\mathsf{T}, b:\mathsf{F}, c:\mathsf{T}\}, \{a:\mathsf{F}, b:\mathsf{T}, c:\mathsf{F}\}, \\ \{a:\mathsf{T}, b:\mathsf{T}, c:\mathsf{F}\}, \{a:\mathsf{F}, b:\mathsf{F}, c:\mathsf{T}\} \end{array} \right\}$$

We thus have

$$(a \Leftrightarrow b) \in B \overset{\sim}{+} \neg(b \Leftrightarrow c)$$

but
$$(a \Leftrightarrow b) \notin B \stackrel{m}{+} \neg(b \Leftrightarrow c)$$

Summing up, our suspicion about the claim that model-theoretic revision retains more knowledge than the approach in Sect. 6.3 turns out to be correct.

Nevertheless, I believe that the model-theoretic approach could be profitably used under some circumstances, namely, if only a set of homogeneous data, say observational data, is to be changed. For instance, it could be used in a logical data base setting to revise the data tuples only.

6.4.2 Nonminimal Model-Theoretic Updates

An approach which does not incorporate the notion of minimal change is described in [Winslett, 1986, Winslett, 1987]. As in Dalal's solution, models are pertubed. However, this time the pertubation is not minimal, but all possible permutations of truth-value assignments which verify the proposition to be inserted are taken into account. The underlying intuition is that the new formula describes the state of affairs more accurately than the information already in the knowledge base. The range of an *update request* is not necessarily the entire set of models but can be explicitly restricted by a selection clause. Syntactically, an update request has the following form:

$$\text{insert } x \text{ where } y \tag{6.34}$$

with the meaning that the models in which y is true shall be changed such that x becomes true, with x and y being propositions in some logical language. Here, however, we will only consider the propositional case. Thus, when we talk about models, we will mean truth-value assignments to atoms, as in the previous subsection.[13] Starting with a KB consisting of a set of models $K = \{\mathcal{M}_i\}$, a new set of models $K' = \{\mathcal{M}_j'\}$ is created by the following rules:

- If $\not\models_{\mathcal{M}_i} y$, then $\mathcal{M}_i \in K'$.

- Otherwise, *all possible* models $\mathcal{M}_i^*$ become elements of K' which differ from $\mathcal{M}_i$ only on the truth valuations of atoms mentioned in x such that x is satisfied.

As an example, let us assume that a knowledge base K is characterized by the two models $\mathcal{M}_1 = \{a : \mathsf{T}, b : \mathsf{T}, c : \mathsf{F}\}$ and $\mathcal{M}_2 = \{a : \mathsf{T}, b : \mathsf{F}, c : \mathsf{T}\}$. An update

$$\text{insert } a \vee b \text{ where } c \tag{6.35}$$

---

[13]In [Winslett, 1987], matters are much more complicated because the language is first-order. However, for the model-theoretic updates only existentially quantified and unquantified formulas are considered. Arbitrary quantified formulas come into play only when integrity constraints and closed world axioms are taken into account. These, however, are not updated model-theoretically. The former restrict model pertubations, i.e., they are never changed, while the latter are adjusted after updates. All in all, one could categorize the approach viewed in its entirety as "hybrid" because more than only model-theoretic considerations are taken into account. Here, however, we will talk only about the model-theoretic update part.

would then lead to a KB K' such that $\mathcal{M}_1$ and $\mathcal{M}_2$ are among the new models – the former because $\not\models_{\mathcal{M}_1} c$, and the latter because $a \vee b$ is already satisfied by $\mathcal{M}_2$. Additionally, we get the models $\mathcal{M}_3 = \{a : \mathsf{T}, b : \mathsf{T}, c : \mathsf{T}\}$ and $\mathcal{M}_4 = \{a : \mathsf{F}, b : \mathsf{T}, c : \mathsf{T}\}$ which are generated from $\mathcal{M}_2$ by creating all possible truth valuations varying the truth values of a and b such that $a \vee b$ is true.

This example demonstrates some of the salient features of Winslett's proposal. First, the syntactic formulation of an update request has an influence on the update operation. As spelled out in the rules above, the truth-valuations for atoms *mentioned* in the formula to be inserted change, and thus logically equivalent but syntactically different expressions may have different effects. So, for instance, if we had requested the insertion of $(a \vee b) \wedge (c \vee \neg c)$, which is logically equivalent to the expression to be inserted in the update request (6.35), then we would have gotten a different result – the truth-valuation of c would be varied. Second, this means that this kind of belief revision does not change a knowledge base minimally in the sense that new information is added if it does not contradict old information. Third, as is shown in [Winslett, 1987] and is evident from what has been said so far, we do not need a pair of modification operations (contraction and revision), but the insert operation alone is the only operation necessary to reach any data base state from a given state. The "deletion" of a proposition x can always be accomplished by inserting $(x \vee \neg x)$.

Although this brief sketch of the nonminimal model-theoretic approach to belief revision sounds somewhat odd (at least to me), it has some pleasing properties. If we start off with an incomplete data base characterized by a finite theory base, it is possible to represent updated data bases by theories which grow only linearly with the number of updates. Moreover, Winslett argues that this style of modifications captures the intention of a user (in a data base setting) better than a minimal-change approach because the effects of update operations depend mainly on the form of the insert operation and only minimally on the data base, making it easy for a user to predict the outcome of an update operation [Winslett, 1987, Chapter 8].

6.5 Nonmonotonic Reasoning

The problem we have studied in the previous three sections was how a logical theory (or set of models, or knowledge base, or data base) could be changed in order to reflect some externally specified requirement. Most of the solutions we came up with implied *nonmonotonic* modifications of the original theory,[14] i.e., some propositions present in the original theory are not part of the modified theory. This property leads quite naturally to the question of how these operations relate to the discipline of nonmonotonic reasoning as studied in AI [Ginsberg, 1987], which is used to formalize common-sense reasoning. As we will see, there is an overlap, but the issues addressed and the underlying intentions are quite different.

---

[14]Actually, only the *theory expansion* operation defined by equation (6.4) changes a KB monotonically.

Common-sense reasoning is a kind of reasoning which is very difficult to formalize using classical logics. Despite the fact that most people justify their reasoning with the phrase "that is logical," analyzing their arguments reveals that common-sense reasoning employs more than logically sound inferences. In order to formalize this reasoning in AI, different formalisms have been developed, all of which are nonmonotonic in nature – they do not respect the monotonicity requirement on the consequence operation (cf. equation (6.3)). The reason behind this is that *defeasible* inferences – tentative guesses – should be possible.

One might ask, why is it necessary to develop formalisms for making guesses? Would it not be a better idea to make all the implicit assumptions which go into a common-sense inference explicit and use a standard logic calculus then? Of course, this seems to be possible in principle. However, there are some problems in exhaustively listing *all* implicit assumptions. Any rule about change in the world can be invalidated by an almost infinite number of incidents – a problem called the *qualification problem* [McCarthy, 1980]. For instance, "If I load a gun and pull the trigger, the bullet will be fired," will be usually a correct assumption. However, there are a number of conceivable circumstances under which this assumption is incorrect: the powder is wet, the gun is broken, etc. There is an even a larger number of inconceivable circumstances which could invalidate this assumption.

A related problem is the *frame problem*[15] [McCarthy and Hayes, 1969], which might be stated as "What conditions still hold after an action has been performed?" Although this might sound trivial, the problems become obvious if we try to formalize the notion of *action* and *history*, as done in [McCarthy and Hayes, 1969] using a *situation calculus*. We are faced with the problem of explicitly and exhaustively stating which conditions are unaffected by all conceivable actions.

In the following, I will briefly (and only intuitively) characterize the two most popular formalisms developed in this context and relate them to the logic of theory change as described above.

6.5.1 Circumscription

Assume you parked your car somewhere. It seems natural to conclude that the car is still where you left it. This is, however, by no means a logically valid conclusion because all sorts of things might have happened to your car – it might have been stolen, towed away, etc. Thus, you may be forced to withdraw the conclusion that the car is still there (especially if you come back to an empty parking space). The general pattern of this kind of reasoning seems to be that one starts off with a theory about something and denies (for some important aspect of it) anything which is not derivable from the theory – an assumption which may be invalidated as one learns more. A simple form of inference which follows this pattern is based on the *closed world assumption* (as introduced in Sect. 3.3.1). Any atomic formula not present in the theory base is assumed to be false. A

---

[15]Note that this problem has nothing to do with *frame* representation languages as discussed in Sect. 3.1.2!

more general form of the closed world assumption is *predicate completion* [Clark, 1978] as used in PROLOG. Yet a more general form of this kind of inferences is *circumscription* as introduced by McCarthy [1980, 1986]. Actually, there is not only one form of circumscription, but a number of different circumscription techniques have been developed [Genesereth and Nilsson, 1987, Chap. 6]. All of these approaches, when viewed from a model-theoretic perspective, consider only some minimal models instead of using all models in order to determine the truth value of a proposition. Proof-theoretically, this amounts to adding some formula to the original theory – in the case of circumscription, a second-order formula. We will not go into the formal details of these things, however.

6.5.2 Default Theories

Another form of common-sense reasoning is the rule-of-thumb approach, e.g., if something is a bird, it is legitimate to assume that it can fly when there is no evidence to the contrary. Formalizing such reasoning processes led to the development of *default theories* [Reiter, 1980] – consisting of an ordinary first-order theory base and a set of *default rules*, like the one concerning the flying capabilities of birds. These default rules are not considered as part of the object language, but as additional *inference rules*, i.e., as a kind of meta-theoretical device not belonging to the object-level theory.

Formally, a *default theory* consists of a pair $T = (W, D)$, W a set of first-order sentence in some language $\mathcal{L}$ and D a set of *default rules* of the form:

$$\frac{\alpha : M\beta_1 \dots M\beta_m}{w} \tag{6.36}$$

with α, β_i, and w well-formed formulas in $\mathcal{L}$. The intuitive idea is that if α can be proven and it is *consistent* to assume that all of the β_i can hold individually, then w may be inferred. This idea is formalized by the notion of *extensions of default theories*, which are defined by the fixed-points of an operator Γ. $\Gamma(S)$, with S an arbitrary subset of propositions $S \subseteq \mathcal{L}$, is defined as the smallest set such that:

(D1) $W \subseteq \Gamma(S)$,

(D2) $\Gamma(S)$ *is a closed first-order theory,*

(D3) *If* $(\alpha : M\beta_1 \dots M\beta_m/w) \in D$, $\alpha \in \Gamma(S)$, *and* $\neg\beta_1, \dots \neg\beta_m \notin S$ *then* $w \in \Gamma(S)$.

An extension E of a default theory is then a fixed-point of Γ, i.e.:

$$\Gamma(E) = E$$

While default theories in general are difficult to deal with – there is currently no idea what a proof theory might look like for such theories – there are a number of special cases which are more easily dealt with. In particular, so-called *normal default theories* which contain only default rules of the form $(\alpha : M\beta/\beta)$ are better behaved. An example for such a normal default is the informal rule concerning birds given above, which could be expressed formally as:

$$\frac{\text{Bird}(x) : \ M \ \text{Fly}(x)}{\text{Fly}(x)} \tag{6.37}$$

As may be evident from the brief sketch above, default theories and circumscription aim at similar goals, and it even seems possible to use them for the same purposes. As it turns out, however, the relationship between the two approaches is very complex, and neither one subsumes the other. They give similar results only in some simple cases [Etherington, 1987].

6.5.3 Default Theories, the Logic of Theory Change, and the Knowledge Base Revision Problem

Although we did not dive into the formal peculiarities of circumscription and scratched only the surface of default theories, it should be evident that the *intentions* behind nonmonotonic formalisms and the logic of theory change are quite different. In the former case, we are interested in making tentative conclusions which may be subject to revision when more information is acquired, while in the latter case, we are interested in the evolution of a theory over time. Nevertheless, as shown in [Ginsberg, 1986] diagnostic reasoning can be modeled by reasoning in default theories as well as by theory base revision as described in Sect. 6.3, employing a relevance function ρ_2, i.e., a function with three degrees of epistemic relevance.

Briefly sketched, in diagnosis from first principles, a system and its behavior is described by the first-order part of a default theory, while the assumptions that all components work as expected are represented by default rules of the form $(: M q_i / q_i)$. The latter are subject to revision when observations contradict them. Using a theory change approach, one would assign second degree relevance to all propositions in the first-order part of the default theory, first degree to all q_i's, and zero degree to all other propositions. Obviously, if one adds a proposition representing an observation which does not contradict the propositions in the first order-part of the default theory or the propositions with the relevance degree 2, respectively, then the q_is are revised in both approaches.

This overlap between reasoning in default theories and reasoning using the logic of theory change demonstrates some of the points where, I believe, the theory change approach is superior to reasoning in default theories. First, default theories are comprised of two ontologically quite distinct parts: a usual first-order theory on one hand and a set of default rules on the other. The first part is considered immune against revision, while the rules in the default part may be subject to revision. In the theory change approach, we do not have such a distinction but may freely distribute degrees of epistemic relevance or may use other means to decide what is the best way to revise a theory. In particular, it is even possible to switch to another choice function and consider another set of propositions as more relevant. In our example of diagnosing faults, we may come to suspect that not the devices are faulty, but that connections are broken, which would simply amount to assigning a different degree of epistemic relevance to propositions. In a default theory framework, this would amount to a radical reformulation of the entire default theory! Second, while in a default theory one has only the choice between encoding a proposition as a regular first order sentence or as a default rule, in the theory change approach, it is possible to use an arbitrary number of different degrees of epistemic relevance – permitting a more fine-grained selection of likely diagnoses.

Besides these considerations, it is evident that the logic of theory change corresponds much better to the intuitions about knowledge base revision spelled out in Sect. 2.3.2. While default logic and circumscription aim only at formalizing defeasible inferences which are subject to revision, the logic of theory change addresses the problem of continually changing a knowledge base. Although it is not obvious how to apply the theoretical results to the problem of terminological knowledge base revision, at least it provides a sound conceptual framework in which solutions may be evaluated.

6.6 Reason-Maintenance Techniques

While in the previous sections we viewed belief revision from a theoretical point of view, in this section we will survey the essential ideas behind the *implementation techniques* supporting belief revision, called *reason-maintenance* or *belief revision techniques*. These techniques address the following problems [Martins, 1987]:

- the *inference problem*: deriving new beliefs from old ones.

- the problem of *disbelief propagation*: identifying beliefs which become arguable when other beliefs have changed.

- the *revision problem*: resolving contradictions by minimal mutilation of the set of beliefs.

- the *nonmonotonicity problem*: dealing with nonmonotonically justified beliefs – beliefs which depend on the disbelief of something else.

As should be obvious, these problems are mutually independent to a certain degree. In fact, most *reason-maintenance systems* (RMS) provide solutions for only a subset of this list.

Relating these problems to our theoretical discussion in the previous sections, we note that the *inference problem* is not a problem of only belief revision, but of any reasoning process. What constitutes the problem in a RMS is that a RMS has to keep track of derivations in order to be able to solve the *disbelief propagation problem*: identifying beliefs which may become arguable if their ultimate premises are disbelieved. For this purpose, the RMS needs information about how a belief was derived in the first place. Two principal solutions for the inference problem are possible: integrating the inference algorithm into the overall system or providing an interface to the outside world which allows the inference algorithm to communicate with the RMS. In fact, even if the inference algorithm is integrated into the RMS, as in the case of RUP (a system, which will be described in Sect. 6.6.3), an interface (called *noticers, demons, consumers, proof monitors,* etc.) is usually provided to the outside world in order to signal that a new belief was derived or that an old belief has been given up, giving the embedding system a chance to act accordingly.

The third point above – the *revision problem* – is then the really essential point in belief revision from a conceptual perspective: how do we change a theory in order to deal with contradictions? As we have seen in Sections 6.2 – 6.4, this is only one half of the problem because *revision* and *contraction* are two sides of the same coin. However, it should be noted that the relation between *revision* and *contraction* as described in Sect. 6.2, as well as all other theoretical results, hold only as long as we deal with monotonic inferences. If nonmonotonic inferences are employed, all the theoretical results described in Sections 6.2 and 6.3 become rather useless – the assumption of monotonicity of the consequence operation is very crucial.

This leads us the last problem in the list, namely, coping with *nonmonotonicity*, which complicates matters a lot. However, as exemplified by the reflections in Sect. 6.5.3, it is often possible to model the nonmonotonic reasoning process by theory revision instead of employing a nonmonotonic logic of some sort, which has the advantage of separating the standard logical inferences from the meta-theoretical inferences about changing theories. In fact, a substantial number of RMS follow this lead, as we will see.

6.6.1 Monotonic Data-Dependency Networks

One of the basic problems for any AI system maintaining a model about the world is that *derived beliefs* may become arguable when the fundamental reasons for them, the *premises*, vanish. Actually, this becomes a problem only if derived beliefs are *explicitly* stored. If all inferences are only performed on demand – at query-time, then there is no problem at all. However, if intermediate results are cached (as described in [Van Marcke, 1986]) or most of the inferences are performed at assert-time, which sometimes is necessary for reasons of efficiency and pragmatics (as we have seen in Sections 4.4 and 4.5), then the problem of maintaining derived beliefs must be solved somehow. Of course, there is a very simple and clean solution to this problem: If something changes, all derived beliefs are given up, and everything is computed from scratch again. Although clean and simple, this solution is also very inefficient. Giving up a premise or adding a new one usually affects only a very small subset of the derived beliefs. For this reason, the entire problem of belief revision could be seen as an internal version of the *frame problem* described above, as noted in [de Kleer, 1984].

In order to identify derived beliefs which may be affected by a change, it is necessary to do some kind of bookkeeping, which is called *data-dependency network management* [Charniak et al., 1980, Chap. 16]. A data-dependency network (DDN) is a directed graph $G = (V, E)$, with the set of *vertices* V composed of two disjoint sets, the nodes N, intended to denote believed propositions, and the *justifications* J, intended to denote sets of propositions used in a derivation.[16] The *edges* E point either from nodes to justifications or from justifications to nodes, i.e., $E \subseteq (N \times J) \cup (J \times N)$.

If there is a link from a justification j to a node n, we say that j *supports* n. If there is a link from a node n to a justification j, we say that n *participates* in the justification j. A justification without incoming edges is called a *premise justification*, and a node supported by a premise justification is called a *premise*.

As an example, let us assume the following propositions:

$$a \equiv \mathsf{Man(FRED)}$$
$$b \equiv \mathsf{Person(FRED)}$$
$$c \equiv \mathsf{Human(FRED)}$$
$$d \equiv (\forall x : \mathsf{Man}(x) \Rightarrow \mathsf{Human}(x))$$
$$e \equiv (\forall x : \mathsf{Human}(x) \Rightarrow \mathsf{Person}(x))$$
$$f \equiv (\forall x : \mathsf{Person}(x) \Rightarrow \mathsf{Human}(x))$$

If we assume $\{a, d, e\}$ as the set of premises, after some (first-order predicate logic) inferences, we end up with the set $\{a, b, c, d, e\}$ of believed propositions. A DDN recording the inferences would look like Fig. 6.1, with nodes depicted as circles and justifications as squares.

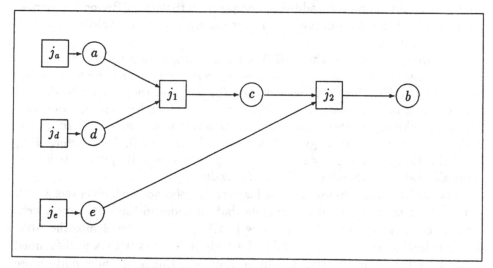

Fig. 6.1. A Simple Data-Dependency Network

Employing such a network, it is easy to identify beliefs which should go away when a particular premise does. A simple procedure for removing derived beliefs which are no longer justified can be given as follows:

---

[16]If we want to talk about a DDN as a graph we use the terms *vertex* and *edge*, while if we want to focus on the interpretation of a graph as a DDN, we use the terms *node*, *justification*, and *link*.

1. If a justification j is removed, then check whether the nodes $\{n_j\}$ which the justification supported have another justification. Remove all nodes which do not have an alternate justification.

2. Remove the justifications which the removed nodes pointed to.

3. If in the previous step a justification got removed, call the entire procedure recursively.[17]

Let us assume that we might lose confidence in the fact that every Human is a Person, i.e., we would like to retract the proposition e. In order to do so, we delete the premise justification j_e. Now, because e is not longer justified, e is deleted, and, following that, j_2 has to go away as well. The recursive call then removes b, and we are done.

All this is very simple and also efficient. Because nodes and justifications are only "visited" when they are going to be deleted, in the worst case (when everything has to be removed) the algorithm performs linearly in the number of vertices of the DDN. In the average case, the number of deletions m is, of course, much smaller: $m \ll \|V\|$.

Unfortunately, this is not the entire story. There are cases conceivable where the simple algorithm sketched above may fail to remove some beliefs which are not *well-founded* – beliefs which cannot be derived any longer from the set of premises. For instance, if we added the proposition that every Person is a Human (proposition f) to the set of premises in our example then we would end up with the DDN in Fig. 6.2.

Removing the premise that FRED is a Man (proposition a) would correctly remove justification j_1, but the derived beliefs b and c would not be touched because both still have justifications – despite the fact that they cannot be derived from the premises. If we want to take care of such unfounded beliefs, more complicated machinery is necessary. One way to detect and handle such situations is the *current support* strategy as described in [Doyle, 1979, McAllester, 1982, Goodwin, 1982]. For any node, a *current support* – one of its justifications – is maintained and is guaranteed to be *well-founded*.

The initial move is to use the first justification of a node which enters a DDN as the node's current support. Assuming that all nodes in the DDN have a well-founded current support before the new justification is inserted into the DDN, this new justification clearly provides the node it justifies with a well-founded support. When a justification has to be removed, things are now quite more complicated than in the above algorithm because the current support has to be maintained. This could be done as follows:

1. If a justification is to be removed and it is not the current support of any node, just remove it and exit.

---

[17]Actually, we do not have to remove the nodes and justifications, but instead could merely mark them as currently unbelieved. This could save some computations if there is a fair chance that we might come back to a node and believe it again.

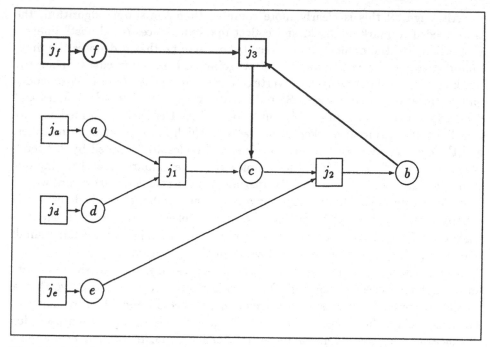

Fig. 6.2. A Cyclic Justification Structure

2. If a justification is the current support of some node n_1, remove it and mark node n_1 and all justifications n_1 participates in. If any of marked justifications is the current support of some node n_2, apply step 2 recursively.

3. Now check for all marked nodes whether there is still an unmarked justification and, if so, apply step 4 for each such node. After that, go to step 5.

4. Use the unmarked justification j_u as the new current support, unmark the node n_u, and propagate the new status. In other words, unmark, if possible, all justifications the node n_u participates in and check whether any of the unmarked justifications can be used as a new current support for some marked node. If so, apply this step recursively.

5. Delete all nodes and justifications which are still marked.

Applying this algorithm to our example, we first have to say what the current supports are. Following the rule about selecting a current support when a new justification is entered, the only justification which is *not* a current support is j_3. If we remove j_a, then a and thus also j_1 will be marked in step 2. Because j_1 is the current support of c, c and j_2 will be marked in the recursive application of step 2, and by another recursive application, b and j_3 are marked. Since j_3 is not a current support of a node, the recursion stops here. If we now try to reestablish current supports, we note that none of the marked nodes can be provided with new supports, and thus, they and all marked justifications are wiped out.

Although all this is clearly more complex than the simple algorithm, the time needed to mark, unmark, and collect marked vertices is "almost" linearly proportional to the number of vertices. Let us assume that d denotes the maximal degree – the maximal number of outgoing and incoming edges. Then the marking step (step 2) visits any vertex at most once. Assume that m nodes and justifications were marked. Step 3 iterates once over all marked nodes and checks for each node at most d justifications. Step 4 is only performed as long as a label changes from marked to unmarked, which happens at most m times, and the checks it performs on justifications and nodes are bounded by d. Step 5 is again bounded by m. Thus, the complexity of the unmarking and wiping out step is something like $O(d \times m)$. Comparing this with the first algorithm, we see that the current algorithm is more expensive. The number of marked vertices is usually larger in this algorithm than the number of vertices deleted in the first algorithm. Furthermore, the maximal degree, although in most cases fairly small [Goodwin, 1982], can considerably slow down the algorithm.

Summarizing, it would evidently be an advantage if it were possible to guarantee that no cycles can appear. Thus, it is worth the effort to prove that a particular application has such a property or, if this is impossible, to take precautions against the creation of cycles. The latter technique has been used, for instance, in a reason-maintenance system, called ITMS, integrated in a expert system for diagnosis [Puppe, 1987].

6.6.2 Nonmonotonic Data-Dependency Networks

The DDNs we analyzed in the previous subsection contained only monotonic justifications, i.e., all nodes participating in a justification were believed nodes. If we want to maintain dependency networks which also take *disbeliefs* into account, the problem becomes more difficult. First of all, we have to distinguish among the incoming links of justifications between links which come from nodes which have to be believed and links which come from nodes which have to be disbelieved in order to validate the justification. The corresponding sets of nodes participating in a justification are usually called the IN-set and OUT-set, respectively. Second, we cannot throw away disbelieved nodes, as in the previous subsection, because the disbelief in a node may be used in a justification. This implies that we have to maintain a labeling of nodes which tells us whether they are currently believed (IN) or disbelieved (OUT).

Putting it more formally, a nonmonotonic DDN has the structure of a monotonic DDN. Additionally, the set of edges from nodes to justifications is partioned into OUT-EDGE and IN-EDGE. Furthermore, there is a *labeling function B* from the set of vertices into the set {IN, OUT, UNDET} with the intuitive meaning that a node labeled OUT is disbelieved, a node labeled IN is believed, and a node labeled UNDET is something we cannot say much about. Similarly, justifications are labeled IN if they are valid, OUT if they are invalid, and UNDET if the state is undetermined. Whether a justification is valid or not follows the intuitive meaning of the nodes in the OUT and IN sets. A justification is valid if all nodes in the IN-set are believed nodes and all nodes in the OUT-set are disbelieved nodes. It is invalid if one of the nodes in the IN-set is a disbelieved node or one of the nodes in the OUT-set is a believed node.

With these conventions, it is possible to define what it means to have a *complete*, *consistent*, and *well-founded* labeling. A labeling is called *complete* if all vertices are either IN or OUT. The labeling is called *consistent* if each IN node has at least one valid justification and each OUT node has only invalid justifications. The labeling is called well-founded if it is possible to trace back the reasons for a node being IN to the believed premises – similar to the notion of well-foundness introduced in the previous subsection.

Before the problem of updating such a network is sketched, a brief example might be in order. Taking from Sect. 6.5 our bird which probably can fly who we will call TWEETY following the tradition of AI literature, let us assume the following propositions:

$$a \equiv \text{Bird(TWEETY)}$$
$$b \equiv \text{Fly(TWEETY)}$$
$$c \equiv (\text{Bird}(x) : M\text{Fly}(x)/\text{Fly}(x))$$

Assuming that $\{a, c\}$ is our default theory, a nonmonotonic DDN including the default conclusion c would look like Fig. 6.3 – the links in OUT-EDGE are marked by a small black circle at the arrow head.

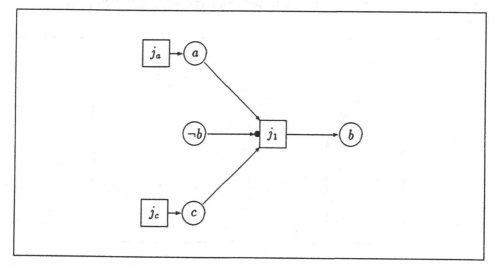

Fig. 6.3. A Nonmonotonic Data-Dependency Network

A complete, consistent, and well-founded labeling for this network would be one which assigned IN to all vertices except to $\neg b$, which must be OUT. Modifications in such a nonmonotonic DDN follow approximately the same line as sketched in the previous section. If the labeling of a justification changes from IN to OUT and the justification is the current support of a node or if the labeling changes from OUT to IN and thus changes a node from OUT to IN, something has to be done. First, all labels which might be affected (using

the current support strategy) are replaced by UNDET. Second, a relabeling
procedure starts. This procedure tries to turn the leftover partial labeling into
a new complete, consistent, and well-founded labeling. Relabeling is, of course,
more complex than unmarking in the monotonic case. As can be shown, the
problem of finding a complete and consistent labeling is equivalent to the famous
satisfiability problem for propositional expressions – and, thus, NP-complete.
Fortunately, however, it is possible to identify very large and reasonable classes
of nonmonotonic DDNs which are considerably better behaved.

   One class of such reasonable networks can be characterized by the absence
of so-called *odd nonmonotonic loops*. These are paths in the graph from a node
to itself such that an odd number of nonmonotonic justifications are involved. A
simple case is the left network in Fig. 6.4. This is also an example of a network
for which no consistent labeling can be found. Assuming that a is IN, then the
justification j_1 is invalid, and thus a must be OUT. Conversely, assuming that
a is OUT leads to the conclusion that it must be IN. Although odd loops are
not a sufficient condition for prohibiting a consistent labeling, they nevertheless
make the computation of labelings very difficult. Without them, it is possible
to compute a new labeling with an $O(d \times m^2)$ algorithm, d the maximal degree
of vertices, and m being the number of vertices to be labeled [Goodwin, 1982].
Because odd loops are also "odd" from a conceptual point of view, it seems
legitimate to ban them from DDNs – and the algorithm described by Goodwin
does just that. Odd loops are detected, and the algorithm complains about
them.[18]

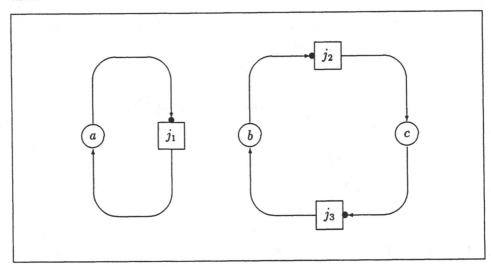

Fig. 6.4. Odd and Even Nonmonotonic Loops

   Excluding odd loops from the DDN leaves only the even ones – an example
is the left network in Fig. 6.4. These structures do not have the property of
excluding consistent labelings, but they permit *multiple* consistent labelings. In

---

[18]We will not go into the details of the algorithm. The only interesting point here is the
computational complexity.

our example, either $\mathcal{B}(b) = $ IN and $\mathcal{B}(c) = $ OUT, or $\mathcal{B}(b) = $ OUT and $\mathcal{B}(c) = $ IN is possible. If it is possible to dispense with both kinds of nonmonotonic loops,[19] the complexity given above can even be even reduced to $O(d \times m)$, which is just the same as in the monotonic case!

6.6.3 Justification-Based Reason Maintenance

The first domain-independent system based on the notion of data-dependency networks was Doyle's *truth-maintenance system* (TMS)[20] [Doyle, 1979], which initiated considerable research efforts in this direction and led to the development of a number of similar systems.

Besides the maintenance of the nonmonotonic DDNs as described in the previous subsection, a number of other interesting ideas utilizing the DDN were incorporated into the TMS, including *dependency-directed backtracking, generation of explanations*, and more. Although very useful, these features were later recognized as distinct and isolatable from the basic idea of the TMS – namely, maintenance of a DDN. Goodwin designed a facility called *proof monitors*, which react to changes of the belief status of a node. These proof monitors are then used to realize *dependency-directed backtracking* and *conditional proofs* – the latter usable for the generation of explanations [Goodwin, 1982].

From a problem-solving point of view, the technique of *dependency-directed backtracking* – a term coined by Stallman and Sussman [1977] – is certainly the most important one. In a problem-solving task, for instance, scheduling, configuration, or analysis of faults, a fairly large search space usually has to be explored. A straightforward technique to accomplish this is ordinary, chronological backtracking – the control strategy used in PROLOG. Choices are made one after the other, and if it becomes obvious after a particular choice that the solution cannot be reached with the particular set of choices done so far, the last decision is retracted and an alternative is explored. If at a choice point all alternatives are exhausted, the choice point before is revisited, and the same strategy is applied. Backtracking using this strategy may explore some subsets of alternatives more than once, even if this particular subset is responsible for prohibiting a solution. A better strategy is, of course, to record a failure and the reasons for it, avoiding reexploration of already recognized bad combinations of alternatives.

This is precisely the technique employed in the TMS for solving the *revision problem* mentioned in the beginning of this section. If, after an input to the TMS, a node which has been labeled as *contradictory* by the program using the TMS becomes believed, the TMS tries to track down the reasons for the belief of the

---

[19]The only loops permitted are the *monotonic* ones!

[20]A note on terminology might be in order here. Although *truth maintenance system* is clearly a misnomer, as admitted by Doyle [1979, p. 232] himself – it is not the *truth* of but *reasons* for beliefs or disbeliefs which are maintained – the term *truth maintenance* seems to have an overwhelming persistence in the literature. Other, more adequate terms used to describe these system are *belief revision systems* [Martins, 1987] – which I do not like because *belief revision* is a more general term, as we have seen in this chapter – or *reason maintenance system*, which I have adopted throughout. When referring to Doyle's reason maintenance system, however, the acronym TMS will be used.

contradiction. Because premises are beliefs the TMS cannot change, it tries to blame *assumptions* for the contradiction. An *assumption* in the TMS is a believed node which is nonmonotonically justified. Out of the set of *assumptions* supporting the contradiction directly or indirectly through monotonic justifications, one *culprit* is chosen and is forced to be disbelieved by inserting new justifications and nodes which summarize the reasons for the contradiction being IN. The details of this process will be omitted here because this process is quite complex.

Viewing such a behavior from the outside, it can be interpreted as finding one of the maximal sets of assumptions such that no contradiction arises after input of a new node x. Thus, in a weak sense this behavior is similar to finding a set in $B \downarrow x$. If assumptions are of the form "belief p if $\neg p$ is disbelieved", then, of course, by the arguments made in Sect. 6.5.3, the parallel is quite obvious. However, assumptions can take an arbitrary form, and, furthermore, the TMS does not incorporate the notion of logical closure but relies on the inferences done by the embedding system. Even in the case that the assumptions are in the form as described above, the parallel is still only approximate.

A RMS which fits better into the theoretical framework established in the previous sections is the RMS component of McAllester's RUP system [McAllester, 1980]. RUP is a radical departure from the TMS in that only monotonic justifications are maintained and that the inference algorithm is integrated into the system.

The logic supported by RUP is ordinary propositional logic.[21] The inference algorithm used is invoked at assert-time and employs a technique which could be called *propositional constraint propagation* of truth-values. Viewing it from a theorem proving angle, it can be characterized as *unit resolution* (e.g. [Genesereth and Nilsson, 1987, Sect. 5.2.]), and since refutation based on unit resolution is incomplete, the system does not detect all possible contradictions.

Ignoring the incompleteness, let us analyze the basic operations of the RMS. First of all, it is possible to enter propositions as premises by an ASSERT operation. Such an input can be either consistent with the propositions accumulated so far or it can be inconsistent, i.e., the inference algorithm has already deduced its falsity. In the former case, the new proposition is added, and new truth-values are propagated (which can lead to the detection of a contradiction). In the latter case or when an inserted proposition leads to a contradiction, the source of the inconsistency is sought, using the current support justifications which are tracked down to the set of premises causing the contradiction. One (or more) of these propositions have to be abandoned (by the system or by the user) in order to remove the contradiction. Interpreting this strategy in the terms of theory revision, it could be called a *maxichoice revision on a theory base*.[22] Interestingly, McAllester also proposes including "likelihood classes" of premises with

---

[21] Actually, in RUP a facility called *noticers* are used, which are similar to proof monitors mentioned above and which can be used to derive new ground formulas from universal implications. Thus, a limited form of first-order predicate logic is supported as well.

[22] Note that such a strategy can be interpreted as if a choice function had been specified which is *transitively relational*, i.e., RUP implements a revision scheme which satisfies all the Gärdenfors Postulates [Nebel, 1989a].

different degrees of relevance, which very much resembles our notion of *epistemic relevance* in Sect. 6.3. However, McAllester does not consider the idea of implementing a schema similar to the base revision operation $\tilde{+}$. The main reason is probably that unit resolution cannot deal with the disjunctions created by such an operation in a sensible way.

Complementary to the ASSERT operation, a RETRACT operation removes premises. While ASSERT is a full-fledged revision operation (modulo incompleteness of the inference algorithm), RETRACT is a contraction operation limited to premises. However, it is possible to define a general contraction operation by first ASSERTing the negation of the proposition to be removed and then RETRACTing the previously ASSERTed proposition.

6.6.4 Assumption-Based Reason Maintenance

Although the kind of RMS described in the previous section proved to be quite valuable and was used in a number of applications,[23] a number of deficiencies became obvious when such systems were used in problem solving contexts, in particular for qualitative reasoning. The "conventional" RMS – also called *justification-based* RMS because of its reliance on justifications for the reason-maintenance process – is inefficient in terms of space and time. Most importantly, it is impossible to compare the outcomes of different sets of assumptions [de Kleer, 1984]. The problem of inefficiency results from the "clever" dependency-directed backtracking strategy, which prunes the search tree but costs a lot of bookkeeping overhead. As de Kleer [1984, p. 79] put it:

> Very simple problems fill up all the memory of Symbolics LM-2 or 3600 in short order ... Timing analysis shows that the reasoner spends the majority of its time in the backtracking algorithms. The term "non-monotonic" reasoning is a misnomer as far as memory is concerned: the number of justifications grows monotonically as problem solving proceeds.

Due to these criticisms, de Kleer proposes an alternative architecture for RMS, which he calls *assumption-based* RMS. The essence of the idea is to label nodes with the set of assumptions which were used in the derivation of the node. This means that a node is neither believed or disbelieved, but believed relative to some context which is determined by sets of assumptions used in the derivation of the node. Here, assumptions are not nonmonotonically justified beliefs – de Kleer's approach is fundamentally monotonic – but arguable premises which may turn out to be wrong. This architecture avoids the inefficiency of dependency-directed backtracking and permits comparison of solutions achieved under different sets of assumptions – which is very important for qualitative reasoning. Of course, dispensing with backtracking means that the different states are held in parallel, and thus even more space will be used – in principle. The

---

[23]For instance, RUP was used in the CAKE system [Rich, 1982, Rich, 1985], and TMS was used in the rule-based problem solving system AMORD [de Kleer et al., 1977].

concrete implementation, called ATMS [de Kleer, 1986a], however, implements the labeling of nodes very efficiently in terms of space and time by using bit-vectors for the representation of sets. Although this does not solve the problem for arbitrarily large problem spaces, ATMS turns out to be usable for all practical cases. De Kleer [1986a, p. 152] claims that problems with 1000 assumptions are well within the abilities of ATMS

Interpreting de Kleer's system in the framework of theory revision, the ATMS computes to a certain degree the maximal sets of assumption which do not conflict with the basic premises (a point noted also in [de Kleer, 1986b, p. 222]).

6.6.5 Utilizing Reason-Maintenance Techniques in Knowledge Base Revision

Although the problem of knowledge base revision has not been rigorously defined so far, and only some intuitions were spelled out in Sections 1.3 and 2.3.4, it should be clear that the reason-maintenance techniques described are not *a priori* usable for knowledge base revision.

First of all, RMS's were designed to be used in a *problem-solving* context. In other words, RMS's are used to explore the problem space given by a problem description in order to find one or all feasible solutions (a plan, a diagnosis, or whatever). For this purpose, backtracking techniques – in the case of justification-based RMS's – or a kind of *breadth-first search* – in the case of assumption-based RMS's – are employed. Even though we might view the problem of changing a knowledge base according to some requirement as similar to finding a solution in a planning or diagnosis task, we probably do not want to invoke expensive search algorithms.

Second, all propositions in a RMS are retained once generated, and perhaps marked as being disbelieved or no longer derivable. This is certainly something we do not intend when changing a knowledge base which is supposed to be static except perhaps when an explicit change is required. In this case, it seems more reasonable to "garbage collect" all propositions which are no longer derivable, particularly so if it is very unlikely that the nonderivable propositions will be again derived. Otherwise, the above cited comment of de Kleer which states that although the KB is changed nonmonotonically, the amount of memory consumed grows monotonically applies.

Summarizing, the techniques of identifying propositions which are no longer derivable are undoubtly useful in a knowledge base revision context. However, the utility of the other techniques described is arguable. However, we will defer a more detailed discussion of these problems until after the problem of terminological revision has been analyzed.

7. The Revision Problem in Terminological Systems

For terminological knowledge bases, revision services do not seem to be strictly necessary, because terminological knowledge should be static. Although this might be correct as a first approximation, applications often require the revision even of terminological knowledge. After a brief discussion of the reasons for revisions, a number of principles are formulated which any knowledge base revision facility should follow. Based on that, the subproblems of revising terminological knowledge bases are analyzed. In order to get an impression how these problems have been solved previously, the revision facilities of different terminological systems are evaluated, revealing that the solutions offered are not fully satisfactory.

Accounting for these criticisms, an attempt is made to apply the logic of theory change to the problem of terminological revision. As it turns out, a straightforward adaption fails because of the restricted expressiveness of terminological representation formalisms. Looking deeper reveals that it is not the representation formalism which is to blame, but that the underlying reason for the failure seems to be that the pragmatics of terminological representation do not match the assumptions behind the logic of theory change.

These reflections result in a view of terminological revision as minimal modifications of definitions viewed in isolation. Using this view, a small set of terminological revision operations is specified.

Finally, we take a quick look at the revision problem in hybrid system and discuss the interaction between terminological and assertional knowledge in the revision process.

7.1 Terminologies in Flux

In an idealized environment, one could assume that every piece of knowledge put into a KB is accurate and thus never needs to be retracted. However, things appear to be different in the real world. It can happen that an input to a KB is wrong – it does not describe the world as it is – or that a piece of knowledge becomes outdated because the world has changed.

Terminological knowledge does not seem to be fallible in this respect at first sight. This kind of knowledge is purely *analytic* in nature and, thus, does not say anything about the state the world is in. Therefore, one would hardly expect that a terminological knowledge base has to be revised because of changes in the world or because it does not model the world accurately.

7.1.1 Terminologies, Analytic Knowledge, and Revisions

The above point of view, however, neglects the fact that terminology does indeed form an important part of our world, although not of the *extensional* world. Terminology serves the purpose of permitting communication. Therefore, we might run into the above mentioned problems even with terminological knowledge bases.

First, when entering a terminology into a knowledge base, it is easy to make a mistake. For instance, we might misunderstand how a technical term is defined. In denying that this problem has anything to do with representation of terminological knowledge, but only with our own imperfect understanding, one could devise some sort of special tool, say, a *knowledge base editor*, for this problem. However, if we employ a terminological representation system as part of a discovery system, such as AM [Lenat, 1982], or as part of a knowledge acquisition system, such as the NANOKLAUS system [Haas and Hendrix, 1983], then we had better be able to correct "misdefinitions." It is not very satisfying to read that "NANOKLAUS currently has no provision for unlearning. Therefore, if a new assertion causes an inconsistency because a previous assertion was not correct, there is no provision for withdrawing the incorrect assertion" [Haas and Hendrix, 1983, p. 411].

Second, terminology changes over time. In particular, categories defined by social or legal institutions are instable. Imagine a term Small-team, which is defined by the management division as a Team with less than than six members. Let us assume that only such teams get involved in advanced research tasks. However, after the next management meeting, the definition of what a Small-team is might change, although the contingent rule that advanced research tasks should be assigned only to those teams may still be valid.

We may try to do away with this problem by denying that relationships between terms defined by social or legal institutions are analytic. Consequently, these relationships should not be represented by using a terminological representation formalism. We may even go one step further and, adopting Quine's [1963] arguments, question whether the notion of *analytic truth* makes any sense at all. Thus, if terminological formalisms are only capable of representing some "nonsensical" relationships, what are they good for?

This radical position leads nowhere. It neither solves the posed problem nor does it really account for Quine's arguments. Quine argued only against the position that there can be any analytic truth in ordinary language or in science because terms are not strictly defined but intertwined with experience and subject to change: "...no statement is immune to revision" [Quine, 1963, p. 43]. However, he admitted, of course, that a statement can become true because of inherent lexical or because of factual conditions. The only point he made is that the boundary is not as sharp as was supposed by others and that this boundary may even change. Thus, we should be prepared for changes in terminologies and had better provide a representation system with appropriate services.

7.1.2 General Principles for Knowledge Base Revision

Before we analyze the problems coming up in the context of revising terminological knowledge bases, it may be worthwhile to identify the general principles to which any sensible knowledge base revision facility should adhere. These cover, of course, the Gärdenfors Postulates to some extent, but are aimed at capturing more than only knowledge representation systems employing a superset of propositional logic as their representation language.

As discussed in Sect. 2.3.2, we will assume one operation – TELL – which adds new knowledge to a knowledge base, perhaps removing conflicting information if necessary, and another one – FORGET – which removes knowledge from the knowledge base, resembling theory revision and theory contraction as discussed in the last chapter. Here, we will refer to them collectively as *knowledge base revision operations*, or just *revision operations*. Abstractly, such operations can be specified as functions from the *set of all possible knowledge bases* $\mathcal{KB}$ and *revision request expressions* of a *request language* $\mathcal{L}$ into the set of all possible knowledge bases:

$$\text{TELL}: \mathcal{KB} \times \mathcal{L} \;\;\rightarrow\;\; \mathcal{KB}$$
$$\text{FORGET}: \mathcal{KB} \times \mathcal{L} \;\;\rightarrow\;\; \mathcal{KB}$$

Any such pair of revision operations should satisfy the following principles:

(K1) *Adequacy of the request language*: The request language should be interpretable in terms of the interpretation rules for the representation formalism the KB employs.

(K2) *Independence of syntax*: If the revision request expressions of two revision operations are equivalent in meaning, then the respective operations should have the same effect on the KB.

(K3) *Closure*: Any revision operation on a KB should lead to a new, uniquely determinable state representable by the representation formalism employed.

(K4) *Success*: Any revision operation should be successful, i.e., after a TELL operation, the revision request expression should be derivable from the KB. Conversely, after a FORGET, operation the revision request expression should not any longer be derivable from the KB – provided the expression is not derivable from the empty KB.

(K5) *Minimal change*: The change of the KB by a revision operation should be as minimal as possible – according to some measure of minimality.

(K6) *Efficiency*: Revision operations shall be as efficient as possible. In particular, the computational complexity should not be harder than the complexity of the associated inference algorithms.

The first of these principles, *adequacy of request language*, seems to be almost self-evident. If the revision operations were not interpretable in terms of the representation language, then the question would be what we are requesting to revise. However, as we will see in the next section, it is possible to ignore this principle – a move which leads to a number of problems which have nothing to do with the original problem of revising a knowledge base.

If we follow the first principle, the second one – which resembles the preservation postulate ($\div 5$) – is also self-evident. If we can assign meaning to revision requests in terms of the semantics of the representation formalism used, then we certainly want two requests equivalent in meaning to have the same effect. Again, though evident, it seems possible to have different opinions on that. The nonminimal model-theoretic approach to revision described in Sect. 6.4.2 violates this principle. On the other hand, as we have seen in Sect. 6.4.1, it is also possible to have an even stronger opinion on this matter; namely, that revision operations should also be independent of the syntactical form of the knowledge base.

The third principle – the counterpart to the closure postulate ($\div 1$) – turns out to be the one which creates most of the problems in the context of terminological revision. Of course, a trivial way to satisfy (K3) is to ignore all revision operations leading to an unrepresentable knowledge base. However, this would violate (K4) or (K5).

Principle (K4) tells us that any revision operation with a meaningful revision request expression should be successful – similar to to the success postulate ($\div 4$). Actually, revision operations which violate this principle should not be called TELL or FORGET because they obviously do not accomplish what the names promise.

The fifth principle captures the essence of belief revision. Any revision operation should be accomplished by a minimal change of the KB. As we have seen in the last chapter, defining the distance between two knowledge states is the crucial point. Three of the Gärdenfors Postulates circumscribe just this principle. The inclusion postulate ($\div 2$) assures that nothing previously unknown should enter the theory when a contraction is performed, the recovery postulate ($\div 6$) gives a lower bound on any contraction by requesting "recovery," and the vacuity postulate ($\div 3$) captures the limiting case that there is nothing to remove. However, although the postulates are plausible, they do not necessarily lead to meaningful theory change operations, as shown by Theorems 6.1 and 6.2. Pragmatic considerations are necessary to give the notion of "minimal change" a real meaning.

Finally, in a computational context, revision operations should be performed efficiently. As pointed out in the last chapter, there are evidently some inherent complexity problems in belief revision. However, there was no hint that revision algorithms have to be harder than inference algorithms in terms of computational complexity. Thus, a property we will require as a minimum is that revision should be as easy as inference. Clever implementation techniques are, of course, also desirable.

7.1.3 Problems in Revising a Terminology

The first obvious problem in terminological revision is selecting an appropriate *request language*. If we reconsider the syntax definition of $\mathcal{TF}$, we see that term introductions could be used as revision request expressions. However, although we can assign a meaning to such an expression, it is not clear what TELL or FORGET operations should do on such expressions.

As already pointed out, the *closure* principle is the most problematic one. One reason is that in a terminological formalism we do not have anything similar to negation or disjunction on a propositional level – a point creating problems when aiming at something similar to a theory base contraction operation. However, there are other reasons for not subscribing to the theory change approach when revising terminological knowledge bases. Terminological knowledge simply seems not be revisable along the lines discussed in the last chapter.

Even accepting a different sense of revision, we still should try to keep the *closure* principle, however. This means that any change operation should lead to well-defined KB. As can be seen from the definition of the terminological formalism in Chap. 3, there are only a few cases we have to take care of. First, we should avoid multiple introductions of the same atomic term. As we will see, this can be handled in a very natural way. Second, the problematical case mentioned in Chap. 3 – terminological cycles – have already been solved in Chap. 5. Third, we should take care of unintroduced atomic terms. However, this problem can be solved by adopting the natural convention that each such term is a top-level primitive term.

Finally, we have the problem of performing revision operations on a terminological knowledge base as efficiently as possible. This topic, however, will be postponed to Chap. 8.

7.2 Previous Solutions

Instead of developing a solution from scratch, it might be helpful to study previous solutions. These could be classified as following:

- *network editors*, which operate directly on the network used to implement a terminological knowledge base,

- *knowledge-base editors*, which modify a terminology using a special purpose editor with dedicated edit operations,

- *functional, symbol-level approaches*, which offer a small set of operations for modifications of a terminological knowledge base on the symbol level, and

- *functional, knowledge-level approaches*, which view a terminological knowledge base as a set of possible subsumption relationships which are to be modified. However, only additions of new concept definitions are permitted in this context.

None of these solutions is fully satisfactory because they do not support modifications of parts of term definitions as described in Sect. 1.3. They all seem to operate on a too coarse-grained level. Moreover, most of them operate on a shallow, syntactical level, making it difficult to get an idea of what revision operations really *mean*, and the only approach which is genuinely connected with the semantics of the representation formalism cannot be extended straightforwardly to deal with revision.

7.2.1 Network Editing Approaches

Accepting that revisions of terminologies are necessary, a first idea realizing these operations might be to manipulate the network used to implement the role and concept taxonomies and the various relationships between concepts and roles – an approach pursued in the BACK system [von Luck et al., 1987, Peltason et al., 1987]. For example, modifying a value restriction could be carried out by modifying a directed link between two concepts. However, although this approach seems natural when creating a concept taxonomy by incrementally adding nodes and links to a network, there are some serious problems.

First of all, deletions in a network are problematical. If, for instance, a concept node which is used as a value restriction by another concept is deleted, then it is not obvious how to proceed. Either such operations should be prohibited, or they should lead to the deletion of the concept using the deleted concept as a value restriction. Otherwise the deletion of a value restriction might result in a "dangling reference."

Second, there are a number of problems when the distinction between *literal* and *derived* links in a network is not maintained – as in the BACK system. For instance, inheritance of value restrictions can lead to the insertion of some links which cannot be deleted. Trying to delete such an inherited link leads to the immediate reinsertion of the link by inheritance.

The situation becomes even worse if a manually constructed network is classified using a classification procedure as described in Sect. 4.4.2. In this case, some links expressing superconcept relationships are deleted and others are added. However, the meaning of the superconcept links is changed. Before classification they meant something similar to conceptual containment, but afterwards they mean immediate subsumption, i.e., necessary set inclusion of extensions. For this reason, modifications after classification have a different meaning than before. The difference becomes obvious when we add a restriction to the concept Small-team in Figure 3.2, which represents the literal relationships between concepts of our "team" terminology, and to the same concept in Figure 1.2, which depicts the derived relationships of the same terminology. In the former case, the restriction would not be inherited by Modern-team because there is no superconcept link between the concepts. In the latter case, however, there exists a superconcept link between Small-team and Modern-team and, thus, there is the question of whether the link should be used for inheritance. In the BACK system, this link is used for inheritance – i.e., instead of distinguishing between the two different kinds of superconcept links (description-forming and immediate subsumption), they are merged into one, confusing matters a lot [Brachman, 1983]. Despite the fact that such an approach leaves the semantic grounds laid down in the previous three chapters, it also violates the intuitions behind terminological knowledge representation.

Summarizing, there are two main problems with the network editing approach. First, in adopting the network metaphor, we may run into the problem that deletions are problematical. Second, when dropping the distinction between literal and derived properties, we confuse matters a lot. While the latter problem can be easily solved by maintaining the distinction between literal term introductions and derived properties of the terminology, the former problem seems to be a conceptual problem solvable only by choosing a different level on which things are revised.

7.2.2 Knowledge Base Editing

The prototypical example of a knowledge base editor for a terminological representation system is KREME [Abrett and Burstein, 1987].[1] KREME is intended to be an editor for multiple knowledge representation formalisms, but here we will focus only on the facilities for editing terminological knowledge bases, employing a representation formalism closely related to NIKL. However, KREME is not built on top of the NIKL system because NIKL does not support arbitrary modifications of the knowledge base, but only additions of new concept definitions.

Besides abilities of knowledge *presentation*, i.e., *browsing* and *navigating* through a KB (see also [Kindermann and Quantz, 1988]), KREME offers a large set of operations to modify an existing terminology. This includes *adding* new concepts and roles, *modifying* the definitions of existing concepts and roles by a structure-oriented editor, *deleting* concepts and roles, and *renaming* concepts and roles. All changes to a KB are incorporated into the KB by *reclassifying* the changed concepts or roles and all other objects which depend on them after an edit operation has been explicitly finished by the user.

While adding and modifying concepts or roles are relatively straightforward, *local* operations – they would amount to supplying a new right hand side of a term introduction in $\mathcal{TF}$ – deleting and renaming are more problematic operations since these are *global* operations on a terminology.

Renaming a term means that *all* occurrences of one particular term in a terminology are replaced by another one. This does not change any semantic relationships in the terminology[2] but affects only how a given concept is accessed from the outside world. Thus, we will consider the issue of naming and renaming as extrinsic to a terminology and ignore it in the following (but cf. Sect. 7.2.4), assuming that the problem can be solved by employing some level of indirection in accessing terms or by a sequence of other modification operations.

---

[1]A similar knowledge base editor is incorporated in QUIRK [Bergmann and Gerlach, 1987], but it does not offer as many edit operations as KREME.

[2]Of course, in case of a name clash, i.e., when the new name is already used in a terminology, this would have dramatic consequences. However, this is probably an illegal operation.

In contrast to renaming a term, deleting a concept or role is an operation which changes semantic relationships. However, it is not quite clear what is meant by "deleting a term." Abrett and Burstein [1986] propose three different delete operations in:[3]

- The term introduction as well as any occurrence of the term in other definitions are deleted. If the concept was used as a value restriction in a definition, a new concept is sought, e.g. a superconcept of the deleted concept, which may require user interaction.

- The term introduction as well as all subsumed terms are deleted.

- The term introduction is deleted, and all occurrences of the term are replaced by the right hand side of the deleted concept introduction.

None of these operations seems particularly convincing. In fact, the idea of "deleting" a concept or role seems to be somewhat arguable. What do we mean by that? The last alternative suggests that we want to forbid the usage of the particular atomic term but want to retain the "meaning," i.e., the definition. The former two alternatives are somewhat vague. They seem to lead to a reduced terminology both without the term and without the original meaning of the term. However, it is quite unclear under what circumstances one would like to use these operations. "Deleting something," a very common operation in computer science, requires that the thing to be deleted has "object character," a property which terms in terminologies do not seem to possess.

Besides edit operations, KREME offers some support for the knowledge acquisition process in form of plausibility tests. During the classification of new objects or reclassification of changed objects, some checks are performed to detect implausible states. These include:

- a check whether all concepts and roles mentioned in a definition are already introduced, and if the check fails, the user can introduce the undefined terms.

- a check whether an *actual, computed* value restriction is equivalent to an introduced, atomic concept. If this is not the case, the user can introduce a new atomic concept to denote the actual value restriction, or the user may change the definition of the concept used as the *literal* value restriction such that it becomes a subconcept of the concept used as the value restriction of a superconcept.

In order to make the last point a little more vivid, let us analyze the terminology in Figure 7.1 – an example borrowed from [Abrett and Burstein, 1986].

When computing the actual value restriction of the role inlet-valve for the concept Two-port-tank by performing inheritance, it becomes obvious that this

---

[3]In the later paper [Abrett and Burstein, 1987], however, the issue of deleting concepts is only briefly sketched.

$$
\begin{array}{ll}
\text{inlet-valve} & \dot{\leq} \ \text{anyrelation} \\
\text{Valve} & \dot{\leq} \ \text{Anything} \\
\text{Two-port-device} & \doteq \ \text{(all inlet-valve Valve)} \\
\text{Stop-Valve} & \dot{\leq} \ \text{Anything} \\
\text{Tank} & \doteq \ \text{(all inlet-valve Stop-valve)} \\
\text{Two-port-tank} & \doteq \ \text{(and Two-port-device Tank)}
\end{array}
$$

Fig. 7.1. A Missing Superconcept Relationship

is the conjunction of Valve and Stop-valve, a concept conjunction which does not have a name yet. Although this is quite reasonable and absolutely compatible with the semantics of the representation formalism, it may be a hint that something is missing. For this reason, KREME offers the user the opportunity to create a concept with the definition (and Valve Stop-Valve) or to make Stop-Valve a subconcept of Valve, which would be just the right thing in our case. Briefly described, the KREME classifier was made *interactive* – driven by knowledge acquisition heuristics.[4]

Summing up, KREME seems to be a very flexible and powerful tool for editing terminological knowledge bases. Nevertheless, there are some shortcomings when viewed in light of the requirements on a knowledge base interface as spelled out in Sect. 1.1. Particularly, it does not seem to be possible to evaluate the operations supported by KREME against the principles in Sect. 7.1.2:

- KREME mixes user interaction and knowledge base operations so that the borderline between them appears to be fuzzy. In particular, KREME incorporates knowledge acquisition heuristics into inferences, which might be adequate in a knowledge base editing context, but precludes the application of KREME as a subsystem in a knowledge acquisition system, as e.g. NANOKLAUS. Additionally, it makes the modification or extension of these heuristics difficult.

- It does not seem to be possible to interpret the entire set of edit operations as knowledge base revision operations. In particular, the *delete* and *rename* operations seem to be arguable. Neither their intuitive nor their formal meaning appears to be plausible.

7.2.3 Adding and Deleting Definitions

In trying to reduce the set of edit operations described above to a small set of well-defined revision operations on terminological knowledge bases, one may come up with the following set of operations:

---

[4]For another approach with even more interactive capabilities integrated in the classifier, albeit one employing a simpler terminological representation language, cf. [Finin and Silverman, 1986].

- *add* a term introduction to a terminology,

- *delete* a term introduction from a terminology.

As a matter of fact, in a recently developed representation system, in LOOM [MacGregor and Bates, 1987], this set has been implemented [MacGregor, 1988b]. Employing these operations, it is possible to give an entirely functional specification of a terminological knowledge base, albeit on a purely syntactical level, i.e., the knowledge base is viewed as a collection of symbolic term introductions rather than as a body of knowledge. Using this idea, it is possible to give a very compact formal description of the intended behavior of a representation system. In order to do so, let us first define what we mean by a *term table*:

Definition 7.1 (Term Table) *Let $\mathcal{A}_C$ and $\mathcal{A}_R$ be (infinite) sets of atomic concepts and atomic roles, respectively. Then the function S with*

$$S : \mathcal{A}_C \rightarrow \{ \doteq, \dot{\leq} \} \times \mathcal{TF}_C$$
$$S : \mathcal{A}_R \rightarrow \{ \doteq, \dot{\leq} \} \times \mathcal{TF}_R$$

is called a term table. *The special term table S_0 with*

$$\forall c : c \in \mathcal{A}_C \Rightarrow S_0[c] = \langle \dot{\leq}, \mathsf{Anything} \rangle$$
$$\forall r : r \in \mathcal{A}_R \Rightarrow S_0[r] = \langle \dot{\leq}, \mathsf{anyrelation} \rangle$$

is called the empty term table.

Based on this definition, it is easy to give a functional, symbol-level specification for a terminological knowledge representation system. A KB is a tuple consisting of a term table and a set of unordered pairs denoting disjoint declarations of concepts, the set of all KBs denoted by $\mathcal{KB}$. Obviously, for any KB there is a corresponding terminology and vice versa. The terminology corresponding to a particular $k \in \mathcal{KB}$ is denoted by $\mathcal{T}(k)$. Following the arguments in Sect. 2.3.2, four operations are defined on such knowledge bases, namely, INITKB, TELL, FORGET, and ASK, with TELL and ASK appearing in three different flavors corresponding to the types of introductions we can make:

$$\text{NEWKB:} \ \rightarrow \ \mathcal{KB} \tag{7.1}$$
$$\text{TELL}_C : \mathcal{KB} \times \mathcal{A}_C \times \{ \dot{\leq}, \doteq \} \times \mathcal{TF}_C \ \rightarrow \ \mathcal{KB} \tag{7.2}$$
$$\text{TELL}_R : \mathcal{KB} \times \mathcal{A}_R \times \{ \dot{\leq}, \doteq \} \times \mathcal{TF}_R \ \rightarrow \ \mathcal{KB} \tag{7.3}$$
$$\text{TELL}_{dis} : \mathcal{KB} \times \mathcal{TF}_C \times \mathcal{TF}_C \ \rightarrow \ \mathcal{KB} \tag{7.4}$$
$$\text{FORGET}_C : \mathcal{KB} \times \mathcal{A}_C \ \rightarrow \ \mathcal{KB} \tag{7.5}$$
$$\text{FORGET}_R : \mathcal{KB} \times \mathcal{A}_R \ \rightarrow \ \mathcal{KB} \tag{7.6}$$
$$\text{FORGET}_{dis} : \mathcal{KB} \times \mathcal{A}_C \times \mathcal{A}_C \ \rightarrow \ \mathcal{KB} \tag{7.7}$$
$$\text{ASK}_{\dot{\prec}} : \mathcal{KB} \times \mathcal{TF}_T{}^2 \ \rightarrow \ \{yes, no\} \tag{7.8}$$

NEWKB should deliver a KB consisting of the empty term table S_0 and an empty set of disjointness-pairs, TELL should replace an entry in the term table by a new definition, FORGET deletes a definition by entering the expression for an undefined term, and ASK infers the entailed subsumption relations. In order to describe the effects of these operation formally, let $f_{[x/y]}$ denote a function which is identical to f except at the point x, where the value of f is y:

$$\text{NEWKB}[] \stackrel{\text{def}}{=} \langle S_0, \emptyset \rangle \tag{7.9}$$

$$\text{TELL}_C[\langle S, d \rangle, c, op, cexpr] \stackrel{\text{def}}{=} \langle S_{[c/\langle op, cexpr \rangle]}, d \rangle \tag{7.10}$$

$$\text{TELL}_R[\langle S, d \rangle, r, op, rexpr] \stackrel{\text{def}}{=} \langle S_{[r/\langle op, rexpr \rangle]}, d \rangle \tag{7.11}$$

$$\text{TELL}_{dis}[\langle S, d \rangle, c_1, c_2] \stackrel{\text{def}}{=} \langle S, (d \cup \{\{c_1, c_2\}\}) \rangle \tag{7.12}$$

$$\text{FORGET}_C[\langle S, d \rangle, c] \stackrel{\text{def}}{=} \langle S_{[c/\langle \stackrel{.}{\le}, \text{Anything} \rangle]}, d \rangle \tag{7.13}$$

$$\text{FORGET}_R[\langle S, d \rangle, r] \stackrel{\text{def}}{=} \langle S_{[r/\langle \stackrel{.}{\le}, \text{anyrelation} \rangle]}, d \rangle \tag{7.14}$$

$$\text{FORGET}_{dis}[\langle S, d \rangle, c_1, c_2] \stackrel{\text{def}}{=} \langle S, (d \setminus \{\{c_1, c_2\}\}) \rangle \tag{7.15}$$

$$\text{ASK}_{\preceq}[k, x, y] \stackrel{\text{def}}{=} \begin{cases} yes & if\ x \preceq_{T(k)} y \\ no & otherwise \end{cases} \tag{7.16}$$

There are not too many exciting things to say about this functional specification. Most of it is buried in the expression "$x \preceq_{T(k)} y$" in equation (7.16).

There are a few notable points, though. The first thing is that the *objects* we manipulate are not *terms* but *term introductions*, which seems more natural for a terminology. Thus, we do not get the idea that terms themselves are objects which can be deleted – and so avoid the blind alley of trying to figure out what it could mean to "delete a term."

Second, we note that we could do without the FORGET$_C$ and FORGET$_R$ operations because the corresponding TELL operations can be used to achieve the same effect if supplied with the appropriate parameters. In fact, LOOM offers just TELL operations [MacGregor, 1988b].

The above reflections demonstrate that though we started off with a pure symbol-level view, it is nevertheless possible to characterize the semantic consequences of the operations. Evaluating this approach using (K1)–(K5), we note that most principles are satisfied. The revision request expressions clearly have a meaning; they are just term introductions and disjointness expressions in the case of TELL operations. Thus, (K1) is satisfied for TELL operations. With FORGET operations, the situation is more problematic. However, as mentioned above, we can do without FORGET operations – ignoring disjointness restrictions for the moment. Any revision operation leads to a well-defined new KB – provided we apply the analysis of Chap. 5. Thus, (K3) is satisfied. Additionally, all TELL expressions are successful in that the subsumption relationships expressed by the term introduction entered into the KB are derivable afterwards. Moreover, if two term introductions are semantically equivalent, then the semantic effects – the subsumption relationships – are the same. Hence, (K2) and (K4) are satisfied. Actually, the only problem is (K5). Although we did not specify any notion of minimal change, it seems that a KB change triggered by a TELL is nonminimal.

This would not be too bad if it turned out that the notion of minimal change does not make sense in the framework of terminological representation. However, if we consider the examples given in the Introduction, we see that *incremental additions* or *deletions* of *parts of a term introduction* seem to be plausible operations. Of course, it is easy to achieve the effect of an incremental addition or deletion by the TELL operation specified above – provided the right revision request expressions are specified. However, we are forced to input knowledge which is represented already. Moreover, from an implementational point of view, deleting and adding a term introduction is more expensive than deleting or adding only parts of a term introduction (as we will see in Chap. 8).

7.2.4 Modifications Viewed as Additions

Although the specification in the last section seems to be at least partly reasonable, it is possible to have a radically different view on what it could mean to modify terminologies. Until now, we have not differentiated between a term and its name because from a semantic point of view such a distinction does not seem to be necessary. However, when talking about operations on terminologies, we have already left semantic ground and have entered the land of *pragmatics*. Thus, it may be worthwhile to reflect about the intentions behind the *use* of a name.

There are (at least) two different interpretations possible when a name is used to refer to something in a formal system (as argued in [Patel-Schneider et al., 1985, p. 4] and [Finin and Silverman, 1986, p. 107]), namely:

- *reference by meaning*, i.e., when a name is used, it refers to the current meaning (definition), and the reference is immediately resolved on input so that later modifications do not have any effect on the entered expression;

- *reference by name*, i.e., the usage of a name has the purpose of referring to something (e.g. a definition) which may change.

In order to illustrate the effects of the two different perspectives,[5] let us assume that the definition of Team in Figure 3.4 is changed, so that instead of requiring two members, a Team can now consist of only one member. Interpreting the knowledge base under the *reference by name* principle this change would also affect the definition of Small-team, i.e., Small-teams require only one member as well. Actually, the functional specification in the last section just formalizes this perspective. If, however, the knowledge base is interpreted under the *reference by meaning* principle the change would not affect Small-teams, which would still be required to consist of at least two members.

If we would like to formalize such a behavior, we could use the specification given in the last section, except that for each TELL expression, the *expanded*

---

[5]Obviously, these two perspectives are roughly similar to the two evaluation strategies for parameters in programming languages which are called *reference by value* and *reference by name*.

defining form – using only primitive components – should be entered into the term table.

In essence, the *reference by meaning* perspective amounts to viewing a re-definition of a concept (or role) as an additional definition not affecting the rest of the terminological knowledge base. For this reason, it avoids a large number of problems accompanying the *reference by name* perspective. First, using the *reference by meaning* principle, it is impossible to create terminological cycles because the usage of a name always refers to the *current* meaning and thus neither a direct circular term introduction, e.g.

$$A \doteq (\text{and } A\ B)$$

nor an indirect circular introduction can result in a "meaning cycle." The names on the right hand side are simply "evaluated" before the name on the left hand side gets its (new) meaning. Second, on the implementational level, we are never forced to take care of assert-time inferences which may become invalid.

Although the principle of *reference by meaning* allows for a simple and elegant implementation of revision operations, it does not seem to capture the intuitive understanding of what a modification in a terminological knowledge base amounts to. The reason for this mismatch is that the occurrence of a concept name seems to denote more than just the current definition. To put it semi-formally, in our example, the use of Team in the definition of Small-team is done with the *intention* that in any *possible terminology* the meaning of Team is part of the concept Small-team (until this is explicitly denied).

Of course, situations are conceivable in which revisions according to the *reference by meaning* principle do meet the intentions of somebody building up a knowledge base. This, however, would mean that a concept name has been used simply to refer to a given structure – usage of a name to refer to this structure has just been coincidental.

In summary, we are not able to decide on formal grounds which principle is "better," but it seems that the intentions behind definitions are better matched by the *reference by name* principle. In fact, I do not know of any system using the other principle as a *documented* feature for knowledge base revision. However, an older NIKL version offered it as an undocumented feature for modifying classified concepts – a fact I discovered once by accident when I was trying to revise a terminological KB with the *reference by name* principle in mind. KRYPTON seems to offer both modes as undocumented features for the terminological part of the KB as far as I can tell from the program listing [Pigman, 1984b].

7.2.5 A Functional, Knowledge-Level Approach

What we have analyzed so far was more or less the manipulations of symbols, and the meaning of the manipulations could only be derived indirectly. In this section we will investigate an alternative approach: the functional, knowledge-level approach to the specification of a representation system [Levesque, 1984a] as used for the KRYPTON system [Brachman et al., 1985]. In this approach, the knowledge the system possesses at any instance of time is described using the possible subsumption relations (and truth valuations for the assertional part, which we will ignore here). Furthermore, any interaction with the system, such as giving more knowledge to the system or asking what it knows, is performed as a function on this abstract body of knowledge. Thus, this specification abstracts not only from any implementational structures but also from concrete symbolic structures used to express the knowledge.

Using the function types (7.1)–(7.8)[6] introduced in the last subsection, we can define the effect of the functions on terminological knowledge bases following closely the approach in [Brachman et al., 1985].

$$\text{NEWKB}[] \stackrel{\text{def}}{=} \{\preceq \mid \preceq \text{ is a subsumption relation}\} \qquad (7.17)$$

$$\text{TELL}_C[k, c, \stackrel{.}{\le}, cexpr] \stackrel{\text{def}}{=} \{\preceq \in k \mid c \preceq cexpr\} \qquad (7.18)$$

$$\text{TELL}_C[k, c, \stackrel{.}{=}, cexpr] \stackrel{\text{def}}{=} \{\preceq \in k \mid c \preceq cexpr \wedge cexpr \preceq c\} \qquad (7.19)$$

$$\text{TELL}_R[k, r, \stackrel{.}{\le}, rexpr] \stackrel{\text{def}}{=} \{\preceq \in k \mid r \preceq rexpr\} \qquad (7.20)$$

$$\text{TELL}_R[k, r, \stackrel{.}{=}, rexpr] \stackrel{\text{def}}{=} \{\preceq \in k \mid r \preceq rexpr \wedge rexpr \preceq r\} \qquad (7.21)$$

$$\text{TELL}_{dis}[k, c_1, c_2] \stackrel{\text{def}}{=} \{\preceq \in k \mid \forall x \in \mathcal{TF}_C : (\text{and } c_1\, c_2) \preceq x\}^7 \qquad (7.22)$$

$$\text{ASK}_{\preceq}[k, x, y] \stackrel{\text{def}}{=} \begin{cases} yes & if \ \forall \preceq \in k : x \preceq y \\ no & otherwise \end{cases} \qquad (7.23)$$

The first thing one notes is probably that there is no FORGET operation. It was not present in [Brachman et al., 1985] – and there are good reasons for this omission, as we will see in the next section. The second important point is that the semantics of the terminological formalism comes into play in equation (7.17) by referring to *the set of subsumption relations of all possible terminologies*. Any TELL operation simply selects a more specific set of these relations, i.e., it restricts the set of possible terminologies. The more knowledge acquired, the more the set of possibilities shrinks.

The rationale behind the functional, knowledge-level specification is spelled out in [Levesque, 1984a]. The main intuition behind the formalization of a knowledge-level KB is that it describes possible world structures – among which we expect to find the world we are trying to describe – which in the course of getting more information becomes more restricted. World structures in this approach are truth assignments of propositions – abstracting from interpretations. In the setting of terminological knowledge bases, this amounts to an abstraction from semantic structures resulting in sets of subsumption relations.

In this specification, "the actual syntactic form of the definition of p is not considered to be relevant; what counts is the relationship between p and all other *gterms*" [Brachman et al., 1985, p. 535]. However, it abstracts not only from the actual syntactic form of a definition but also from the "reasons" for

---

[6]In the original paper [Brachman et al., 1985] TELL and ASK are called DEFINE and SUBSUMES, respectively.

[7]Note that *disjointness* can be reduced to *incoherency* of the conjunction of the disjoint concepts, which in turn is equivalent to the fact that the conjunction is subsumed by *all* possible concepts because it necessarily has the smallest – the empty – extension.

subsumption relations, i.e., all terminologies with the same entailed subsumption relation are considered as equivalent. For example, the two terminologies in Figure 7.2 are indistinguishable on the knowledge level – they entail identical subsumption relations.

First Terminology:

A $\doteq$ (and B C)

D $\dot\leq$ (and A E)

Second Terminology:

A $\doteq$ (and B C)

D $\dot\leq$ (and B C E)

Fig. 7.2. Two Terminologies Equivalent on the Knowledge Level

This example demonstrates that a FORGET operation undoing the effects of a particular definition as specified in Sect. 7.2.3 cannot be defined. On the knowledge level, there is simply no way to tell whether a certain subsumption relationship is the result of a particular definition or not.

We could, of course, try to revise the subsumption relations directly. A FORGET operation would then be defined in terms of eliminating certain subsumption relationships. Assuming, for instance, that k is the knowledge-level KB corresponding to the terminologies in Figure 7.2, then we might request that the subsumption relationship between A and D should not hold any longer:

$$\text{FORGET}_C[k, \text{D} \preceq \text{A}] \tag{7.24}$$

Obviously, such an operation would be something like a theory contraction in terms of the theoretical framework presented in the last chapter. However, it is not fully clear whether the results of the last chapter are really applicable – a problem we will address in the next section.

7.3 A Framework for Terminological Revision

After studying what has been done so far in the area of modifying terminological knowledge bases, it seems that none of the solutions are fully satisfactory. All of them violate at least one of the principles presented in Sect. 7.1.2, and the most promising approach for knowledge base revision – the functional, knowledge-level approach – does not support FORGET operations.

As we see in the next subsection, we cannot capture terminological revision in terms of the logic of theory change without a considerable modification of the representation language. However, such a modification runs counter to the philosophy of terminological representation spelled out in Chap. 3. Reflecting on the pragmatics of terminological knowledge leads us to view a term defining expression – the right hand side of a term introduction – as a set of *essential meaning components*, components which can be added and removed.

7.3.1 Terminological Revision Viewed as Belief Revision

Trying to relate the knowledge-level approach to the theoretical framework of belief revision presented in the previous chapter, we may view the FORGET operation as a base contraction operation and the TELL operation as a base revision operation. Clearly, as in the case of theory change operations, we would like to take the symbol-level into account, using it for determining the epistemic relevant entities. As a first approximation, we will use the term introductions as the set of epistemic relevant propositions.

However, there are a number of problems. First, a terminological knowledge base can never become inconsistent. Although, it is possible that a concept can be *incoherent*, i.e., its extension is necessarily empty, this does not lead to an inconsistent KB, a terminology without any admissible semantic structure. Actually, this means that the TELL operation can be seen as a theory expansion operation since anything is consistent with a terminological KB. Second, connected with the first problem, there is no counter part to disjunction or negation in a terminology. It is simply impossible to *state* negated subsumption, like

$$\neg(D \preceq A)$$

or disjunctive subsumption relationships, such as

$$(D \preceq A) \vee (B \preceq C)$$

The Gärdenfors Postulates for contraction do not refer to disjunction or negation. However, the construction presented in Sect. 6.3 relied heavily on both of them. Even the model-theoretic approach described in Sect. 6.4.1 makes use of them when it comes to the symbolic transformation required to accomplish the model-theoretic update. The reason for this need is obvious. There are usually many maximal subsets of propositions which accomplish a contraction request, and because one does not want to select a single solution, all of them are taken disjunctively. For instance, in order to accomplish the FORGET request (7.24) in the second terminology displayed in Figure 7.2, one could either delete the introduction of A or the one of D. Since there is no measurement of which deletion is "better," it is probably best to use the disjunction of both introductions. This, however, cannot be done in a terminological formalism. Although terminological formalisms which support a concept-disjunction operator are conceivable, they would not help in the general case. They would permit disjunctive concept descriptions of the form

$$(\text{or } A \; B)$$

but not disjunctive concept introductions, such as

$$(A \doteq X) \vee (D \doteq Y)$$

Moreover, in order to satisfy the recovery postulate ($\div 6$), we would have to introduce negated concept introductions as well.

These reflections show that a contraction operation on subsumption relationships similar to the base contraction operation described in Sect. 6.3 would require a substantial extension of the representation formalism – an extension which seems not to fit into the framework of terminological representation. In a terminology, object descriptions are taken as unambiguous and definite, and subsumption relationships are *derived* from the descriptions. There is simply no room for stating disjunctive term introductions as in the example above.

7.3.2 Terminological Revision as Revision of Literal Definitions

Looking for the deeper reasons of the failure of the logic of theory change, we see that the pragmatics of terminological representation are probably responsible. If we imagine a system similar to the one described in the Introduction, i.e., a kind of database system employing a terminological formalism as its database definition language and if we allow for knowledge base revision in the overall system, then we certainly would require the term introductions to be unrevisable, except when it is *explicitly* requested. Entering an assertional item should never lead to a revision of the terminological knowledge. In some sense, it seems that terminological knowledge is epistemically most relevant – even immune against revision. The same holds true for other applications, for instance, the ones mentioned in Chap. 3. In those applications, an input to the assertional subcomponent of the system should never lead to a change of the terminological knowledge.

The reason is that the represented terminological knowledge is the basis for communication, the *vocabulary* used to interact with the world. Of course, we have to face the possibility that the definition of a term is inaccurate because of a misunderstanding or a change of meaning over time. However, it is the *definition* of a term, not the *subsumption relationship* between terms, which is "wrong." Moreover, the definition is not wrong in the sense that it does not match the facts, but only in the sense that somebody may have a different understanding. Carnap, trying to characterize the nature of analytic postulates (A-postulates), which correspond to what we have called "term introductions," put it as follows [Carnap, 1966, p. 263]:

> Always bear in mind that A-postulates, although they seem to do so, do not tell anything about the actual world. Consider, for example, the term "warmer". We may wish to lay down an A-postulate to the effect that the relation designated by this term is asymmetric. ... If someone says he has discovered two objects A and B, of such a nature that A is warmer than B, and B is warmer than A, we would not respond by saying: "How surprising! What a wonderful discovery!" We would reply: "You and I must have different understandings of the word 'warmer'."

This means that instead of a belief revision operation as discussed in the previous chapter it is more appropriate to try to come to a new mutual agreement about the meaning of a term. We might take an unwanted subsumption relationship between two terms as an indication that one or more term definitions have to be changed. The revision operation itself, however, should only act on term definitions and only after it has been determined which term definitions have to be changed in which way. Otherwise an accurate term definition might be changed, and thus even more misdefinitions are introduced into the terminological knowledge base. The appropriate level for such revision operations is obviously the level of *literal* term definitions.[8]

The symbol-level approach described in Sect. 7.2.3 seems to come very close to this idea. The only arguable point in this solution is that in order to make a small change to a term definition, the entire definition has to be reentered. The other way around, symbol-level changes as described in Sect. 7.2.3 changes the KB (on the symbol-level) more than necessary. However, this shortcoming can be circumvented if we can give a sensible and semantically sound definition of what the *essential meaning components* (see [Carnap, 1966, p. 263]) are that make up the meaning of a concept.

Definition 7.2 (Simple Concept) *A $\mathcal{TF}$ concept expression is called a* simple concept *if it does not contain any* and *operators.*

A simple concept does not contain any conjunction of concepts, neither on the top-level nor in an embedded expression. For instance,

$$\text{(all R (atleast 1 Q))}$$

is a simple concept, while

$$\text{(and X (atleast 1 Q))}$$

is not. Obviously, simple concepts are very similar to linear concepts as introduced in Sect. 4.3.2, except that the last expression is not a primitive component but an atomic concept or a number restriction. Furthermore, the function UNFOLD defined in Def. 4.8 applied to $\mathcal{TF}$ concept expression yields sets of simple concepts such that the conjunction over the set is equivalent to the original concept.

Proposition 7.1 *Let c be an arbitrary $\mathcal{TF}$ concept. Then for any terminology $\mathcal{T}$ and any semantic structure $\langle \mathcal{D}, \mathcal{E} \rangle$ of $\mathcal{T}$:*

$$\mathcal{E}[c] \;=\; \mathcal{E}[(\text{and } \text{UNFOLD}(c))]$$

---

[8]In other contexts, these pragmatic assumptions may turn out to be wrong. For instance, the task of learning concepts from examples is not based on explicit, literal changes of a description, but on finding fitting descriptions for given examples by employing rules of generalization etc. [Diettrich and Michalski, 1983]. Nevertheless, even in this case it is not subsumption relationships which are manipulated, but symbolic descriptions. In this sense, the approach to terminological revision described here may be employed as an interface to a knowledge representation system in such a learning system.

Based on this decomposition of defining expressions into essential meaning components,[9] we are able to refine the symbol-level revision approach to set-theoretical modifications of simple concepts participating in a concept definition. Instead of viewing the defining expression in a term introduction as one monolithic expression, we take the perspective of a defining expression being a set of simple concept expressions. Thus, a TELL operation does not add a new definition to the knowledge base, perhaps also removing an old one, but rather adds a set of simple concepts set-theoretically to an already present definition. Similarly, a FORGET operation removes the elements which appear in the revision request expression from the set of simple concepts making up a concept definition. In the following, this idea is put in formal terms.

Definition 7.3 (Simple Concept Term Table) *Let $\mathcal{A}_C$ and $\mathcal{A}_R$ be the (infinite) set of atomic concepts and atomic roles, respectively. Let TF_S be the set of simple concept expressions according to Def. 7.2. Then the function S with*

$$S: \mathcal{A}_C \;\rightarrow\; \{\,\dot{=},\,\dot{\leq}\,\} \times 2^{TF_S}$$
$$S: \mathcal{A}_R \;\rightarrow\; \{\,\dot{=},\,\dot{\leq}\,\} \times 2^{TF_R}$$

is called a simple concept term table. *Moreover, let S^1 be S projected to the first component, and S^2 be S projected to the second component. The special simple concept term table S_0 with*

$$\forall c:\; c \in \mathcal{A}_C \Rightarrow S_0[c] \;=\; \langle\,\dot{\leq},\emptyset\,\rangle$$
$$\forall r:\; r \in \mathcal{A}_R \Rightarrow S_0[r] \;=\; \langle\,\dot{\leq},\emptyset\,\rangle$$

is called the empty simple concept term table.

As in Sect. 7.2.3, we will take $\mathcal{T}(k)$ to denote a terminology corresponding in a natural way to a knowledge base consisting of a simple concept term table and a disjointness set. The operations we define on such knowledge bases are slightly different from the ones presented in Sect. 7.2.3 because now we will change the defining expression and the status of a term – *primitive* or *defined* – separately.

$$\text{NEWKB}[] \;\overset{\text{def}}{=}\; \langle S_0, \emptyset \rangle \tag{7.25}$$

$$\text{TELL}_C[\langle S, d \rangle, c, =] \;\overset{\text{def}}{=}\; \langle S_{[c/\langle \dot{=}, S^2[c] \rangle]}, d \rangle \tag{7.26}$$

$$\text{TELL}_C[\langle S, d \rangle, c, cexpr] \;\overset{\text{def}}{=}\; \langle S_{[c/\langle S^1[c],(S^2[c] \cup \mathcal{F}[cexpr]) \rangle]}, d \rangle \tag{7.27}$$

$$\text{TELL}_R[\langle S, d \rangle, r, =] \;\overset{\text{def}}{=}\; \langle S_{[r/\langle \dot{=}, S^2[r] \rangle]}, d \rangle \tag{7.28}$$

$$\text{TELL}_R[\langle S, d \rangle, r, rexpr] \;\overset{\text{def}}{=}\; \langle S_{[r/\langle S^1[r], \{rexpr\} \rangle]}, d \rangle \tag{7.29}$$

$$\text{TELL}_{dis}[\langle S, d \rangle, c_1, c_2] \;\overset{\text{def}}{=}\; \langle S, (d \cup \{\{c_1, c_2\}\}) \rangle \tag{7.30}$$

---

[9] The decomposition of concepts into conjunctions of simple concepts obviously relies on the restricted expressiveness of TF. However, if expressively more powerful languages are used, it should be possible to find a similar notion of decomposition.

$$\text{FORGET}_C[\langle \mathcal{S}, d\rangle, c, =] \stackrel{\text{def}}{=} \langle \mathcal{S}_{[c/\langle \stackrel{.}{\leq}, \mathcal{S}^2[c])\rangle]}, d\rangle \tag{7.31}$$

$$\text{FORGET}_C[\langle \mathcal{S}, d\rangle, c, cexpr] \stackrel{\text{def}}{=} \langle \mathcal{S}_{[c/\langle \mathcal{S}^1[c],(\mathcal{S}^2[c]\setminus\mathcal{F}[cexpr])\rangle]}, d\rangle \tag{7.32}$$

$$\text{FORGET}_R[\langle \mathcal{S}, d\rangle, r, =] \stackrel{\text{def}}{=} \langle \mathcal{S}_{[r/\langle \stackrel{.}{\leq}, \mathcal{S}^2[r])\rangle]}, d\rangle \tag{7.33}$$

$$\text{FORGET}_R[\langle \mathcal{S}, d\rangle, r, rexpr] \stackrel{\text{def}}{=} \langle \mathcal{S}_{[r/\langle \mathcal{S}^1[r],(\mathcal{S}^2[r]\setminus\{rexpr\})\rangle]}, d\rangle \tag{7.34}$$

$$\text{FORGET}_{dis}[\langle \mathcal{S}, d\rangle, c_1, c_2] \stackrel{\text{def}}{=} \langle \mathcal{S}, (d \setminus \{\{c_1, c_2\}\})\rangle \tag{7.35}$$

$$\text{ASK}_{\preceq}[k, x, y] \stackrel{\text{def}}{=} \begin{cases} yes & if\ x \preceq_{T(k)} y \\ no & otherwise \end{cases} \tag{7.36}$$

Before we discuss the pros and cons of the presented revision approach, a few comments might be in order. The first thing we note is that the specification of NEWKB, TELL$_{dis}$, FORGET$_{dis}$, and ASK$_{\preceq}$ do not differ from the specification given in Sect. 7.2.3. The operations on roles and concepts are, however, completely different. In equations (7.26), (7.28), (7.31), and (7.33) the *status* of a term is manipulated, i.e., whether it is defined or primitive, while in equations (7.27) and (7.32) simple concept expressions are added or removed from a set of simple simple concepts characterizing a defining expression. In the case of roles, there is a slight anomaly in that the revision request expression of a TELL operation in (7.29) replaces an already present expression. However, taking the restricted expressiveness of $\mathcal{TF}$ into account, there is no other reasonable way. Replacing the old expression is the only means of guaranteeing success, and it is a minimal change in that it does not change more than necessary – on the level of simple term expressions.

7.3.3 Properties of the Literal Revision Approach

When evaluating the solution described in the last subsection, it seems to be necessary to analyze the level of simple concepts on which the revision operations are defined. Obviously, this level lies between the syntax and the semantics of terms. It abstracts from arbitrary syntactic distinctions, such as ordering of subexpressions, embedded conjunctions, and multiple occurrences of the same simple concepts, but does not consider all terms which have the same meaning in one terminology as equivalent. So, for instance, in the terminology

$$A \stackrel{.}{=} (\text{and } B\ C)$$
$$D \stackrel{.}{=} (\text{and } A\ C)$$

the sets of simple concepts characterizing the respective defining expressions are different, although they have the same extension. However, this is not an accidental distinction but seems to meet the intuitions. As I argued in Sect. 7.2.4, the literal parts of a defining expression of a term should be part of the meaning of a term in any possible terminology. The level of simple concepts accomplishes just that. The set of simple concepts characterizing the defining expression of D contains A and C in any terminology. Thus, the level of simple concepts formalizes the notion of equivalence of concept expressions when viewed in isolation, i.e., equivalence regardless of a terminology. However, there is one exception. If a concept expression is incoherent in every terminology or contains a value restriction which is incoherent in every terminology, then two expressions semantically equivalent in every terminology may still be characterized by different sets of simple concepts. For example,

$$\text{(and (atleast 2 R) (atmost 1 R))} \qquad (7.37)$$

although having an empty extension in any terminology, is not necessarily equivalent to other incoherent concepts on the level of simple concepts.

However, the distinction made on the the level of simple concepts again seems to be reasonable. Although the expression (7.37) is semantically equivalent to any other incoherent concept, the *reason* for the incoherency can only be found by considering the simple concepts which make up the concept expression. While this reason for the incoherency is not important when we view the expression (7.37) as static and unchangeable, it plays a role when viewed from a dynamic angle. If we intend to revise the concept expression, for instance, by removing one of the number restrictions, we probably want to retain the other number restriction.

Essentially, the level of simple concepts seems to capture everything which we consider as important distinctions between concepts, and it abstracts from all unimportant, coincidental, purely syntactical distinctions. Moreover, interpreting a terminological knowledge base on this level, all the requirements presented in Sect. 7.1.2 are satisfied trivially. The important question in this context is how far the principles are satisfied on the semantic level, i.e., on the level of subsumption relationships, as well.

The first of the principles presented in Sect. 7.1.2, *adequacy of the request language*, is evidently satisfied. Although we do not manipulate term introductions or subsumption relationships, the expressions still can be interpreted in the formalism. The principle (K2) – revision request expressions with the same meaning should lead to identical effects – is satisfied to the extent described above. All concept expressions which have identical extension in any terminology and which do not contain incoherent subexpressions are equivalent on the level of simple concepts, and have thus the same effect on a knowledge base. As regards (K3), the *closure* principle, it is impossible to introduce a term more than once and terminological cycles do not present any semantical problem – thus, this principle is satisfied.

With regard to (K4) and (K5), the situation is more problematic. The *success* principle (K4) is unconditionally satisfied for TELL operations in the sense that after a TELL operation the expression to be added to a term definition subsumes the term. For FORGET operation, however, this does not hold in general. For instance, if we request to remove (atleast 2 member) from Small-team in the by now famous "team" terminology, the number restriction on the member role would still be inherited from Team. As argued above, however, revision operations are intended to operate on individual defining expressions, and thus the success should be measured on this level as well – and on this level the operations are successful in most cases. After a FORGET operation, the expression to be removed no longer subsumes the term defining expression if both are viewed in isolation – and if the original expression and the expression to be removed are not incoherent. Summarizing, in a weak sense, (K4) is satisfied. However, there are cases when FORGET is unsuccessful on the semantic level. With (K5), the *minimal change* principle, the situation is similar. A TELL operation might add a simple concept which is already inherited and thus change the knowledge base more than necessary, but when we view the expression in isolation, there is no other choice.

Actually, I would regard FORGET operations which are unsuccessful on the semantic level, TELL operations which add something already derivable, and TELL operations which lead to incoherent concepts as *legal* but as *implausible* revision requests (see also Sect. 8.3). They indicate that the assumptions about the state of the terminological knowledge base are most probably invalid, a fact which should be taken as a starting point for interaction between the agent issuing the terminological revision operation and the terminological representation system. However, this is something which has more to do with knowledge acquisition than with knowledge representation, and, thus, we will touch on this issue only briefly in Sect. 8.3. Summarizing, I strongly believe that the literal revision approach described above suffices to cover all cases where terminological revisions appear to be necessary.

In order to justify this claim, it might be helpful to reconsider the examples given in the Introduction. In the first example, the "atmost"-restriction on the member role of the Small-team was requested to be decreased to three. Translating this to a formal revision request on the "team" terminology T, it might look like as follows:

$$\text{TELL}_C[T, \text{Small-team}, (\text{atmost 3 member})]$$

resulting in an addition of the requested number restriction to the defining expression of the concept Small-team. A Modern-team would thus no longer be a Small-team.

In the second example, for Modern-team, the "atmost" restriction on the member role should be changed to ten. Taking this request literally, one could try:

$$\text{TELL}_C[T, \text{Modern-team}, (\text{atmost 10 member})]$$

leading to the addition of the requested number restriction to the definition of Modern-team, although without any semantic effect. The Modern-team concept has already a stronger number restriction on the member role. Actually, I would regard such an operation as an *implausible revision operation* which should lead to further interaction.[10] The effect of this operation becomes visible only if the the stronger restriction is removed from the definition of Modern-team, before or after the above TELL operation:

$$\text{FORGET}_C[T, \text{Modern-team}, (\text{atmost 5 member})]$$

---

[10]What should be noted is that though the operation is implausible, even under a revision scheme which is more oriented towards belief revision as described in the previous chapter, the semantic effect would be the same because the addition of something which can be already derived does not change anything.

In the third example, somebody requested a change for the value restriction of the member role for the concept **Modern-team** as follows:

$$\textrm{TELL}_C[\mathcal{T}, \textsf{Modern-team}, (\textsf{all member Man})]$$

Such an operation leads to an incoherent concept definition because the **leader** role, which is a subrole of **member**, is restricted to **Woman**. However, from a semantic point of view, there is nothing wrong with incoherent concepts. Again, I would regard this as an implausible, but legal operation, which should lead to further interactions. In a belief revision context, one might be tempted to remove the (least epistemically relevant) propositions leading to the incoherency, e.g. the subrole introduction of **leader**, the value restriction on the **leader** role, or both. However, since the incoherency is probably based on a misunderstanding of the term, it seems to be more reasonable to come to a new mutual understanding instead of trying to find a description which differs minimally. As argued above, such an implicit revision will most probably lead to other misunderstandings in the future.

The fourth example given in Sect. 1.3 is (intentionally) somewhat on the wrong track. We requested to "delete" the concepts **Man** and **Woman** because the distinction between them were no longer considered as meaningful. First of all, as discussed in Sect. 7.2.2, it does not seem to be meaningful to delete concepts. Second, it is not even necessary. The intention of dropping the distinction between **Man** and **Woman** can be easily accomplished by "replacing" **Woman** and **Man** by **Human** in all concepts which use them, in our case only the **Modern-team** concept. This can be done either manually for all concepts, or preferably as a kind of "macro operation" defined on the entire knowledge base.

Finally, the last example presented in Sect. 1.3

$$\textrm{TELL}_C[\mathcal{T}, \textsf{Human}, (\textsf{all offspring Human})]$$

was the reason I investigated terminological cycles in Chap. 5 in the first place.

Before we now end the conceptual analysis of revision in terminological systems, we will briefly discuss the revision problem in the context of hybrid systems, providing a partial answer to the question posed in the Introduction of how assertional and terminological knowledge interact in revision processes.

7.4 Revision in Hybrid Representation Systems

While we have so far concentrated our discussion on the problem of revising terminological knowledge, it might be interesting to study the revision problem in the broader context of hybrid representation systems. Actually, one intention behind working out a formally sound solution for the problem of terminological revision was to provide a framework for the maintenance of assertional knowledge when terminological changes are permitted. With the solution described in Sect. 7.3.2, it is possible to describe such a maintenance process which is formally sound and intuitively plausible, as we will see below.

Conceiving a hybrid representation system employing a terminological formalism and an assertional one, for instance $\mathcal{TF}$ and $\mathcal{AF}$, let us assume knowledge base revision operations which act on the TBox and on the ABox, named TELL^T, FORGET^T, TELL^A, and FORGET^A, respectively. The two former operations should be defined as described in Sect. 7.3.2, while the two latter should be something similar to theory change operations as discussed in the last chapter.

As argued in Sect. 7.3.2, TELL^A and FORGET^A should never lead to any modification of the TBox. This means that terminological knowledge is not only epistemically more relevant than assertional knowledge, but also that it is immune against revision – against revision concerning the description of the world.[11] Thus, if an assertion is to be entered which is inconsistent with the TBox alone, i.e., if there are no models respecting the terminology for the assertion to be entered, the assertion should be rejected. If the assertion is inconsistent with the ABox interpreted in light of the TBox, then the ABox has to be revised using one of the strategies described in the last chapter – taking the TBox as unrevisable.

Revisions in the ABox as described are straightforward, at least conceptually. The interesting problem is what should be done with the ABox if the TBox is revised. TELLing and FORGETing parts of defining expressions have the obvious intuitive meaning of restricting or relaxing, respectively, the conditions under which a term may be applied to an object. TELLing or FORGETing the *defined* status of a term simply means that all necessary and sufficient conditions are given or that only necessary conditions are supplied, respectively. Using these intuitive meanings of terminological revision operations, it is easy to derive consequences of terminological change operations for the ABox.

FORGET^T operations result simply in invalidating some hybrid inferences based on the withdrawn part of the defining expression on one hand. On the other hand, it may allow recognizing some objects as belonging to the extension of the now more weakly defined concept. For instance, if we decide to forget that every **leader** of a modern team has to be a **Woman**, then any role filler of the **leader** role which had not been explicitly stated to be a **Woman** can no longer believed to be a **Woman**. On the other hand, any **Team** with at least one **leader** and not more than four **members** can now be considered being a **Modern-team**, regardless of the sex of the **leader**. In any case, a FORGET^T operation can never lead to an inconsistency. If an ABox has models respecting the terminology in the TBox, a FORGET^T operation simply makes more models possible.

For TELL^T operations, we have the opposite situation. A TELL^T may permit some new hybrid inferences to be drawn, based on the added part of the defining expression of some term. Additionally, some objects previously believed to belong to the extension of a concept may, after the TELL^T operation, turn out not to be in the extension of the concept any longer. Most seriously, a TELL^T can lead to inconsistencies. For instance, if we have in our ABox an assertion that

---

[11]As pointed out before, in a concept learning context, one would probably like the opposite behavior, i.e., terminological knowledge to be considered less epistemically relevant than assertional knowledge.

TEAM-X is a Modern-team with four members, and we TELL^T the TBox that Modern-teams have at most three members, then the ABox becomes inconsistent with respect to the TBox. The obvious way to deal with such inconsistencies is to revise the ABox with respect to the new TBox. Technically speaking, any object which is predicated to belong to the extension of a modified concept has to be revised according to the added expression, which results in ferreting out the inconsistency introduced by the TELL^T operation.

Summarizing, revision in hybrid systems does not seem to present deeper conceptual problems and is easy to understand on an intuitive level. However, a necessary prerequisite is that we permit for revisions of parts of term introductions, as described in Sect. 7.3.2. If we had adopted the scheme discussed in Sect. 7.2.3 – revising a definition by deleting and reinserting it – this would not have been so straightforward.

Changing the point of view on the problem, the solution presented in this section may be used as another argument in favor of using hybrid representation formalisms. In Chap. 3 we introduced a terminological formalism with the arguments that factoring out terminological knowledge makes it possible to impose organizational principles on a knowledge base and that it leads to efficient special-purpose inference techniques. Moreover, if the restricted assertional formalism is used to form a hybrid representation formalism, as in our case, the boundary between the two formalisms is quite clear, and the purposes of the subformalisms are evident.

The situation is a little different if first-order predicate logic is employed as the assertional formalism, as e.g. in the KRYPTON case. Although one can still argue that the distinction between assertional and terminological knowledge supports the organization of a knowledge base and permits efficient special-purpose inference techniques, everything expressible in the terminological formalism may as well be expressed in the assertional formalism. This situation often gives rise to heated discussions whether it is really worthwhile to consider such a formalism as hybrid or "simply" as a different view on first-order predicate logic. *Hybrid formalisms may be convenient for expressing a given body of knowledge* and may even be used to speed up the inference process. However, the knowledge expressed is the same regardless of whether a hybrid formalism is used or everything is expressed in pure first-order logic.

Although this argument is correct in a formal sense – on the knowledge level representation formalisms are irrelevant – it makes, of course, a difference how knowledge can be expressed. This is not only a matter of convenience and organization but has also to do with the pragmatics of the represented knowledge. As the reflection about revision in terminological representation systems has shown, terminological knowledge seem not to be revisable along the lines one would revise assertional knowledge. This means that although from a static point of view there may be no difference between the knowledge represented in an assertional formalism and the knowledge represented in a terminological formalism, fundamental differences become visible if we analyze the properties of the dynamics of a hybrid representation formalism.

8. Terminological Reason Maintenance

Having analyzed revision operations in terminological representation systems from a conceptual point of view, we will now try to identify appropriate implementation techniques. As a first approximation, there are two two simple but inefficient solutions. If we are not interested in assert-time inferences and do all reasoning at query-time, there is no problem at all. After a revision of the terminological knowledge base as described in Sect. 7.3.2, all subsumption tests will work on the new terminology without any problems. However, as argued in Sect. 4.4.2, there are a number of good reasons to perform assert-time inferences in terminological representation systems.

Accepting that premise, we have the problem that some assert-time inferences may become invalid after a revision operation and that new ones have to be made. A brute-force solution would be to throw away everything derived after a revision operation and to start computing all subsumption and immediate subsumption relationships from scratch. However, as noted in Sect. 6.6.1, a small change to a knowledge base usually affects only a small fraction of inferred propositions – a fact we should take advantage of when designing a system.

In the following section, we will analyze what kind of assert-time inferences should be taken care of and what kind of reason-maintenance technique is most appropriate for our problem. In particular, we will try to analyze the trade-off between recording inferences and recomputation. Based on this analysis, a technique for combining a simple data-dependency network and invariants derivable from semantic properties of terminologies related by revision operations will be described in Sect. 8.2. Finally, in Sect. 8.3, we will briefly discuss how such a terminological revision system can be embedded in a knowledge acquisition system.

8.1 Incremental Classification

Essentially, what has been said above implies that the *classification process* should work *incrementally*. For each revision request, the classifier should update the affected parts of the concept and role taxonomy. Note that this is quite different from making classification *interactive*, as described in [Finin and Silverman, 1986]. *Interactive classification*, as defined by Finin and Silverman, means that the inferences made during classification are used to drive the interaction with the user – based on some heuristics, e.g. that two atomic concepts with different names should not be equivalent in a terminology. While such a facility seems to be a good idea for knowledge acquisition, it precludes the application of the knowledge base revision facility in a broader context, and it is not clear how to specify a clean interface between classification and knowledge acquisition heuristics – as we already noted when discussing the KREME system [Abrett and Burstein, 1987] in Sect. 7.2.2.

Incremental classification is in some sense easier than interactive classification because it is based "only" on the semantics of the representation formalism and ignores all issues connected with heuristics concerning knowledge acquisition. Nevertheless, incremental classification is not trivial. Lipkis even seems to believe that it is almost impossible [Lipkis, 1982, p. 134]:

> Once a concept has been established as part of the taxonomy, the classifier assumes it will not be changed or deleted, as the effects of such changes on other concepts in the network are, in general, unpredictable.

Indeed, the classifiers implemented in KL-ONE and NIKL do not allow for incremental changes of concept definitions. The only revision operation they permit is the addition of a new, previously undefined and unused atomic concept. As a consequence, working with these systems resembles the time-consuming *edit-compile-test* cycle one has to follow in conventional compiler-based software development environments – despite the fact that the development of knowledge-based systems is usually performed experimentally and requires strong interactive capabilities.

Of course, the citation above is either too pessimistic or merely represents a statement about the particular implementation of the classifier used in KL-ONE. With the definition of what a legal revision operation is (as given in the previous chapter) and the specification of the semantics of the representation formalism, it is obvious that a revision operation does not result in a completely unpredictable and chaotic change of the concept taxonomy. Rather, some inferences made in the classification process become invalid and others become possible – a fact calling for some form of *reason maintenance*.

8.1.1 What Kind of Reason Maintenance Do We Need?

As pointed out in Sect. 6.6.5, we do not need the full power of reason maintenance systems for a knowledge base revision facility. We want neither dependency-directed backtracking as in justification-based RMS nor the breadth-first search technique employed in assumption-based RMS. The reason is that we do not have to find a minimal consistent set of assumptions or to track down inconsistencies and get rid of them by chosing alternatives – as is needed in a problem-solving context. We are merely interested in identifying propositions which can no longer be derived and, conversely, sets of propositions which can be used to derive something new. Furthermore, we want to retain as many of the inferences made as possible. In a nutshell, we only need data-dependency network maintenance techniques, as described in Sect. 6.6.1 and 6.6.2.

However, what kind of DDN is required? Is it enough to have a simple monotonic, cycle-free DDN, or is it necessary to employ nonmonotonic DDNs containing cycles? Reconsidering the inferences necessary to compute the concept taxonomy as described in Sect. 4.1 and 4.4, in particular the classification process, leads to the conclusion that some inferences are indeed nonmonotonic in the sense that they can be invalidated by TELL operations.

As already noted in Sect. 3.2.6, the *immediate subsumption* relation is non-monotonic with respect to the addition of new concept introductions. Thus, it is also nonmonotonically changed by a $TELL_C$ operation on an undefined atomic concept. However, the story is even worse. The subsumption relation is also nonmonotonic with respect to the $TELL_C$ operations we defined. Assuming two concepts, c and c' with $c \preceq_T c'$, a $TELL_C$ operation on c' can easily invalidate the subsumption relationships between c and c'. Thus, if we intend to record and maintain *every* atomic inference step in the classification process, we have to employ a nonmonotonic DDN. Although it seems unlikely that classification requires circular justifications, we will take a closer look at the entire problem, identifying each atomic inference step and describing the necessary justifications.

8.1.2 Recording and Justifying Terminological Inferences

Instead of analyzing the classification algorithm as described in Sect. 4.4, we will analyze a simplified model first. Let us assume that in order to compute immediate subsumption, only the subsumption relation between concepts is used, i.e., instead of inserting a concept in a directed graph, the directed graph is computed from the subsumption relation. Moreover, subsumption between terms will be computed directly from subsumption between the respective p-terms. Thus, no anonymous concepts for conjoined value restrictions are created as in the classification algorithm described in Sect. 4.4.

Given these assumptions, the inference steps of the classification process are the following:

1. The replacement of atomic terms by their normal-form definitions by applying the function EXP.

2. The normalization of expanded p-terms by using the NORM algorithm.

3. The structural comparison between two p-terms by using the COMPARE algorithm.

4. Computation of immediate subsumption according to Definition 3.16.

Actually, steps 2 and 3 can be further decomposed into atomic inference steps according to the rules (N1)–(N8) and (C1)–(C6) as specified in NORM and COMPARE, respectively. Using this model, we can justify all the atomic steps as follows.

Each occurrence of a normal-form definition which replaces an atomic term in a term expression can be *justified* by the term introduction of the atomic term. Each subexpression in a normalized p-term created by step (Ni) can be justified by the subexpressions of the unnormalized expression involved in forming a normalized subexpressions. Based on these justifications, revision operations could be handled in the following way. If a subexpression is added to the normal-form definition of an atomic term, then perhaps some new subexpression in normalized p-terms can be derived. Conversely, if a subexpression of a normal-form definition of an atomic concept is deleted, then some subexpressions in the normalized p-term become *unjustified*, and some recomputation is necessary.

Coming now to the structural comparison between p-terms, subsumption between p-terms can be justified by the fact that *for each* subexpression of the first p-term, we find *some* subexpression in the second p-term such that one of the rules in COMPARE is satisfied. This means that besides the relationships between subexpressions in the two p-terms, a crucial justification for subsumption is that the subsuming p-term has just the subexpressions it has and no more. If something is added to the previously subsuming p-term, it is necessary to find a corresponding subexpression in the previously subsumed p-term in order to justify continued subsumption. Thus, if something is added to a subsuming p-term, the recorded subsumption relationship will become possibly invalid, and for the new subexpression, a corresponding subexpression has to be found in the subsumed expression. Conversely, if we add something to a subsumed p-term, the subsumption relationship computed previously is unarguably valid. For deletions, of subexpression in p-terms the converse relationships hold.

In order to compute the immediate subsumption relation (i.e., the concept taxonomy), we also need the complement of subsumption, nonsubsumption. That is for each pair of p-terms p, q such that p does not subsume q, this relationship has to be recorded and justified by a subexpression in p for which no corresponding subexpression in q can be found. Additionally, parallel to the subsumption case, the nonsubsumption relationship has to be justified by the fact that q has only the subexpressions it has and no more.

Based on the subsumption and nonsubsumption relation between introduced atomic terms, immediate subsumption between two atomic terms t and t' computed using Definition 3.16 has to be justified by the fact that no introduced atomic term "lies between" t and t' and that the terminology contains only the introduced atomic terms it actually contains. In the event that a term introduction is changed, a new term is added, the immediate subsumption relation becomes possibly invalid and must be reestablished on the base of the updated subsumption relation.

Note that no circular justifications are necessary. Terminological cycles, which were not mentioned explicitly, would be handled by the extended subsumption algorithm. Thus, although we have nonmonotonic justifications, the DDN we would have to employ is still very simple.

Carrying over this result to the classification algorithm described in Sect. 4.4, we would have to add some more steps and modify some steps of the inference recording technique described above. In step 1, only the top-level atomic concepts would be expanded, and, in step 2, NORM would be applied to these partially expanded expressions. For concepts acting as value restrictions, anonymous terms would be introduced – justified by the particular value restriction – and these anonymous concepts would be treated in the same way. Recording of inferences according to COMPARE would then act only on primitive concept components, roles, and value restrictions for which subsumption is justified by the chains of immediate subsumption relationships between them established previously. This means that the justifications for subsumption and immediate subsumption are intertwined.

Furthermore, if we follow the strategy proposed in Sect. 4.4, inserting concepts into the concept taxonomy by testing subsumption only until we find the set of immediate subsumers and immediate subsumees, we will not record *all* subsumption inferences but will justify the immediate subsumption relationships between a newly inserted concept and the immediate subsumers and subsumees by previously established immediate subsumption relationships. Since immediate subsumption depends on more premises than subsumption, it may pay to compute and justify the entire subsumption relation, as well (perhaps only temporarily before a revision operation is executed).

8.1.3 Redundancy and Functional Equivalence

Although it is possible to employ a DDN in order to support terminological reason maintenance as sketched above, there are good arguments against such a straightforward adaption of reason maintenance techniques to our problem. Analyzing the structure of recorded inferences and of the necessary justifications reveals that the recorded inferences are either trivial, i.e., in terms of computational costs, it does not pay to record the inferences, or they are justified in a way such that recomputation is necessary in most cases, anyway.

Subsumption and immediate subsumption both depend on justifications of the form "nothing else is in the term or terminology." Such justifications are, however, invalidated by almost all revisions. Furthermore, recording the subsumption relationships between subexpressions of normalized terms does not save very much when recomputations are necessary. In the simplified model, as well as in the case of full classification, we would have to record

1. identity of primitive components

2. subsumption between roles

3. numerical relationships between number restrictions

4. subsumption relations between value restrictions, which are complex subexpressions in the case of the simplified model and anonymous concepts in the classification model.

These relationships are, however, almost instantaneously computable from the expressions itself. Although following the CSUB algorithm, we would need $O(|q|)$ steps to find a subexpression in a term q, we could reduce this to almost constant time by using indexing or hashing techniques. Recording subsumption relations between subexpressions would thus not enhance the efficiency. On the contrary, the overhead for recording and maintaining inferences would cost more in terms of space and time than what could be saved by recording subsumption relationships!

This reflection shows that the straightforward combination of a terminological reasoner and a DDN does not lead to the result desired. Most of the structure we could make use of in a DDN is already part of the implementational data-structure in a terminological representation system. Thus, what we should do is to exploit this structure, aiming at a system which is *functionally equivalent* to a DDN, instead of employing a full-fledged DDN, which would result in redundancy and mere overhead.

8.2 Invariants of Revision Operations

The key idea in a "hybrid" approach to terminological revision as envisioned above – exploiting the already computed structures of semantic relationships in a terminology and combining this with DDN techniques where necessary – is to identify as many *invariants* between *terminologies related by revision operations* as possible. These invariants can then be used for recomputing the changed relationships without relying on explicitly recorded atomic inference steps.

8.2.1 Terminologies Related by Revision Operations

When analyzing the general relation between two terminologies which are related by a revision operation as defined in the previous chapter, it becomes obvious that it is possible to identify a large number of relationships between concepts and roles which are necessarily invariant for a given operation on a given term. In particular, if we have a TELL or FORGET operation on some atomic term t, then for any terms s and s' which do not use t, i.e., $s \not\rightarrow t$ and $s' \not\rightarrow t$, the subsumption relationships between s and s' will not change. This means, only for t and all terms using t directly or indirectly, the subsumption relationships have to be recomputed.

However, this is not all that can be said. There are also a number of relationships between terms which stay valid. In order to analyze these relationships, let us adopt the following conventions. If T is a terminology, then T' shall denote the revised terminology. Furthermore, t shall be the atomic term on which the revision operation acts. In the case when we have a TELL$_{dis}$ or FORGET$_{dis}$, we will have two terms which are directly affected, and which will be denoted by t and t'. Furthermore, the variables o and o' will be used for denoting atomic terms which do not use t or t', and n and n' will be used for denoting atomic terms which use t or t'.

One relationship which seems to stay invariant is $n \preceq_T o$ for a TELL$_C$ operation and $n \not\preceq_T o$ for a FORGET$_C$ operation. However, we have to be careful. If the *defined* status is added to a concept introduction, this could mean that a *disjointness* restriction becomes irrelevant, resulting in the removal of the term Nothing as a value restriction in the corresponding p-term, which may lead to the result that we cannot conclude from $n \preceq_T o$ that $n \preceq_{T'} o$ is valid.

In general, there are two problematic situations we have to take care of, namely, the presence of Nothing as a value restriction or as the normalized form of a concept expression, and the presence of restriction-circular concepts.[1] In any of these situations, a revision operation may change the subsumption relation in a way which runs counter to the intuition that TELLing only makes the affected terms more specialized and that FORGETing has the opposite effect. Table 8.1 lists all possible cases and relationships we encounter when revising a concept. Additionally, the exception conditions are all specified.

Operation	$n \preceq o$	$n \npreceq o$	$n \preceq n'$	$n \npreceq n'$	$o \preceq n$	$o \npreceq n$
$\text{TELL}_C(\ldots,=)$	$\sqrt{}^a$	$\sqrt{}$	$\sqrt{}^a$	$\sqrt{}^{a,c}$	$\sqrt{}$	
$\text{TELL}_C(\ldots,cexpr)$	$\sqrt{}$		$\sqrt{}^c$			$\sqrt{}$
$\text{TELL}_{dis}(\ldots)$	$\sqrt{}$	$\sqrt{}^b$	$\sqrt{}^b$	$\sqrt{}^b$	$\sqrt{}^b$	$\sqrt{}$
$\text{FORGET}_C(\ldots,=)$	$\sqrt{}$	$\sqrt{}^b$	$\sqrt{}^{b,c}$	$\sqrt{}^b$		$\sqrt{}$
$\text{FORGET}_C(\ldots,cexpr)$		$\sqrt{}$		$\sqrt{}^c$	$\sqrt{}$	
$\text{FORGET}_{dis}(\ldots)$	$\sqrt{}^a$	$\sqrt{}$	$\sqrt{}^a$	$\sqrt{}^a$	$\sqrt{}$	$\sqrt{}^a$

[a]Except part of one the concepts was equivalent to Nothing before the operation.
[b]Except part of one the concepts becomes equivalent to Nothing after the operation.
[c]Except one of the concepts is restriction-circular.

Tab. 8.1. Invariants of Revision Operations

Each tick ($\sqrt{}$) marks an invariant of a revision operation except for the cases explicitly given in the footnotes. For instance, the operation $\text{TELL}_C[\mathcal{T}, t, cexpr]$ leads to $o \npreceq_{\mathcal{T}'} n$ if we had $o \npreceq_{\mathcal{T}} n$, and there is no exception to this rule. Instead of giving proofs for all the invariants, in the next two subsections, we will only sketch the arguments leading to the ticks in the upper two rows of Table 8.1 – leaving it to the reader to verify the other rows by using similar arguments.

Parallel to revision operations on concepts, we could try to identify invariants for revision operations on roles. However, since the update of the role taxonomy is almost trivial, it does not pay to fill up the space with a table specifying the role invariants. Furthermore, there are not that many invariants for relationships between concepts after a role revision , unfortunately. Studying the subsumption algorithm in Sect. 4.1.1, we see that changing relationships between roles may either specialize or generalize a concept using this role. Thus, there is not much to say about the relationship between concepts after a role revision, except that we know that $o \preceq_{\mathcal{T}'} o'$ and $o'' \npreceq_{\mathcal{T}'} o'''$ holds if we had $o \preceq_{\mathcal{T}} o'$ and $o'' \npreceq_{\mathcal{T}} o'''$, respectively.

8.2.2 Making a Primitive Concept Defined

Adding the status of being a defined concept to a concept definition amounts to deleting a primitive component in the corresponding p-concept and, perhaps, deleting a disjointness marker, which may lead to changing a concept from incoherent to coherent. Furthermore, for any concept not using the revised concept,

[1]Component-circular concepts are not problematic. As the descriptive semantics tells us, they are simply equivalent to primitive concepts. When introducing or removing such a cycle, we should be careful. However, they do not present problems, as we will see below.

it follows that the corresponding p-concept does not contain the deleted primitive component and disjointness marker. For this reason, in the normal case, we can infer $n \preceq_{T'} o$ from $n \preceq_T o$. However, this holds only if no subexpression of the p-concept corresponding to n contains the term **Nothing** resulting from a disjointness restriction on the revised primitive concept. If this is the case, a subsumption relationship between n and o based on the subsumption between a subexpression of o and a **Nothing**-subexpression in n can be invalidated. For the complementary relation, $n \npreceq_T o$, things are easier. The removal of part of a concept or value restriction in the p-term corresponding to n can never lead to a nonsubsumption relationship being changed into a subsumption relationship. Hence, in this case, we can unconditionally infer $n \npreceq_{T'} o$.

In the case when we consider the change of subsumption relationships between concepts which are both affected by the revision, we see that in the normal case, subsumption and nonsubsumption are invariant. If we have $n \preceq_T n'$ and we remove primitive components and disjointness markers, then either we remove them in corresponding subexpressions, or they did not contribute to the subsumption relationship, anyway. However, similar to the case analyzed above, the implicit removal of a disjointness restriction can invalidate this invariant. Furthermore, if we have a restriction-circular concept, there are some problems. Subsumption will not be affected by a cycle, but nonsubsumption is not always preserved. Consider the following example:

$$X \;\; \dot{\leq} \;\; (\text{all } r\, X)$$
$$Y \;\; \dot{=} \;\; (\text{all } r\, X)$$

Here, we have $Y \npreceq_T X$. However, adding the defined status to X leads to the equivalence between X and Y.

Finally, in the first row, we have the two cases that before the revision operation, $o \preceq_T n$ or $o \npreceq_T n$. If there was a subsumption relation in the unrevised terminology – which must rest on the fact that some subexpression in the p-term corresponding to o is **Nothing**, which is subsumed by the primitive component to be removed in the p-term corresponding to n – the removal of primitive parts in the p-term corresponding to n cannot invalidate the subsumption relationship. On the other hand, the removal of a primitive component in n can establish subsumption, provided this was the only subexpression not present in o.

As should be obvious, component-circular concepts are not relevant if we add a defined status to a concept. All concepts in the cycle would be equivalent to a hypothetical primitive concept, and since such a cycle is neither created nor eliminated by such a revision operation, such cycles are irrelevant.

8.2.3 Adding an Expression to a Concept Definition

Adding a concept expression to a concept definition amounts to restricting the extension, i.e., the revised concept is subsumed by more concepts than before. This also holds for all affected concepts, i.e., all concepts using the revised concept in the definition. For this reason, the first tick in the first row should be obvious.

The only problematic case might be that the addition results in a component-circular concept introduction. In this case, the descriptive semantics tells us that the entire cycle results in a primitive concept which is more specialized than all concepts participating in the cycle. Thus, the invariant holds for the introduction of component-circular concepts as well. Conversely, the relation $n \not\sqsubseteq_T o$ is, of course, not invariant. Adding something to the definition of n can very well establish subsumption between n and o.

Subsumption between two affected concepts continues to hold, except we have a restriction-circular concept, e.g.

$$X \doteq (\text{all } r\, X)$$
$$Y \doteq (\text{all } r\, X)$$

Adding a concept expression to the definition of X leads to the fact that $X \not\sqsubseteq_{T'} Y$. If the two concepts are not restriction-circular, however, then the addition of the subexpression either will be at corresponding places in the two corresponding p-terms since there was a subsumption relationship before, or the subsumed concept contains a Nothing-subexpression at the place were the revised atomic concept is mentioned in the subsuming p-term. Nonsubsumption between two affected concepts obviously does not hold because the added concept expression can easily establish subsumption between two concepts which were unrelated before.

Finally, there are the last two columns in the second row, which are in a sense symmetrical to the first two columns. Adding something to a subsuming p-term can easily lead to the fact that a previous subsumption relationship is invalidated. On the other hand, the addition of a concept expression to some definition can never lead to the fact that this concept subsumes some previously nonsubsumed concept.

8.2.4 Exploiting the Invariants in Reclassification

If we maintained the subsumption relation in a terminology, it would now be easy to identify the individual relationships which become arguable by a revision operation and to check these by recomputing subsumption for the identified pairs of atomic concepts. However, not the subsumption, but the immediate subsumption relation is usually recorded.

Using the most basic invariants, namely, that the subsumption relation on all unaffected terms is invariant, the following strategy may be applied. All terms which use the revised term t and the revised term t itself are spliced out off the taxonomies. After that, the normalized form of those terms is recomputed and reinserted into the taxonomies.[2] As is easy to see, this simple strategy can be extended in order to exploit the invariants of Table 8.1 as well. When reinserting the affected terms into the concept taxonomy, the invariant subsumption relationships can be used to save a large number of subsumption tests. For this

---

[2]This actually is the strategy used in KREME [Abrett and Burstein, 1987] and LOOM [MacGregor, 1988b].

purpose, the invariant subsumption relationships between affected and unaffected concepts as well as between two affected concepts should be temporarily saved before the affected concepts are removed from the taxonomy.

This means that the task of saving recomputations is done by exploiting invariants instead of relying on a general DDN. The only point where we need a DDN is the identification of affected concepts. Actually, the relation necessary to identify affected atomic concepts is identical to the usage relation – and is for this reason easily computable from the concept definitions itself. Employing a DDN for this purpose, however, saves the effort of searching through all definitions. Thus, we do not need any nonmonotonicity or cyclic justifications. The DDN we have to use is a noncyclic, monotonic one.

The general conclusion we can draw from the reflections in the last two sections on implementation techniques for terminological reason maintenance is that when we know how revision operations can effect the knowledge base, in particular, when we know about invariants without explicitly recording them, then the use of a general-purpose RMS will be much less efficient than the careful combination of DDN techniques and invariants. Although this may sound almost trivial, the idea of solving the revision problem by a dedicated and isolatable component seems so overwhelmingly convincing that it may take some time to discover what the real meaning (in terms of computational resources) behind the final note in [Doyle, 1979, p. 269] is: "the overhead required to record justifications for every program belief might seem excessive."

Although the computational complexity in cycle-free DDNs is reasonable, the real costs can be very high. I discovered this fact when implementing a prototype of a terminological revision system which handles terminological cycles and revision operations, which led to the investigation of invariants between terminologies related by a revision operation.

There are two points to consider here. First, terminological revision differs considerably from the problems Doyle and others propose to use a RMS for. Second, the concrete implementation was carried out in SYMBOLICS-PROLOG, and this implementation of PROLOG (as well as many other PROLOG implementations) has the property that recording something in the database usually costs a lot of time compared to other operations, e.g. unification and backtracking. For this reason, in PROLOG, it often pays to recompute something instead of recording an assert-time inference. Nevertheless, maintaining the immediate subsumption relation leads to a considerable speed-up compared to computing immediate subsumption from scratch, and exploiting the invariants in revision also saves a significant amount of time when reclassifying concepts affected by a revision operation.

8.3 Supporting Knowledge Acquisition

So far, we have intentionally ignored all issues concerning knowledge acquisition and have focussed on the formal and implementational aspects of revising terminological knowledge bases. This means that we have the freedom to apply the system in every context where a revision facility is required – be it in machine learning, in knowledge acquisition, or simply in maintaining the terminological part of a hybrid representation system. In this section, we will discuss how the revision facility might be integrated into a knowledge acquisition system.

First, we should note that the separation of issues connected with representation and revision on one hand and the problems of knowledge acquisition on the other hand avoids a number of problems and confusions usually present in approaches which do not distinguish between these issues. For instance, the "empirical semantic" approach [Reimer, 1985, Reimer, 1986] (already mentioned in Sect. 2.2.1) does not aim at describing what the contents of a knowledge base is supposed to denote in the external world but imposes *integrity constraints* on the use of certain representation constructs [Reimer, 1985, Sect. 3.3]: "Representation constructs are required to reflect the empirical regularities which are holding in some domain of discourse. This way the possibility of representing illegal knowledge is reduced and (semantic!) integrity is increased." The problem with such an approach is that it is clear neither what the "empirical regularities" of representation constructs are, nor what "illegal" knowledge is. The net effects are that it remains unclear what the representation constructs refer to and that the specification of the representation language and of the representation system is overloaded with restrictions which belong conceptually to a user interface.

Furthermore, imposing "integrity constraints" on a representation language may lead to restrictions which are difficult by a user to understand and are most probably unnecessary – if the syntax is designed carefully. The investigation of terminological cycles in Chap. 5 was motivated mainly by this fact and the idea that a system should be "liberal" with respect to seemingly weird user inputs. Instead of complaining about a particular revision request, the system should simply point out the consequences and perhaps indicate what is unusual about the revision request. For instance, component-circular concepts seem to be really nonsense – and for this reason one might be tempted to ban them from a terminological knowledge base. However, the user may have had in mind to cut this cycle somewhere else, in any case. Thus, forbidding component-circular concepts would force the user to take an unmotivated detour. Nevertheless, taking a liberal standpoint does not imply that the user should not get any feedback. For this reason, some conditions for detecting

- implausible state of a knowledge bases and

- implausible revision requests

will be specified, whereby implausibility will mostly be justified by the fact that a *shorter* and *less complex* expression would be able to achieve the same *semantic effect*. These conditions might be seen as "integrity constraints" in the sense described above. However, they are not absolute and one can even say there is a grading of plausibility, as opposed to the binary decision of either accepting or rejecting a user input.

As we have seen in the previous chapter, all revision requests lead to well-formed and meaningful knowledge bases. However, based on the rule given above that it is more desirable to use a short and simple expression than a long and complicated one to achieve a given semantic effect, it is possible to identify some, more or less, implausible parts of a terminological knowledge base:

- *Component-circular concepts* and *roles* are implausible since the semantic effect could be expressed more succinctly by a primitive concept using all the non-circular restrictions.

- *incoherent concepts* are implausible because they cannot be used to describe anything or to define new *plausible* concepts. Most likely, the user has overlooked some disjointness restriction or conflicting number restrictions.

- Similarly, *incoherent value restrictions* are implausible. The simplest way to express that a role cannot be filled is to use an "atmost" restriction of 0.

- The presence of *two atomic concepts equivalent with respect to subsumption* is implausible since one of them would be enough to achieve anything which could be done with the two concepts.

- Concept definitions mentioning *role restrictions already inherited* are somewhat implausible because the definition is more complex than necessary.

Using these conditions, a revision request can be judged to be implausible if it leads to a partly implausible knowledge base. However, as already pointed out in Sect. 7.3.3, there are more cases which can be regarded as implausible. In particular, all revision requests which are not successful on the semantic level or which are more complex than necessary can be regarded as implausible:

- Any revision request leading to an implausible state is implausible.

- Any TELL operation adding something which is already a literal part of the knowledge base is implausible.

- Any FORGET operation trying to remove something which is not a literal part of the knowledge base is implausible.

- Any FORGET operation not removing the subsumption relation between the removed expression and the revised concept is implausible. Note that this implies that the revised concept was implausible!

- Any FORGET operation leading to Anything or anyrelation is implausible.

As is easy to see, these conditions could be checked by subsumption tests and inspection of the simple concepts making up a concept definition. Moreover, the conditions specified could easily be formulated as formal rules which could be used to drive a user interface, which would give us the flexibility to change and extend this set of rules in order to meet different demands.

I hope to have shown by the discussion above that distinguishing between the formal process of revising a knowledge base and the heuristic part of supporting the user in a knowledge acquisition context enables us to to achieve a better and deeper understanding of both problems.

9. Summary and Outlook

Knowledge representation formalisms should be declarative, i.e., they should have a semantics that is process independent. However, when such formalisms are put to use, the processing aspect becomes very important. Focusing on this aspect, technical contribution were made in two areas, namely, reasoning and revision, studied in the context of KL-ONE-based hybrid representation systems.

9.1 Technical Contributions

Starting with a KL-ONE-based terminological knowledge representation formalism (called $\mathcal{TF}$), a model-theoretic semantics inspired by [Brachman and Levesque, 1984] was used to analyze some of the semantic properties of the formalism. In particular, it was shown that it is possible to abstract from the semantic structures induced by a (cycle-free) terminology without changing the possible extensions of defined terms. For this reason, subsumption in terminological languages can be reduced to subsumption in term-forming languages (Theorem 3.3). This holds even when primitive concepts and disjointness restrictions are permitted because they can be eliminated without an effect on the relevant semantic structure of a terminology (Theorem 3.1). Additionally, a simple assertional formalism (called $\mathcal{AF}$) was introduced resulting together with $\mathcal{TF}$ in a hybrid representation formalism closely resembling the formalism used in the BACK system. A unified model-theoretic semantics for the overall formalism was specified, and a hybrid entailment relation was defined. Based on this formalization, it was shown that $\mathcal{TF}/\mathcal{AF}$ is a conservative extension of $\mathcal{TF}$ (Theorem 3.6).

Using the formal semantics, I showed that the subsumption problem in the term-forming language underlying $\mathcal{TF}$ is decidable (Theorem 4.3), but co-NP-hard (Theorem 4.5) and specified an incomplete subsumption algorithm which detects all obvious subsumption relationships in polynomial time (Theorem 4.2). Unfortunately, however, this complexity result is not valid for subsumption determination in terminological languages. This problem is co-NP-hard even for very small terminological languages (Corollary 4.3). Concerning hybrid inferences, I noted that an important inference had been ignored in similar systems, and proved that employing this inference leads to completeness of the hybrid inference algorithm in the limiting case that the world description is, roughly speaking, vivid in the sense of [Levesque, 1986] (Theorem 4.10). Although this is a rather weak characterization, it seems to be a reasonable and desirable property.

Finally, I tackled a problem usually ignored, namely, how to deal with terminological cycles. Evaluating three different styles of semantics led to the conclusion that the descriptive semantics, which does not prefer least or greatest semantic structures, is the most plausible one. Based on this style of semantics, I showed that subsumption in $\mathcal{TF}$ remains decidable (Theorem 5.3) and discussed how to extend the inference algorithms.

Although inference is the most important aspect when using a knowledge representation formalism, a knowledge representation system which is simply a mechanized deductive calculus is not very useful for practical purposes. Since the world changes, it is necessary to change knowledge bases as well – a requirement which motivates the second topic – revision.

Based on a survey of current approaches in this field, it was shown that the solutions proposed for updates of logical data bases and for counterfactual reasoning can be reconstructed in the logic of theory change employing a notion of epistemic relevance (Theorem 6.3). This reconstruction demonstrated that reason maintenance is only an implementational notion and needs not to be used as a primitive in a theoretical framework of belief revision, contrary to the opinion other authors seem to have. Furthermore, I argued that belief revision as implemented in the reason maintenance system RUP can be conceived as a special case of this scheme, which gives a formal characterization of the revision process implemented in the assertional component of KL-TWO.

Using the rationality postulates of the logic of theory change, a set of general requirements for knowledge base revision was developed (Sect. 7.1.2). These requirements were employed to evaluate previous solution to the problem of revising terminologies. As it turns out, none of them fulfill all requirements. However, an attempt to use the logic of theory change in order to solve the problem also did not lead to a satisfying solution. First, in order to apply the logic of theory change to terminological knowledge, the representation formalism must be considerably extended. Second, taking pragmatics of terminological knowledge into account, the logic of theory change seems not to be the appropriate tool for terminological revision. For these reasons, I adopted an approach which aims at minimal changes on the symbolic level, abstracting from arbitrary syntactic distinctions, though (Sect. 7.3). One crucial property of this solution, namely, the closure property of the revision operation, relies on the fact that terminological cycles are legal and meaningful. Based on this result, I discussed how terminological revision can be combined with the theory change approach in order to design an intuitive plausible and simple model of revision in hybrid systems (Sect. 7.4).

Adopting the notion of minimal changes on the symbolic level, some possible implementation techniques were explored. A straightforward implementation based on a RMS is apparently too inefficient, which led to the analysis of invariants of terminological revision operations (Table 8.1). Using these and a simple data-dependency network is obviously more efficient than employing a general-purpose RMS. Finally, I sketched a mechanism how to integrate such a system into a knowledge acquisition tool with the main emphasis on detecting implausible states and revision requests, contrasting this with an approach of enforcing "integrity."

9.2 Open Problems

There are a number of problems that are still open and some directions of investigation I did not pursue. The most obvious question is the one resulting from the analysis of subsumption determination in terminological languages in Sect. 4.3.2:

1. Are some of the provably intractable term-subsumption problems well-behaved in most cases occuring in practice?

A second, more theoretical problem is the computational complexity of subsumption determination in cyclic terminologies. If an appropriate fixed point semantics (least or greatest) is used, the PSPACE-completeness result for NDFA equivalence will probably carry over to subsumption in terminologies, i.e. subsumption is probably PSPACE-hard. For the descriptive semantics, NDFA equivalence cannot be straightforwardly reduced to subsumption. Thus:

2. What is the increase in computational complexity when moving from cycle-free to cyclic terminologies and does it depend on the style of the semantics?

Another open problem is in how far the conditional completeness result for realization (Theorem 4.10) can be generalized:

3. What are the minimal requirements on the terminological language, on the algorithms, and on the form of the assertional knowledge base to achieve the conditional completeness results?

More generally, it seems to be necessary to develop theoretical tools and techniques to analyze and describe incomplete reasoners[1] and to develop more general methods to combine different representation and reasoning systems in order to create useful and predictable hybrid systems. As a matter of fact, hybrid systems employing limited reasoners will probably not be accepted if we are unable to show that their reasoning capabilities satisfy some reasonable criteria.[2]

Turning to revision, there are also some loose ends. First, there is the question of what the formal relationships between the notion of epistemic relevance introduced in this work and epistemic entrenchment as introduced in [Gärdenfors and Makinson, 1988] is. Although it is clear that in general it is impossible to construct an epistemic entrenchment function for a given epistemic relevance function (because base contraction does not satisfy postulate ($\div$8)), the question is:

---

[1] The approach of analyzing expressively limited formalisms and weak semantics as described in [Levesque, 1988] is one obvious direction. However, I believe that additional criteria have to be developed which are more oriented towards application requirements.

[2] For instance, in [Smoliar and Swartout, 1988], the incomplete terminological reasoner NIKL is criticized and rejected as a knowledge representation tool partly because of the lack of a description of its reasoning capabilities.

4. Under which circumstances is it possible to construct an epistemic entrenchment function corresponding to a given epistemic relevance function?

Furthermore, there is the question of how to formalize iterated revision and contraction. The logic of theory change deals only with the case of revising a theory given some measure of relevance but does not give a hint how this measure is to be updated by a change operation. However, this is necessary if more than one change operation shall be applied to a knowledge base.

Finally, evaluating the solution to the problem of terminological revision, there are, of course, a number of pragmatic settings where other strategies are conceivable, which gives raise to the question of whether the logic of theory change can be exploited in such settings. As a general direction, I believe that the further investigation of properties of belief revision are necessary for the design of future representation systems because real systems will have to cope with a changing world and the correction of wrong assumptions.

A. The Universal Term-Forming Formalism $\mathcal{U}$

Below, the syntax and semantics of all term-forming operators of $\mathcal{U}$ [Patel-Schneider, 1987a] is given (some of the operators have been renamed and others have been omitted without changing the expressiveness, though).

$$
\begin{aligned}
\langle concept \rangle \quad ::= \quad & \langle atomic\text{-}concept \rangle \mid \\
& (\text{and } \langle concept \rangle^+) \mid \\
& (\text{or } \langle concept \rangle^+) \mid \\
& (\text{not } \langle concept \rangle) \mid \\
& (\text{all } \langle role \rangle \langle concept \rangle) \mid \\
& (\text{atleast } \langle number \rangle \langle role \rangle) \mid \\
& (\text{atmost } \langle number \rangle \langle role \rangle) \mid \\
& (\text{rvm } \langle role \rangle \langle role \rangle) \mid \\
& (\text{sd } \langle concept \rangle \langle binding \rangle^+)
\end{aligned}
$$

$$
\begin{aligned}
\langle binding \rangle \quad ::= \quad & (\subseteq \langle role \rangle \langle role \rangle) \mid \\
& (\supseteq \langle role \rangle \langle role \rangle)
\end{aligned}
$$

$$
\begin{aligned}
\langle role \rangle \quad ::= \quad & \langle atomic\text{-}role \rangle \mid \\
& (\text{androle } \langle role \rangle^+) \mid \\
& (\text{orrole } \langle role \rangle^+) \mid \\
& (\text{notrole } \langle role \rangle) \mid \\
& (\text{comp } \langle role \rangle^+) \mid \\
& \text{self} \mid \\
& (\text{inv } \langle role \rangle) \mid \\
& (\text{range } \langle role \rangle \langle concept \rangle) \mid \\
& (\text{trans } \langle role \rangle)
\end{aligned}
$$

$$
\langle number \rangle \quad ::= \quad \langle non\text{-}negative\ integer \rangle
$$

The specification of the semantics is done by specifying the equations for the extension function. $\mathcal{D}$ and $\mathcal{E}$ are the domain and the extension function as defined in Definition 3.2. c and c_i denote concepts, b and b_i denote bindings, and

r and r_i denote roles.

$$\mathcal{E}[(\text{and } c_1 \ldots c_n)] = \bigcap_{i=1}^{n} \mathcal{E}[c_i]$$

$$\mathcal{E}[(\text{or } c_1 \ldots c_n)] = \bigcup_{i=1}^{n} \mathcal{E}[c_i]$$

$$\mathcal{E}[(\text{not } c)] = \mathcal{D} \setminus \mathcal{E}[c]$$

$$\mathcal{E}[(\text{all } r\, c)] = \{x \in \mathcal{D} \mid \forall y : \langle x, y \rangle \in \mathcal{E}[r] \Rightarrow y \in \mathcal{E}[c]\}$$

$$\mathcal{E}[(\text{atleast } n\, r)] = \{x \in \mathcal{D} \mid \|\{y \in \mathcal{D} \mid \langle x, y \rangle \in \mathcal{E}[r]\}\| \geq n\}$$

$$\mathcal{E}[(\text{atmost } n\, r)] = \{x \in \mathcal{D} \mid \|\{y \in \mathcal{D} \mid \langle x, y \rangle \in \mathcal{E}[r]\}\| \leq n\}$$

$$\mathcal{E}[(\text{rvm } r_1\, r_2)] = \{x \in \mathcal{D} \mid \forall y : \langle x, y \rangle \in \mathcal{E}[r_1] \Rightarrow \langle x, y \rangle \in \mathcal{E}[r_2]\}$$

$$\mathcal{E}[(\text{sd } c\, b_1 \ldots b_n)] = \{x \in \mathcal{D} \mid \exists y \in \mathcal{E}[c] \wedge \langle x, y \rangle \in \bigcap_{i=1}^{n} \mathcal{E}[b_i]\}$$

$$\mathcal{E}[(\subseteq\ r_1\, r_2)] = \{\langle x, y \rangle \in \mathcal{D} \times \mathcal{D} \mid \forall z \in \mathcal{D} : \langle x, z \rangle \in \mathcal{E}[r_1] \Rightarrow \langle y, z \rangle \in \mathcal{E}[r_2]\}$$

$$\mathcal{E}[(\supseteq\ r_1\, r_2)] = \{\langle x, y \rangle \in \mathcal{D} \times \mathcal{D} \mid \forall z \in \mathcal{D} : \langle y, z \rangle \in \mathcal{E}[r_2] \Rightarrow \langle x, z \rangle \in \mathcal{E}[r_1]\}$$

$$\mathcal{E}[(\text{androle } r_1 \ldots r_n)] = \bigcap_{i=1}^{n} \mathcal{E}[r_i]$$

$$\mathcal{E}[(\text{orrole } r_1 \ldots r_n)] = \bigcup_{i=1}^{n} \mathcal{E}[r_i]$$

$$\mathcal{E}[(\text{notrole } r)] = (\mathcal{D} \times \mathcal{D}) \setminus \mathcal{E}[r]$$

$$\mathcal{E}[(\text{comp } r_1 \ldots r_n)] = \mathcal{E}[r_1] \circ \mathcal{E}[r_2] \circ \ldots \circ \mathcal{E}[r_n]$$

$$\mathcal{E}[\text{self}] = \{\langle x, y \rangle \in \mathcal{D} \times \mathcal{D} \mid x = y\}$$

$$\mathcal{E}[(\text{inv } r)] = \{\langle x, y \rangle \in \mathcal{D} \times \mathcal{D} \mid \langle y, x \rangle \in \mathcal{E}[r]\}$$

$$\mathcal{E}[(\text{range } r\, c)] = \mathcal{E}[r] \cap (\mathcal{D} \times \mathcal{E}[c])$$

$$\mathcal{E}[(\text{trans } r)] = (\mathcal{E}[r])^+$$

B. Overview of Formalisms and Systems

This appendix gives an overview of the computational complexity (with respect to term-subsumption) of some term-forming languages described in the literature and surveys the features of implemented hybrid systems employing terminological formalisms. For this purpose, some more term-forming operators are needed. In the following, c and c_i denote concepts, r and r_i denote roles, and rl and rl_i denote lists of roles or the role self.

$$(\text{single } r) \stackrel{\text{def}}{=} (\text{atmost } 1\ r)$$

$$(\text{some } r) \stackrel{\text{def}}{=} (\text{atleast } 1\ r)$$

$$(\text{c-some } r\ c) \stackrel{\text{def}}{=} (\text{atleast } 1\ (\text{range } r\ c))$$

$$(\text{c-atleast } n\ r\ c) \stackrel{\text{def}}{=} (\text{atleast } n\ (\text{range } r\ c))$$

$$(\text{domain } r\ c) \stackrel{\text{def}}{=} (\text{inv } (\text{range } (\text{inv } r)\ c))$$

$$(\text{l-rvm } (rl_1)\ (rl_2)) \stackrel{\text{def}}{=} (\text{rvm } (\text{comp } rl_1)\ (\text{comp } rl_2))$$

$$(\text{eq-rvm } (rl_1)\ (rl_2)) \stackrel{\text{def}}{=} (\text{and } (\text{rvm } (\text{comp } rl_1)\ (\text{comp } rl_2)) \\ (\text{rvm } (\text{comp } rl_2)\ (\text{comp } rl_1)))$$

Additionally, we will assume a restricted concept negation operator "a-not" defined on primitive components only, such as the one used in $\mathcal{NTF}$, and a restricted role-value-map operator "fl-rvm" that is defined only over role-chains using single-valued roles (or features). Using the term-forming operators of $\mathcal{U}$ and the operators defined above, Table B.1 summarizes all published complexity results concerning subsumption in term-forming languages.

Name	Concept-Forming Operators	Role-Forming Operators	Complexity of Subsumption, Remarks, and References
$\mathcal{FL}^-$	and, all, some		polynomial [Levesque and Brachman, 1987]
	and, all, some, rvm, fl-rvm	inv	polynomial [Donini et al., 1989]
$\mathcal{FL}$	and, all, some	range	co-NP-hard [Levesque and Brachman, 1987]
$\mathcal{ALE}$	and, all, c-some, a-not		NP-complete without a-not still NP-complete [Donini et al., 1989]
$\mathcal{ALU}$	and, or, a-not, all, c-some		co-NP-hard without all and c-some, subsumption is still co-NP-hard [Schmidt-Schauß and Smolka, 1989]
$\mathcal{ALC}$	and, or, not, all, c-some		PSPACE-complete [Schmidt-Schauß and Smolka, 1989]
$\mathcal{NTF}_T$	and, all, atleast, atmost	androle	co-NP-hard without androle but with c-atleast still co-NP-hard Section 4.2.2 and [Nebel, 1988]
	and, all, atleast atmost	androle, range	polynomial for four-valued semantics [Patel-Schneider, 1989a]
$\mathcal{R}$		androle, notrole, comp, self	undecidable [Schild, 1988]
NIKL$^-$	and, all, some, single, l-rvm	range, inv	undecidable without inv still undecidable [Patel-Schneider, 1989b]
KL-ONE*	and, all, eq-rvm		undecidable (subsumes the above result) [Schmidt-Schauß, 1989]

Tab. B.1. Complexity Results for Various Term-Forming Languages

The next table surveys the features of hybrid systems based on KL-ONE as far as there are descriptions of implemented systems in the literature. However, often there are different versions with different terminological formalisms. Moreover, sometimes the expressiveness is restricted in a way that makes it hard to give a concise description in the framework established so far. For instance, in most systems role-forming expressions are only permitted on the right hand side of role introductions. This does not affect the principal expressivity provided roles can be introduced as defined roles (i.e. by using $\doteq$), but it makes a difference if only primitive roles are allowed. Additionally, sometimes extensions which do not contribute to the terminological expressiveness (e.g. attributes, integer arithmetic, individual concepts) as described in Section 3.4.1 are part of terminological formalism.

Worse yet, most systems are inferentially incomplete—except for KRYPTON, CLASSIC, and MESON—even to a degree that a term-forming or restriction operator is never used for making any inference. Thus, should such operators be included in a system description or not? Furthermore, even if one would describe only those operators which have some inferential impact, it is still unclear to which extent they are employed in making inferences.

For all of these reasons, any survey of existing hybrid systems based on KL-ONE has an arguable value. It is a documentation of what people find useful to include in such systems, but it is by no means a description of what has been achieved in terms of designing hybrid systems that are inferentially complete, or even only almost complete, or incomplete in a principled way. Taking all of this into account, I decided to describe the systems as completely as possible by enumerating the straightforward terminological operators and giving a rough sketch of the assertional formalism. However, all idiosyncratic features that I do not consider as essential have been left out.

In order to describe the systems as completely as possible, another restriction operator has to be mentioned, namely, the **cover** operator which is used to state that the extension of one concept is *completely covered* by the extension of a set of other concepts, i.e. something like

$$\mathcal{E}[c] = \mathcal{E}[c_1] \cup \ldots \cup \mathcal{E}[c_n]$$

System	TBox		ABox
	Concepts	Roles	Remarks and References
KL-ONE	$\doteq$, $\leq$, and, all, atleast, atmost, sd, l-rvm	$\leq$	Individual Concepts, Wires, Nexus, and Contexts [Brachman and Schmolze, 1985]
KL-TWO	$\doteq$, $\leq$, disjoint, cover, and, all, atleast, atmost, l-rvm	$\doteq$, $\leq$, androle, inv, domain, range	Variable-free predicate logic with equality, but without UNA and number restriction. Updates supported by RUP. [Vilain, 1985, Vilain, 1983]
KRYPTON	$\doteq$, and, all	$\doteq$, comp	First-order predicate logic (theorem prover) [Brachman et al., 1985, Pigman, 1984a]
KANDOR	$\doteq$, $\leq$, disjoint and, all, c-atleast, atmost	$\leq^a$	Similar to $\mathcal{AF}$, but no number restrictions. Implicit exhaustivity assumption for all roles with specified role-fillers. [Patel-Schneider, 1984]
CLASSIC	$\doteq$, $\leq$, disjoint, and, all, atleast, atmost, fl-rvm		Similar to $\mathcal{AF}$, but instead of number restrictions, exhaustivity of role-fillers can be explicitly specified. [Borgida et al., 1989]
BACK	$\doteq$, $\leq$, disjoint, and, all, atleast, atmost, rvm^b	$\leq^c$	Similar to $\mathcal{AF}$ plus disjunction of role-fillers. [Nebel and von Luck, 1988, von Luck et al., 1987]

[a]It is possible to restrict the range of primitive roles.
[b]Note that rvm take only roles as arguments—not role-chains!
[c]It is possible to restrict the domain and range of primitive roles.

Tab. B.2. Features of Hybrid Systems Based on KL-ONE

System	TBox		ABox
	Concepts	Roles	Remarks and References
MESON	$\doteq$, $\dot{\leq}$, disjoint, and, all, atleast, atmost		Similar to $\mathcal{AF}$ plus a facility to state universal implications [Owsnicki-Klewe, 1988]
LOOM	$\doteq$, $\dot{\leq}$, disjoint, cover, and, all, atleast, atmost, rvm	$\doteq$, $\dot{\leq}$, androle, inv, domain, range, comp, self, trans	Similar to $\mathcal{AF}$ (but no number restriction or exhaustivity of role-fillers) plus universal implications. Updates supported by object-centered RMS [MacGregor, 1988a, MacGregor and Bates, 1987]
QUIRK & QUARK	$\doteq$, $\dot{\leq}$, and, all, atleast, atmost, l-rvm	$\doteq$, $\dot{\leq}$, androle, inv, domain, range	Propositional formalism employing time intervals and belief contexts [Bergmann and Gerlach, 1987, Poesio, 1988b]
SPHINX	$\doteq$, $\dot{\leq}$, disjoint, cover[a], and, all	$\doteq$, $\dot{\leq}$, comp, androle[b], domain, range	Horn logic with "negation as failure" (i.e. Prolog) [Han et al., 1987]
SB-ONE	$\doteq$, $\dot{\leq}$, disjoint, cover, and, all, atleast, atmost, l-rvm	$\dot{\leq}$[c]	Similar to $\mathcal{AF}$[d] [Kobsa, 1989, Kalmes, 1988]

[a]Disjointness and covering can only be stated in combination.
[b]There are some nonobvious restriction for the androle operator.
[c]It is possible to restrict the domain and range of primitive roles.
[d]The SB-ONE ABox is still under construction.

Tab. B.3. Features of Hybrid Systems Based on KL-ONE (continued)

Bibliography

[Abarbanel and Williams, 1987] Robert M. Abarbanel and Michael D. Williams. A relational representation for knowledge bases. In L. Kerschberg, editor, *Expert Database Systems—Proceedings From the 1st International Conference*, pages 191–206, Benjamin/Cummings, Menlo Park, Cal., 1987.

[Abrett and Burstein, 1986] Glenn Abrett and Mark H. Burstein. The BBN laboratories knowledge acquisition project: KREME knowledge editing environment. Bolt, Beranek, and Newman, Inc., Cambridge, Mass., 1986.

[Abrett and Burstein, 1987] Glenn Abrett and Mark H. Burstein. The KREME knowledge editing environment. *International Journal of Man-Machine Studies*, 27(2):103–126, 1987.

[Aït-Kaci, 1986] Hassan Aït-Kaci. An algebraic semantics approach to the effective resolution of type equations. *Theoretical Computer Science*, 45:293–351, 1986.

[Alchourrón and Makinson, 1982] Carlos E. Alchourrón and David Makinson. On the logic of theory change: contraction functions and their associated revision functions. *Theoria*, 48:14–37, 1982.

[Alchourrón et al., 1985] Carlos E. Alchourrón, Peter Gärdenfors, and David Makinson. On the logic of theory change: partial meet contraction and revision functions. *Journal of Symbolic Logic*, 50(2):510–530, June 1985.

[Allen, 1983] James F. Allen. Maintaining knowledge about temporal intervals. *Communications of the ACM*, 26(11):832–843, November 1983. Also published in [Brachman and Levesque, 1985].

[Allgayer and Reddig, 1986] Jürgen Allgayer and Carola Reddig. Processing descriptions containing words and gestures—a system architecture. In C.-R. Rollinger and W. Horn, editors, *GWAI-86 und 2. Österreichische Artificial-Intelligence-Tagung*, pages 119–130, Springer-Verlag, Berlin, West Germany, 1986.

[Arens et al., 1988] Yigal Arens, Lawrence Miller, Stuart C. Shapiro, and Norman K. Sondheimer. Automatic construction of user-interface displays. In *Proceedings of the 7th National Conference of the American Association for Artificial Intelligence*, pages 808–813, Saint Paul, Minn., August 1988.

[Bachant and McDermott, 1984] Judith Bachant and John McDermott. R1 revisited: four years in the trenches. *The AI Magazine*, 5(3):21–32, 1984.

[Barr and Feigenbaum, 1979] Avron Barr and Edward A. Feigenbaum, editors. *The Handbook of Artificial Intelligence*. Volume 1, Pitman, London, England, 1979.

[Belnap, 1977] Nuel D. Belnap. A useful four-valued logic. In G. Epstein and J. M. Dunn, editors, *Modern Uses of Multiple-Valued Logics*, pages 30–56, Reidel, Dordrecht, Holland, 1977.

[Bergmann and Gerlach, 1987] Henning Bergmann and Michael Gerlach. *QUIRK: Implementierung einer TBox zur Repräsentation von begrifflichem Wissen*. WIS-

BER Memo 11, 2nd ed., Project WISBER, Department of Computer Science, Universität Hamburg, Hamburg, West Germany, June 1987.

[Bergmann and Paeseler, 1986] Henning Bergmann and Annedore Paeseler. Wissensakquisition für das natürlichsprachliche Zugangssystem HAM-ANS. In H. Stoyan, editor, *GWAI-85. 9th German Workshop on Artificial Intelligence*, pages 295–299, Springer-Verlag, Berlin, West Germany, 1986.

[Bjørner, 1980] Dines Bjørner, editor. *Abstract Software Specification*. Springer-Verlag, Berlin, West Germany, 1980.

[Bobrow, 1986] Daniel G. Bobrow. Concluding remarks from the Artificial Intelligence perspective. In M. L. Brodie and J. Mylopoulos, editors, *On Knowledge Base Mangement Systems*, pages 569–574, Springer-Verlag, Berlin, West Germany, 1986.

[Bobrow and Stefik, 1981] Daniel G. Bobrow and Mark J. Stefik. *The LOOPS Manual*. Technical Report KB-VLSI-81-13, Xerox Palo Alto Research Center, Palo Alto, Cal., 1981.

[Bobrow and Winograd, 1977] Daniel G. Bobrow and Terry Winograd. An overview of KRL-0, a knowledge representation language. *Cognitive Science*, 1(1):3–46, January 1977. Also published in [Brachman and Levesque, 1985].

[Bobrow et al., 1986] Daniel G. Bobrow, Sanjay Mittal, and Mark J. Stefik. Expert systems: perils promise. *Communications of the ACM*, 29(9):880–894, September 1986.

[Borgida, 1985] Alexander Borgida. Language features for flexible handling of exceptions in information systems. *ACM Transactions on Database Systems*, 10(4):565–603, December 1985.

[Borgida et al., 1989] Alexander Borgida, Ronald J. Brachman, Deborah L. McGuinness, and Lori Alperin Resnick. CLASSIC: a structural data model for objects. In *Proceedings of the 1989 ACM SIGMOD International Conference on Mangement of Data*, pages 59–67, Portland, Oreg., June 1989.

[Brachman, 1978] Ronald J. Brachman. Structured inheritance networks. In W. A. Woods and R. J. Brachman, editors, *Research in Natural Language Understanding, Quarterly Progress Report No. 1, BBN Report No. 3742*, pages 36–78, Bolt, Beranek, and Newman Inc., Cambridge, Mass., 1978.

[Brachman, 1979] Ronald J. Brachman. On the epistemological status of semantic networks. In N. V. Findler, editor, *Associative Networks: Representation and Use of Knowledge by Computers*, pages 3–50, Academic Press, New York, N.Y., 1979. Also published in [Brachman and Levesque, 1985].

[Brachman, 1983] Ronald J. Brachman. What IS-A is and isn't: an analysis of taxonomic links in semantic networks. *IEEE Computer*, 16(10):30–36, October 1983.

[Brachman, 1985] Ronald J. Brachman. 'I lied about the trees' or, defaults and definitions in knowledge representation. *The AI Magazine*, 6(3):80–93, 1985.

[Brachman and Levesque, 1982] Ronald J. Brachman and Hector J. Levesque. Competence in knowledge representation. In *Proceedings of the 2nd National Conference of the American Association for Artificial Intelligence*, pages 189–192, Pittsburgh, Pa., August 1982.

[Brachman and Levesque, 1984] Ronald J. Brachman and Hector J. Levesque. The tractability of subsumption in frame-based description languages. In *Proceedings of the 4th National Conference of the American Association for Artificial Intelligence*, pages 34–37, Austin, Tex., August 1984.

[Brachman and Levesque, 1985] Ronald J. Brachman and Hector J. Levesque, editors. *Readings in Knowledge Representation.* Morgan Kaufmann, Los Altos, Cal., 1985.

[Brachman and Levesque, 1986] Ronald J. Brachman and Hector J. Levesque. The knowledge level of a KBMS. In M. L. Brodie and J. Mylopoulos, editors, *On Knowledge Base Mangement Systems*, pages 9–12, Springer-Verlag, Berlin, West Germany, 1986.

[Brachman and Levesque, 1987] Ronald J. Brachman and Hector J. Levesque. Tales from the far side of KRYPTON. In L. Kerschberg, editor, *Expert Database Systems—Proceedings From the 1st International Conference*, pages 3–43, Benjamin/Cummings, Menlo Park, Cal., 1987.

[Brachman and Schmolze, 1985] Ronald J. Brachman and James G. Schmolze. An overview of the KL-ONE knowledge representation system. *Cognitive Science*, 9(2):171–216, April 1985.

[Brachman and Smith, 1980] Special issue on knowledge representation. February 1980.

[Brachman et al., 1983] Ronald J. Brachman, Richard E. Fikes, and Hector J. Levesque. KRYPTON: a functional approach to knowledge representation. *IEEE Computer*, 16(10):67–73, October 1983. A revised version appears in [Brachman and Levesque, 1985].

[Brachman et al., 1985] Ronald J. Brachman, Victoria Pigman Gilbert, and Hector J. Levesque. An essential hybrid reasoning system: knowledge and symbol level accounts in KRYPTON. In *Proceedings of the 9th International Joint Conference on Artificial Intelligence*, pages 532–539, Los Angeles, Cal., August 1985.

[Brodie and Mylopoulos, 1986a] Michael L. Brodie and John Mylopoulos. Knowledge bases versus databases. In M. L. Brodie and J. Mylopoulos, editors, *On Knowledge Base Management Systems*, pages 83–86, Springer-Verlag, Berlin, West Germany, 1986.

[Brodie and Mylopoulos, 1986b] Michael L. Brodie and John Mylopoulos, editors. *On Knowledge Base Management Systems.* Springer-Verlag, Berlin, West Germany, 1986.

[Brodie and Zilles, 1980] Michael L. Brodie and Stephen N. Zilles, editors. *Proceedings of the Pingree Park Workshop on Data Abstraction, Databases and Conceptual Modelling*, Pingree Park, Colo., 1980. Published as SIGART Newsletter (No. 74), SIGMOD Record 11(2), and SIGPLAN Notices 16(1).

[Brodie et al., 1984] Michael L. Brodie, John Mylopoulos, and Joachim W. Schmidt, editors. *On Conceptual Modelling.* Springer-Verlag, Berlin, West Germany, 1984.

[Brown, 1986] Harold I. Brown. Sellars, concepts and conceptual change. *Synthese*, 6:275–307, 1986.

[Carbonell, 1970] Jaime R. Carbonell. AI in CAI: an artificial intelligence approach to computer-aided instruction. *IEEE Transactions on Man-Machine Systems*, 11(4):190–202, 1970.

[Carey and DeWitt, 1986] Michael J. Carey and David J. DeWitt. Extensible database systems. In M. L. Brodie and J. Mylopoulos, editors, *On Knowledge Base Mangement Systems*, pages 315–330, Springer-Verlag, Berlin, West Germany, 1986.

[Carnap, 1966] Rudolf Carnap. *Philosophical Foundations of Physics.* Basic Books, New York, N.Y., 1966.

[Chandrasekaran et al., 1988] B. Chandrasekaran, Ashok Goel, and Dean Allemang. Connectionism and information—processing abstractions. *The AI Magazine*, 9(4):25–42, 1988.

[Charniak et al., 1980] Eugene Charniak, Christopher K. Riesbeck, and Drew V. McDermott. *Artificial Intelligence Programming*. Erlbaum, Hillsdale, N.J., 1980.

[Christaller, 1985] Thomas Christaller. *Eine Entwicklung generischer Kontrollstrukturen aus kaskadierten ATNs*. PhD thesis, Universität Hamburg, Hamburg, West Germany, 1985.

[Clark, 1978] K. Clark. Negation as failure. In H. Gallaire and J. Minker, editors, *Logic and Databases*, pages 293–322, Plenum Press, New York, N.Y., 1978.

[Clocksin and Mellish, 1981] William F. Clocksin and Christopher S. Mellish. *Programming in Prolog*. Springer-Verlag, Berlin, West Germany, 1981.

[Collins and Quillian, 1970] Alan M. Collins and M. Ross Quillian. Failitating retrieval from semantic memory: the effect of repeating part of an inference. In A. F. Sanders, editor, *Acta Psychologica 33 Attention and Performance III*, North-Holland, Amsterdam, Holland, 1970.

[Corella, 1986] Francisco Corella. Semantic retrieval and levels of abstraction. In L. Kerschberg, editor, *Expert Database Systems—Proceedings From the 1st International Workshop*, pages 91–114, Benjamin/Cummings, Menlo Park, Cal., 1986.

[Dalal, 1988] Mukesh Dalal. Investigations into a theory of knowledge base revision: preliminary report. In *Proceedings of the 7th National Conference of the American Association for Artificial Intelligence*, pages 475–479, Saint Paul, Minn., August 1988.

[D'Aloisi et al., 1988] D. D'Aloisi, O. Stock, and A. Tuozzi. An implementation of the propositional part of KRAPFEN, a hybrid knowledge representation system. In Z. W. Ras and L. Saitta, editors, *Methodologies for Intelligent Systems*, Volume 3, pages 200–209, North-Holland, Amsterdam, Holland, 1988.

[Date, 1981] C. J. Date. *An Introduction to Database Systems*. Addison-Wesley, Reading, Mass., 3rd edition, 1981.

[Davidson, 1967] Donald Davidson. The logical form of action sentences. In N. Rescher, editor, *The Logic of Decision and Action*, pages 81–95, University of Pittsburgh Press, Pittsburgh, Pa., 1967.

[Davis, 1982] Randall Davis. Teiresias: applications of meta-level knowledge. In R. Davis and D. B. Lenat, editors, *Knowledge-Based Systems in Artificial Intelligence*, pages 229–485, McGraw-Hill, New York, N.Y., 1982.

[Davis and King, 1984] Randall Davis and Jonathan J. King. The origin of rule-based systems in AI. In B. G. Buchanan and E. H. Shortliffe, editors, *Rule Based Expert Systems—The MYCIN Experiments of the Stanford Heuristic Programming Project*, pages 20–52, Addison-Wesley, Reading, Mass., 1984.

[de Kleer, 1984] Johan de Kleer. Choices without backtracking. In *Proceedings of the 4th National Conference of the American Association for Artificial Intelligence*, pages 79–85, Austin, Tex., August 1984.

[de Kleer, 1986a] Johan de Kleer. An assumption-based TMS. *Artificial Intelligence*, 28(2):127–162, March 1986. Also published in [Ginsberg, 1987].

[de Kleer, 1986b] Johan de Kleer. Problem solving with the ATMS. *Artificial Intelligence*, 28(2):197–224, March 1986.

[de Kleer and Williams, 1987] Johan de Kleer and Brian C. Williams. Diagnosing multiple faults. *Artificial Intelligence*, 32(1):97–130, April 1987. Also published in

[Ginsberg, 1987].

[de Kleer et al., 1977] Johan de Kleer, Jon Doyle, Guy L. Steele, Jr., and Gerald J. Sussman. AMORD: explicit control of reasoning. In *Symposium on Artificial Intelligence and Programming Languages*, pages 116–125, August 1977. The Proceedings are published as SIGPLAN Notices 16(2) and SIGART Newsletter (No. 64). The article appears also in [Brachman and Levesque, 1985].

[Diettrich, 1986] Thomas G. Diettrich. Learning at the knowledge level. *Machine Learning*, 1:287–316, 1986.

[Diettrich and Michalski, 1983] Thomas G. Diettrich and Ryszard S. Michalski. A comparative review of selected methods for learning from examples. In R. S. Michalski, J. G. Carbonell, and T. M. Mitchell, editors, *Machine Learning—An Artificial Intelligence Approach*, pages 41–81, Tioga, Palo Alto, Cal., 1983.

[Donini and Lenzerini, 1988] Francesco M. Donini and Maurizio Lenzerini. TermLog: a logic for terminological knowledge. In Z. W. Ras and L. Saitta, editors, *Methodologies for Intelligent Systems*, Volume 3, pages 408–417, North-Holland, Amsterdam, Holland, 1988.

[Donini et al., 1989] Francesco M. Donini, Bernhard Hollunder, Maurizio Lenzerini, Alberto Marchetti Spaccamela, Daniele Nardi, and Werner Nutt. *The Frontier of Tractability for Concept Description Languages*. DFKI-Report, DFKI, Kaiserslautern, West Germany, 1989. In preparation.

[Dörre and Eisele, 1989] Jochen Dörre and Andreas Eisele. Determining consistency of feature terms with distributed disjunctions. In D. Metzing, editor, *GWAI-89. 13th German Workshop on Artificial Intelligence*, pages 270–279, Springer-Verlag, Berlin, West Germany, 1989.

[Doyle, 1979] Jon Doyle. A truth maintenance system. *Artificial Intelligence*, 12(3):231–272, 1979. Also published in [Webber and Nilsson, 1981] and in [Ginsberg, 1987].

[Doyle and London, 1980] Jon Doyle and Philip London. A selected descriptor-indexed bibliography to the literature on belief revision. *SIGART Newsletter*, (No. 71):7–23, 1980.

[Doyle and Patil, 1989] Jon Doyle and Ramesh S. Patil. *Language Restrictions, Taxonomic Classifications, and the Utility of Representation Services*. Technical Memo MIT/LCS/TM-387, Laboratory for Computer Science, Massachusetts Institute of Technology, Cambridge, Mass., May 1989.

[Dreyfus, 1981] Hubert L. Dreyfus. From micro-worlds to knowledge-representation: AI at an impasse. In J. Haugeland, editor, *Mind Design*, pages 161–204, MIT Press, Cambridge, Mass., 1981. Also published in [Brachman and Levesque, 1985].

[Edelmann and Owsnicki, 1986] Jürgen Edelmann and Bernd Owsnicki. Data models in knowledge representation systems: a case study. In C.-R. Rollinger and W. Horn, editors, *GWAI-86 und 2. Österreichische Artificial-Intelligence-Tagung*, pages 69–74, Springer-Verlag, Berlin, West Germany, 1986.

[Ernst and Newell, 1969] George W. Ernst and Allen Newell. *GPS: A Case Study in Generality and Problem-Solving*. Academic Press, New York, N.Y., 1969.

[Etherington, 1987] David W. Etherington. Relating default logic and circumscription. In *Proceedings of the 10th International Joint Conference on Artificial Intelligence*, pages 489–494, Milan, Italy, August 1987.

[Fagin et al., 1983] Ronald Fagin, Jeffrey D. Ullman, and Moshe Y. Vardi. On the semantics of updates in databases. In *2nd ACM SIGACT-SIGMOD Symposium* on *Principles of Database Systems*, pages 352–365, Atlanta, Ga., 1983.

[Fagin et al., 1986] Ronald Fagin, Gabriel M. Kuper, Jeffrey D. Ullman, and Moshe Y. Vardi. Updating logical databases. *Advances in Computing Research*, 3:1–18, 1986.

[Fahlman, 1979] Scott E. Fahlman. *A System for Representing and Using Real-World Knowledge*. MIT Press, Cambridge, Mass., 1979.

[Fikes, 1982] Richard E. Fikes. Highlights from KloneTalk: display-based editing and browsing, decompositions, qua concepts and active role value maps. In J. G. Schmolze and R. J. Brachman, editors, *Proceedings of the 1981 KL-ONE Workshop*, pages 90–105, Cambridge, Mass., 1982. The proceedings have been published as BBN Report No. 4842 and Fairchild Technical Report No. 618.

[Finin and Silverman, 1986] Timothy W. Finin and David Silverman. Interactive classification as a knowledge acquisition tool. In L. Kerschberg, editor, *Expert Database Systems—Proceedings From the 1st International Workshop*, pages 79–90, Benjamin/Cummings, Menlo Park, Cal., 1986.

[Freeman et al., 1983] Michael Freeman, Donald McKay, Lewis Norton, and Martha Palmer. *KNET: A Logic-Based Associative Network Framework for Expert Systems*. Technical Report, Research & Development Division, SDC—A Burroughs Company, Paoli, Pa., 1983.

[Frisch, 1988] Alan M. Frisch, editor. *Proceedings of the 1988 Workshop on Principles of Hybrid Reasoning*, St. Paul, Minn., August 1988.

[Frixione et al., 1988] M. Frixione, S. Gaglio, and G. Spinelli. Proper names and individual concepts in SI-nets. In *Proceedings of the 8th European Conference on Artificial Intelligence*, pages 208–213, Munich, West Germany, August 1988.

[Gärdenfors, 1988] Peter Gärdenfors. *Knowledge in Flux—Modeling the Dynamics of Epistemic States*. MIT Press, Cambridge, Mass., 1988.

[Gärdenfors and Makinson, 1988] Peter Gärdenfors and David Makinson. Revision of knowledge systems using epistemic entrenchment. In M. Vardi, editor, *Proceedings of the 2nd Workshop on Theoretical Aspects of Reasoning about Knowledge*, Morgan Kaufmann, Los Altos, Cal., 1988.

[Garey and Johnson, 1979] Michael R. Garey and David S. Johnson. *Computers and Intractability—A Guide to the Theory of NP-Completeness*. Freeman, San Francisco, Cal., 1979.

[Genesereth and Nilsson, 1987] Michael R. Genesereth and Nils J. Nilsson. *Logical Foundations of Artificial Intelligence*. Morgan Kaufmann, Los Altos, Cal., 1987.

[Ginsberg, 1986] Matthew L. Ginsberg. Counterfactuals. *Artificial Intelligence*, 30(1):35–79, October 1986.

[Ginsberg, 1987] Matthew L. Ginsberg, editor. *Readings in Nonmonotonic Reasoning*. Morgan Kaufmann, Los Altos, Cal., 1987.

[Goldberg and Robson, 1983] Adele Goldberg and David Robson. *Smalltalk-80: The Language and its Implementation*. Addison-Wesley, Reading, Mass., 1983.

[Goodwin, 1982] James W. Goodwin. *An Improved Algorithm for Non-monotonic Dependency Net Update*. Research Report LiTH-MAT-R-82-83, Software Systems Research Center, Linköping Institute of Technology, Linköping, Sweden, August 1982.

[Haas and Hendrix, 1983] Norman Haas and Gary G. Hendrix. Learning by being told: acquiring knowledge for information management. In R. S. Michalski, J. G. Carbonell, and T. M. Mitchell, editors, *Machine Learning—An Artificial Intelligence Approach*, pages 405–428, Tioga, Palo Alto, Cal., 1983.

[Habel, 1983] Christopher Habel. Logische Systeme und Repräsentationsprobleme. In B. Neumann, editor, *GWAI-83. 7th German Workshop on Artificial Intelligence*, pages 118–142, Springer-Verlag, Berlin, West Germany, 1983.

[von Hahn et al., 1980] Walther von Hahn, Wolfgang Hoeppner, Anthony Jameson, and Wolfgang Wahlster. The anatomy of the natural language dialogue system HAM-RPM. In L. Bolc, editor, *Natural Language Based Computer Systems*, pages 119–254, Hanser/MacMillan, Munich, West Germany, 1980.

[Han et al., 1987] Sangki Han, D. W. Shin, Y. Kim, Y. P. Jun, S. R. Maeng, and J. W. Cho. *A Logic Programming Approach To Hybrid Knowledge Representation*. Technical Report CAL-TR-008, Department of Computer Science, Korea Advanced Institute of Science and Technology, Seoul, Korea, October 1987.

[Härder et al., 1987] Theo Härder, Nelson Mattos, and Bernhard Mitschang. Abbildung von Frames auf neuere Datenmodelle. In K. Morik, editor, *GWAI-87. 11th German Workshop on Artificial Intelligence*, pages 396–405, Springer-Verlag, Berlin, West Germany, 1987.

[Haugeland, 1981] John Haugeland, editor. *Mind Design*. MIT Press, Cambridge, Mass., 1981.

[Haugeland, 1985] John Haugeland. *Artificial Intelligence—The Very Idea*. MIT Press, Cambridge, Mass., 1985.

[Hayes, 1974] Patrick J. Hayes. Some problems and non-problems in representation theory. In *AISB Summer Conference*, pages 63–79, Sussex, England, 1974. Also published in [Brachman and Levesque, 1985].

[Hayes, 1977] Patrick J. Hayes. In defence of logic. In *Proceedings of the 5th International Joint Conference on Artificial Intelligence*, pages 559–565, Cambridge, Mass., 1977.

[Hayes, 1980] Patrick J. Hayes. The logic of frames. In D. Metzing, editor, *Frame Conceptions and Text Understanding*, pages 46–61, deGruyter, Berlin, West Germany, 1980. Also published in [Brachman and Levesque, 1985] and [Webber and Nilsson, 1981].

[Hayes, 1985] Patrick J. Hayes. Naive physics I: ontology for liquids. In J. R. Hobbs and R. C. Moore, editors, *Formal Theories of the Commonsense World*, pages 71–108, Ablex, Norwood, N.J., 1985.

[Hendrix, 1979] Gary G. Hendrix. Encoding knowledge in partitioned networks. In N. V. Findler, editor, *Associative Networks: Representation and Use of Knowledge by Computers*, pages 51–92, Academic Press, New York, N.Y., 1979.

[Hendrix, 1986] Gary G. Hendrix. Q&A: already a success? In *Proceedings of the 11th International Conference on Computational Linguistics*, pages 164–166, Bonn, West Germany, August 1986.

[Hobbs, 1985] Jerry R. Hobbs. Ontological promiscuity. In *Proceedings of the 23rd Annual Meeting of the ACL*, pages 61–69, Chicago, Ill., 1985.

[Hobbs and Moore, 1985] Jerry R. Hobbs and Robert C. Moore. *Formal Theories of the Commonsense World*. Ablex, Norwood, N.J., 1985.

[Hoeppner et al., 1983] Wolfgang Hoeppner, Thomas Christaller, Heinz Marburger, Katharina Morik, Bernhard Nebel, Michael O'Leary, and Wolfgang Wahlster. Beyond domain-independence: experience with the development of a German natural language access system to highly diverse background systems. In *Proceedings of the 8th International Joint Conference on Artificial Intelligence*, pages 115–121, Karlsruhe, West Germany, August 1983.

[IntelliCorp, 1985] *IntelliCorp KEE Software Development System: User's Manual.* IntelliCorp, Mountain View, Cal., 1985.

[Israel, 1983] David J. Israel. The role of logic in knowledge representation. *IEEE Computer*, 16(10):37–42, October 1983.

[Kaczmarek et al., 1986] Thomas S. Kaczmarek, Raymond Bates, and Gabriel Robins. Recent developments in NIKL. In *Proceedings of the 5th National Conference of the American Association for Artificial Intelligence*, pages 978–987, Philadelphia, Pa., August 1986.

[Kaczmarek et al., 1983] Thomas S. Kaczmarek, William Mark, and Norman K. Sondheimer. The Consul/CUE interface: an integrated interactive environment. In *Proceedings of the CHI'83 Conference on Human Factors in Computing Systems*, pages 98–102, Boston, Mass., ACM, December 1983.

[Kalmes, 1988] Joachim Kalmes. *SB-Graph User Manual (Release 0.1)*. Technical Memo 30, Department of Computer Science, Universität des Saarlandes, Saarbrücken, West Germany, December 1988.

[Kanellakis and Mitchell, 1989] Paris C. Kanellakis and John C. Mitchell. Polymorphic unification and ML typing. In *Proceedings of the 16th ACM Symposium on Principles of Programming Languages*, pages 5–15, January 1989.

[Kasper, 1987] Robert T. Kasper. A unification method for disjunctive feature descriptions. In *Proceedings of the 25th Annual Meeting of the ACL*, pages 235–242, Stanford, Cal., 1987.

[Kasper and Rounds, 1986] Robert T. Kasper and William C. Rounds. A logical semantics for feature structures. In *Proceedings of the 24th Annual Meeting of the ACL*, pages 257–265, New York, N.Y., 1986.

[Kindermann and Quantz, 1988] Carsten Kindermann and Joachim Quantz. Wissenspräsentation und -repräsentation. In W. Hoeppner, editor, *GWAI-88. 12th German Workshop on Artificial Intelligence*, pages 206–210, Springer-Verlag, Berlin, West Germany, 1988.

[Kobsa, 1988] Alfred Kobsa. Report on a KL-ONE workshop. *KI*, 88(1):15–16, 1988.

[Kobsa, 1989] Alfred Kobsa. The SB-ONE knowledge representation workbench. In *Preprints of the Workshop on Formal Aspects of Semantic Networks*, Two Harbors, Cal., February 1989.

[Kowalski, 1980] Robert A. Kowalski. Contribution to the SIGART Newsletter special issue on knowledge representation. *SIGART Newsletter*, (No. 70):44, February 1980.

[Kuhn, 1970] Thomas S. Kuhn. *The Structure of Scientific Revolutions*. Chicago University Press, Chicago, Ill., 2nd edition, 1970.

[Lehnert and Wilks, 1979] Wendy Lehnert and Yorick Wilks. A critical perspective on KRL. *Cognitive Science*, 3(1):1–28, January 1979.

[Lenat, 1982] Douglas B. Lenat. AM: discovery in mathematics as heuristic search. In R. Davis and D. B. Lenat, editors, *Knowledge-Based Systems in Artificial Intelligence*, pages 3–225, McGraw-Hill, New York, N.Y., 1982.

[Levesque, 1984a] Hector J. Levesque. Foundations of a functional approach to knowledge representation. *Artificial Intelligence*, 23(2):155–212, 1984.

[Levesque, 1984b] Hector J. Levesque. A logic of implicit and explicit belief. In *Proceedings of the 4th National Conference of the American Association for Artificial Intelligence*, pages 198–202, Austin, Tex., August 1984.

[Levesque, 1986] Hector J. Levesque. Making believers out of computers. *Artificial Intelligence*, 30(1):81–108, October 1986.

[Levesque, 1988] Hector J. Levesque. Logic and the complexity of reasoning. *Journal of Philosophical Logic*, 17:355–389, 1988.

[Levesque and Brachman, 1985] Hector J. Levesque and Ronald J. Brachman. A fundamental tradeoff in knowledge representation and reasoning (revised version). In R. J. Brachman and H. J. Levesque, editors, *Readings in Knowledge Representation*, pages 41–70, Morgan Kaufmann, Los Altos, Cal., 1985.

[Levesque and Brachman, 1986] Hector J. Levesque and Ronald J. Brachman. Knowledge level interfaces to information systems. In M. L. Brodie and J. Mylopoulos, editors, *On Knowledge Base Mangement Systems*, pages 13–34, Springer-Verlag, Berlin, West Germany, 1986.

[Levesque and Brachman, 1987] Hector J. Levesque and Ronald J. Brachman. Expressiveness and tractability in knowledge representation and reasoning. *Computational Intelligence*, 3:78–93, 1987.

[Levi, 1977] Isaac Levi. Subjunctives, dispositions and chances. *Synthese*, 34:423–455, 1977.

[Lewis, 1973] David K. Lewis. *Counterfactuals*. Harvard University Press, Cambridge, Mass., 1973.

[Lipkis, 1982] Thomas Lipkis. A KL-ONE classifier. In J. G. Schmolze and R. J. Brachman, editors, *Proceedings of the 1981 KL-ONE Workshop*, pages 128–145, Cambridge, Mass., 1982. The proceedings have been published as BBN Report No. 4842 and Fairchild Technical Report No. 618.

[Liskov and Zilles, 1974] Barbara Liskov and Stephen N. Zilles. Programming with abstract data types. *SIGPLAN Notices*, 9(4):50–59, 1974.

[Lovasz, 1973] L. Lovasz. Coverings and colorings of hypergraphs. In *Proceedings of the 4th Southeastern Conference on Combinatorics, Graph Theory, and Computing*, pages 3–12, Utilitas Mathematics Publishing, Winnipeg, Ont., 1973.

[von Luck, 1986] Kai von Luck. Semantic networks with number restricted roles or another story about Clyde. In C.-R. Rollinger and W. Horn, editors, *GWAI-86 und 2. Österreichische Artificial-Intelligence-Tagung*, pages 58–68, Springer-Verlag, Berlin, West Germany, 1986.

[von Luck et al., 1988] Kai von Luck, Bernhard Nebel, and Hans-Jochen Schneider. Some aspects of knowledge-base management systems. In G. Rahmstorf, editor, *Wissensrepräsentation in Expertensystemen*, pages 146–157, Springer-Verlag, Berlin, West Germany, 1988.

[von Luck et al., 1986] Kai von Luck, Bernhard Nebel, Christof Peltason, and Albrecht Schmiedel. BACK to consistency and incompleteness. In H. Stoyan, editor, *GWAI-85. 9th German Workshop on Artificial Intelligence*, pages 245–257, Springer-Verlag, Berlin, West Germany, 1986. An extended version of this paper is available as: *The BACK System*. KIT Report 29, Department of Computer Science, Technische Universität Berlin, 1985.

[von Luck et al., 1987] Kai von Luck, Bernhard Nebel, Christof Peltason, and Albrecht Schmiedel. *The Anatomy of the BACK System*. KIT Report 41, Department of Computer Science, Technische Universität Berlin, Berlin, West Germany, January 1987.

[MacGregor, 1988a] Robert MacGregor. A deductive pattern matcher. In *Proceedings of the 7th National Conference of the American Association for Artificial Intelligence*, pages 403–408, Saint Paul, Minn., August 1988.

[MacGregor, 1988b] Robert MacGregor. Personal communications. 1988.

[MacGregor and Bates, 1987] Robert MacGregor and Raymond Bates. *The Loom Knowledge Representation Language*. Technical Report ISI/RS-87-188, University of Southern California, Information Science Institute, Marina del Rey, Cal., 1987.

[Maida, 1987] Anthony S. Maida. Frame theory. In S. C. Shapiro, editor, *Encyclopedia of Artificial Intelligence*, pages 302–312, Wiley, Chichester, England, 1987.

[Maida and Shapiro, 1982] Anthony S. Maida and Stuart C. Shapiro. Intensional concepts in propositional semantic networks. *Cognitive Science*, 6(4):291–330, 1982. Also published in [Brachman and Levesque, 1985].

[Makinson, 1985] David Makinson. How to give it up: a survey of some formal aspects of theory change. *Synthese*, 62:347–363, 1985.

[Makinson, 1987] David Makinson. On the status of the postulate of recovery in the logic of theory change. *Journal of Philosophical Logic*, 16:383–394, 1987.

[Mann and Matthiessen, 1983] William C. Mann and Christian M. I. M. Matthiessen. *Nigel: A Systemic Grammar for Text Generation*. Technical Report ISI/RR-83-105, University of Southern California, Information Science Institute, Marina del Rey, Cal., February 1983.

[Mann et al., 1985] William C. Mann, Yigal Arens, Christian M. I. M. Matthiessen, Shari Naberschnig, and Norman K. Sondheimer. Janus abstraction structure—draft 2. Draft paper, University of Southern California, Information Science Institute, Marina del Rey, Cal., October 1985.

[Marburger and Nebel, 1983] Heinz Marburger and Bernhard Nebel. Natürlichsprachlicher Datenbankzugang mit HAM-ANS: Syntaktische Korrespondenz, natürlichsprachliche Quantifizierung und semantisches Modell des Diskursbereiches. In J. W. Schmidt, editor, *Sprachen für Datenbanken*, pages 26–41, Springer-Verlag, Berlin, West Germany, 1983.

[Marburger and Wahlster, 1983] Heinz Marburger and Wolfgang Wahlster. Case role filling as a side effect of visual search. In *Proceedings of the 1st Conference of the European Chapter of the Association for Computational Linguistics*, pages 188–195, Pisa, Italy, 1983.

[Mark, 1982] William Mark. Realization. In J. G. Schmolze and R. J. Brachman, editors, *Proceedings of the 1981 KL-ONE Workshop*, pages 78–89, Cambridge, Mass., 1982. The proceedings have been published as BBN Report No. 4842 and Fairchild Technical Report No. 618.

[Martelli and Montanari, 1982] Alberto Martelli and Ugo Montanari. An efficient unification algorithm. *ACM Transactions on Programming Languages and Systems*, 4(2):258–282, April 1982.

[Martins, 1987] João P. Martins. Belief revision. In S. C. Shapiro, editor, *Encyclopedia of Artificial Intelligence*, pages 58–62, Wiley, Chichester, England, 1987.

[Martins and Shapiro, 1986] João P. Martins and Stuart C. Shapiro. Theoretical foundations for belief revision. In J. Y. Halpern, editor, *Theoretical Aspects of Reasoning About Knowledge, Proceedings of the 1986 Conference*, pages 383–398, Morgan Kaufmann, Los Altos, Cal., 1986.

[Masterman, 1962] Margaret Masterman. Semantic message detection for machine translation, using an interlingua. In *Proceedings of the 1961 International Conference on Machine Translation of Languages and Applied Linguistic Analysis*, pages 438–475, London, England, 1962.

[Mays et al., 1987] Eric Mays, Chidanand Apté, James Griesmer, and John Kastner. Organizing knowledge in a complex financial domain. *IEEE Expert*, 2(3):61–70, 1987.

[Mays et al., 1988] Eric Mays, Chidanand Apté, James Griesmer, and John Kastner. Experience with K-Rep: an object-centered knowledge representation language. In *Proceedings of IEEE CAIA-88*, pages 62–67, March 1988.

[McAllester, 1980] David A. McAllester. *An Outlook on Truth Maintenance*. AI Memo 551, AI Laboratory, Massachusetts Institute of Technology, Cambridge, Mass., August 1980.

[McAllester, 1982] David A. McAllester. *Reasoning Utility Package User's Manual*. AI Memo 667, AI Laboratory, Massachusetts Institute of Technology, Cambridge, Mass., April 1982.

[McCarthy, 1968] John McCarthy. Programs with common sense. In M. Minsky, editor, *Semantic Information Processing*, pages 403–418, MIT Press, Cambridge, Mass., 1968. Also published in [Brachman and Levesque, 1985].

[McCarthy, 1977] John McCarthy. Epistemological problems in artificial intelligence. In *Proceedings of the 5th International Joint Conference on Artificial Intelligence*, pages 1038–1044, Cambridge, Mass., 1977. Also published in [Webber and Nilsson, 1981] and in [Brachman and Levesque, 1985].

[McCarthy, 1980] John McCarthy. Circumscription—a form of non-monotonic reasoning. *Artificial Intelligence*, 13(1–2):27–39, 1980. Also published in [Webber and Nilsson, 1981] and in [Ginsberg, 1987].

[McCarthy, 1986] John McCarthy. Applications of circumscription to formalizing common-sense knowledge. *Artificial Intelligence*, 28:89–116, 1986. Also published in [Ginsberg, 1987].

[McCarthy and Hayes, 1969] John McCarthy and Patrick J. Hayes. Some philosophical problems from the standpoint of artificial intelligence. In B. Meltzer and D. Michie, editors, *Machine Intelligence*, Volume 4, pages 463–502, Edinburgh University Press, Edinburgh, Scotland, 1969. Also published in [Webber and Nilsson, 1981].

[McCoy, 1984] Kathleen F McCoy. Correcting object-related misconceptions: how should the system respond? In *Proceedings of the 10th International Conference on Computational Linguistics*, pages 444–447, Stanford, Cal., July 1984.

[McDermott, 1976] Drew V. McDermott. Artificial intelligence meets natural stupidity. *SIGART Newsletter*, (No. 57):4–9, April 1976. Also published in [Haugeland, 1981].

[McDermott, 1978] Drew V. McDermott. Tarskian semantics, or no notation without denotation! *Cognitive Science*, 2(3):277–282, July 1978.

[McDermott, 1987] Drew V. McDermott. A critique of pure reason. *Computational Intelligence*, 3(3):151–160, August 1987.

[Metzing, 1980] Dieter Metzing, editor. *Frame Conceptions and Text Understanding*. deGruyter, Berlin, West Germany, 1980.

[Michie, 1982] Donald Michie. Game-playing programs and the conceptual interface. *SIGART Newsletter*, (No. 80):64–70, April 1982.

[Minsky, 1975] Marvin Minsky. A framework for representing knowledge. In P. Winston, editor, *The Psychology of Computer Vision*, pages 211–277, McGraw-Hill,

New York, N.Y., 1975. An abridged version has been published in [Haugeland, 1981], [Metzing, 1980], and [Brachman and Levesque, 1985].

[Moore, 1986] Johanna D. Moore. NIKL workshop summary, 15–16 July 1986, Boston. University of Southern California, Information Science Institute, Marina del Rey, Cal., October 1986.

[Moore, 1982] Robert C. Moore. The role of logic in knowledge representation and common sense reasoning. In *Proceedings of the 2nd National Conference of the American Association for Artificial Intelligence*, pages 428–433, Pittsburgh, Pa., August 1982. Also published in [Brachman and Levesque, 1985].

[Moser, 1983] M. G. Moser. An overview of NIKL, the new implementation of KL-ONE. In *Research in Knowledge Representation and Natural Language Understanding, BBN Report No. 5421*, pages 7–26, Bolt, Beranek, and Newman Inc., Cambridge, Mass., 1983.

[Mylopoulos and Levesque, 1984] John Mylopoulos and Hector J. Levesque. An overview of knowledge representation. In M. L. Brodie, J. Mylopoulos, and J. W. Schmidt, editors, *On Conceptual Modelling*, pages 3–18, Springer-Verlag, Berlin, West Germany, 1984.

[Mylopoulos et al., 1980] John Mylopoulos, Philip A. Bernstein, and Harry K. T. Wong. A language facility for designing interactive database-intensive systems. *ACM Transactions on Database Systems*, 5(2):185–207, 1980.

[Nebel, 1985] Bernhard Nebel. How well does a vanilla loop fit into a frame? *Data & Knowledge Engineering*, 1(2):181–194, 1985. Also available as KIT Report 30, Department of Computer Science, Technische Universität Berlin, October 1985.

[Nebel, 1988] Bernhard Nebel. Computational complexity of terminological reasoning in BACK. *Artificial Intelligence*, 34(3):371–383, April 1988. Also available as KIT Report 43, Department of Computer Science, Technische Universität Berlin, April 1987.

[Nebel, 1989a] Bernhard Nebel. A knowledge level analysis of belief revision. In R. J. Brachman, H. J. Levesque, and R. Reiter, editors, *Proceedings of the 1st International Conference on Principles of Knowledge Representation and Reasoning*, pages 301–311, Toronto, Ont., May 1989.

[Nebel, 1989b] Bernhard Nebel. On terminological cycles. In *Preprints of the Workshop on Formal Aspects of Semantic Networks*, Two Harbors, Cal., February 1989. The proceedings will be published by Morgan Kaufmann. A preliminary version is available as KIT Report Department of Science, Technische Universität Berlin, November 1987.

[Nebel, 1989c] Bernhard Nebel. Terminological reasoning is inherently intractable. *Artificial Intelligence*, 1989. To appear. Also available as IWBS Report 82, IBM Germany Scientific Center, IWBS, Stuttgart, West Germany, October 1989.

[Nebel and von Luck, 1987] Bernhard Nebel and Kai von Luck. Issues of integration and balancing in hybrid knowledge representation systems. In K. Morik, editor, *GWAI-87. 11th German Workshop on Artificial Intelligence*, pages 114–123, Springer-Verlag, Berlin, West Germany, 1987. Also available as KIT Report 46, Department of Computer Science, Technische Universität Berlin, July 1987.

[Nebel and von Luck, 1988] Bernhard Nebel and Kai von Luck. Hybrid reasoning in BACK. In Z. W. Ras and L. Saitta, editors, *Methodologies for Intelligent Systems*, Volume 3, pages 260–269, North-Holland, Amsterdam, Holland, 1988.

[Nebel and Marburger, 1982] Bernhard Nebel and Heinz Marburger. Das natürlich-sprachliche System HAM-ANS: Intelligenter Zugriff auf heterogene Wissens- und Datenbasen. In J. Nehmer, editor, *GI-12. Jahrestagung*, pages 392–402, Springer-Verlag, Berlin, West Germany, 1982.

[Nebel and Smolka, 1989] Bernhard Nebel and Gert Smolka. Representation and reasoning with attributive descriptions. In K.-H. Bläsius, U. Hedtstück, and C.-R. Rollinger, editors, *Sorts and Types in Artificial Intelligence*, Springer-Verlag, Berlin, West Germany, 1989. To appear. Also available as IWBS Report 81, IBM Germany Scientific Center, IWBS, Stuttgart, West Germany, September 1989.

[Nebel and Sondheimer, 1986] Bernhard Nebel and Norman K. Sondheimer. NIGEL gets to know logic: an experiment in natural language generation taking a logical, knowledge-based view. In C. Rollinger and W. Horn, editors, *GWAI-86 und 2. Österreichische Artificial-Intelligence-Tagung*, pages 75–86, Springer-Verlag, Berlin, West Germany, 1986. Also available as KIT Report 36, Department of Computer Science, Technische Universität Berlin, July 1986.

[Neches et al., 1985] Robert Neches, William R. Swartout, and Johanna D. Moore. Explainable (and maintainable) expert systems. In *Proceedings of the 9th International Joint Conference on Artificial Intelligence*, pages 382–389, Los Angeles, Cal., August 1985.

[Newell, 1982] Allen Newell. The knowledge level. *Artificial Intelligence*, 18(1):87–127, 1982. Also published in *The AI Magazine*, 2(2), 1981.

[Nilsson, 1980] Nils J. Nilsson. *Principles of Artificial Intelligence*. Tioga, Palo Alto, Cal., 1980.

[Owsnicki-Klewe, 1988] Bernd Owsnicki-Klewe. Configuration as a consistency maintenance task. In W. Hoeppner, editor, *GWAI-88. 12th German Workshop on Artificial Intelligence*, pages 77–87, Springer-Verlag, Berlin, West Germany, 1988.

[Patel-Schneider, 1984] Peter F. Patel-Schneider. Small can be beautiful in knowledge representation. In *Proceedings of the IEEE Workshop on Principles of Knowledge-Based Systems*, pages 11–16, Denver, Colo., 1984. An extended version including a KANDOR system description is available as AI Technical Report No. 37, Palo Alto, Cal., Schlumberger Palo Alto Research, October 1984.

[Patel-Schneider, 1986] Peter F. Patel-Schneider. A four-valued semantics for frame-based description languages. In *Proceedings of the 5th National Conference of the American Association for Artificial Intelligence*, pages 344–348, Philadelphia, Pa., August 1986.

[Patel-Schneider, 1987a] Peter F. Patel-Schneider. *Decidable, Logic-Based Knowledge Representation*. PhD thesis, University of Toronto, Toronto, Ont., May 1987. Computer Science Department, Technical Report 201/87.

[Patel-Schneider, 1987b] Peter F. Patel-Schneider. A hybrid, decidable, logic-based knowledge representation system. *Computational Intelligence*, 3(2):64–77, May 1987.

[Patel-Schneider, 1989a] Peter F. Patel-Schneider. A four-valued semantics for terminological logics. *Artificial Intelligence*, 38(3):319–351, April 1989.

[Patel-Schneider, 1989b] Peter F. Patel-Schneider. Undecidability of subsumption in NIKL. *Artificial Intelligence*, 39(2):263–272, June 1989.

[Patel-Schneider et al., 1984] Peter F. Patel-Schneider, Ronald J. Brachman, and Hector J. Levesque. ARGON: knowledge representation meets information retrieval. In

Proceedings of the 1st Conference on Artificial Intelligence Applications, pages 280–286, Denver, Col., 1984.

[Patel-Schneider et al., 1985] Peter F. Patel-Schneider, Victoria Pigman Gilbert, and Ronald J. Brachman. *Hybrid Knowledge Representation Systems*. AI Working Paper, Schlumberger Palo Alto Research, Palo Alto, Cal., July 1985.

[Paterson and Wegman, 1978] M. S. Paterson and M. N. Wegman. Linear unification. *Journal of Computer and System Sciences*, 16:158–167, 1978.

[Peltason, 1987] Christof Peltason. The scheme of Posidonius—using taxonomic reasoning in design. In D. Sriram and R. A. Adey, editors, *Proceedings of the 2nd International Conference on Applications of AI in Engineering*, pages 299–314, Cambridge, Mass., August 1987. Also available as KIT Report 55, Department of Computer Science, Technische Universität Berlin, September 1987.

[Peltason et al., 1987] Christof Peltason, Kai von Luck, Bernhard Nebel, and Albrecht Schmiedel. *The User's Guide to the BACK System*. KIT Report 42, Department of Computer Science, Technische Universität Berlin, Berlin, West Germany, January 1987.

[Peltason et al., 1989] Christof Peltason, Albrecht Schmiedel, Carsten Kindermann, and Joachim Quantz. *The BACK System Revisited*. KIT Report 75, Department of Computer Science, Technische Universität Berlin, Berlin, West Germany, September 1989.

[Pigman, 1984a] Victoria Pigman. *KRYPTON: Description of an Implementation, Vol. 1*. AI Technical Report 40, Schlumberger Palo Alto Research, Palo Alto, Cal., December 1984.

[Pigman, 1984b] Victoria Pigman. *KRYPTON: Description of an Implementation, Vol. 2*. AI Technical Report 41, Schlumberger Palo Alto Research, Palo Alto, Cal., December 1984.

[Pletat and von Luck, 1989] Udo Pletat and Kai von Luck. Knowledge Representation in LILOG. In Karl-Hans Bläsius, Uli Hedtstück, and Claus Rollinger, editors, *Sorts and Types in Artificial Intelligence*, Springer-Verlag, Berlin, West Germany, 1989. To appear. Also available as IWBS Report 90, IBM Germany Scientific Center, IWBS, Stuttgart, West Germany, November 1989.

[Poesio, 1988a] Massimo Poesio. Dialog-oriented A-boxing. Project WISBER, Department of Computer Science, Universität Hamburg, Hamburg, West Germany, 1988. In preparation.

[Poesio, 1988b] Massimo Poesio. Toward a hybrid representation of time. In *Proceedings of the 8th European Conference on Artificial Intelligence*, pages 247–252, Munich, West Germany, August 1988.

[Puppe, 1987] Frank Puppe. Belief revision in diagnosis. In K. Morik, editor, *GWAI-87. 11th German Workshop on Artificial Intelligence*, pages 175–184, Springer-Verlag, Berlin, West Germany, 1987.

[Quillian, 1966] M. Ross Quillian. *Semantic Memory*. PhD thesis, Carnegie Institute of Technology, Pittsburgh, Pa., 1966. BBN Report AFCRL-66-189, Bolt, Beranek, and Newman Inc., October 1966.

[Quillian, 1967] M. Ross Quillian. Word concepts: a theory and simulation of some basic semantic capabilities. *Behavioral Science*, 12:410–430, 1967. Also published in [Brachman and Levesque, 1985].

[Quine, 1963] Willard Van Orman Quine. Two dogmas of empiricism. In W. V. O. Quine, editor, *From a logical point of view*, pages 20–46, Harper, New York, N.Y.,

1963. Reprint of the 2nd edition. The 1st edition has been published by Harvard University Press, 1953.

[Reddy, 1988] Raj Reddy. Foundations and grand challenges of artificial intelligence. *The AI Magazine*, 9(4):9–21, 1988.

[Reimer, 1985] Ulrich Reimer. A representation construct for roles. *Data & Knowledge Engineering*, 1(3):233–252, 1985.

[Reimer, 1986] Ulrich Reimer. A system-controlled multi-type specialization hierarchy. In L. Kerschberg, editor, *Expert Database Systems—Proceedings From the 1st International Workshop*, pages 173–187, Benjamin/Cummings, Menlo Park, Cal., 1986.

[Reiter, 1980] Raymond Reiter. A logic for default reasoning. *Artificial Intelligence*, 13(1):81–132, April 1980. Also published in [Ginsberg, 1987].

[Reiter, 1984] Raymond Reiter. Towards a logical reconstruction of relational database theory. In M. L. Brodie, J. Mylopoulos, and J. W. Schmidt, editors, *On Conceptual Modelling*, pages 191–233, Springer-Verlag, Berlin, West Germany, 1984.

[Reiter, 1987] Raymond Reiter. A theory of diagnosis from first principles. *Artificial Intelligence*, 32(1):57–95, April 1987. Also published in [Ginsberg, 1987].

[Rich, 1982] Charles Rich. Knowledge representation languages and predicate calculus: how to have your cake and eat it too. In *Proceedings of the 2nd National Conference of the American Association for Artificial Intelligence*, pages 193–196, Pittsburgh, Pa., August 1982.

[Rich, 1985] Charles Rich. The layered architecture of a system for reasoning about programs. In *Proceedings of the 9th International Joint Conference on Artificial Intelligence*, pages 540–546, Los Angeles, Cal., August 1985.

[Rich, 1983] Elaine Rich. *Artificial Intelligence*. McGraw-Hill, New York, N.Y., 1983.

[Richens, 1958] R. H. Richens. Interlingua machine translation. *Computer Journal*, 1(3):144–147, October 1958.

[Roberts and Goldstein, 1977] R. Bruce Roberts and Ira P. Goldstein. *FRL Users' Manual*. AI Memo 409, AI Laboratory, Massachusetts Institute of Technology, Cambridge, Mass., 1977.

[Robinson, 1965] J. A. Robinson. A machine-oriented logic based on the resolution principle. *Journal of the ACM*, 12(1):23–41, 1965.

[Rollinger, 1980] Claus-Rainer Rollinger. Readtime-Inferenzen für Semantische Netze. In C.-R. Rollinger and H.-J. Schneider, editors, *Inferenzen in natürlichsprachlichen Systemen der künstlichen Intelligenz*, pages 115–150, Einhorn, Berlin, West Germany, 1980.

[Rumelhart and McClelland, 1986] David E. Rumelhart and James L. McClelland, editors. *Parallel Distributed Processing: Exploration in the Microstructure of Cognition*. MIT Press, Cambridge, Mass., 1986.

[Schank, 1973] Roger C. Schank. Identification of conceptualization underlying natural language. In R. C. Schank and K. M. Colby, editors, *Computer Models of Thought and Language*, pages 187–247, Freeman, San Francisco, Cal., 1973.

[Schefe, 1982] Peter Schefe. Some fundamental issues in knowledge representation. In W. Wahlster, editor, *GWAI-82. 6th German Workshop on Artificial Intelligence*, pages 42–62, Springer-Verlag, Berlin, West Germany, 1982.

[Schefe, 1987] Peter Schefe. On definitional processes in knowledge reconstruction systems. In *Proceedings of the 10th International Joint Conference on Artificial Intelligence*, pages 509–511, Milan, Italy, August 1987.

252   Bibliography

[Schild, 1988] Klaus Schild. *Undecidability of U.* KIT Report 67, Department of Computer Science, Technische Universität Berlin, Berlin, West Germany, October 1988.

[Schild, 1989] Klaus Schild. *Towards a Theory of Frames and Rules.* Master's thesis, Department of Computer Science, Technische Universität Berlin, Berlin, West Germany, 1989. To appear as a KIT Report.

[Schmidt-Schauß, 1989] Manfred Schmidt-Schauß. Subsumption in KL-ONE is undecidable. In R. J. Brachman, H. J. Levesque, and R. Reiter, editors, *Proceedings of the 1st International Conference on Principles of Knowledge Representation and Reasoning*, pages 421–431, Toronto, Ont., May 1989.

[Schmidt-Schauß and Smolka, 1989] Manfred Schmidt-Schauß and Gert Smolka. Attributive concept descriptions with unions and complements. *Artificial Intelligence*, 1989. To appear. Also available as IWBS Report 68, IBM Germany Scientific Center, IWBS, Stuttgart, West Germany, June 1989.

[Schmiedel et al., 1986] Albrecht Schmiedel, Kai von Luck, Bernhard Nebel, and Christof Peltason. *'Bitter Pills'—A Case Study in Knowledge Representation.* KIT Report 39, Department of Computer Science, Technische Universität Berlin, Berlin, West Germany, August 1986.

[Schmolze, 1989a] James G. Schmolze. *The Language and Semantics of NIKL.* Technical Report 89-4, Department of Computer Science, Tufts University, Medford, Mass., September 1989.

[Schmolze, 1989b] James G. Schmolze. Terminological knowledge representation systems supporting n-ary terms. In R. J. Brachman, H. J. Levesque, and R. Reiter, editors, *Proceedings of the 1st International Conference on Principles of Knowledge Representation and Reasoning*, pages 432–443, Toronto, Ont., May 1989.

[Schmolze and Brachman, 1982] James G. Schmolze and Ronald J. Brachman, editors. *Proceedings of the 1981 KL-ONE Workshop.* BBN Report 4842, Bolt, Beranek, and Newman Inc., Cambridge, Mass., 1982. Also available as AI Technical Report 4, Schlumberger Palo Alto Research, May 1982.

[Schmolze and Israel, 1983] James G. Schmolze and David J. Israel. KL-ONE: semantics and classification. In *Research in Knowledge Representation and Natural Language Understanding, BBN Technical Report, No. 5421*, pages 27–39, Bolt, Beranek, and Newman Inc., Cambridge, Mass., 1983.

[Schmolze and Lipkis, 1983] James G. Schmolze and Thomas Lipkis. Classification in the KL-ONE knowledge representation system. In *Proceedings of the 8th International Joint Conference on Artificial Intelligence*, pages 330–332, Karlsruhe, West Germany, August 1983.

[Schubert et al., 1979] Lenhart K. Schubert, Randolph G. Goebel, and Nicholas J. Cercone. *The Structure and Organization of a Semantic Network for Comprehension and Inference*, pages 121–175. Academic Press, New York, N.Y., 1979.

[Shapiro, 1979] Stuart C. Shapiro. The SNePS semantics network processing system. In N. V. Findler, editor, *Associative Networks: Representation and Use of Knowledge by Computers*, pages 179–203, Academic Press, New York, N.Y., 1979.

[Shapiro and Rapaport, 1986] Stuart C. Shapiro and William J. Rapaport. SNePS considered as a fully intensional semantic network. In *Proceedings of the 5th National Conference of the American Association for Artificial Intelligence*, pages 278–283, Philadelphia, Pa., August 1986.

[Simmons, 1973] Robert F. Simmons. Semantic networks: their computation and use for understanding english sentences. In R. C. Schank and K. M. Colby, editors, *Computer Models of Thought and Language*, pages 63–113, Freeman, San Francisco, Cal., 1973.

[Sloman, 1985] Aaron Sloman. Why we need many knowledge representation formalisms. In M. Bramer, editor, *Research and Development in Expert Systems*, Cambridge University Press, Cambridge, England, 1985.

[Smith, 1982] Brian C. Smith. *Reflection and Semantics in a Procedural Language*. PhD thesis, Massachusetts Institute of Technology, Cambridge, Mass., 1982. Report MIT/LCS/TR-272.

[Smoliar and Swartout, 1988] Stephen W. Smoliar and William R. Swartout. A report from the frontiers of knowledge representation. University of Southern California, Information Science Institute, Marina del Rey, Cal., October 1988. Draft paper.

[Smolka, 1989a] Gert Smolka. *Feature Constraint Logics for Unification Grammars*. IWBS Report 93, IBM Germany Scientific Center, IWBS, Stuttgart, West Germany, November 1989.

[Smolka, 1989b] Gert Smolka. A feature logic with subsorts. *Journal of Logic Programming*, 1989. To appear. Also available as LILOG Report 33, IBM Germany Scientific Center, IWBS, Stuttgart, West Germany, May 1988.

[Sondheimer and Nebel, 1986] Norman K. Sondheimer and Bernhard Nebel. A logical-form and knowledge-base design for natural language generation. In *Proceedings of the 5th National Conference of the American Association for Artificial Intelligence*, pages 612–618, Philadelphia, Pa., August 1986.

[Sowa, 1987] John F. Sowa. Semantic networks. In S. C. Shapiro, editor, *Encyclopedia of Artificial Intelligence*, pages 1011–1024, Wiley, Chichester, England, 1987.

[Stallman and Sussman, 1977] Richard M. Stallman and Gerald J. Sussman. Forward reasoning and dependency directed backtracking in a system for computer-aided circuit analysis. *Artificial Intelligence*, 9(2):135–196, 1977.

[Stalnaker, 1968] Robert C. Stalnaker. A theory of conditionals. In N. Rescher, editor, *Studies in Logical Theory*, Oxford University Press, Oxford, England, 1968. Also published in E. Sosa, editor, *Causation and Conditionals*, Oxford University Press, Oxford, 1975, and in W. Harper, R. Stalnaker, and G. Pearce, editors, *IFS*, Reidel, Dordrecht, 1981.

[Stickel, 1985] Mark E. Stickel. Automated deduction by theory resolution. In *Proceedings of the 9th International Joint Conference on Artificial Intelligence*, pages 1181–1186, Los Angeles, Cal., August 1985.

[Stoy, 1977] J. E. Stoy. *Denotational Semantics: The Scott-Strachey Approach to Programming Language Theory*. MIT Press, Cambridge, Mass., 1977.

[Stoyan, 1987] Herbert Stoyan. Künstliche Intelligenz—Sprachen und Systeme. *computer magazin*, 16(3):68–71, 1987.

[Swartout and Neches, 1986] William R. Swartout and Robert Neches. The shifting terminological space: an impediment to evolvability. In *Proceedings of the 5th National Conference of the American Association for Artificial Intelligence*, pages 936–941, Philadelphia, Pa., August 1986.

[Szolovits et al., 1977] Peter Szolovits, Lowell B. Hawkinson, and William A. Martin. *An Overview of OWL, A Language for Knowledge Representation*. Technical Report MIT/LCS/TM-86, Laboratory for Computer Science, Massachusetts Institute of Technology, Cambridge, Mass., June 1977.

[Tarski, 1935] Alfred Tarski. Der Wahrheitsbegriff in den formalisierten Sprachen. *Studia Philosophica Comentarii Societatis philosophicae Polonorium*, 1:261–405, 1935. Reprinted in K. Breka and L. Kreiser (eds.), Logik-Texte, Akademie-Verlag, Berlin, East Germany, 1971.

[Tarski, 1955] Alfred Tarski. A lattice-theoretical fixpoint theorem and its applications. *Pacific Journal of Mathematics*, 5:285–309, 1955.

[Tou et al., 1982] Frederick N. Tou, Michael D. Williams, Richard E. Fikes, Austin Henderson, and Thomas Malone. RABBIT: an intelligent database assistant. In *Proceedings of the 2nd National Conference of the American Association for Artificial Intelligence*, pages 314–318, Pittsburgh, Pa., August 1982.

[Touretzky, 1986] David S. Touretzky. *The Mathematics of Inheritance Systems*. Morgan Kaufmann, Los Altos, Cal., 1986.

[Van Marcke, 1986] Kris Van Marcke. A parallel algorithm for consistency maintenance in knowledge representation. In *Proceedings of the 7th European Conference on Artificial Intelligence*, pages 278–290, Brighton, England, July 1986.

[Vilain, 1983] Marc B. Vilain. Assertions in NIKL. In *Research in Knowledge Representation and Natural Language Understanding, BBN Report, No. 5421*, pages 45–79, Bolt, Beranek, and Newman Inc., Cambridge, Mass., 1983.

[Vilain, 1985] Marc B. Vilain. The restricted language architecture of a hybrid representation system. In *Proceedings of the 9th International Joint Conference on Artificial Intelligence*, pages 547–551, Los Angeles, Cal., August 1985.

[Vilain, 1987] Marc B. Vilain. Personal communication. April 1987.

[Vilain and Kautz, 1986] Marc B. Vilain and Henry A. Kautz. Constraint propagation algorithms for temporal reasoning. In *Proceedings of the 5th National Conference of the American Association for Artificial Intelligence*, pages 377–382, Philadelphia, Pa., August 1986.

[Wahlster, 1981] Wolfgang Wahlster. *Natürlichsprachliche Argumentation in Dialogsystemen*. Springer-Verlag, Berlin, West Germany, 1981.

[Waterman, 1986] Donald A. Waterman. *A Guide to Expert Systems*. Addison-Wesley, Reading, Mass., 1986.

[Webber and Bobrow, 1980] Bonnie Lynn Webber and Robert J. Bobrow. Knowledge representation for syntactic/semantic processing. In *Proceedings of the 1st National Conference of the American Association for Artificial Intelligence*, pages 316–323, Stanford, Cal., August 1980.

[Webber and Nilsson, 1981] Bonnie Lynn Webber and Nils J. Nilsson, editors. *Readings in Artificial Intelligence*. Tioga, Palo Alto, Cal., 1981.

[Weber, 1987] Andreas Weber. Updating propositional formulas. In L. Kerschberg, editor, *Expert Database Systems—Proceedings From the 1st International Conference*, pages 487–500, Benjamin/Cummings, Menlo Park, Cal., 1987.

[Weinreb and Moon, 1981] Daniel Weinreb and David A. Moon. *Lisp Machine Manual*. Massachusetts Institute of Technology, Cambridge, Mass., 4th edition, 1981.

[Wellman and Simmons, 1988] Michael P. Wellman and Reid G. Simmons. Mechanisms for reasoning about sets. In *Proceedings of the 7th National Conference of the American Association for Artificial Intelligence*, pages 398–402, Saint Paul, Minn., August 1988.

[Wiederhold, 1986] Gio Wiederhold. Knowledge versus data. In M. L. Brodie and J. Mylopoulos, editors, *On Knowledge Base Management Systems*, pages 77–82, Springer-Verlag, Berlin, West Germany, 1986.

[Wiederhold et al., 1987] Gio Wiederhold, Surajit Chaudhuri, Waqar Hasan, Michael G. Walker, and Marianne S. Winslett. Architectural concepts for large knowledge bases. In K. Morik, editor, *GWAI-87. 11th German Workshop on Artificial Intelligence*, pages 366–385, Springer-Verlag, Berlin, West Germany, 1987.

[Wilensky, 1984] Robert Wilensky. KODIAK: a knowledge representation language. In *Proceedings of the 6th Annual Conference of the Cognitive Science Society*, pages 344–353, Boulder, Col., 1984.

[Winograd, 1972] Terry Winograd. *Understanding Natural Language*. Academic Press, New York, N.Y., 1972.

[Winograd, 1975] Terry Winograd. Frame representations and the declarative/procedural controversy. In D. G. Bobrow and A. M. Collins, editors, *Representation and Understanding: Studies in Cognitive Science*, pages 185–210, Academic Press, New York, N.Y., 1975. Also published in [Brachman and Levesque, 1985].

[Winslett, 1986] Marianne S. Winslett. Is belief revision harder than you thought? In *Proceedings of the 5th National Conference of the American Association for Artificial Intelligence*, pages 421–427, Philadelphia, Pa., August 1986.

[Winslett, 1987] Marianne S. Winslett. *Updating Databases with Incomplete Information*. PhD thesis, Stanford University, Stanford, Cal., January 1987. Technical Report STAN-CS-87-1143.

[Winston, 1975] Patrick H. Winston. Learning structural descriptions from examples. In P. H. Winston, editor, *The Psychology of Computer Vision*, pages 157–209, McGraw-Hill, New York, N.Y., 1975. Also published in [Brachman and Levesque, 1985].

[Winston, 1984] Patrick H. Winston. *Artificial Intelligence*. Addison-Wesley, Reading, Mass., 2nd edition, 1984. A German translation has been published as: *Künstliche Intelligenz*, Addison-Wesley, Bonn, 1987.

[Winston and Horn, 1981] Patrick H. Winston and Berthold K. P. Horn. *LISP*. Addison-Wesley, Reading, Mass., 1981.

[Wong and Mylopoulos, 1977] Harry K. T. Wong and John Mylopoulos. Two views of data semantics: data models in artificial intelligence and database mangement. *INFOR*, 15(3):344–383, 1977.

[Woods, 1975] William A. Woods. What's in a link: foundations for semantic networks. In D. G. Bobrow and A. M. Collins, editors, *Representation and Understanding: Studies in Cognitive Science*, pages 35–82, Academic Press, New York, N.Y., 1975. Also published in [Brachman and Levesque, 1985].

[Woods, 1983] William A. Woods. What's important about knowledge representation. *IEEE Computer*, 16(10):22–29, October 1983.

Subject Index

Boldface page numbers refer to definitions.

Author Index

Italic page numbers refer to *et al.* citations which do not contain the author's name. Numbers in boldface indicate the page on which the complete reference is given.

Abarbanel, R. M., 32, **237**
Abrett, G., 4, 193, 193, 214, 221, **237**
Alchourrón, C. E., 29, 153, 156–159, **237**
Allemang, D., *16*, **240**
Allen, J. F., 23, 91, **237**
Allgayer, J., 62, **237**
Apté, C., *4*, *47*, **247**
Arens, Y., 63, *70*, **237**, **246**
Aït-Kaci, H., 70, **237**

Bachant, J., 4, **237**
Barr, A., 13, 18, **237**
Bates, R., 47, *50*, *61*, 72, *91*, *101*, 101, *119*, 119, 196, 235, **244**, **246**
Belnap, N. D., 28, **237**
Bergmann, H., 25, 47, 64, 193, 235, **237**, **238**
Bernstein, P. A., *32*, **248**
Bjørner, D., 19, **238**
Bobrow, D. G., 4, 23, 31, 40, 41, **238**
Bobrow, R. J., 58, 62, **254**
Borgida, A., 47, 64, 71, 92, 96, 153, 234, **238**
Brachman, R. J., 4–6, 11, 12, 15, 20, 21, 25, 26, 28, 29, 32, *32*, 37, 41–47, *47*, 48–50, 52, 58, 62, 63, *64*, *66*, 68, *71*, 71, 90, 91, *92*, 96, *96*, *104*, 119, 146, 193, *198*, 199, 200, 225, 232, 234, *234*, **238**, **239**, **245**, **249**, **250**, **252**
Brodie, M. L., 29, 30, 32, **239**
Brown, H. I., 135, **239**
Burstein, M. H., 4, 193, 194, 214, 221, **237**

Carbonell, J. R., 38, **239**
Carey, M. J., 32, **239**
Carnap, R., 203, 204, **239**

Cercone, N. J., *39*, **252**
Chandrasekaran, B., 16, **240**
Charniak, E., 176, **240**
Chaudhuri, S., *31*, *32*, **255**
Cho, J. W., *47*, *235*, **243**
Christaller, T., *17*, 17, *24*, *25*, **240**, **243**
Clark, K., 173, **240**
Clocksin, W. F., 11, **240**
Collins, A. M., 38, **240**
Corella, F., 62, 63, **240**

D'Aloisi, D., 47, **240**
Dalal, M., 168, 169, **240**
Date, C. J., 20, **240**
Davidson, D., 70, **240**
Davis, R., 17, 24, **240**
DeWitt, D. J., 32, **239**
de Kleer, J., 153, 176, 185, 186, **240**, **241**
Diettrich, T. G., 29, 33, 204, **241**
Donini, F. M., 47, 232, **241**
Doyle, J., 97, 151, 178, 183, *185*, 222, **241**
Dreyfus, H. L., 16, **241**
Dörre, J., 97, **241**

Edelmann, J., 47, 64, 91, 96, **241**
Eisele, A., 97, **241**
Ernst, G. W., 11, **241**
Etherington, D. W., 174, **241**

Fagin, R., 153, 156, 157, 160, 161, 163, 165, 167, 169, **241**, **242**
Fahlman, S. E., 20, **242**
Feigenbaum, E. A., 13, 18, **237**
Fikes, R. E., *26*, *32*, *45*, *46*, 47, *49*, **239**, **242**, **254**
Finin, T. W., 195, 198, 213, **242**
Freeman, M., 47, **242**

Lecture Notes in Computer Science